Abstracts of

Bucks County, Pennsylvania

LAND RECORDS

1711-1749

June D. Brown

HERITAGE BOOKS
2008

HERITAGE BOOKS
AN IMPRINT OF HERITAGE BOOKS, INC.

Books, CDs, and more—Worldwide

For our listing of thousands of titles see our website at
www.HeritageBooks.com

Published 2008 by
HERITAGE BOOKS, INC.
Publishing Division
100 Railroad Ave. #104
Westminster, Maryland 21157

Copyright © 1998 June D. Brown

Other books by the author:
Abstracts of Cecil County, Maryland Land Records 1673-1751
Abstracts of Cecil County, Maryland Land Records, 1734-1753

All rights reserved. No part of this book may be reproduced or transmitted in any form or by any means, electronic or mechanical, including photocopying, recording or by any information storage and retrieval system without written permission from the author, except for the inclusion of brief quotations in a review.

International Standard Book Numbers
Paperbound: 978-1-58549-023-3
Clothbound: 978-0-7884-7582-5

CONTENTS

Introduction v

Map of Bucks and Part of Philadelphia Counties, taken from Holmes's
  "Map of the Improved part of the Province of Pennsylvania." vi

Land Records 1

Index 197

INTRODUCTION

Bucks County was one of Pennsylvania's original counties. In 1685 its boundary with Philadelphia County ran along the east side of Potquessin Creek from its mouth on the Delaware River northwest to near its source and continued in the same direction along the west side of Southampton and Warminster townships. The Delaware River formed its southeast and northeast boundaries while its northwest boundary was determined by Indian treaties. See Thomas Holme's *Map of the Improved Part of the Province of Pennsylvania in America* on the following page.

For a thorough discussion of the complex history of the administration of the land under William Penn see Donna Bingham Munger, *Pennsylvania Land Records. A History and Guide for Research*. Published by Scholarly Resources, Inc. (1991).

In this work we have included references to all persons found in the records. Our primary goal was to reveal information useful to genealogical research. We have eliminated the proforma legal requirements and also the specific descriptions of the metes and bounds of the tracts - all for reasons of economy. The omission of specific descriptions of the boundaries is indicated by ellipsis (...). Dates shown include acknowledgement (Ackn:), registration at the court (Reg:) or recordation (Rec:). Witnesses are indicated by "Wit:." The reader is invited to acquire complete copies of the records through the county court or by ordering microfilm through a local Family History Center (LDS).

F. Edward Wright
Westminster, Maryland
1998

1711-1731
Deed Book A, Vol. 2

P. 1   Deed. James Shattick, for £250, to Henry Nelson of Bucks Co., yeoman, 550 acres of land. Thomas Constable, late of Listeard, Cromwell Co., gent., conveyed to James Shattick 18 Dec 1703, 550 acres of woodland in Bucks Co. bounded on the northeast by Neshaminy Creek at a corner of Newtown Township and southeast by the land of Thomas Musgrove, deceased, then by Bridgeman's land. Said land by patent dated 26 Apr 1708 was confirmed to James Shattick and recorded in Patent Book A, Vol 4, pg 81. Made 18 May 1710. Wit: Justinian Fox, Henry Comly, Joseph Wilcox. Ackn: 1 Jan 1711 in presence of John Wildman and John Cutter. Rec: 8 Dec 1713. JP: Thomas Watson; Rec. Deeds: Jeremiah Langhorne.

P. 4   Deed. John Rowland of Bristol, gent., and Thomas Biddle of the same place, inholder, affirm their presence when Thomas Coats of Philadelphia Co., yeoman, and Elizabeth his wife, for £65, convey to John Baldwin of Bristol, miller, a 200 acre tract of land on the east side of Neshaminy Creek beginning on a corner of John Baldwin's land then south by land of the late John Otter and by land of William Clark. Said land part of land granted to Samuel Allen, late of Bucks Co., deceased, by patent under hands of William Markham and John Goodson dated 28 Nov 1689 and recorded in Bucks Co. Book A, Vol 1, pgs 289-290. Samuel Allen by deed dated 7 Jun 1692 sold the land to Elizabeth Pegy and it was recorded in Bucks Co. Book A, Vol 1, pg 349. Made 24 Sep 1710. Wit: Joseph Welch, Thomas Biddle, John Rowland. Ackn: 24 Dec 1713. JP: Thomas Stevenson. Rec. Deeds: Jeremiah Langhorn.

P. 8   Deed. John Griffith of Southampton, Bucks Co., cordwainer, for £250, conveys to James Carter, of the same place, blacksmith, 200 acres of land in Southampton by Neshaminy Creek and at a corner of Samuel Griffith's land on the southeast at a line of Ralph Draycot's and by Kings Road leading from the Falls of Philadelphia and then by John Swift's land to Mill Creek. Said land part of 500 acres granted by patent to Christopher Taylor dated 15th da 5th mo 1684. Christopher Taylor conveyed the land to his son Israel Taylor by deed dated 7th da 2nd mo 1685 and recorded at Philadelphia in Book C, Vol 3, pg 63. Israel Taylor granted 290 acres of the land to John Griffith by deed dated 22 Mar 1696 and recorded in Bucks Co. Book B, Vol 1, pgs 131-132 and the 200 acres being conveyed to James Carter is part of this 290 acres. John Griffith reserves for himself and his wife Katherine the east end of the dwelling house with the adjacent field, garden and meadow containing about 3 acres. Made 26th da 10th mo 1706. Ackn: 16 Dec 1713. Wit: John Hayhurst of Southampton, yeoman, and John Cutter [Cutler?] of Middletown, yeoman. JP: Joseph Kirkbride. Rec. Deeds: Jeremiah Langhorne.

P. 11   Deed. Barnard Christian of Bergen Co., New Jersey, yeoman, for £50 and for good will and natural affection, conveys to his son Barnard Barnson of Bucks Co., yeoman, 274 acres in Bucks Co. bounded on the northeast by Thomas Atkinson's land, then south by Johanne Blacker's land and by land of Edward Pennington's. Thomas Groom sold the land to Barnard Christian by deed dated 29 Sep 1707. The deed is recorded in Bucks Co. Book C, Vol 1, pg 346. Made 20 Sep 1712. Wit: Christian Barnson, Bartholomew Jacobs, both of Middletown, yeomen, and Jeremiah Langhorne. Ackn: 17 Jun 1714.

P. 13   Deed. Samuel Boron of Flushing, Long Island, New York, yeoman, conveys to Thomas Marriott of Bristol, for £37.10s, a lot in Bristol beginning at Phineas Pemberton's corner by Mill Street then by William Croasdale's land and east to Market Street. Said land Anthony Burton, yeoman of Bucks Co., conveyed to Samuel Boron by deed dated 22 Jun 1696 and recorded in Bucks Co. Book B, Vol 1, pgs 88-89. Made 18 Apr 1713. Wit: Edward Kempe. Ackn: 17 Mar 1713. Wit: Samuel Carpenter of Philadelphia, merchant, and William Watson of Bristol, shopkeeper. JP: Joseph Kirkbride; Rec. Deeds: Jeremiah Langhorne.

P. 15   Deed. Daniel Burges and John Burges of Bucks Co., yeoman and carpenter, convey to Samuel Burges of the same place, carpenter, each of their third of 100 acres of land in Bristol. Daniel, John and Samuel Burges had jointly purchased the 100 acres from John Rowland of Bucks Co., yeoman, by indenture dated 30 March 1705. Made 20 Dec 1709. Wit: Edward Kemp, John Hutchinson, Richard Hill. Ackn: 17 Sep 1713. JP: Thomas Stevenson. Rec. Deeds: Jeremiah Langhorne.

P. 16   Deed. John Hall of Bristol, cooper, and Rebecca his wife, for £6, to Thomas Marriott of Bristol, sadler, 6½ acres in Bristol bounded by the lands of Jacob Pellison, John Baldwin, John Hall, Samuel Carpenter, John Royton and William Atkinson. Said land part of 116 acres granted to John Hall by patent dated 9 Apr 1713. Made 26 Feb 1713. Wit: Edward Oland, John Cutter [Cutler?] and William Watson. Ackn: 17 Mar 1713. JP: Joseph Kirkbride. Rec. Deeds: Jeremiah Langhorne.

P. 18   Release. Richard Eayre of Burlington Co., NJ, and Elizabeth Eayre his wife and relict of John Brock, late of Bucks Co., deceased, for £30, to Ralph Brock of Bucks Co., millwright and son of Elizabeth, 1,000 acres. Said land property of John Brock, former husband of said Elizabeth, by indenture of lease and release dated 2 and 3 Mar 1681, which John Brock died possessed of. Made 3 Nov 1713. Wit: John A. Tinings, Richard R. Bowen.

P. 19   Deed. Thomas Stevenson of Bensalem, yeoman, and Sarah his wife, for £130, 125 acres in Bensalem to Harman Vansand of the same place, yeoman. Johannes Vansand of the same place and Lea his wife by deed dated 17 May 1714 conveyed to Thomas Stevenson 125 acres in Bensalem bounded by lands belonging to said Stevenson and said Vansand and Joseph Growdon. Made 26 May 1713. Wit: James Smyth, Edward Kempe, Jeremiah Langhorne. Ackn: 31 May 1714. JP: Francis White. Rec. Deeds: Jeremiah Langhorne.

P. 21   Deed. Ralph Brock of Makefield, millwright and son and heir of John Brock, for £300, to John Lambert of Nottingham, NJ, yeoman, 223 acres in Makefield aside the Delaware River by Samuel Overton's land and by the land of Joseph Clews, deceased. Said land part of 1,000 acres granted by indenture of lease and release dated 2 and 3 Mar 1681 to John Brock, late of Makefield, deceased. Made 10 Dec 1713. Wit: Grace Langhorne, Jacob Helstyn, Jeremiah Langhorne. Ackn: 12 Nov 1713. JP: Thomas Watson. Rec. Deeds: Jeremiah Langhorne.

P. 23   Deed. James Yates of Newtown, Bucks Co., yeoman, and Agnes his wife, for £16.10s, to Daniel Doan of the same place, carpenter, 22 acres in Newtown beginning at Henry Nelson's line on the west side of the Newtown-to-Bristol road and by Newtown Creek. Said land part of land granted to Israel Taylor by patent dated 18 Feb 1692 and was sold by Israel Taylor to James Yates 14th da 2nd mo 1698. Made 2 Jan 1713. Wit: Ezra Croasdale, Daniel Jackson, Samuel Hilborn. Ackn: 18 Jan 1713. JP: John Rowland. Rec. Deeds: Jeremiah Langhorne.

P. 25   Deed. George Slater of Makefield, yeoman, and Sarah his wife, to Samuel Burges of Bristol, Bucks Co., carpenter, for £92, 103 acres of land in Makefield on the River Delaware and by Henry Margerum's land, then south to Joseph Kirkbride's land and north by the land late of William Bealurs. Said land Jane Kirkbride and Thomas Kirkbride, executors of Matthew Kirkbride, late of Makefield, deceased, conveyed by deed dated 5 Nov 1709 to George Slater. Made 17 Jun 1714. Wit: Joseph Kirkbride, Peter

Webster, William Biles. JP: Willoughby Warder. Rec. Deeds: Jeremiah Langhorne.

P. 26   Deed.   John Burges of Bristol, carpenter, for £71, to George Clough of Bristol, boulter, a lot with a warehouse or bolting house near the mills late of Samuel Carpenter's in Bristol bounded on the south and east with lands late belonging to Samuel Carpenter and on the west by a wharf joining the mill and on the north by the street. Said lot was conveyed to John Burges by Samuel Carpenter by indenture dated 3 Jul 1710. Made 1 Nov 1714. Wit: Joseph Bond, James Moon, William Atkinson. Ackn: 23 Nov 1714. Rec: 19 Mar 1714.

P. 28   Mortgage.   Joseph White of Bristol, carpenter, for £60.10s, to Hannah Carpenter, widow and executrix of Samuel Carpenter, late of Philadelphia, merchant, deceased, a lot in Bristol adjoining the garden and dwelling house of the late Samuel Carpenter. Made 21 Apr 1714. Wit: George Clough, John Hall, Jeremiah Langhorne. Ackn: 22 May 1714. JP: John Rowland. Rec. Deeds: Jeremiah Langhorn.

P. 31   Deed.   John Swift of Southampton, yeoman, for £600, to Robert Heaton, Jr. of Middletown, yeoman, 340 acres beginning at a post in John Naylor's line on the north side of the highway leading from the Falls to Philadelphia and running northwest by Thomas Harding's land and by Samuel Allen's line and by Christopher Wealtherill's land to Mill Creek then down to James Carter's corner and by Ralph Draycott's line. 100 acres of said land was granted to John Swift from Israel Taylor by deed dated 26th da 1st mo 1690, being part of 1,000 acres which was granted to Israel Taylor by Christopher Taylor, his father, and 60 of these acres were conveyed to John Swift by Israel Taylor 29 May 1695, part of 500 acres granted to Israel Taylor by his father by deed dated 17th da 2nd mo 1685 and 50 acres granted to John Swift by John Griffith by deed dated 22 Mar 1696 and recorded in Bucks Co. Book B, Vol 1, pgs 131-132, being part of the said 500 acres, and 130 acres conveyed to John Swift from Barbara Blangdon by deed dated 10 May 1701 which was granted to Barbara by Elizabeth Bennett, relict of Edmund Bennett, by deed dated 14 Feb 1697. Made 10th da 11th mo 1710. Wit: William Stockdell, John Swift, Jr., John Cutter. Rec: 19 Mar 1714.

P. 32   Deed.   Henry Paxson of Marsh Township, for love and good will and natural affection and because Henry Paxson is moving, to his nephew Henry Paxson, Jr. of Falls Township, yeoman, 450 acres in Marsh by the River Delaware and by Paxson and Beakes land. 250 acres of this land was granted to Henry Paxson by deed from William Croasdale and recorded in

Bucks Co. Book C, Vol 1, pg 170 and 200 acres is part of 250 acres granted to Henry Paxson by deed from Jeremiah Langhorne. Made 1 May 1714. Wit: John Plumley, Mary Plumley, Jeremiah Langhorne. Ackn: 1 May 1714. JP: Francis White. Rec. Deeds: Jeremiah Langhorne.

P. 33 Deed. William Stockdale of Southampton, husbandman, and his wife Dorothy, for £141, to Thomas Stackhouse of Middletown, yeoman, 150 acres of land in Middletown by Neshaminy Creek at Henry Nelson's corner, then northeast to Thomas Musgrave's land, and bounded on the south by John Croasdale's land and by Joseph Wildman's land. 90 of these acres were granted to William Stockdale from Henry Nelson by deed dated 12 Feb 1713 and these 90 acres were part of a tract conveyed to Henry Nelson from James Shattick by deed dated 18 May 1710 and was granted to James Shattick by patent dated 26 Apr 1708. The other 60 acres were conveyed to William Stockdale from Joseph Wildman by deed dated 11 Sep 1711 and is part of 220 acres granted to Joseph Wildman from John Martindale and his wife Mary by indenture dated 13 Apr 1709 and was conveyed to Martindale by patent dated 12 Apr 1709. Made 6 Mar 1713. Wit: William Watson, John Cutter. Ackn: 17 Mar 1713. JP: Joseph Kirkbride. Rec. Deeds: Jeremiah Langhorne.

P. 35 Deed. John Enoch of Philadelphia Co., yeoman, and his wife Britta; John Johnson of Bristol in Bucks Co., weaver; Peter Johnson of Bristol, laborer; Matts Murton of Philadelphia Co., yeoman, and Brita his wife, for £177, to John Johnson of Bristol, yeoman, 100 acres of land in Bristol by Neshaminy Creek and a corner of the land late of John Town's and by John Johnson's land. Said land part of 520 acres granted to John Clawson, father of said John Johnson, by patent dated 1 Jul 1684. Made 10 Apr 1713. Wit: Joseph Thatcher, Joseph Large, Joseph Thatcher [sic], Jeremiah Langhorne, Peter Chamberlin, Henry Mitchell, Duck Alborsbrult, Benjamin Barkes.

P. 38 Deed. George Vansand of Bensalem, yeoman, and Micah his wife, for £150, to Thomas Stevenson of the same place, yeoman, 150 acres in Bensalem by the River Neshaminy opposite the house formerly belonging to Edward Carter. Stophell Vansand, Cornelius Vansand, Harman Vansand, Albert Vansand, Johannes Vansand and Garret Vansand by deed conveyed the said 150 acres to George Vansand and Jacobus Vansand and the deed was recorded in Book C, Vol 1, pg 258. By indenture of lease and release Jacobus Vansand conveyed the land to George Vansand 1 and 2 Apr 1711. Made 17 May 1714. Wit: Jeremiah Langhorne, James Smyth, Stophfell

Vansand. Ackn: 17 May 1714. JP: Francis White. Rec. Deeds: Jeremiah Langhorne.

P. 41   Deed. Harman Vansand of Bensalem, gent., and Elizabeth his wife, for £29.15s, to Thomas Stevenson of the same place, gent., a tract of land containing 29 acres and 3 rods beginning "at a stone about a gunshot below the dam on the west side of the Run." Said land part of a piece of land which Thomas Stevenson sold to Harman Vansand. Made 13 May 1714. Wit: James Smyth, Jeremiah Langhorne. Ackn: 31 May 1714. JP: Francis White. Rec. Deeds: Jeremiah Langhorne.

P. 43   Deed. Cornelius Vansand and Derica his wife, for £163.6s.8p, to Thomas Stevenson of Bensalem, gent., 150 acres in Bensalem and by the River Neshaminy at a corner of George Vansand's land and on the line of Thomas Stevenson's land, formerly John Tatham's. Said land part of 5,000 acres Joseph Growdon of Bensalem, yeoman, purchased by indenture of lease and release dated under the hand and seal of William Penn 24 and 25 October 1681 and Joseph Growdon sold the said 150 acres to Cornelius Vansand 13 Oct 1699, recorded in Book B, pgs 225-226. Made 4 May 1714. Wit: Francis White, James Smyth. Ackn: 14 May 1714. JP: Francis White. Rec. Deeds: Jeremiah Langhorne. Signed Cor. Vansand and Derica A. Vansandt [sic].

P. 45   Deed. Johannes Vansand of Bucks Co., yeoman, and Leah his wife for £150 to Thomas Stevenson of the same place, gent., 125 acres of land in Bensalem bordering on Stevenson's line and by Harman Vansand's land and on the north by Joseph Growdon's land. Said land recorded in Book C, Vol 1, pgs 191-193. Made 17 May 1714. Wit: Jeremiah Langhorne, Stopfell Vansand. Rec: 18 Mar 1714. Signed: John Vansand and Leah O. Vansand.

P. 47   Deed. William Smith of Darby in Chester Co., yeoman, for £200, to Thomas Davids of Bucks Co., yeoman, 400 acres of land bordered by Southampton's land, by Thomas Potter's land, by James Claypoole's land, and by Arthur Cook's land. Said land George Willard of Chester Co. and John Shaw of Bucks Co., yeoman, by deed dated 17 May 1697 granted to William Smith. Made 21 Jan 1708. Wit: Edward Evans, Joshua Lawrence, David Lloyd, Griffith Jones. Ackn: 17 Nov 1713. JP: Joseph Kirkbride. Rec. Deeds: Jeremiah Langhorne. Wit: Edward Evans of Philadelphia, joiner, and Joshua Lawrence of the same place, gent. Signed: William S. Smith.

P. 49   Deed. William Atkinson of Bristol, tailor, and Mary his wife, for £9.10s, to Benjamin Harris of Bristol, wheelwright, a tract of 4 acres in

Bristol beginning at a corner of Samuel Burges' lot and on the west by Thomas Bills' land. Said land granted by deed from John Hall of Bristol, cooper, and Rebecca his wife to William Atkinson and recorded in Book D, Vol 1, pg 436 [295 written in above 436.] Made 24 Jul 1714. Wit: Thomas Biddle, William Watson, Peter Fearon. Rec: 12 Mar 1714.

P. 50   Deed. Samuel Hough of Newtown, carpenter, for £77, to John Stackhouse of Middletown, yeoman, 300 acres of land in Newtown beginning at a post in Thomas Revell's line and bordering the Wrightstown lands, William Bennett's land, and the said Samuel Hough's land. This land is part of 564 acres which Israel and Joseph Taylor, sons and heirs of Christopher Taylor, deceased, sold to Samuel Hough by deed dated the 2nd day of this month and acknowledged this day. Made 10th da 4th mo 1702. Wit: William Biles, Jr., Andrew Heath, David Lloyd. Rec: 12 Mar 1715 by Jeremiah Langhorne.

P. 51   Release. George Dunkan of Bensalem, yeoman, for £200, to Alexander Mood of the same place, yeoman, 184 acres in Bensalem on Postquequick Creek bordering William Dunkan's land, Francis Searle's line and Samuel Scott's land. William Dunkan by deed dated 30 Dec 1708 conveyed the land to George Dunkan. Made 3 Aug 1714. Wit: Thomas Stevenson, John Hutchinson, Jeremiah Langhorne. Rec: 13 Mar 1714.

P. 54   Deed. Daniel Jackson of Bucks Co., fuller, for £100, to Edward Kemp, schoolmaster of Bucks Co., "a plantation on which I now dwell" in Middletown containing 128 acres beginning at the end of Smith's Shop and fronting the stone schoolhouse by the King's Road and bordering William Paxson's land on the northwest. This land was formerly granted to Robert Carter by patent dated 28 Dec 1684 by James Claypool and Robert Turner, Commissioners for William Penn. After Robert Carter's decease the land was allotted to his son John Carter by order of an Orphans Court held 14 Mar 1690. Said land was later sold by deed dated 12 Mar 1696 to John Smith by John Carter, being first released from the rest of the children of Robert Carter by another Orphans Court held 1 Oct 1689, and is recorded in Book B, Vol 1, pgs 126-127. John Smith sold the land by deed dated 10 Oct 1700 to Daniel Jackson and it is recorded in Book C, Vol 1, pgs 21-22. Made 10 Mar 1714. Wit: Thomas Watson, Francis White, Jeremiah Langhorne. Rec: 13 Mar 1714.

P. 55   Deed. Francis Searle of Bensalem, yeoman, for 5 shillings and natural affection and because Francis Searle is moving, to Arthur Searle, son of Francis Searle, 100 acres in Bensalem bordering Joseph Growdon's land.

This land part of 400 acres granted to Francis Searle from Joseph Growdon by deed dated 1st da 6th mo 1697 and recorded in Book B, Vol 1, pg 145. Made 29th da 8th mo 1714. Wit: Alexander Mood, Edmund Dunkan, George Dunkan. Rec: 14 Mar 1714.

P. 57   Release. John Clark of Bucks Co., gent., for £80, to Robert Shaw of the same County, yeoman, 114½ acres on the River Delaware bordering land late of Stephen Beaks and by land formerly John Lufs. This land was conveyed by indenture dated 30 Dec 1708 by Samuel Beakes of said County to John Clark. Made 15 Dec 1710. Wit: George Hulme, Jr., Jeremiah Langhorn, Matt Hughes. Rec: 14 Mar 1714.

P. 58   Deed. William Homer of Bristol, yeoman, and Elizabeth his wife, who are moving, for £195.8s, to Samuel Carpenter of Philadelphia Co., merchant, 156 acres of land beginning at a corner post of John Otter's land, part of a 262 acre tract which was originally patented to William Sanford by William Markham and John Goodson, two of the late Commissioners of William Penn, dated 7th da 11th mo 8th year of the Proprietary Government. William Sanford dispersed the land in his Last Will and Testament by these words: "I give unto my eldest son William Sanford half the land whereon I now live and the other half to my son William Homer to be equally divided betwixt them both houses meadows and orchards to them and their heirs forever and if in case my eldest son William die and have no children neither son nor daughter then to be divided amongst my two children Mary and Esther And also if my son William Homer die without issue and have no children then his part of the land shall be equally divided as aforesaid and in case they all die without issue to fall to the next heirs" as in and by the same recited testament bearing date the 24th day of Mar 1689. Sometime after William Sanford made his will, but before his death, he conveyed 106 acres of the said land to Henry Burchan. Henry Burchan conveyed the land to Samuel Carpenter. William Sanford died so seized in his estate as aforesaid and his son William Sanford is also deceased. Sanford's other son William Homer has children. Mary and Esther, daughters of William Sanford, by the names of Mary Burge and her husband Henry Burge of Philadelphia Co., husbandman, and Esther Preston and her husband Amos Preston of Buckingham, Bucks Co., tailor, had conveyed to William Homer their share of the land. William Homer reserves a piece of burying ground where his father-in-law is buried containing four perches square. Made 16 Dec 1713. Rec: 15 Mar 1714.

P. 61   Deed. Nicholas Randall of Bucks Co., carpenter, for £150 to John Swift of Philadelphia, gent., four tracts of land containing 175 acres. John

Swift conveyed to Nicholas Randall 100 acres in Southampton beginning at a corner of John Jones' land and by Derrick Cruson's land and bordering the Philadelphia County line, acknowledged and recorded in Book D, Vol 1, pg 5. By another deed, John Swift conveyed to Nicholas Randall 25 acres of land bordered by George Tatham's land which was recorded 15 Mar 1703. Margery Jennings of Alton in Southampton Co. in England, widow, by her attorney Peter Chamberlain of Peniel in Philadelphia Co., yeoman, by deed dated 20 Jun 1708 granted to Nicholas Randall 25 acres of land bordered by the lands of Thomas Catchill and George Jackman. Also James Jacob of Philadelphia, cordwainer, by deed dated 28 May 1698 granted to Nicholas Randall 25 acres of land and the deed is recorded in Book B, pg 192. Made 17 Mar 1713. Wit: Henry Mitchell, Jeremiah Langhorne. Ackn: 17 Mar 1713. JP: Joseph Growdon. Rec. Deeds: Jeremiah Langhorn.

P. 65   Deed. Thomas Stevenson of Bensalem, gent., and Sarah his wife, for £350, convey to Thomas Walmsley of the same place, yeoman, 888 acres of land by Andrew Heath's and William Large's land and on the northwest by Nathaniel Broomly's land and southwest by John Reynolds' and Edward West's land. 688 acres of this land is part of 1,100 acres which Isaac Decow of Burlington, NJ, yeoman, by deed dated 16 Jan 1712 granted to Thomas Stevenson. Samuel Hough of Newtown, yeoman, conveyed the other 200 acres to Thomas Stevenson by deed dated 10 Dec 1712. And also another tract of land in Newtown by the Town Common and a corner of William Buckman's land and by Samuel Hough's land containing 250 acres which Mitchell Luff of Bristol, chairmaker and son and heir of Mitchell Luff, late of Bristol, yeoman, deceased, by deed dated 10 Dec 1712 and recorded in Book D, Vol 1, pg 226, conveyed to Thomas Stevenson, making the entire conveyance a total of 1,138 acres. Made 20 Apr 1713. Wit: Charles Levalley, William Beale, Thomas Knight. Rec: 23 Mar 1714.

P. 68   Deed. Samuel Carpenter of Philadelphia, merchant, for £38, to John Burges of Bristol, carpenter, a house and the ground upon which it stands used as a warehouse and bolting house now in the possession of said John Burges and located near Samuel Carpenter's mills in Bristol, bordering the wharf and the street, and free use of the wharf for landing and loading goods and the free use of a passage between the land and the mill. Made 3 Jul 1710. Wit: Israel Pemberton, John Carpenter, John Rogson. Rec: 23 Mar 1714.

P. 69   Deed. Thomas Cutler of Southampton, yeoman, for £250, to Francis Searle of Bensalem, yeoman, 25 acres bordering Joseph Growdon's land called Weskittetts and a 220 acre patent, altogether 245 acres. Joseph

Growdon of Trevose, gent., by indenture dated 12 Oct 1692 conveyed to Edmund Cutler of Southampton, deceased, 25 acres. After Edmund Cutler's decease the land descended to Thomas Cutler, eldest son and heir of Edmund Cutler. Edward Shippen, Griffith Owen, Thomas Story and James Logan, Commissioners for William Penn, by patent dated 28 Oct 1701 granted 220 acres bounded by Joseph Tomlinson's land, John Naylor's land and the town of Bensalem, to Thomas Cutler. Made 9 Sep 1713. Wit: John Cutler, Edward Smout, William Biles. Rec: 24 Mar 1714.

P. 71   Deed. Joseph Growdon of Philadelphia, gent., for £45, to Francis Searle of Bensalem, yeoman, a 275 acre tract of land in Bensalem lying by the lands of Thomas Walmsley, Clause Johnson, Abell Hingston, and Thomas Stevenson. Said land part of 5,000 acres granted to Joseph Growdon by William Penn by indenture of lease and release dated 24 and 25 Oct 1681. Made 20 Feb 1711. Wit: Jeremiah Langhorne, Sara [?] Growdon. Rec: 24 Mar 1714.

P. 73   Deed. John Scarborough of Solebury, yeoman, and Mary his wife, for £58, to Samuel Pickering of Solebury, yeoman, 200 acres in Solebury bordering Henry Paxson's land and is part of 820 acres which Jacob Holcombe by indenture recorded in Book D, Vol 1, pg 175 [129 written above 175] conveyed to John Scarborough. Made 8 Feb 1714. Wit: John Bye, Edward Corn, Mary Scarborough, Richard Lundy. Rec: 24 Mar 1714.

P. 74   Deed. Robert Heaton, Jr. of Southampton, yeoman, and Grace his wife, and Robert Heaton, Sr. of Middletown, yeoman, and Alice his wife, for £450, convey to Jonathan Woolston of Middletown, yeoman, 384 acres in Middletown by Neshaminy Creek and by lands of James Sutton, Henry Johnson Vandicke, Thomas Thwaits and Cuthbert Hayhurst and by the road that leads from Newtown to Bristol. Said land is part of 584 acres which Edward Shippen, Griffith Owen and James Logan, Commissioners for William Penn, conveyed by patent dated 9 Jul 1705 and recorded at Philadelphia in Patent Book A, Vol 3, pg 76 to Robert Heaton, Jr. Made 30 Jan 1712. Wit: Thomas Stackhouse, William Biles, Jeremiah Langhorne. Rec: 27 Mar 1715.

P. 76   Mortgage. John Addington of Bristol, yeoman, for £30 plus interest due in 1722, to William White of Falls Township, yeoman, for 100 acres of land in Bristol beginning near John Headly's line and bordering the lands of George White, Daniel Jackson, Thomas Watson, Thomas Terry and Edmond Lovett. Edmond Lovett of Bristol , yeoman, by deed recorded in Book C, Vol 1, pg 193, conveyed the land to John Addington. Made 25

Mar 1715. Wit: John Sotcher, Jeremiah Langhorne, William Strutt. Rec: 29 Mar 1715. Payment acknowledged 20 Apr 1722 by Jeremiah Langhorne.

P. 79   Deed. John Swift of Philadelphia, glazier, and Frances his wife, for £400, to Jacob Izelstein of Bucks Co., yeoman, a total of 618 acres in three tracts of land, the first tract of 250 acres in Philadelphia Co. bordering the land of John Jones, deceased, and Richard Wood's land and the lands late of William Dilwin's, Nicholas More's and John Jennings'. This land was conveyed by Thomas Fairman of Philadelphia Co., gent., to Anna Salter in her lifetime by indenture dated 24th da 5th mo 1686 and recorded at Philadelphia in Book E1, Vol 5, pg 401. Anna Salter sold the land to Thomas Lloyd, late of the same place, gent., deceased, who by his Last Will and Testament dated 10th da 7th mo 1694, named his wife Patience Lloyd, his son Mordecai Lloyd, his son-in-law Isaac Norris and kinsman David Lloyd executors. Patience renounced her executorship and son Mordecai Lloyd died before the Will was proved. As executors, the named Isaac Norris and David Lloyd by deed dated 13 Jun 1702 sold the land to John Swift and the deed was acknowledged in court 12 Oct 1702.

Another tract of land in Philadelphia Co. bordering Thomas Lloyd's land and by the Manor of Moreland containing 143 acres was part of 500 acres out of the "over plus land of Moreland" and was conveyed to Thomas Fairman by warrant dated 10th da 5th mo 1689. This 500 acres was part of 1,100 acres that fell to the share of Thomas Hooton in right of his wife Elizabeth, one of the daughters of William Stanley, deceased, purchaser of 5,000 acres in Pennsylvania. The said 500 acres was sold to Thomas Fairman in his lifetime by Thomas Hooton with the consent of his wife Elizabeth by deed dated 11th da 4th mo 1689 and is recorded at Philadelphia in Book D2, Vol 4, pg 35. The said Elizabeth, with her now husband Alexander Paxton of Philadelphia, merchant, by deed dated 3 Jul 1702 sold the 1,100 acres of land to Thomas Fairman. Thomas Fairman by deed dated 4 Jul 1702 sold 143 acres of the tract to John Swift.

Both tracts, the first of 250 acres and the second of 143 acres were confirmed to John Swift by patent from the Commissioners for William Penn dated 7 Jul 1702 and recorded at Philadelphia in Patent Book A, Vol 2, pgs 340-342.

The third tract of land, beginning near Richard Wood's land, contained 225 acres. This tract was granted by warrant dated 12th da 1st mo 1684 to John Luffe in right of William Smith of Bramham House, of whom the said John Luffe purchased the same. By his Last Will and Testament dated 27 Sep 1684 John Luffe named his wife Jane his sole executrix and left instructions to sell the land for the payment of his debts and the maintenance of herself and his child. John's said child died in infancy and

the widow Jane Luffe agreed to sell the land to James Jacob of Philadelphia, cordwainer. Jane then married Philip Howell of Philadelphia, tailor, and afterwards died before a deed of conveyance was made to the said James Jacob, who had already paid for the land. John and Jane Luffe both died without a living child, and the land descended to their heirs. By Patent of Confirmation dated 5th da 2nd mo 1689, the Commissioners of Propriety granted the land together with other lands to the heirs, executors and administrators of John Luffe. Philip Howell, the last husband of Jane's, and Thomas Peart of Philadelphia, blacksmith, and Mary his wife, who was formerly the wife of Richard Hilliard of the same place, carpenter, deceased, being the heirs of John and Jane Luffe, confirmed that James Jacob had paid to Jane the full sum agreed upon for the land. Therefore, Philip Howell and Thomas and Mary Peart by indenture dated 30 Jul 1696, conveyed the land, together with other lands, to James Jacob. James Jacob then sold the 225 acres to Nicholas Randall of Bucks Co., yeoman. Nicholas Randall by deed dated 5th da 1st mo 1702 conveyed the land to John Swift.
    Made 12 Oct 1711. Wit: Abraham Carliell, Elizabeth Taylor, Joseph Wilcox. Frances Swift confirmed her willing participation in the sale of the property in Philadelphia to Justice Joseph Wilcox. Rec: 29 Mar 1715.

P. 84 Lease. Jacob Islestone of Southampton, yeoman, for 5 shillings, to Andreas VanBuskirk of Bergin, NJ, two tracts of land containing 619 acres. The first tract of land in Philadelphia County beginning next to the lands of John Jones, deceased, and Richard Wood and the lands late of William Dilwin, Nicholas Moore and John Jennings contains 394 acres and the other tract beginning in the line of the above mentioned property and bordered by John Morris', William Gregory's and Joseph Kirle's land, contains 225 acres. John Swift of the City of Philadelphia, glazier, by deed dated 12 Oct 1711 granted these tracts of land to Jacob Islestone. Made 29 Nov 1714. Wit: Robert Colbert, Thomas Todd, Jeremiah Langhorne.

P. 86 Release. Jacob Islestone of Southampton, yeoman, for £300, to Andreas VanBuskirk of Bergin, NJ, gent., 619 acres of land [as described in the above entry] now in the actual possession of Andreas VanBuskirk by virtue of a lease made to him for one year. Made 10 Nov 1714. Wit: Robert Cobbert [sic], Thomas Todd, Jeremiah Langhorne. Rec: 4 Apr 1715.

P. 88 Deed. John Hall of Bristol, cooper, for £60, to Joseph White of the same place, carpenter, 50 acres of land in Bristol by the River Delaware at Jacob Pellison's corner and by Hogg Run. Said land part of 116 acres granted to John Hall by patent dated 9 Apr 1713 by Richard Hill, Isaac Norris and James Logan, Commissioners for William Penn and recorded at

Philadelphia in Patent Book A, Vol 4, pg 335. An addendum states agreement that John Hall and his heirs shall have access from John Hall's other lands which border this tract to the River Delaware. Made 6 Feb 1714. Wit: William Paxson, Joseph Bond, James Allen, Benjamin Wright and Jeremiah Langhorn. Rec: 4 Apr 1715.

P. 91   Deed. Jasper Terry of Bristol, yeoman, eldest son and heir of Thomas Terry, deceased, and Susanna Terry, wife of Jasper Terry, for £72.10s, to John Bowne of Bucks Co., husbandman. Confirmed by patent from William Penn dated 24th da 1st mo 1701 and recorded at Philadelphia in Patent Book A, Vol 2, pgs 57-58 to Thomas Terry, 100 acres of land in Bristol beginning at a corner of Edmond Lovett's land and by the lands of John Hiett, Anthony Burton, and Phineas Pemberton. Made 22 Oct 1714. Wit: William Baldwin, Edmond Lovett, Edmond Lovett, Jr. Rec: 7 Apr 1715.

P. 92   Deed. John Hall of Bristol, cooper, for £30, to Joseph White of the same place, carpenter, a meadow in Bristol by Hogg Run and at a corner of James Allen's meadow containing about 2½ acres, being the residue of 116 acres granted to John Hall by patent from William Penn dated 9 Apr 1713 and recorded at Philadelphia in Patent Book A, Vol 4, pg 335. Made 26 Jul 1715. Wit: Joseph Bond, Henry Tomlinson, Jeremiah Langhorn. Rec: 19 Sep 1715.

P. 93   Deed. Thomas Knight of Bensalem, yeoman, for £6, to Thomas Knight, Jr., eldest son of the said Thomas Knight, 8 acres and 12 perches of land in Bensalem beginning at a corner of Thomas Knight, Jr.'s other land and by Nehemiah Allen's land. Said land part of land formerly belonging to Joseph Kirle, late of Philadelphia, deceased, and taken in payment for a debt due to Thomas Knight the elder and conveyed to him by the court. Made 4 Aug 1715. Wit: William W. Baker, John Baker, James Pain. Rec: 19 Nov 1715.

P. 94   Deed. Richard Hill of Philadelphia, gent., for £150, to John Burges of Bucks Co., carpenter, 283 acres in Falls Township beginning at John Clark's corner and bordering the lands of Daniel Burges, Joseph Kirkbride, Roger Moon, Samuel Dark and Robert Harvey. This land is part of land formerly granted to James Hill by William Penn by indenture of lease and release dated 27 Jul 1681. The land was granted to Richard Hill by Richard Hill, son and heir of James Hill, and his wife Agnes by indenture dated 7th da 3rd mo 1712 and recorded at Philadelphia in Book E, Vol 8, pg 205. Made 6 Jun 1715. Wit: James Logan, Samuel Burges, Roger Moone.

P. 96   Deed. George White of Bristol, yeoman, for £10.10s, to John Hall of the same place, cooper, a lot in Bristol on the southwest side of Mill Street and at a corner of the lot late of Richard Burges and running alongside Mill Creek to a lot formerly Hardman's. Made 17 Jan 1715. Wit: George Clough, Otter Otterson, Jeremiah Langhorn.

P. 98   Lease. Jeffry Pollard of Bristol, merchant, and Rebecca his wife, for 10 shillings, to Pentecost Teague of Philadelphia, merchant, 150 acres beginning at a corner of John Otter's land and bounded by lands of John Closson, the widow Bladgen, and William Croasdale. Made 29 Nov 1716. Wit: Jeremiah Langhorne, Thomas Mogridge, Thomas Clark, George Fitzwater. Rec: 1 Mar 1716.

P. 99   Release. Jeffry Pollard of Bristol, merchant, and Rebecca his wife, for £166, to Pentecost Teague of Philadelphia, merchant, 150 acres of land beginning at a corner of John Otter's land and bounded by the lands of John Clauson, the widow Blagdon, and William Croasdale. This land part of a tract that William Penn by patent dated 18 May 1686 granted to James Boyden, late of Bucks Co., yeoman, deceased, 541 acres of land by Neshaminy Creek near Samuel Allen's land. James Boyden made his Last Will and Testament dated 1 Aug 1699, leaving the land to his son James Boyden, to be his after the decease of his (James the father's) wife Margaret, who has since deceased. James Boyden the son granted the land to Jeffry Pollard by deed dated 27 Feb 1705. Made 30 Nov 1716. Wit: Jeremiah Langhorn, Thomas Mogridge, Thomas Clark, George Fitzwater. Rec: 1 Mar 1716.

P. 102   Lease. Henry Paxson, Jr. of Marsh Township, yeoman, for 5 shillings, to Bartholomew Jacobs of Middletown, yeoman, 280 acres of land in Falls Township beginning by John Dark's land and bordering the lands of Edward Lucas and John Webster. Said land part of 380¾ acres which James Paxson, father of Henry Paxson, granted to Henry by deed recorded in Book D, Vol 1, pgs 123-124. Made 19 Feb 1716. Wit: William Biles, John Plumly, Jeremiah Langhorne. Rec: 2 Mar 1716.

P. 103   Release. Henry Paxson, Jr. of Marsh Township, yeoman, for £147, to Bartholomew Jacobs of Middletown, yeoman, 280 acres of land in Falls Township, land now in the possession of Bartholomew Jacobs [same land as described in previous entry for P. 102.] Made 20 Feb 1716. Wit: William Biles, John Plumly, Jeremiah Langhorn. Rec: 2 Mar 1716.

P. 105   Deed. Samuel Carpenter of Philadelphia, merchant, for £22.10s, to Richard Mountain of Bristol, husbandman, a lot in Bristol beginning by John Baldwin's corner and by the road leading to Newtown. Said lot part of land which William Penn's Commissioners granted by patent dated 26 May 1706 and recorded at Philadelphia in Patent Book A, Vol 3, pg 290 to Samuel Carpenter. Made 1 Nov 1710. Wit: John Baldwin, Samuel Large, Joseph White.

P. 106   Deed. Hannah Carpenter of Philadelphia, widow and sole executrix of Samuel Carpenter, deceased, for £8, to Richard Mountain of Bristol, husbandman, a lot in Bristol by the road leading to Newtown and the corner of Richard Mountain's other lot and by Samuel Carpenter's land, containing 2 acres. Said land part of that granted by patent dated 26 May 1706 to Samuel Carpenter and recorded at Philadelphia in Patent Book A, Vol 3, pg 290. Made 1 May 1716. Wit: Joseph Bond, George Clough, Samuel Baker.

P. 107   Deed. Ann Kaighin, daughter of John and Ann Kaighin of Gloucester Co., NJ, for £275, to William and Abraham Alberson of the same place, yeomen, and Joseph Satterwaite of Byberry in Pennsylvania and Rebecca his wife, who before her marriage was Rebecca Alberson, 417 acres of land on the Delaware River and Poquessin Creek and bounded also by lands lately belonging to John Gilbert and Joseph Growdon. Walter Forrest of Byberry in his Last Will and Testament dated 18th da 1st mo 1691/2 gave to Ann his wife (who later became the wife of John Kaighin and mother to Ann) one half of his lands and mills at Byberry. In Nov 1694, the lands were sold to William, Abraham and Rebecca Alberson. William Alberson's wife named as Mary. Made 13 Oct 1715. Wit: Tobias Griscom, Tobias Holloway, Joseph Dole.

P. 109   Mortgage. Daniel Jackson of Bucks Co., yeoman, for securing the payment of £200, a plantation to Samuel Preston of Philadelphia, merchant and guardian for Deborah Puckle, daughter of Nathaniel Puckle, who made his Last Will and Testament 8 Jul 1706 leaving his estate to be divided between his wife Anne and his daughter Deborah, and made Samuel Preston and Francis Cooke (since deceased) guardians of Deborah until she be of age or married. Said plantation bounded by the lands of Henry Paxson, Robert Carter, Henry Pawlins, William Paxson, Edward Kemp, George White, and by the Falls Township line containing 120 acres. Made 14 Dec 1716. Wit: Thomas Watson, Thomas Stevenson, Andrew Hamilton. Rec: 8 May 1717.

P. 110　　Appointment. The Honorable Charles Gookin, Esq., Lt. Gov. of the Counties of Newcastle, Kent and Sussex, empowers Jeremiah Bass, Esq., to practice law. Made 28 Mar 1712. Rec: 9 May 1717.

P. 111　　Mortgage. Jefry Pollard of Bristol Township, merchant, and Rebecca Pollard, for £96, to Miriam Boyden of Philadelphia, widow, 391 acres in Bristol by Neshaminy Creek and John Clauson's land and to a corner of Pentecost Teague's land and by lands of John Otter and Samuel Allen, full payment to be made on 1 Dec 1717. Made 1 Dec 1716. Wit: Jeremiah Langhorn, Thomas Mogridge, Thomas Clark. Rec: 10 May 1717.

P. 113　　Deed. Joseph Growdon of Philadelphia, merchant, for £149, to James Harrison of Bensalem, husbandman, 271 acres in Bensalem on the northwest side of Neshaminy Creek and at a corner of land formerly John Bowen's and by lands of Joshua Nicholls and Nathaniel Hardin and then by Claus Johnson's corner and Samuel Allen's line. Said land part of 600 acres laid out to Robert Fairman and conveyed to Joseph Growdon by deed from Thomas Fairman, attorney to Robert Fairman. Made 24th da 5th mo 1708. Wit: Lawrence Growdon, John Cutler, Samuel Scott. Rec: 2 Oct 1717.

P. 113　　Mortgage. James Harrison of Bensalem, yeoman, for £34.14s.2p, to William Carter of Philadelphia, blockmaker, 271 acres of land in Bensalem on the northwest side of Neshaminy Creek [same land as described in previous entry for P. 113.] The full sum plus interest to be paid on or before 27 Apr 1718. Made 27 Apr 1717. Wit: Charles Brockden, Chas. Osborne. Signed: James Harrison. Rec: 2 Oct 1717.

P. 115　　Lease. Oddy Brock of Philadelphia Co., yeoman, for 5 shillings, to Joseph Jones of Philadelphia, gent., the use of 155¾ acres of land in Bucks Co. bounded by Bensalem Township and by Cobus Vanzant's land for one whole year. Made 6 Oct 1718. Wit: John McComb, William Moore, Joseph Wilcox. Ackn: 10 Feb 1718. JP: Joseph Bond. Rec: 23 Mar 1718. Rec. Deeds: Jeremiah Langhorne.

P. 116　　Mortgage. Oddy Brock, for £144.16s.6p received from Joseph Jones, land now in the possession of Joseph Jones [same land as described in previous entry for P. 115.] A payment of £9.6s.10p to be paid in full on or before 1 Oct 1719, the same again in 1720 and a final payment of £126.2s.10p residue to be paid on or before 1 Oct 1721. Made 7 Oct 1718. Wit: John McComb, William Moore, Joseph Wilcox. Rec: 28 Mar 1719. On 18 Apr 1722 Joseph Jones appeared before Jeremiah Langhorne, Recorder of Deeds, and acknowledged full payment from Oddy Brock.

P. 119   Mortgage. Jeffrey Pollard of Bristol, merchant, and Rebecca his wife, to secure a debt of £96, to Miriam Boyden of Philadelphia, widow, 391 acres in Bristol Township along side Neshaminy Creek near John Clauson's land and bordering the lands of Pentecost Teague, John Otter and Samuel Allen. To be repaid 1 Dec 1717. Made 1 Dec 1716. Wit: Jeremiah Langhorne, Thomas Mogridge, Thomas Clark. Ackn: 11 Dec 1716. JP: Thomas Watson. Rec: 30 May 1717. Rec. Deeds: Jeremiah Langhorne.

P. 123   Lease. Joseph Growdon of Bensalem, esq., and Ann his wife, for 10 shillings, to Jacob Kolluck of "Sussex County upon Delaware," merchant, two water grist mills or corn mills known by the name of Richlieu Mills in Bensalem, and also the bolting mills which adjoin the plantation formerly Nicholas Williams' and lastly in the possession of James Carver, containing 2 acres, and including the mill gear, implements, ponds, and dams, for one full year from this day. Made 15 Sep 1718. Wit: Samuel Bulkley, Isaac Warner, Jeremiah Langhorne. Rec: 3 Feb 1719/20.

P. 124   Release. Joseph Growdon and Ann his wife, for £156, to Jacob Kolluck. [Mills as described in previous entry for P. 123.] Made 16 Sep 1718. Wit: Samuel Bulkley, Isaac Warner, Jeremiah Langhorne. Rec: 16 Feb 1719/20.

P. 127   Defeasance. Between Jacob Kolluck of the County of Sussex upon Delaware, merchant and Joseph Growdon of Bensalem Township, Bucks Co., esq. Joseph Growdon to pay to Jacob Kolluck the full sum of £218.7s.6p: £12.9s.6p on 16 Sep 1719; same in 1720, 1721, and again in 1722. The sum of £168.9s.6p residue to be paid on 16 Sep 1723. [Concerning the same mills as described in previous entries for P. 123 and P. 124.] Made 16 Sep 1718. Wit: Samuel Bulkley, Isaac Warner, Jeremiah Langhorne. Rec: 21 Feb 1719/20.

P. 130   Lease. Nathan Stanbury of Philadelphia, merchant, for 5 shillings paid to him by Nathaniel Walton of Byberry, yeoman, 500 acres of land beginning at a corner formerly John Tatham's and on the southwest by lands late of Benjamin Furley's and bounded on the northeast by the Proprietor's land, leased to Walton for one full year. Made 10 Mar 1718. Wit: ____ Moore, William Betredge, Jno. Sisom. Rec: 21 Feb 1719/20.

P. 131   Release. Nathan Stanbury, for £225, to Nathaniel Walton land in Walton's possession. [Same land as described in previous entry for P. 130.] John Cook of Frankford in Philadelphia Co., yeoman, son and heir of Arthur

Cook, late of Frankford, deceased, by deed conveyed the 500 acres to Nathan Stanbury. 11 Mar 1718. Wit: _____ Moor, Wm. Betredge, Jno Sisom.

P. 133   Deed. William Biles of Bucks Co., yeoman, for 20 shillings and for natural affection, to John Biles, son of William Biles, land and plantation in Falls Township containing 300 acres. This land was formerly conveyed to William Biles by Henry Baker, yeoman, deceased, dated 1st da 7th mo 1698 and recorded in Book B, Vol 1, pgs 205-206. Made 24th da 3rd mo 1707. Wit: Anne Biles, Thomas Pilston, William Biles, Jr. Rec: 25 Apr 1720.

P. 134   Deed. Joseph Frost of Charlestown, Middlesex Co., MA, yeoman, for £250, to James Goold of Boston, Suffolk Co., MA, mariner, 400 acres of land in Newtown, Bucks Co., PA, bounded on the south by Shadrack Walley's land. Said land lately belonged to John Frost of Newtown, deceased, and was bequeathed by him to Joseph Frost, his brother Edmund Frost, and sister Elizabeth Francis by his Last Will and Testament dated 20th da 8th mo 1716. Hannah Frost, wife of Joseph Frost, freely gives up her right of dowery. Made 10 Mar 1718/9. Wit: John Mann, Caleb Call. Rec: 26 Apr 1720.

P. 136   Deed. Richard Hill of Philadelphia, gent., for £150, to John Burges of Bucks Co., carpenter, 283 acres of land in Falls Township beginning at John Clark's corner, by Daniel Burges' land, north by Joseph Kirkbride's land, east by Roger Moon's land, northeast by the land of Samuel Dark, and finally southeast by Robert Harody's land. This land was part of a larger quantity of land formerly granted to James Hill by indenture of lease and release dated 27 Jul 1681 and was granted to Richard Hill by Richard Hill, son and heir of James Hill, and Agnes, his wife by indenture dated 7th da 3rd mo 1712 and recorded at Philadelphia in Book E7, Vol 8, pg 205. Made 6 Jun 1715. Wit: James Logan, Samuel Burges, Roger Moon. Rec: 26 Apr 1720.

P. 137   Deed. John Hough of Middletown, yeoman, for £100, to Samuel Hornibroock of the same place, cordwainer, 150 acres of land in Middletown bounded by John Hough's land on the north, by Musgrove's line, across Cove Creek, and on the east by John Cawley's land, part of two tracts that John Hough came to own through Jonathan Scarfe, late of Middletown, deceased, who granted by deed to John Rumford, late of Middletown, weaver, 145 acres of land in Middletown, recorded in Book B, Vol 1, pgs 283-284. John Rumford and Mary, his wife, by deed dated 1 May 1714, granted the land to John Hough. The second tract of 250 acres of land in Middletown is that which Jonathan Scarfe by deed dated 10th da 12th mo

1698 granted to John Hough and is recorded in Book B, Vol 1, pgs 217-218. Made 25 May 1719. Wit: Joseph Kirkbride, Jr., Thomas Maybury, Jeremiah Langhorne. Rec: 27 Apr 1720.

P. 140   Mortgage.   Samuel Horneybroock of Middletown, cordwainer, for £60.9s, to Toby Leech of Philadelphia Co., gent., 150 acres of land in Middletown [same land as described in previous entry for P. 137.] Made 29 Jan 1719. Joseph Kirkbride, Jr., Thomas Maybury, Jeremiah Langhorne. Ackn: 18 Mar 1719. JP: John Hall. Rec: 28 Apr 1720. Rec. Deeds: Jeremiah Langhorne.

P. 142   Defeasance.   Toby Leech of Philadelphia Co., gent., to Samuel Horneybroock of Bucks Co., cordwainer, 150 acres in Middletown [same land as described in previous two entries for P. 137 and P. 140.] The sum of £60.9s to be paid on or by 2 Feb 1722. Made 29 Jan 1719. Wit: Joseph Kirkbride, Jr., Thomas Maybury, Jeremiah Langhorne. Ackn: 18 Mar 1719. JP: John Hall. Rec: 29 Apr 1720. Rec. Deeds: Jeremiah Langhorne.

P. 144   Power of Attorney.   Benjamin Borden of Newport, Rhode Island and Providence Plantation in New England, mariner, appoints Joseph Kirkbride of Bucks Co., PA, yeoman attorney to divide a moiety of 1,000 acres of land. Said land that which by the Last Will and Testament of John Borden, late of Portsmouth, RI, yeoman and father of Benjamin Borden, was bequeathed to Benjamin Borden and his brother William Borden to be equally divided between them. Benjamin Borden directs Joseph Kirkbride to sell his 500 acres of the land. Made 24 Aug 1720. Wit: Samuel Holmes, Thomas Richardson. Rec: 1 Nov 1720.

P. 144   Deed.   John Dawson of Solebury, yeoman, and Katharine his wife, for £100, to Thomas Heed of the same place, yeoman, 100 acres in Solebury beginning in Henry Paxson's line and by Jos. Pike's land. Said land part of a 223 acre patent made to Sarah Jackson, then wife of Tobias Dymock, late deceased, dated 12 Jan 1704. Ralph Jackson of Philadelphia, whitesmith, and Sarah his wife, and Francis Hardin of Philadelphia, merchant, by indentures of lease and release dated 1 and 2 Dec 1719, conveyed the land to John Dawson. Made 8 Aug 1720. Wit: Joseph Kirkbride, Thomas Brown, Thomas Canby. Rec: 11 Feb 1720/1.

P. 146   Lease.   Sarah Stevenson of Bensalem, widow of Thomas Stevenson, deceased, and Joseph Kirkbride of Falls Township, yeoman, executors of Thomas Stevenson, for 5 shillings lease for one whole year to John and Thomas James of Bucks Co., yeoman, 1,000 acres beginning at a corner by Thomas Suite's line. Made 14 Nov 1720. Wit: Thomas Watson, William Biles, Jeremiah Langhorne. Ackn: 15 Nov 1720. JP: Thomas Watson. Rec: 14 Feb 1720/1. Rec. Deeds: Jeremiah Langhorne.

P. 147   Release.   Sarah Stevenson of Bensalem, widow of Thomas Stevenson, deceased, and Joseph Kirkbride of Falls Township, yeoman, executors of Thomas Stevenson, for £200, 1,000 acres beginning at a corner by Thomas Suite's line to the lands of John James and Thomas James. A deed of lease and release was made by William Penn to Thomas Hudson of Makefield in Great Britain for 5,000 acres in Bucks Co. and recorded in Book A, Vol 1, pgs 240-249. Thomas Hudson, by his attorney William Biles of Bucks Co., yeoman, conveyed the land to William Lawrence, John Talman, Joseph Thorne, Samuel Thorne and Benjamin Field, all of Long Island, gents., and the deed was recorded in Book B, Vol 1, pgs 285-287. Benjamin Field conveyed his share of 1,000 acres of the land to Thomas Stevenson by deed dated 10 Jun 1719. Thomas Stevenson appointed his wife Sarah Stevenson and Joseph Kirkbride his executrix and executor. Isaac Norris, Richard Hill and James Logan, Commissioners, by warrants dated 11 Dec 1719 and 14 Oct 1720 directed Jacob Taylor, surveyor, to survey the land for Sarah Stevenson which survey was recorded in the Surveyor General's office on pg 112. Made 14 Nov 1720. Wit: Thomas Watson, William Biles, Jeremiah Langhorne. Ackn: 15 Nov 1720. JP: Thomas Watson. Rec: 17 Feb 1720/1. Rec. Deeds: Jeremiah Langhorne.

P. 150   Lease.   Made between Hannah Carpenter of Philadelphia, widow and executrix of Samuel Carpenter, Sr., late of Philadelphia, merchant, deceased; Samuel Carpenter of the same place, merchant and one of the sons of Samuel Carpenter, Sr.; John Carpenter of the same place, merchant and the other son of Samuel Carpenter, Sr.; and William Fishborn of the same place, merchant and Hannah his wife and daughter of Samuel Carpenter, Sr., for 5 shillings, to Joseph Bond of Bristol, two islands, one called Burdens Little Island and the other Burdens Great Island in Bristol on the Delaware River near the old mill where the creek empties into the river and by the lands of Daniel Pegg, Henry Tomlinson, Jeffrey Pollard, Richard Mountain, John Baldwin and by the road leading to Neshaminy Ferry containing 815¼ acres, but excluding the burying ground and allowing passageway for access to Mill Street. Made 1 May 1716. Wit: Charles Brockdon, Nathaniel French, George Shier, Jos. Fox. Rec: 4 Nov 1721.

P. 151   Release.   Hannah Carpenter, et al, for £1,250, to Joseph Bond. [Same parties and land as described in previous entry for P. 150.] Part of the said land was granted to Samuel Carpenter, Sr. by patent dated 26 May

1706 from Edward Shippen, Griffith Owen, Thomas Story and James Logan, late Commissioners for William Penn and recorded at Philadelphia in Patent Book A, Vol 3, pg 290 on 9th da 6th mo 1706. Another part of the land was conveyed to Samuel Carpenter, Sr. by Thomas Bills of Seowsbury [sic] in Monmouth Co., NJ, weaver, by indenture dated 4 Nov 1710. The residue of the land was granted to Samuel Carpenter, Sr. by William Homer of Bristol, yeoman, and Elizabeth his wife, by indenture dated 16 Dec 1713. Samuel Carpenter, Sr. made his will 6 Apr 1714, naming his wife Hannah sole executrix and after her decease his children Samuel Carpenter, John Carpenter, William Fisburn and his wife Hannah executors. Made 2 May 1716. Wit: Nathaniel French, George Shiers, Charles Brockden, Jos. Fox.

P. 155   Lease. Charles Brockden of Philadelphia, gent., and his wife Susannah, for 5 shillings, to Thomas Morris of Moreland, Philadelphia Co., yeoman, 300 acres in Hilltown, Bucks Co., beginning by Thomas Cain's line. Made 7 Apr 1721. Wit: Charles Osburne, Jos. Watson, Sarah Wright. Rec: 16 Nov 1721.

P. 156   Release. Charles Brockden, et al, for £85, to Thomas Morris. [Same land and people as in previous entry for P. 155, but mentions that part of the land was formerly William Hingstone's.] 500 acres of said land was conveyed to Charles Brockden, then of Bensalem, gent., by John Rowland of Bristol, merchant, by indenture of lease and release dated 16 Jun 1711 and recorded in Book D, Vol 1, pgs 447-449 and was then confirmed by patent from William Penn dated 9th da 2nd mo 1712 and recorded at Philadelphia in Patent Book A, Vol 5. Made 8 Apr 1721. Wit: Charles Osborn, Jos. Watson, Sarah Wright. Rec: 21 Nov 1721.

P. 158   Release. Nicholas Vandergrift of Bucks Co., yeoman, and his wife Barentye, for £171.10s, to Jacob Kolluck of Lewis Town, in the County of Sussex upon Delaware, cooper, 215 acres on the River Delaware and by Frederick Vandergrift's land. Joseph Growdon of Philadelphia, gent., by deed dated 1st da 1st mo 1697 conveyed the land to Nicholas Vandergrift and it was recorded in Book B, Vol 1, pg 151 on 10 Dec 1697. Made 21 Apr 1713. Wit: Jacob Levering, Joa. Lawrence. Rec: 21 Nov 1721.

P. 160   Deed. Mary Kolluck, widow and executrix of Jacob Kolluck, for £150, to Foulkert Vandergrift of Bucks Co., yeoman. Indenture and lease to be paid by a certain date now past, remain unpaid and indenture becomes indefeasible. [Specific land not described, but refers to interests of Nicholas Vandergrift.] Made 9 Jun 1721. Wit: Samuel Preston, Charles Brockden, Jos. Watson, Willoughby Warder. Rec: 25 Nov 1721.

P. 161   Mortgage. John Johnson of Bucks Co., yeoman, and Margaret his wife, for £160 plus interest to be paid on or before 8 Jun 1723, to Benjamin Duffield of Philadelphia, tanner, for 2 tracts of land. The first by Neshaminy Creek containing 520 acres. The second also by Neshaminy Creek and containing 209 acres. Made 8 Jun 1721. Wit: Cosbar Wislar, Jos. Lawrence, Isa Browne. Ackn:19th da 8th mo 1721. JP: Joseph Bond. Rec.Deeds: Jeremiah Langhorne. Memo: 26 Aug 1751 Thomas Whitton, surviving executor of Benjamin Duffield, acknowledged receipt of the principal money and interest due on the mortgage. Rec.Deeds: Law. Growdon.

P. 164   Deed. Henry Nelson of Middletown, yeoman, for £93, to John Wildman of the same place, yeoman, 220 acres in Middletown beginning on Jonathan Scarfe's line and by John Hough's land. Part of 440 acres granted to Henry Nelson by indenture tripartite dated 4th da 8th mo 1718 by William Musgrove, surviving son of Thomas Musgrove, deceased, and Evan Evans and Elizabeth, his wife, daughter of the said Thomas Musgrove. By indenture of partition dated 20 Jan 1712 the trustees of Thomas Musgrove, deceased, allotted to William Musgrove his share of the land. Made 10 Nov 1718. Wit: Euclydes Longshore, Thomas Stackhouse, Jr. Rec: 21 Dec 1721.

P. 165   Lease. Thomas Hillborn of Newtown, yeoman, for 5 shillings, to Robert Hillborn, son of Thomas Hillborn, 250 acres in Newtown alongside Newtown Creek and Thomas Hillborn's meadow and by John Frost's line. Said land part of two tracts conveyed to Thomas Hillborn, one from Margaret Cook and John Cook by indenture tripartite dated 7th da 9th mo 1701 and recorded in Book C, Vol 1, pg 61 and confirmed to Margaret Cook by patent. The other tract conveyed to Thomas Hillborn from Samuel Baker, son and heir of Henry Baker, deceased, by deed dated 12th da 9th mo 1700 and recorded in Book C, Vol 1, pg 34. Made 21 Oct 1717. Wit: Abrm. Chapman, Thomas Maybury. Rec: 22 Dec 1721.

P. 166   Release. Thomas Hillborn, for 10 shillings, for natural affection he has for his son and because he is moving, two tracts of land, to Robert Hillborn. [Same land as described in previous entry for P. 165.] The first tract of land was formerly confirmed to Margaret Cook by patent dated 21st da 8th mo 1701 and recorded at Philadelphia in Patent Book A, Vol 2. The other tract of land was conveyed to Henry Baker from John Otter by deed dated 4th da 4th mo 1694 and recorded in Bucks Co. Book B, Vol 1, pg 89. The land was conveyed to John Otter by patent. Made 22 Oct 1717. Wit: Abraham Chapman, Tho. Maybury. Rec: 22 Dec 1721.

P. 168   Release. Clause Johnson (son of John Clauson of Bucks Co., cooper, deceased) for consideration that he is moving, quit claims the estate right he has to his father's estate, to John Johnson of Bucks Co., yeoman. Made 13 May 1721. Wit: Benj. Paschall, John Wilson, Charles Read. Rec: 22 Dec 1721.

P. 168   Release. George Townsend of Oyster Bay, Queens Co., on the Island of Nassaw in the Colony of New York, yeoman, for 10 shillings, to Samuel Bound of Flushing, Queens Co., New York, yeoman, quit claims all his rights of a 500 acre tract of land in Bucks Co. by Neshaminy Creek and near land formerly Robert Turner's. Said land was formerly granted to John Bowne, deceased, by patent dated 10th da 2nd mo 1688. Samuel Bowne conveyed the land to his cousin Hannah Willets, now wife of Job Carr, by deed dated 21 June 1696 and recorded in Book B, Vol 1, pgs 95-96. Job Carr and his wife Hannah conveyed the land by deed dated 5 Jan 1714/5. Made 28 Jan 1721. Wit: William Wills, James Townsend, Jacob Willets. Memo: 1 Feb 1720/1 William Wills appeared before Isaac Hicks, Justice of the Peace for Queens Co., and acknowledged the signatures of George Townsend, James Townsend, and Jacob Willis [sic]. Rec: 28 Dec 1721/2.

P. 170   Mortgage. Jonathan Cooper of Wrightstown, yeoman, and Sarah his wife, to secure a debt of £125, to Christopher Topsham of Philadelphia, yeoman, 200 acres in Wrightstown by Neshaminy Creek and bounded on the north by land late of Phineas Pemberton's, on the southeast by the town square and south by land late of Roger Longworth's. Mary Baker, Richard Radcliffe, Edward Radcliffe, William Hayhurst and Rachel his wife and Rebecca Radcliffe by deed recorded in Book E, Vol 1, pgs 411-412 conveyed the land to Jonathan Cooper. To be paid in full by 30 Sep 1723. Made 30 Sep 1719. Wit: Ja. Holcombe, Jno. Worstall, Jer. Langhorne. Rec: 23 Feb 1721/2. On 18 May 1726 Christopher Topsham acknowledged receipt of full payment of £125 plus interest. Rec.Deeds: Jeremiah Langhorne.

P. 172   Lease. Richard Hill of Bristol, cordwainer, for 5 shillings, to Jonathan Wright of Burlington, NJ, tanner, and Thomas Lambert of Nottingham Township, tanner, a tenement and lot in Bristol beginning by the land of Samuel Bown on Mill Street and east to Market Street. Made 18 Nov 1720. Wit: Cha. Brockden, Jos. Fox, Chas. Osborne, Jos. Watson. Rec: 12 Aug 1722.

P. 173   Release. Richard Hill, for £68.7s.3p, to Jonathan Wright and Thomas Lambert, a tenement and lot in Bristol [same property as described in previous entry for P. 172.] Made 19 Nov 1720. Wit: Cha. Brockden, Jos. Fox, Charles Osburne, Jos. Watson. Rec: 17 Aug 1722.

P. 175   Deed. William Croasdell of Bristol, gent., for £50 and affection to his son Richard Hill, of the same place, cordwainer, a lot of land in Bristol bounded by Samuel Bown's land and fronting Mill Street and east to Market Street [same land as described in previous entry for P. 172.] Joseph English, late, yeoman, by deed dated 20 Feb 1695 conveyed 11 acres in Bristol to Anthony Burton and Thomas Brock, both of the said place, yeomen. Burton and Brock by indenture of partition dated 8 Jun 1696 divided the land equally. Burton by deed dated 22 Jun 1696 and recorded in Book B, Vol 1, pgs 84-85 conveyed a lot of the land to William Croasdell. Made 10 Jan 1710. Wit: James Heaton, William Smith, Edward Kempe. Rec: 18 Oct 1722.

P. 176   Mortgage. John Bye of Solebury, shoemaker, for £60, to Thomas Watson of Strobery [sic,] tanner, 438 acres of land in Solebury by John Scarbrough's land, by the Great Spring Tract and by the Manor of Highlands. Thomas Bye of Solebury conveyed the land to John Bye by deed recorded in Book D, Vol 1, pgs 190-191. Full payment plus interest to be paid on or by 14 Jun 1729. Made 14 Jun 1722. Wit: John Hall, Thomas Meredith, Jer. Langhorne. Rec: 20 Oct 1722. Memo: 1729 Thomas Watson acknowledged receipt of full payment. Rec. Deeds: Jeremiah Langhorne.

P. 178   Lease.   John Walley of Newtown, yeoman, son and heir of Shadrach Walley, deceased, for 5 shillings, to Thomas Winder of Amwell, Hunterdon Co., NJ, 600 acres of land in Newtown bounded on the southwest by John Hough's land. Made 16 Nov 1721. Wit: Stophel Vansant, Christian Barnetvanhood, Jer. Langhorne. Rec: 20 Oct 1722.

P. 179   Release. John Walley, for £240, to Thomas Winder, 600 acres in Newtown. [Same parties and land as described in above entry for P. 178.] Said land is part of 618 acres which Edward Shippen, Griffith Owen and James Logan, William Penn's Commissioners, conveyed to Shadrach Walley by patent dated 16 Jul 1705 and recorded at Philadelphia in Patent Book A, Vol 3, pg 93. Made 17 Nov 1721. Wit: Stophel Vansand, Christian Barnsonvanhorne, Jeremiah Langhorne. Rec: 30 Jan 1722.

P. 181   Lease. Barnard Christian of Bergen, NJ, yeoman, for 5 shillings, to Abraham Vanhorn of Bucks Co., yeoman, 290 acres bounded by land formerly William Cutter's and by John Clark's and Christian Barnson's land. Made 6 May 1722. Wit: Christian Barnetvanhorn, Hans Vanbreskirk, Jeremiah Langhorne. Rec: 1 Feb 1722.

P. 182 Release. Bernard Christian, for £110, to Abraham Vanhorn. [Same parties and land as described in previous entry for P. 181.] Christian Barnson conveyed the land to Bernard Christian by indenture dated 9 and 10 Dec 1719. Made 7 May 1722. Wit: Christian Barnetvanhorn, Hans Vanbreskirk, Jeremiah Langhorne. Rec: 2 Feb 1722.

P. 183 Mortgage. Daniel Hodgson of Bensalem, yeoman, for £100, to John Swift of Philadelphia, gent., 271 acres in Bensalem by Neshaminy Creek and by land formerly John Bowen's, by John Nicholls' land, by the land laid out for Nathaniel Harding, by Claus Johnson's corner and by Samuel Allen's line. James Harrison conveyed the land to Daniel Hodgson by lease and release dated 9 and 10 Jul 1722. To be paid in full plus interest on or before 31 Aug 1725. Made 31 Aug 1723. Wit: Richard Glover, Wm. Atkinson, Margaret Atkinson. Rec: 18 Feb 1723/4.

P. 184 Lease. John Baker of Bensalem, yeoman, for 5 shillings, to Johannes Vanhorn of Warminster, yeoman, 107 acres and 52 perches in Bensalem beginning by Thomas Knight's land, by land late of William Baker, deceased, and late of William Williams, deceased, and by Francis Candonet's land [See index, Gandovet, Francis.] Made 20 Apr 1722. Wit: Johannes Vandegrift, Benj. Jones, Jeremiah Langhorne. Rec: Mar 1723.

P. 186 Release. John Baker of Bensalem, yeoman, for £74, to Johannes Vanhorn of Warminster, yeoman, 107 acres and 52 perches in Bensalem. [Same land as described above in previous entry for P. 184.] Francis Candonet of Philadelphia, practitioner in phisick, and Mary his wife, by deeds of lease and release dated 15 and 16 Nov 1717, conveyed the land to John Baker. Made 21 Apr 1722. Wit: Johannes Vandegrift, Benj. Jones, Jeremiah Langhorne. Rec: 21 Mar 1723/4. [See index, Gandovet, Francis.]

P. 188 Release of Mortgage. Daniel Jackson of Bucks Co., yeoman, and Hannah his wife, for 5 shillings and because they are moving, to Roger Edmunds of Philadelphia, mariner, and Deborah his wife. James Claypoole and Robert Turner, former Commissioners for William Penn, deceased, leased 250 acres to Robert Carter by patent dated 28th da 10th mo 1684 and recorded in Book B, Vol 1, pg 125., Carter to pay 1 English silver penny for every acre on the first day of the first month of every year at the town of Springetbury in Bucks Co. Robert Carter died intestate and the land was allotted to John Carter, husbandman and son of Robert Carter, as his share of his father's estate by the records of the Orphans Court held in Bucks Co. 1st da 8th mo 1689.

John Carter, by deed dated 12th da 1st mo 1696 and recorded in Book B, Vol 1, pg 126, conveyed the land to John Smith of Bucks Co., blacksmith. John Smith then sold the land to Daniel Jackson by deed dated 10th da 8th mo 1700 and recorded in Book C, Vol 1, pgs 21-22. By indenture dated 14 Dec 1716 and recorded in Book A, Vol 2, pg 109, Daniel Jackson conveyed 120 acres to Samuel Preston, then of Philadelphia, merchant, the part of the above mentioned 250 acres that borders Robert Carter's, Henry Paxson's, Henry Paulin's, William Paxon's, Edward Kempe's, and George White's land and by the line of Falls Township. By indenture dated 12 Mar 1721 Samuel Preston, then of Passyunck Township in Philadelphia Co., merchant, conveyed the land to Rodger Edmonds and Deborah his wife with the proviso that Daniel Jackson could seize the land if default of payment occurs. Payment was not made on time, and Daniel Jackson redeemed the property. Made 31 May 1722. Wit: Benj. Vining, Lewis Jolly. Rec: 31 Aug 1724.

P. 190   Lease. Niell Grant of Bucks Co., husbandman, for 5 shillings for one year, to John Lambert of Burlington Co., NJ, gent., 200 acres by lands laid out to Thomas Bond and Thomas Hodson. Made 12 Mar 1724. Wit: Wm. Biles, James Crowley. Rec: 20 May 1725.

P. 191   Release. Niell Grant, for £230, to John Lambert. [Same parties and land as described in above entry for P. 190.] Thomas Dure, late of Bucks Co., weaver, deceased, by deed recorded in Book C, Vol 1, pg 5, conveyed the land to James Moon of Bristol, husbandman. James Moon conveyed the land to Niell Grant by deed recorded in Book D, Vol 1, pg 132. Made 13 Mar 1724. Wit: William Biles, James Crowley. Rec: 20 May 1725.

P. 192   Lease. George Brown of Falls Township, yeoman, for 5 shillings for one year, to Henry Paxson of Solebury, yeoman, 250 acres of land in Solebury by Paxson's land, by land formerly Stephen Beake's, and by Samuel Beake's land. Made 19 Jan 1724. Wit: Thomas Pilling, John Brown, Wm. Atkinson. Rec: 3 Jun 1725.

P. 193   Release. George Brown, for £70, to Henry Paxson. [Same persons and property as described in above entry for P.192.] James Carter conveyed the land to George Brown by deed dated 24 Feb 1709 and recorded in Book D, Vol 1, pg 116 [122 is written above 116.] Made 20 Jan 1724. Wit: Thomas Pilling, John Brown, Wm. Atkinson. Rec: 3 Jun 1725.

P. 194   Lease. George Pownall of Solebury, yeoman, for 5 shillings, to Reuben Paxson of Bucks Co., son of William Paxson, late of New Castle Co., yeoman, 238¾ acres in Solebury by the land of Randall Spakeman and by Bassillian Foster's land. Made 20 Nov 1723. Wit: James Hambleton, Thomas Gilbert, Samuel Jones. Rec: 10 Jun 1725.

P. 195   Release. George Pownall, for £60 to Reuben Paxson, 238¾ acres [same parties and land as in above entry for P. 194.] By indenture of lease and release dated 21 and 22 Mar 1681 and recorded at Philadelphia in Book A, Vol 1, pg 130, William Penn conveyed to George Pownall (father of the above named George Pownall) 1,000 acres. George Pownall the father by warrant laid out and surveyed several tracts of the land in Bucks Co. When George Pownall the father died intestate, the land descended to his eldest son Reuben Pownall, brother to the above George Pownall. Reuben Pownall by indentures of lease and release dated 13 and 14 Feb 1710 conveyed 484 acres of the land in Solebury to his brother George. Made 21 Nov 1723. Wit: James Hambleton, Thomas Gilbert, Samuel Jones. Rec: 16 Jun 1725.

P. 197   Deed. William Connoly of Bristol, yeoman, for £40, to Cain Connoly of the Island of St. Christophers in the West Indies, carpenter, one full equal and undivided moiety or half part (the whole to be divided into two equal parts) of land in Bristol. The first part of 87 acres begins by William Dungans line, by the land of John Smith, by John Clay's land and by the River Delaware. The second part contains 50 acres and begins by the River Delaware, runs by the land of Edward Wanton's, by Edward Ratcliff's, and by land formerly belonging to Edward Doyl. Made 29 Jun 1725. Wit: John Cassly, Brett Kirll, Ann Maddox. Rec: 5 Jul 1725.

P. 199   Release. William Musgrove of Derby, Chester Co., cooper, surviving son of Thomas Musgrove, deceased, Evan Evans of Guineth, Philadelphia Co., yeoman, and Elizabeth his wife and daughter of Thomas Musgrove, for £186, to Henry Nelson of Middletown, Bucks Co., yeoman, 440 acres in Middletown. By indenture of lease and release dated 21 and 22 Apr 1682 William Penn conveyed to Henry Bayley of Grindleton, York Co., yeoman, now deceased, 1,500 acres in Pennsylvania. In another indenture of lease and release dated 15 and 16 Dec 1696 Henry Bayley, son and heir of the first Henry Bayley, sold 1,250 acres of the land to Thomas Musgrove of Wharley, York Co., clothier. A 440 acre tract of this land located in Middletown was resurveyed by warrant dated 26 Oct 1702 and begins by Thomas Constable's corner, and by the lands of John Hough, Jonathan Scaife, and William Bridgeman.

Thomas Musgrove's Last Will and Testament devised his land to his wife Hannah and children in their minority. The widow Hannah Musgrove married David Price. Before their marriage, Hannah agreed with the trustees named in her husband's Will that she would accept £100 in lieu of £200 given her by the Will in case of her second marriage in full satisfaction of her share in the estate and £50 for the maintenance and education of Elizabeth and William, the minor children of Thomas Musgrove. The residue of the testators estate was divided between the four children, Thomas, Abraham, Elizabeth and William by indenture tripartite dated 11 Nov 1701 made between David Price and Hannah and the trustees Samuel Carpenter and David Lloyd. Thomas Musgrove, the son, died; the testators debts were paid; and David and Hannah received their £150 out of the estate.

By indenture quadripartite dated 20 Jan 1712, David Price of Merion in the Welsh tract in the Province, yeoman, and Hannah his wife and Abraham Musgrove of Haverford in the Welsh tract, taylor and son of Thomas Musgrove of the first part, William Musgrove of the second part, Elizabeth Musgrove of Haverford, spinster, of the third part, and the trustees Samuel Carpenter and David Lloyd of the fourth part, divided the land. William Musgrove was to pay £30 to Abraham Musgrove by 20 Jan 1715 for the 440 acres. Abraham Musgrove has since died, and the money paid to Gaynor Musgrove, his widow and executrix. The said Elizabeth and William are now of age. Made 4 Oct 1718. Wit: Cha. Brockden, Jos. Fox. Rec: 13 Sep 1725.

P. 202 Deed. Thomas Brown of Buckingham, cordwainer, for £30, and because he is moving, to James Shaw of Buckingham, yeoman, 200 acres in Buckingham beginning by Richard Hill's line, and by the lands of Joseph Paull and Ephraim Fenton. Said land is part of 1,000 acres which Thomas Stevenson, late of Bensalem, gent., by deeds of lease and release conveyed to Thomas Brown. Made 8 Jun 1724. Wit: John Brown, Alexander Brown. Rec: 15 Sep 1725.

P. 204 Deed. Thomas Stevenson of Bensalem, gent., for £200, to Thomas Brown of Buckingham, yeoman, two tracts of land totaling 1,000 acres lying near Buckingham. One tract of 500 acres begins near Francis Plumstead's line and at a corner of the Widow Musgrove's land and by Joseph Paul's land. John Norcross, Jeremiah Scaif, and Jane, his wife, conveyed the said 500 acres to Thomas Stevenson by deed recorded in Book D, Vol 1, pg 261 [182 is written above 261.]

The Commissioners for William Penn, by warrant dated 18 Jun 1714, directed John Cutler, surveyor of Bucks Co., to survey for Thomas Stevenson 250 acres in right of Isaac Decow. By another warrant of the same date, John Cutler was authorized to survey for Thomas Stevenson 250 acres in right of George White. The two tracts joined containing 500 acres also border on the Widow Musgrove's land. Made 11 Aug 1717. Wit: Francis Searl, Thomas Curly, Margaret Johnson. Memo: Received full payment from Thomas Brown 11 Aug 1719. Wit: Francis Searle, Thomas Curry, Margaret Johnson. Rec: 1 Oct 1725.

P. 207   Deed. Ann Kaighin, daughter of John Kaighin of Gloucester Co., NJ and Ann his wife, for £275, to William and Abraham Alberson of the same place, yeoman, and Joseph Satterwait of Byberry and Rebecca his wife, who before her marriage was Rebecca Alberson, 470 acres and the mills near the Delaware River, bounded on the south by Poquessing Creek, on the west by land that belonged to John Gilbert, and on the north by land that belonged to Joseph Growdon. Walter Forrest of Byberry, in his Last Will and Testament dated 18th da 1st mo 1691/2 bequeathed to his wife Ann (who afterwards became the wife of John Kaighin and mother of Ann Kaighin) one half of his land and mills at Byberry. John Kaighin by indenture dated 23 Nov 1694 conveyed the land and mills to William, Abraham and Rebecca Alberson. Wit: Tobias Griscom, Tobias Holloway, and Joseph Dole. Made 13 Oct 1715. Rec: 30 Oct 1725.

P. 208   Deed. William Biles, Sr. of Bucks Co., yeoman, for £150, to William Biles, Jr., son of William Biles, Sr., of the same place, cooper, the farm and land "whereon I now dwell" near the Falls containing 309 acres and bounded by the River Delaware and by the lands of Samuel Darke and Gilbert Wheeler. Made 14 Jun 1698. Wit: Samuel Beakes, Anthony Burton, Richard Hough. Rec: 12 Oct 1726.

P. 209   Lease. Benjamin Borden of Newport, Rhode Island and Providence Plantation in New England, mariner, for 5 shillings, leases for one year to Derick Cruson of Southampton, Bucks Co., yeoman, 500 acres beginning at the Dungan's corner. Said 500 acres an equal moiety of 1,000 acres. Borden's attorney: Joseph Kirkbride. Made 14 Dec 1720. Wit: Pet Evans, Jon. Hall, Jer. Langhorne.

P. 210   Release. Benjamin Borden, for £170, to Derick Cruson, 500 acres [same parties and property as described in previous entry.] John Borden, late of Portsmouth, by his Last Will and Testament dated 24 Feb 1715/6, bequeathed 1,000 acres to his two sons, William Borden and Benjamin Borden. Benjamin Borden filed a Letter of Attorney, recorded in Bucks Co. Book A, Vol 2, pg 144, appointing Joseph Kirkbride his attorney to sell his share of the 1,000 acres. Made 15 Dec 1720. Wit: John Hall, Jer. Langhorne. Rec: 13 Oct 1726.

P. 212   Deed. Jeffry Pollard of Bristol, merchant, and Rebecca his wife, for £195, to Thomas Annis of Philadelphia, mariner. By indenture dated 26 Feb 1723 Jeffry Pollard mortgaged his property to Samuel Carpenter, Jeremiah Langhorne, William Fishbourn and Nathaniel Newlin, appointed Trustees of the General Loan Office of Pennsylvania, all 391 acres of his plantation and lands beginning at Neshaminy Creek and by the lands of John Clauson, Pentecost Teague, John Otter and Samuel Allen. Jeffry Pollard paid the Trustees £20 of the debt and Thomas Annis has agreed to pay the remainder of the mortgage money. Made 1 Sep 1726. Wit: John Noble, Jos. Watson.

P. 214   Deed. Joseph Kirkbride of Falls Township, yeoman, for £80 and because he is moving, to Joseph Worth of Stony Brook, Middlesex Co., NJ, cooper, 400 acres in Bucks Co.
William Penn, deceased, by indenture of lease and release dated 23 and 24 Apr 1683 conveyed to Thomas Hudson of Mansfield, Chester Co., England, gent., 5,000 acres of land in Pennsylvania. By another indenture dated 26th da 12th mo 1683 and recorded in Book A, Vol 1, pgs 240-249, William Penn granted to Thomas Hudson the yearly rent of the 5,000 acres. A warrant dated 26th da 12th mo 1684 surveyed and laid out the 5,000 acres to Thomas Hudson in Bucks Co. adjoining the partition line between Bucks Co. and Philadelphia Co.
By Letter of Attorney dated 16 Aug 1697, proved in open court the 14th da 2nd mo 1698 and recorded in Book B, Vol 2, pgs 183-184, Thomas Hudson authorized William Biles, late of Falls Township, yeoman, his attorney to sell the 5,000 acres. William Biles, by deed dated 1 May 1698 and recorded in Book B, Vol 1, pg 285, sold the 5,000 acres to William Lawrence, gent., John Tallman, Joseph Thorne, Samuel Thorne and Benjamin Field, all of Flushing, Queens Co., Long Island, NY. William Lawrence by deed conveyed to William Fowler of Flushing, NY, 500 acres of the 5,000 acres. William Fowler, deceased, by his Last Will and Testament appointed Jeremiah Fowler of East Chester and William Thorn of Flushing, both in New York, yeoman, his executors to sell the 500 acres, which they did by deed dated 8 May 1722 to Joseph Kirkbride. Made 8 Sep 1722. Wit: Benjamin Eastbourn, Jonathan Carlile. Ackn: 4th da 8th mo 1722. JP: Thomas Watson. RecDeeds: Jeremiah Langhorne. Rec: 18 Nov 1726.

P. 217   Mortgage. Joseph Tomlinson of Makefield, yeoman, and Mary his wife, for £80, to John Shallcross of Oxford, Philadelphia Co., yeoman, 255 acres of land in Makefield beginning by a corner of Thomas Jones' land, then by the lands of Timothy Smith, ___ Scott, Stephen Wilson, and Samuel Stackhouse. Mortgage payment of £84.16s in one payment to be made on or before 1 Sep 1727. Made 1 Sep 1726. Wit: Cha. Brockden, Jos. Watson. Rec: 20 Jan 1726/7.

P. 218   Deed. Joseph Growdon of Bucks Co., gent., for £250, to John Gray of the same place, esq., 1,000 acres near Neshaminy Creek. Made 17 Sep 1685. Wit: Samuel V. Wallige, Isaac Smith, Samuel Fryday. Rec: 22 Feb 1726/7.

P. 220   Deed. John Hall of Bristol, cooper, for £20 and because he is moving, to Charles Levalley of Middletown, cooper, 133 and 1/3 acres of land in Middletown bounded on the north by the land of Bartholomew Jacobs, on the east by the lands of John Johnson and Francis White, on the south by Samuel Carpenter's land and on the west by Neshaminy Creek. Said land is part of 500 acres granted by William Penn's Commissioners by patent dated 8 Feb 1685 to Robert Hall (father of the said John Hall.) The land descended to John Hall, eldest son and heir of Robert Hall, after his father's death. Made 13 Jun 1711. Wit: William Biles, Thomas Biddle, Jeremiah Langhorne. Rec: 22 Feb 1726/7.

P. 222   Deed. Charles Levalley of Middletown, cooper, for £80 and because he is moving, to Thomas Stevenson of Bensalem, merchant, 133 and 1/3 acres of land in Middletown [same land as described in previous entry.] Made 1 Oct 1711. Wit: Susannah Fox, Charles Brockden. Rec: 23 Feb 1726/7.

P. 223   Deed. Francis Searle of Bensalem, yeoman, for £250, to Thomas Stevenson of Bensalem, 275 acres in Bensalem lying by the lands of Thomas Walmsley, Claus Johnson, Abel Hingston, Joseph Growdon and Thomas Stevenson. Joseph Growdon of Philadelphia, esq., by deed dated 20 Feb 1711 conveyed the 275 acres to Francis Searle. Made 22 Aug 1712. Wit: Jer. Langhorne, Grace Langhorne, Joseph Webb. Rec: 25 Feb 1726/7.

P. 224   Deed. By order of a Writ of Vendition Exponas dated 13 Dec 1721, Thomas Biles, esq., Sheriff of Bucks Co., exposes to sale at a Court of Common Pleas to be held 12 Mar 1723 and sells, for £710, to Samuel Bayard of New York City, merchant, all the several tracts of land, mills and buildings that Thomas Stevenson died seized of and left in the possession of his wife, Sarah, also since deceased.
    First, a grist mill plantation containing 581 acres of land near Neshaminy Creek and by the lands of Joseph Growdon, Henry Enoch, Harman Vansant, and by the land late of Francis Searle. This land is part of 1,000 acres which John Tatham, late of Burlington, NJ, gent., son and heir of

John Tatham alias Gray, late of Burlington, deceased, sold by deed dated 24 Jan 1711 and recorded in Bucks Co. Book D, Vol 1, pg 269 [it does not say to whom this land was conveyed, presumably to Thomas Stevenson.]

A plantation in Middle Township bounded by Bartholomew Jacob's land on the north, on the east by John Johnson's and Francis White's land, on the south by Samuel Carpenter's land and on the west by Neshaminy Creek containing 133 and 1/3 acres. This land is part of 500 acres which William Penn's Commissioners conveyed by patent dated 8th da 12th mo 1685 to Robert Hall.

Another tract of land in Bensalem bounded on the southwest by the land late of Thomas Walmsley and by the lands of Claus Johnson, Abel Hinekson, Joseph Growdon and Thomas Stevenson containing 275 acres, which was granted to Thomas Stevenson by Francis Searle of Bensalem, now deceased, by deed dated 20 Feb 1711.

A plantation in Bensalem beginning at Samuel Allen's corner, by Claus Johnson's land, by the lands late of George Phillips and Henry Mitchell, and by Joseph Growdon's land containing 300 acres. A tract in Bensalem bounded by the above described land by the lands of Joseph Growdon and late of Henry Mitchell containing 46 acres. These two tracts were conveyed to Thomas Stevenson by Thomas Walmsley and Mary, his wife, by deed dated 13 Oct 1715.

A plantation in Bensalem by Neshaminy Creek, bounded on the northwest by Claus Johnson's land and the southeast by Joseph Growdon's land containing 77 acres, which was granted to Thomas Stevenson by Michael Headerickson by deed dated 1 Nov 1713.

All the above described tracts of land were in the possession of Thomas Stevenson when he died. At a Court of Common Pleas held 12 Dec 1721 at Bristol, William Trent recovered against Sarah Stevenson, executrix of Thomas Stevenson's estate, a debt of £443.10s and £6.19s.6p. By writ of execution dated at Bristol 14 Jun 1722 the then Sheriff John Hall ordered the estate lands and goods be levied to pay the debts. Sheriff John Hall at a Court of Common Pleas held on 12 Sep 1722 stated that by virtue of a writ he had taken three messuages and 1,412 acres of land in Bensalem and Bristol, which Thomas Stevenson died seized of, being estate assets Sarah Stevenson was to administrate. The seized property did not produce a sufficient yearly income to satisfy the debts of Thomas Stevenson and the lands remained unsold for want of a buyer.

At an inquest the payment of certain sums of money from the estate was ordered: £56.3s and £4.8s.6p damage paid to Samuel Preston. £66 and £4.8s.6p damage to Thomas Thorne and £120 and £3.14s.6p damage also to Thomas Thorne; £61.16s.3p damage to George Emmot and his wife

Mary. Made 20 Jan 1723. Wit: Sarah Cowpland, Jeremiah Langhorne, Jos. Rodman. Rec: 18 Aug 1727.

P. 229   Thomas Walmsley of Bensalem, yeoman, and Mary his wife, for £350, convey to Thomas Stevenson of Bensalem, gent., 300 acres of land in Bensalem beginning at Samuel Allen's corner, by Clause Johnson's line, by the lands late of George Phillips and Henry Mitchell, and by Joseph Growdon's land and another tract of land by the above land containing 46 acres. Joseph Growdon sold these two tracts of land to Thomas Walmsley by two deeds dated 7 Mar 1703 and 10 Dec 1707 and recorded in Book E, Vol 1, pgs 183 and 370. Made 13 Oct 1715. Wit: John Johnson, Anna Merriot, Jer. Langhorne. Rec: 18 Aug 1727.

P. 231   Deed. Jeremiah Dungan of Northampton, yeoman, and Mary his wife, for £350, convey to Benjamin Corson of Stratten Island, Richmond Co., husbandman, 250 acres in Northampton beginning at James Heaton's line and a corner of Clement Dungan's land, then by the lands of Benjamin Jones, Francis Krosen, Peter Yoder and John Addis. James Claypoole and Robert Turner, Commissioners for William Penn, granted to Arthur Cook, late of Frankford, Philadelphia Co., land in Bucks Co. by patent dated 1st da 4th mo 1686. Margaret Cook, widow and executrix of the estate of Arthur Cook, and John Cook, son of Arthur Cook, by deed dated 11th da 1st mo 1699 and recorded in Bucks Co. Book C, Vol 1, pgs 19-20, sold to Clement Dungan and Thomas Dungan 1,000 acres, part of the previous mentioned property. Clement Dungan and Thomas Dungan by deed dated 3 Nov 1711 conveyed part of the 1,000 acres of land to Jeremiah Dungan. Made 19 May 1726. Wit: Benjamin Jones, John Hart, both of Bucks Co., yeoman. Ackn: 1 Oct 1726. JP: Jeremiah Langhorne. Rec: 19 Mar 1727.

P. 233   Mortgage. James MacCollester of Southampton, yeoman, for £30, mortgages to Benjamin Duffield of Philadelphia, tanner, 204 acres of land beginning at the line between Bucks Co. and Philadelphia Co. and by the lands of Evan Evans, Mathew Evans, and Benjamin Griffith. The full sum of £31.16 to be paid on or before 1 Mar 1728. Made 1 Mar 1727. Wit: E. Porue, Gabriel Hinton. Rec: 10 Jun 1728. Rec. Deeds: Jeremiah Langhorne.

P. 235   Mortgage. William Cooper of Southampton, husbandman, for £42.11s.2p mortgages to John Morris of the same place, yeoman, 112½ acres of land bounded by the land of Jacob Heston [Heaton?] and Joseph Kirk. Said land is that which Jan VanBaskirk of Bucks Co., tanner, by indenture of lease and release dated 4 and 5 Dec 1724 conveyed to William Cooper. First payment of £2.5s.7p to be paid to John Morris in his dwelling house by or on 15 Jun 1727 and £40.5s.7p on 15 Jun 1728. Made 15 Jun 1726. Wit: Evan Morris, John Phillips. Rec: 10 Dec 1726. Rec. Deeds: Jeremiah Langhorne.

P. 238   Deed. At an auction held 9 Dec 1727, Thomas Biles, Sheriff, for £200 sold to Edward Pearce of Philadelphia, gent., being the highest bidder, 1,100 acres of land which begins at the line of Wrightstown and a corner of Joseph Claypoole's line and runs by the lands of David Lloyd, Henry Bayley, and Thomas Callowhill. Said land was granted to Mary Crap by Richard Hill, Isaac Morris and James Logan, Commissioners for William Penn by patent dated 17 Apr 1714.

At a Court of Common Pleas held at Newtown, William Robinson recovered against Benjamin Perce and Mary his wife, executrix of the estate of Mary Crap, late of Bucks Co., deceased, £48.6s.5p. In a writ of execution dated at Newtown 16 Jun 1727 Sheriff Thomas Biles was commanded to levy the debts of the estate from Benjamin and Mary Perce in order to have the money for the Court of Common Pleas to be held 15 Sep 1727. An inquest held found that the income from Mary Crap's 1,100 acres of land was not of a sufficient yearly value to satisfy the debts of the estate.

Sheriff Biles seized the 1,100 acres of land that was Mary Crap's estate. As the lands remained unsold for want of a buyer, Sheriff Biles, by writ dated 15 Sep 1727, was commanded to sell the land at public auction to satisfy the debts and present the money at the Court of Common Pleas to be held 14 Dec 1727 at Newtown. Made 16 Dec 1727. Wit: F. Gardinell, John Hyatt, James Gould. Rec: 24 Jul 1728.

P. 240   Lease. Edward Peirce of Philadelphia, gent., for 5 shillings, leases for one year to George Claypoole of the same place, merchant 1,100 acres now in the possession of Benjamin Pearce of Bucks Co. and his wife Mary, administrator of the estate of Mary Crap, who died intestate. Said land in Wrightstown borders the lands of Joseph Claypoole, David Lloyd, Henry Bayley, and Thomas Callowhill. [Same land as described in previous entry.] Made 16 Jan 1727. Wit: William Fishbourn, Israel Pemberton, John Jones. Rec: 2 Aug 1728.

P. 241.   Release. Edward Peirce for £200 paid by George Claypoole. [Same parties and land as in 2 previous entries.] The released premises were lately sold to Edward Peirce by the High Sheriff Thomas Biles after the estate of Mary Crap, deceased, was sued for damages by William Robinson, sadler of Philadelphia. Made 17 Jan 1727. Wit: Wm. Fishbourn, Israel Pemberton, John Jones. Rec: 2 Aug 1728.

P. 243   Deed. Jonathan Cooper of Wrightstown, yeoman, for £300, to Thomas Pursill of Wrightstown, 220 acres in Wrightstown by Neshaminy Creek and at the mouth of Randalls Run and then by Godfrey Kirk's land. By indenture of lease and release dated 21 and 22 Apr 1682, William Penn granted to James Harrison 5,000 acres. James Harrison conveyed 200 of those acres to James Radclift, confirmed by Phineas Pemberton who married Phebe, only daughter and heiress of James Harrison. Mary Baker (widow of James Radclift,) Richard Radclift and Edward Radclift (the two men the only surviving sons of James and Rebecca Radclift) and Rachel Hayhurst and her husband William Hayhurst (the only surviving daughters of James Radclift) by deed 15 Feb 1704 conveyed the 200 acres to Jonathan Cooper. Israel Pemberton (only son of Phineas and Phebe Pemberton) by indenture dated 7 Nov 1710 released the 200 acres to Jonathan Cooper. That 200 acres and another tract joining it was resurveyed and granted to Jonathan Cooper by patent dated 20 Jul 1713, recorded at Philadelphia in Patent Book A, vol 4, pg 362. Made 12 May 1726. Wit: Christopher Topham, Abraham Chapman. Rec: 12 Aug 1728.

P. 245   Deed. Michael Fredrickson of Bensalem, yeoman, because he is moving and for £20, to Thomas Stevenson of the same Co., gent., 77 acres in Bensalem by Neshaminy Creek and Clause Johnson's land and by the land of Joseph Growdon, who by deed recorded in Book C, Vol 1, pg 215 conveyed the land to Michael Fredrickson. Made 21 Nov 1713. Wit: Cornelius Vansant, James Smith, Wm. Beal. Rec: 16 Aug 1728.

P. 247   Mortgage. Josiah Hingston of Philadelphia, merchant, for £80, to Thomas Sober, merchant, of Philadelphia, 200 acres in Hilltown. William Hingston, who died intestate, brother of Josiah and James Hingston, owned 200 acres in Hilltown, Bucks Co. alongside the lands of Colonel Mildways and Charles Brockden. James Hingston by power of attorney dated 27 Oct 1726 authorized his brother Josiah to sell the land. Made 31 May 1728. Wit: Pet Evans, Henry Gonne. Jeremiah Langhorne, attorney for Josiah Hingston. Ackn: 18 Nov 1728. JP: Matthew Hughes. Wit: Peter Evans of Philadelphia, gent. Rec: 26 Nov 1728.

P. 249   Mortgage. George Welsh of Newtown, inholder, to secure a debt of £120, to Henry Nelson and William Brelsford of the same Co., yeomen, a tenement and lot in Newtown two streets removed from the Courthouse. Full payment to be made by or on 13 Mar 1733. Made 13 Mar 1728. Wit: Jer. Langhorne, Abr. Chapman, Joseph Chapman. Rec: 1 Apr 1729.

P. 250 Mortgage. William Carter of Southampton, yeoman, for £50, to Benjamin Duffield of Philadelphia, tanner, 200 acres and a plantation in Southampton by Neshaminy Creek and Mill Creek and by the lands of Samuel Griffith, Ralph Dracott, John Swift, and by the King's Road leading from the Falls to Philadelphia except an undivided third for William's mother Susanna, by the Last Will dated 1 Dec 1714 of her husband, James Carter, deceased. To be paid on or before 13 Feb 1729. Made 13 Feb 1728. Wit: James Carter, Joseph Breintall. Ackn: 14 Feb 1728. Rec: 1 Apr 1729.

P. 252 Deed. Thomas Stackhouse of Middletown, yeoman, for £120, to John Montgomery of Makefield, 100 acres by the lands of Samuel Stackhouse, Henry Gouldney & Co. and John Whitecar. Said land part of 1,200 acres which Francis Richardson of Philadelphia, silversmith, conveyed to Thomas Stackhouse by deed dated 19 Nov 1707 and recorded in Book C, Vol 1, pg 422. Made 25 Oct 1728. Wit: Thomas Dikes, Jer. Langhorne. Rec: 1 Apr 1729.

P. 254 Lease. Thomas Marke of Burlington Co., New Jersey, tanner, for 5 shillings, to John Abraham DeNormandy of Bristol, Bucks Co., merchant, 108 acres in Bristol by the road to Philadelphia and by the lands of Henry Tomlinson, Joseph Bond, and William Fishbourn. Made 18 Apr 1726. Wit: Cesar Godeffroy, Cha. Brockden, Jo. Watson. Ackn: 10 Sep 1728. JP: John Hall. Rec: 1 Apr 1729.

P. 255 Deed. Thomas Marke for £80 to John Abraham DeNormandy [same parties and land as described in previous entry.] 108 acres, part of the land which by indenture of lease and release dated 15 and 16 Apr [year not stated] Samuel Preston Parsyunck of Philadelphia Co., merchant, and his wife Margaret (formerly the widow of Josiah Langdale of Bridlingtonkey, York Co., Great Britain, yeoman, deceased) sold to Thomas Marke 238 acres of land in Bristol bounded by the River Delaware, the flood gates, and the ferry road and by the lands of Henry Tomlinson and Joseph Bond. Made 19 Apr 1726. Wit: Cesar Godeffroy, Cha. Brockden, Jo. Watson. Rec: 1 Apr 1729.

P. 257 Deed. Anthony Burton of Bristol, yeoman, for 5 shillings, to John Abraham DeNormandy of Bristol, merchant, land in Bristol by Radcliffe Street at a corner of Henry Nelson's lot and south to the River Delaware. Made 10 May 1728. Wit: Jno. Anthony DeNormandie, Joseph Peace, Jos. Kirkbride, Jr. Rec: 3 Apr 1729.

P. 258   Release. Anthony Burton for £22 to John Abraham DeNormandy [same parties and land as described above] his half of 11 acres in Bristol. Joseph English of Burlington Co., NJ by deed dated 20th da 12th mo 1695 and recorded in Bucks Co. Book B, Vol 1, pg 57 conveyed to Thomas Brock, late of Bristol, deceased, and Anthony Burton 11 acres in Bristol (which place not yet made into a borough was called Buckingham.) Brock and Burton partitioned the land 8th da 4th mo 1696 (recorded in Bucks Co. Book B, Vol 1, pg 73.) Made 11 May 1728. Jno. Anthony DeNormandie, Joseph Pearce, Jos. Kirkbride, Jr. Rec: 3 April 1729.

P. 261   Deed. Thomas Biles of Bucks Co. for £100 paid by Bartholomew Jacobs of Middle Township, yeoman, one full sixth part of two grist mills with boulting mills and 4 tracts of land in Middle Township, the first tract of 50 acres bounded by Neshaminy Creek by the lands late of George Vansant and on the northeast by Joseph Growdon's land. The second tract of 2½ acres and 11 perches is also by Neshaminy Creek. The third tract lies by Johannes Praul's land, John Plumbly's line and Neshaminy Creek and contains 5 acres and 30 perches. The fourth tract by Neshaminy Creek contains 3¾ acres and 12 perches. Jeremiah Langhorne, Stophel Vansant, John Plumbly and Bartholomew Jacobs, all of Middle Township, conveyed the two grist mills, the boulting mills and the 4 tracts of land by deed dated 25 Sep 1727 to Thomas Biles. Made 13 Sep 1727. Wit: Richard Mitchell, Garret Vandine. Ackn: 2 October 1727. JP: William Paxson. Rec: 3 Apr 1729.

P. 262   Deed. Thomas Biles of Bucks Co. for £100, to Stophel Vansant of Middle Township, yeoman, one full sixth part of two grist mills and 4 tracts of land [as described above.] Made 13 Sep 1727. Wit: Richard Mitchell, Garret Vandine. Ackn: 2 Oct 1727. JP: William Paxson. Rec: 3 Apr 1729.

P. 264   Deed. Thomas Biles of Bucks Co., for £150, to Jeremiah Langhorne of Middle Township, gent., one full fourth part of two grist mills and 4 tracts of land [as described in previous entries above.] Made 13 Sep 1727. Wit: Richard Mitchell, Jarret Vandine. Ackn: 2 Oct 1727. JP: William Paxson. Rec: 3 Apr 1729.

P. 266   Deed. Jeremiah Langhorne, Stophel Vansant, John Plumbley and Bartholomew Jacobs, all of Middle Township, for £500, to Thomas Biles, two grist mills with bolting mills and 4 tracts of land in Middletown [as previously described in entry for P. 261.] Made 25 Sep 1727. Wit: Richard Mitchell, Garret Vandine. Ackn: 2 Oct 1727. JP: William Paxson. Rec: 3 Apr 1729.

P. 268　　Deed. Daniel Hodgson of Bensalem, and Sarah his wife, for £200, to John Swift, esq., of Philadelphia, 271 acres in Bensalem. Joseph Growdon of said city, merchant, by deed dated 24 Jul 1708 and recorded in Bucks Co. Book A, Vol 2, pg 43, conveyed to James Harrison 271 acres of land in Bensalem on the northwest side of Neshaminy Creek and bordering land formerly John Bowen's, by John Nicholas' land, by land laid out to Nathaniel Harding, by Claus Johnson's corner and by Samuel Allen's line. James Harrison by indenture of lease and release dated 9 and 10 July 1722 conveyed the land to Daniel Hodgson. Made 26 Feb 1723/4. Wit: Thomas Pryor, Robert Davies. Rec: 3 Apr 1729. Memo: 27 Sep 1734 Robert Davies of Philadelphia, innkeeper, appeared before Lawrence Growdon, esq., JP and acknowledged his witnessing of the deed. Norton Pryor affirmed the handwriting of his father Thomas Pryor, late of Philadelphia, deceased. Rec: 15 Oct 1754 [sic.]

P. 270　　Lease. Jonathan Taylor of Bucks Co., yeoman, for 5 shillings, to Peter Groom of Middlesex Co., NJ, yeoman, 200 acres by the River Delaware and by William Biles land. Made 9 Jan 1710. Wit: William Hixon, Jacob Wright, John Brierly, Wm. Beakes. Witnesses William Hixson and John Brierly acknowledge their signature on 16 March 1720 before JP Joseph Kirkbride. Rec: 4 Apr 1729.

P. 271　　Release. Jonathan Taylor for £60 to Peter Groom [same land as in above entry.] Made 10 Jan 1710. Wit: William Hixon, Jacob Wright, John Brierly, Wm. Beaks. Rec: 4 Apr 1729.

P. 273　　Deed. George Beale of Wimboro, Surrey Co., Great Britain, yeoman, for 10 shillings, to Jeremiah Langhorne of Bucks Co., gent., 3,000 acres in Pennsylvania. By indenture of lease and release dated 17th and 18th das 11th mo 1701 William Penn conveyed to George Beale 3,000 acres. Made 18 Oct 1718. Wit: William Frazor, Lodowick Christian Sprogell, John Westbrook. Rec: 4 Apr 1729.

P. 274　　Release. George Beale for £120 to Jeremiah Langhorne [same land as in above entry.] Made 18 Oct 1718. Wit: William Frazor, Lodowick Christian Sprogell, John Westbrook. On 6 May 1727, before a Justice of the Peace, William Frazor and Lodowick Christian Sprogell acknowledged their signatures. Rec: 4 Apr 1729.

P. 275　　Lease. Philip Ford, agent for William Penn, for £100, to George Beale near Guilford, County Surry, yeoman, 3,000 acres of land clear of

Indian encumbrances in Pennsylvania between the Rivers of Susquehanna and Delaware. Made 17th da 11th mo 1701. Wit: William Lirkfold, William Beale. Rec: 4 Apr 1729.

P. 276   Release. Philip Ford, agent for William Penn, for £100, to George Beale 3,000 acres [same land as in above entry.] Made 18th da 11th mo 1701. Wit: William Lirkfold, William Beale. Rec: 4 Apr 1729.

P. 276   Lease. Joseph Peckom of Little Comton, Bristol Co, MA, yeoman and executor of John Peckom, his father, late of Little Comton, deceased, for 5 shillings, to James Dyer of the same place, yeoman, 214 acres of land in Southampton, Bucks Co., PA. on Neshaminy Creek by the lands of John Hayhurst, Robert Heaton and Widow Blagdon. Also another tract of 150 acres in Southampton beginning at a corner of Jeremiah Bartholomew's land. Made 1 Feb 1725/6. Wit: William Simans, George Brownell. Rec: 4 Apr 1729.

P. 277   Release. Joseph Peckcom, executor of the estate of John Peckcom, for £900, to James Dyer [same parties and land as in above entry for P. 276.] John Rutledge and Margaret his wife by indenture dated 16 Oct 1722 conveyed both tracts of land containing 364 acres to John Peckcom, now deceased. John Peckcom by his Last Will and Testament dated 1 December 1722, empowered his son Joseph Peckcom executor to sell the land. Made 2 Feb 1725/6. Wit: William Simans, George Brownell. Rec: 4 Apr 1729.

P. 280   Deed. William Carter of Philadelphia, blockmaker, for £34.14s.2p and interest, to Daniel Hodgson of Bristol, Bucks Co., mariner, 271 acres of land in Bensalem on the northwest side of Neshaminy Creek by John Bowen's land, by Joshua Nichol's land, by land laid out to Nathaniel Harding, by Claus Johnson's corner and by Samuel Allen's line. Said land formerly granted by Joseph Growdon of Philadelphia, merchant, to James Harrison of Bensalem, husbandman, by deed dated 24th da 5th mo 1708 and recorded in Bucks Co. Book A, Vol 2, pg 113 [a "5" is written over the #2 for the volume.] James Harrison mortgaged the land to William Carter to secure the payment of £34.14s.2p and then conveyed the mortgage to Daniel Hodgson. Made 5 Feb 1722. Wit: Tho. Yardley, Wm. Paxton, Chas. Brockden, Chas. Osborne. Rec: 10 Apr 1729.

P. 281   Letter of Attorney. James Cooper of Kennett, Chester Co., clothworker, empowers his trusty and well beloved son William Cooper of the same place to act as his attorney to make a deed and to recover from William Briggs, Bucks Co., yeoman, the sum of £5 on 18 Feb, £5 on 16 May and £15 on 16 May 1728 and £15 on 16 May 1729. Made 16 Feb 1726. Wit: Andrew Haydon, James Johnson. Ackn: 18 Feb 1726 when James Johnson confirms his signature before Edward Roberts, a Justice of the Peace for Philadelphia Co.

P. 281　　Lease. Thomas Stevenson of Bensalem, gent., for 5 shillings, to Derick Cruson of Southampton, yeoman, 500 acres of land beginning by Dungan's corner, being one full moiety, or half part of 1,000 acres of land. Made 2 June 1719. Wit: Jos. Hall, Henry Mitchell, Jeremiah Langhorne. Rec: 10 Apr 1729.

P. 282　　Release. Thomas Stevenson to Derick Cruson [same land as in previous entry] for £175. Said land that which William Borden of Newport, Rhode Island, shipwright, by deed dated 2 Aug 1718 conveyed one moiety (or half part) of 1,000 acres to Thomas Stevenson. Made 3 June 1719. Wit: Jos. Hall, Hen. Mitchell, Jer. Langhorne. Memo: Rec'd. from Derick Cruson full sum of £175 14 Dec 1720. Signed: Sarah Stevenson. Wit: Isaac Pennington, Jer. Langhorne. Rec: 10 Apr 1729.

P. 284　　Deed. William Borden of Newport, Rhode Island, shipwright, for £160, to Thomas Stevenson of Bucks Co. one half of 1,000 acres in Bucks Co. beginning at Dungan's corner. Said land is moiety of 2,000 acres granted to Arthur Cook of Frankford, Philadelphia Co., deceased, and Margaret Cook, his widow, and John Cook, his son, both of Philadelphia, sold to John Borden of Portsmouth, Rhode Island, father of William Borden, by deed recorded by the then Recorder of Deeds Jeremiah Langhorne 6 May 1712 in Bucks Co. Book D, Vol 1, pgs 256-257. The 1,000 acres was bequeathed to William Borden and his brother Benjamin Borden by their father John Borden's Will dated 24 Feb 1715/6. Made 2 Aug 1718. Wit: John Hewlet, Oliver Earle in Newport, Rhode Island. JP: Tho. Richardson. Ackn: 24 Aug 1718 when Oliver Earle of Rhode Island, yeoman, appeared before JP Jeremiah Langhorne and swore his presence at the signing of this deed. Rec: 10 Apr 1729.

P. 285　　Mortgage. Richard Hough of Makefield, yeoman, for £160, to John Shallcross of Oxford, Philadelphia Co., yeoman, a plantation and tract of 416 acres and 135 perches by the River Delaware and bordering the land's of Abel Janney, Thomas Janney, Joshua Hoope, Thomas Kirle, Peter Worrall and Andrew Ellet. Payment of £9.12s on 28 Jan 1729, 1730 1731 and 1732 and £169.12s residue on 28 Jan 1733 to be paid to John Shallcross. Made 28 Jan 1728. Wit: Cha. Brockden, Chris Denning. Ackn: 14 Mar 1728/9. JP: Joseph Kirkbride. Rec: 10 Apr 1729.

P. 288   Lease.   Peter Groom of Middlesex Co., NJ, yeoman, for 5 shillings, to Samuel Shoards of Falls Township, cooper, 200 acres of land in Falls Township by the River Delaware and by the lands of William Biles. 21 Aug 1726. Wit: Joseph Peace, John Severns, Tho. Biles. Rec: 10 Apr 1729.

P. 289   Release. Peter Groom to Samuel Shoards [same parties and land as above] for £82.10s. Said land granted by William Penn to Samuel Darke, late of Bucks Co., deceased, by patent dated 31 Mar 1684. Samuel Darke conveyed the land to John Radley of Elizabethtown, NJ, yeoman, by deed dated 18 Aug 1693. John Radley conveyed the land to Edward Guy of NJ, yeoman. Edward Guy died intestate and the 200 acres descended to his eldest son John Guy who sold the land to Isaac Atkinson of Bucks Co., cordwainer, by deed dated 9 Dec 1700. Isaac Atkinson sold the land to Jonathan Taylor, yeoman, by deed dated 9 Dec 1702, who sold it by lease and release dated 9 and 10 Jan 1710 to Peter Groom. Made 25 Aug 1726. Wit: Joseph Peace, John Severns, Tho. Biles. Rec: 10 Apr 1729.

P. 291   Samuel Shoards of Falls Township, cooper, and Sarah his wife, for £95, to Thomas Biles of the same place, gent., 200 acres in Falls Township by the River Delaware and bordering the lands of William Biles. Peter Groom, late of Middlesex Co., NJ, yeoman, conveyed the land to Samuel Shoards by lease and release dated 24 and 25 Aug 1726. Made 23 Dec 1728. Wit: Wm. Saterthwaite, Eliza Saterthwaite, John Beakes. Rec: 10 Apr 1729.

P. 294   Deed. Frederick Vandegrift of Bensalem, yeoman, for £75, to Leonard Vandegrift of the same Co., yeoman, 74 acres beginning at a corner of his brother Nicholas Vandegrift's land on the River Delaware. Made 24 Aug 1705. Wit: Tho. Fairman, Jr., Jacob Groosbeck. Rec: 12 Apr 1729.

P. 295   Deed. Job Carr of Oyster Bay, Queens Co., NY and Hannah his wife, for £132, to George Townsend of the same place, yeoman, 500 acres in Bucks Co. beginning at a corner formerly Robert Turner's by Neshaminy Creek. Said land was formerly granted by patent dated 10th da 2nd mo 1688 to John Bound who died and the land descended to his son Samuel Bound of Flushing, Queens Co., NY who conveyed the land to Hannah Carr by deed dated 27 Jun 1696 and recorded in Bucks Co. Book B, Vol 1, pgs 94-96. Made 5 Jan 1714/5. Wit: Samuel Macorume, Anthony Wright, Nathaniel Townsend, Jacob Townsend. Ackn: 14 Feb 1721 Hannah Carr appeared before John Jackson, esq., Judge, Queens Co., NY and vowed this a voluntary act on her part. Rec: 12 Apr 1729.

P. 296   Deed. Elizabeth Bennett, widow and sole executrix of the Last Will and Testament (dated 5 Sep 1692) of Edmond Bennett, late of Philadelphia, deceased, for £12.10s, to Barbara Blongdon of Bristol in England, widow, 3 tracts of land in Bucks Co., the first 200 acres bordered by the lands of James Boyden and Henry Jones (deceased) which Griffith Jones sold to Thomas Lloyd (deceased.) Said land part of Edmond Bennett's 1,000 acres purchased from the Proprietary. Also 130 acres bordering the lands of Samuel Allen. This land confirmed to Edmond Bennett by patent dated 3 Nov 1690. Also another 160 acres by Neshaminy Creek and Richard Thatcher's land. This land part of 500 acres granted to Edmond Bennett by patent dated 18 Nov 1690. Also 10 acres in Philadelphia. Joseph Mood her attorney. Made 14 Feb 1691. Wit: Edward Shippen, Samuel Carpenter, Joseph Wilcox, David Floyd. Rec'd. full payment 14th da 12th mo 1692/3.

P. 298   Lease.   Bernard Christian of Bergen Co, NJ, for 5 shillings, to Isaac Vanhorn of the same place, yeoman, 276 acres of land in Bucks Co. bordering the lands of Johannes Blacker, Anthony Tomkins, Edward Pennington and Barnard Vanhorn. Made 7 Jun 1722. Wit: Abraham Vanhorn, Lawrence VanBuskirk.

P. 298   Release.   Bernard Christian, for £150, to Isaac Vanhorn [same parties and land as in above entry.] This land part of 550 acres which Thomas Groom of Philadelphia Co. conveyed to Bernard Christian by deed recorded in Bucks Co. Book C, Vol 1, pg 356, 357. Made 8 June 1722. Wit: Abraham Vanhorn, Lawrence VanBuskirk.

P. 300   Deed.   Charles Read, Job Goodson, Evan Owen, George Fitzwater and Joseph Pidgeon of Philadelphia, merchants (Trustees of the Society of Free Traders) for £936, to Jeremiah Langhorne of Bucks Co. 5,200 acres in Bucks Co. bordered by lands of Joseph Kirkbride, George Fitzwater, James Steel, John James, Joseph Hough, Thomas Meredith, and David Williams. Made 25 Mar 1724. Wit: David Evans, Mirick Davis.

P. 301   Deed.   Charles Read, Job Goodson, Evan Owen, George Fitzwater and Joseph Pidgeon, all of Philadelphia, merchants (Trustees of the Society of Free Traders) for £260, to Jeremiah Langhorne of Bucks Co. 2,000 acres of unlocated land late belonging to the said Society. Made 15 Feb 1724/5. Wit: David Evans, Mirick Davies.

P. 303   Mortgage. Thomas Jones of Makefield, yeoman, to secure a debt of £185, to John Sotcher, Joseph Peace and Joseph Kirkbride, Jr., all of Bucks County, yeomen, two tracts of land in Makefield. The first tract is 150 acres and borders the lands of Thomas Hillbourne, Ezra Croasdele, Thomas Stackhouse, Timothy Smith and Thomas Stradling. Edward Shippen of Philadelphia, gent., by indenture of lease and release conveyed the land to Thomas Jones. The other tract of land in Makefield is that which Joseph Tomlinson conveyed to Thomas Jones by indenture of lease and release dated 24 and 25 Mar 1728 contingent with the above mentioned land bounded by the lands of Timothy Smith and containing 100 acres. Made 10 Mar 1728/9. Wit: Robert Edwards, Isabel Hewarth. Ackn: 21 June 1728/9. JP: Matthew Hughes.

P. 306   Deed. William Snowdon of Makefield, yeoman, for £145, to Mahlon Kirkbride of Falls Township, yeoman, 300 acres in Makefield (which John Snowdon of Makefield by deed conveyed to William Snowdon, his son) bounded by the lands of Joseph Burges, John Preestly, Henry Margarum and by lands formerly Thomas Kirkbride's. Made 22 Aug 1724. Wit: James McComb, Richard Kilbran, Joseph Kirkbride, Jr.

P. 309   Deed. William Biles, Sheriff, for £175, to Philip Dracott of Southampton, Bucks County. John Swift of Philadelphia, gent., at the County Court of Common Pleas held at Bristol 10 Dec 1712 recovered from Nicholas Randall, late of Southampton, carpenter and administrator of the estate of Ralph Dracott of Bucks Co., a debt of £150.6s and £15.12s.10p for damages. By writ dated 26 Feb last the Sheriff seized the lands of Ralph Dracott which remained unsold for want of a buyer in order to satisfy the debt due John Swift. Said 178 acres borders the lands of Joseph Tomlinson, Robert Heaton, James Carter, Thomas Stackhouse and John Sands. Made 18 Jun 1713. Wit: Tho. Stevenson, Tho. Watson. Rec: 28 Aug 1729.

P. 310   Deed. Samuel Overton of Nottingham, Burlington Co., NJ, yeoman, and his wife Hannah; his son Constantine Overton of Mansfield, same Co.; and his son Joseph Overton of Nottingham, for 5 shillings a piece paid by John Lambert of Makefield, yeoman, 250 acres in Makefield near the River Delaware by the lands of John Lambert, Ralph Brock and land formerly surveyed for Joseph Hall and later owned by Thomas Tennyclift. Said land is the moiety of 500 acres which Joseph Hall of Congleton, Chester Co., England, shoemaker and brother of Hannah Overton, purchased by deed of lease and release dated 4 and 5 Apr 1682. Joseph Hall conveyed the 250 acres in trust to William Hobson and William Hall, both of Congleton aforesaid by deeds dated 3 and 4 Aug 1683. Made 8 Apr 1715. Wit: Samuel Wilson, William Bougher, Sarah Overton.

P. 311   Deed. Samuel Overton, for £180, to John Lambert [same parties and land as above entry.] Made 9 Apr 1715. Wit: Saml. Wilson, William Bouger, Sarah Overton.

P. 314   Deed. Jeremiah Langhorne of Middletown, for 5 shillings, to Joseph Kirkbride of Falls Township, 3 tracts of land in or near Hilltown. The first tract is 534 acres and bounded by the lands of John James. The second parcel is 1,602 acres. The third tract borders the land of Joseph Hough and Thomas Meredith and contains 443 acres. These three parcels are one moiety of 5,200 acres which Charles Read, Job Goodson, Evan Owen, George Fitzwater and Joseph Pidgeon sold to Jeremiah Langhorne by deed dated 25 Mar 1724 and recorded in Book A, Vol 2, pgs 300-301. Made 15 May 1729. Wit: James Holmes, John Carson.

P. 315   Deed. Jeremiah Langhorne, for £468, to Joseph Kirkbride [same parties and land as in previous entry.] Made 16 May 1729. Wit: James Holmes, John Carson. Ackn: 5 Aug 1729. JP: William Paxson.

P. 317   Ephraim Allen of Salem Co., NJ, yeoman, and Elizabeth his wife, for £46, to John Shellton of Buckingham, Bucks Co., yeoman, 230 acres of land in Buckingham bounded by the lands of Samuel Beake, Paul Wolf and Thomas Carn. Said land was laid out by warrant from Edward Pennington, Surveyor General to Jedediah Allen (father of Ephraim Allen) and part of Nicholas Waln's purchase from William Penn by indenture dated 18 Oct 1686 and recorded in Bucks Co. Book A, Vol 1, pg 76. By his Last Will and Testament, Jedediah Allen bequeathed the land to Ephraim Allen. Made 25 Mar 1713. Wit: Joseph Kirkbride, Mary Kirkbride, James Adams. Ackn: Ephraim Allen appeared before JP Joseph Kirkbride on 10 May 1717.

P. 319   Deed. Thomas Stackhouse of Middletown, yeoman, for £50, to George Mitchell of Wrightstown, yeoman, 119 acres in Wrightstown and bounded by the lands of John Laycock and Samuel Stackhouse, part of 1,200 acres granted to Francis Richardson, deceased, by patent dated 23 Mar 1692 and given by his Last Will and Testament dated 7 July 1688 to Francis, Rebecca and John Richardson, his children and one third part to his wife who has since died. His son John Richardson is also deceased and Thomas Murray and his wife the said Rebecca by deed dated 30 Sep 1707 conveyed the land to Francis Richardson, their brother who sold it to Thomas Stackhouse by deed dated 19 Nov 1707 and recorded in Bucks Co. Book C, Vol 1, pg 42. Made 28 May 1723. Wit: Joseph Chapman, Lanslot Gibson, Joseph Hampton. Ackn: 4 Sep 1723. JP: William Paxson.

P. 321   Lease. Andrew Hamilton of Philadelphia, esq., and Ann his wife, for 10 shillings, to Evan Evans of Hilltown, Bucks Co., yeoman, 250 acres. Made 30 Dec 1728. Wit: James Steel, Richard Lewis, Fra Sherrard.

P. 321   Release. Andrew Hamilton and his wife Ann, for £100, to Evan Evans [see entry above] Benjamin Harrison of Perth Amboy, NJ (son and heir of John Harrison, late of Perth Amboy, deceased) and Rachel his wife sold to Andrew Hamilton the 250 acres which formerly belonged to John Harrison who purchased it from Samuel Thorn of Flushing, NY. Made 31 Dec 1728. Wit: James Steel, Richard Lewis, Fra Sherrard.

P. 323   Deed. Samuel Bayard of New York City, merchant, for £425, to John Rodman, Jr. of Flushing, Queens Co., NY, one-half or moiety of the following lands: a plantation and 581 acres in Bensalem, Bucks Co. near Neshaminy Creek and bordering the lands of Joseph Growdon, Henry Enoch, Harman Vansant, and by lands late of Francis Searle. Said land part of 1,000 acres which John Tatham, late of Burlington, NJ, gent., and son and heir of John Tatham alias Gray, late of Burlington, deceased, sold to Thomas Stevenson on 24 Jan 1711 and recorded in Bucks Co. Book D, Vol 1, pg 269, it being part of the plantation on which Stevenson lived.
    Also 133 and 1/3 acres of land in Middletown bounded by the lands of Bartholomew Jacobs, John Johnson, Francis White, and by the lands late of Samuel Carpenter, which is part of 500 acres that William Penn's Commissioners patented to Robert Hall 8th da 12th mo 1685.
    A third tract of land in Bensalem bounded by the lands of Claus Johnson, Abel Hinkson, Thomas Stevenson and the lands late of Thomas Walmsley containing 275 acres which was sold to Thomas Stevenson by Francis Searle, late of Bensalem, deceased, by deed dated 20 Feb 1711. Another tract of land in Bensalem bordering the lands of Samuel Allen, Claus Johnson, Joseph Growdon, and by the lands late of George Phillips and Henry Mitchell containing 300 acres.
    Also a 46 acre tract in Bensalem bordering the above described property which two tracts were conveyed to Thomas Stevenson by Thomas Walmsley and his wife Mary by deed dated 13 Oct 1715. Another plantation and 77 acres in Bensalem by Neshaminy Creek and bordering lands of Claus Johnson and Joseph Growdon which Stevenson purchased from Michael Frederickson by deed dated 21 Nov 1713.
    All of the above described lands were in the possession of Sarah Stevenson, executrix of the Will of Thomas Stevenson, deceased, and were sold to Samuel Bayard by Sheriff Thomas Biles in order to pay the debts of Thomas Stevenson by deed dated 20 Jan 1723. Made 2 Mar 1723/4. Wit:

Elias Isillteas, Rip Van Dam, Jr., H. Demeyer, Joseph Severns, Obediah Wildey. Rec: 3 Jan 1729.

P. 327   Deed. Thomas Richardson of Newport, RI, merchant, for £330, to John Rodman his (Richardson's) one moiety of 2,500 acres of land in Bucks Co. on Neshaminy Creek which was conveyed to William Stephenson of Burlington, NJ, gent., and Thomas Stephenson of Bucks Co., gent., by Thomas Revel of Burlington Co., NJ, gent. and administrator of the estate of Elizabeth Tatham of Burlington, deceased, widow of John Grey, alias Tatham, deceased. William and Thomas Stephenson sold the land to John Rodman, Jr., then of Flushing, Queens Co., NY, now of Burlington, NJ, gent., and the above named Thomas Richardson, late of West Chester Co., NY, shipwright to each of them one moiety of the 2,500 acre tract by deed dated 8 Sep 1703. Made 15 October 1726. Wit: Adam Lawton, Josiah Foster, Thomas Lawton.

P. 328   Lease. Thomas Stevenson of Bensalem, gent., for 5 shillings to James Rue of Stratten Island, NY, yeoman, 150 acres of land in Bensalem by the River Neshaminy opposite the house formerly Edward Carter's. Made 23 May 1718. Wit: David Wilson, Roger Wilcox, Jer. Langhorne.

P. 329   Release. Thomas Stevenson for £115 to James Rew [sic] [same parties and land as in above entry.] Said land that which George Vansant, late of Bensalem, yeoman, sold to Thomas Stevenson by deed recorded in Book A, Vol 2, pg 38. Made 24 May 1718. Wit: David Wilson, Roger Wilcox, Jer. Langhorne.

P. 331   Lease. Joseph Growdon of Trevose, Bucks Co., for 5 shillings, to James Rue of Stratten Island, NY 160 acres and 30 perches of land in Bensalem by Neshaminy Creek and by James Rue's other land, by land formerly sold to John Grey and by land laid out to Francis Walker and Duncan Williams. Made 26 May 1718. Wit: John Plumley, Samuel Bulkley, Martin Overholts.

P. 331   Release. Joseph Growdon, for £125, to James Rue [same parties and land as above.] This land is part of 5,000 acres which William Penn conveyed to Joseph Growdon by lease and release dated 24 and 25 Oct 1681. Made 25 May 1718. Wit: John Plumly, Samuel Bulkley, Martin Overholts.

P. 333   Power of Attorney.   James Logan, General Receiver of the Province of Pennsylvania, gent., by authority derived from John Penn, Thomas Penn and Richard Penn, Proprietors of the Province, empower

Isaac Pennington of Bucks Co. to collect the quit rents from the freeholders in Bucks Co. at Pennsbury. Given at Philadelphia 10 Mar 1729. Rec: 21 Mar 1729.

P. 333 Lease. Thomas Stevenson of Bensalem, for 5 shillings, to Derick Crusen of Southampton, a full moiety (or half part) of 1,000 acres of land by Dungan's corner. Made 2 Jun 1719. Wit: Jos. Hall, Henry Mitchell, Jer. Langhorne.

P. 334 Mortgage. Joseph Drinker and his wife Mary and William Fisher and his wife Tabitha, all of Philadelphia, for £250, to Henry Lodge and Francis Knowles, also of Philadelphia, executors of the Last Will and Testament of Elizabeth Teague, widow of Pentecost Teague, both deceased, for land in Philadelphia on the north side of Mulberry Street bounded on the north by Widow Peace's lot and on the west by Peter Hiley's house, being part of a larger lot formerly purchased by Pentecost Teague from Andrew Robinson and now in the possession of Joseph Oldmant. Also 150 acres of land near Bristol in Bucks Co. bounded by the land of John Otter, Jeffry Pollard, John Clauson, Widow Blagdon and William Croasdale, which was formerly purchased by Pentecost Teague from Jeffry Pollard and his wife Rebecca. Elizabeth Teague's Will instructed her executors to sell the land and pay £150 to kinswoman Constance Desting, then or late of Marrazion in Cornwall, England, providing that Constance paid to David Richard of Marrazion what was due him for service done to her late husband. The remaining part of the purchase money should apply towards payment of her debts. Made 6 Jan 1729. Wit: Ric. Redman, Peter Stell, John Kinsy, Jr. On 14 Feb 1729 Joseph and Mary Drinker and William and Tabitha Fisher appeared before JP Matt Hughes in order to ascertain that the wives entered this agreement voluntarily. Rec: 29 May 1730.

P. 337 Reservation. William Brilsford of Bucks Co., carpenter, promises to John Plumly, yeoman, the right to fish and fowl on the property he (John Plumly) sold to William Brilsford by indenture of lease and release dated 10 and 11 May 1728 which was a one-sixth part of two water grist mills and bolting mills with four tracts of land, reserving for himself and his heirs liberty to fish and fowl on the premises. However the deed failed to specifically mention the reserve. Made 2 Mar 1729/30. Wit: Tho. Watson, Wm. Atkinson, John Elfreet. Rec: 30 May 1730.

P. 337 Mortgage. Daniel Palmer of Makefield, yeoman, £248.12s.6p paid by Daniel Hoopes of Chester Co., yeoman. Daniel Hoopes and his wife Jane by indenture of lease and release dated 14 and 15 Mar 1728 conveyed to

Daniel Palmer a plantation and 250 acres of land in Makefield plus 151 acres in Makefield bounded on the west by Jonathan Palmer's land. To be paid by yearly installments on 1 March of each year to and including the year 1740. Made 2 Mar 1729/30. Wit: Timothy Cock, Jonathan Palmer. Rec: 27 Aug 1730. Memo: 1 Mar 1750 Daniel Hoopes acknowledged financial satisfaction for the mortgage to Law. Growdon, Recorder.

P. 339   Mortgage. John Linter of Warminster, yeoman, to secure a debt of £160, to John Roberts of Philadelphia, shopkeeper, a plantation and 100 acres of land in Warminster bounded by George Harris' land and by the lands of John Cadwallader and Nicholas Gilbert. Made 29 May 1730. Wit: C. Brockden, William Parsons. Ackn: 13 Jun 1730. JP: Benjamin Jones. Rec: 27 Aug 1730.

P. 341   Power of Attorney. Rev. Robert Sandilands of Speen, Bucks Co., clerk at present in London, make Col. John Hamilton of New York City my true and lawful attorney to sell my property in East Jersey, Pennsylvania or elsewhere. Made 5 Jun 1725 in London. Wit: Anthony Wright of London, Loyd Laehary, Thos. Ruck. George Perttinse, Lord Mayor and Alderman of London. Recorded in Liber D, No. 2, Folio 144, 145.

P. 342   Deed. Nathaniel Donham of Newtown, inholder, for £21, to Thomas Maybury of the same place, blacksmith, and Thomas Maybury, late of Manatamy, Philadelphia Co., hammerman, 10½ acres of land in Newton bordered by Newtown Road at Peter Cloak's land and by Newtown Creek, part of the 50 acres which James Yates of Newtown, yeoman, by deed dated 28 Mar 1729 sold to Nathaniel Donham which are part of 250 acres conveyed to James Yates by Israel Taylor of Bucks Co., chyrurgeon, by deed dated 14 Apr 1693 and recorded in Book B, Vol 1, pg 3. Made 1 Jul 1729. Wit: Thomas Croasdale, John Cartar, Jos. Lupton, James Yates.

P. 343   Deed. Joseph Lupton of Newtown, weaver, for £3, to Thomas Maybury of the same place, blacksmith, and Thomas Maybury late of Manatamy, Philadelphia Co., hammerman, 1 acre of land on Newtown Creek which is part of 50 acres of land in Newtown which Stephen Twining, Nathaniel Twining and John Twining, all of Bucks Co., yeoman, by indenture dated 3 Jun 1721 conveyed to Joseph Lupton. Made 19 Sep 1729. Wit: Timothy Smith, William Croasdale, John Milnor, James Yates, Nathaniel Donham.

P. 344   Deed. John Wally of Newtown, yeoman, for £57.10s, to Joseph Pool of the same place, tailor, 57½ acres by Joseph Pool's land which he bought from William Ashbourn, by Jacob Johnson's land [Sarah is crossed out and Jacob written over it] by Henry Nelson's land and by John Wally's land, part of 200 acres of land in Newtown which John Coat of Newtown, yeoman, by deed dated Aug 1699 conveyed to his son Samuel Coat of Newtown. Samuel Coat by deed dated 10th da 1st mo 1702 sold the land to Shadrach Wally of Newtown. Made 2 Aug 1729. Wit: William Pennock, Jos. Lupton. Ackn. by John Wally 1 May 1731 before Jeremiah Langhorne, JP. Rec: 3 May 1731.

P. 346   Deed.   Peter Lawrence of Constable's Hook, Bergin Co., NJ, yeoman, for £350, conveys to Josiah Ogdon, esq. of Newark, Essex Co., NJ, 285 acres of land in Bucks Co. on the northwest side of Neshaminy Creek and bounded on the south by land formerly belonging to Barnard Christian but now to Christian Pemborne; on the west by land that belonged to Edward Pennington and on the north by land formerly belonging to Anthony Thompkins but now to Mr. Winecope. Made 19 Jun 1731. Wit: James Dyre, Cor. Corson. Ackn. when James Dyre appeared 5 Jun 1731 before Samuel Alling, esq., Justice of the Inferior Court for Essex Co., NJ. Rec: 14 Jul 1731.

P. 347   Division of Park or Town Square, Wrightstown. John Chapman, Benjamin Clark, William Smith, Abraham Chapman, Joseph Chapman, John Penquite, Israel Pemberton, William Trotter, John Parsons, Joseph Ambler, Richard Tunly, Garret Vansant, Peter Johnson, Robert Stutchbury and Nicholas Williams each by deeds have divided into equal portions land in Wrightstown known as Park or Town Square. Made 23 Dec 1719. Also agreeing to the division are James Logan in Philadelphia dated 16 Dec 1719/20. Rec: 4 Oct 1731.

P. 348.   Recorder's Office, Doylestown, PA, January 24, 1902.
"I hereby certify that the foregoing records, which have been recopied and transcribed into this book from the original Deed Book A, Vol 2 which is dilapidated and worn are true and correct copies of instruments of writing therein recorded. In testimony whereof, I have hereunto set my hand and seal of office the day and year aforesaid." Burroughs Michener, Recorder of Deeds.

1723 - 1741
Deed Book B, Vol. 2

P. 1 Lease. Tobias Collett, haberdasher, Daniel Quare, watchmaker, and Henry Goldney, linen draper, all of London, England, for 10 shillings, to Thomas Scott of Makefield, Bucks Co., yeoman, two parcels of land. The first tract of 200 acres bounded by John Hough's line, by John Whitaker's land and by the lands of the three sellers. The second tract bounded by the above described land and containing 100 acres. Made 13 Mar 1722. Wit: Sarah Dimsdall, Jno. Estaugh, Eliza Esnaugh [sic.] Ackn. 13 Jul 1723. JP: Robert Ashton.

P. 1 Release. Tobias Collet, Daniel Quare and Henry Goldney, for £75 to Thomas Scott, two tracts of land [same land as described in above entry] which are part of a total of 7,500 acres of land on the River Delaware in Bucks Co. by John Scriepers land which Edward Shippen, Griffith Owen, Thomas Story and James Logan, Commissioners for William Penn, lately deceased, conveyed to Tobias Collet, Michael Russell of London, Daniel Quare and Henry Goldney, by patent dated 2 Apr 1706 and recorded at Philadelphia in Patent Book A, Vol 3, pg 256. Michael Russell has since died and the three sellers have Russell's share of the land by right of survivorship. Made 14 Mar 1722. Wit: Sarah Dimsdall, Jno. Estaugh, Eliza Estaugh. Ackn: 13 Jul 1723. JP: Rob Ashton. Rec: 6 Dec 1731.
    Memo: John Estaugh of Gloucester Co., NJ, attorney for the sellers, claims the land description is erroneous and sets the true derivation of the title to the premises as part of 5,000 acres on the River Delaware as by warrant dated 17 Aug 1699 and was surveyed for Tobias Collet on the 19th da 6th mo 1709 and bounded by Richard Hough's land, John Clark's land, Thomas Kirl's land, Gilbert Wheeler's land and by the Manor Highland Pidcodor. Wit: Barnard Eaglesfield, Tho. Biles, Henry Hodgly.

P. 3 Mortgage. Bartholomew Jacobs of Middletown, yeoman, for 5 shillings, to Mathew Rue of the same place, yeoman, 500 acres of land on Neshaminy Creek bounded by land late of Robert Hall (deceased), by Francis White's land, by John White's land and by the land of Edward Carter, deceased. Made 26 May 1730. Wit: C. Brockden, William Parsons.

P. 4 Deed. Bartholomew Jacobs, for £775, to Mathew Rue [same parties and land as above entry.] This 500 acres is that which John White conveyed to Bartholomew Jacobs by deed dated 10 Mar 1702 and recorded in Book C, Vol 1, pg 164. Mathew Rue has agreed to pay the residue of the mortgage Bartholomew Jacobs made to the Trustees of the General Loan Office of the Province of Pennsylvania by indenture dated 26 Feb 1723/4. Made 27 May 1730. Wit: C. Brockden, William Parsons. Ackn: 3 Jun 1731. JP: Jeremiah Langhorne. Rec: 5 Jan 1731.

P. 5   Lease. Joseph Kirkbride of Falls Township, gent., and his wife Mary, for 5 shillings, to David Stevens of New Britain, yeoman, 227 acres and 53 perches of land in New Britain bounded by the lands of Jeremiah Langhorne and Simon Mathews. Made 11 Oct 1731. Wit: John Kirkbride, Thomas James, Ja. Holcomb.

P. 5   Release. Joseph Kirkbride, for £116, to David Stevens [same parties and land as above entry.] Said land part of 5,200 acres which Charles Read, Job Goodson, Evan Owen, George Fitzwater and Joseph Pidgeon, all Trustees of the Free Society of Traders, by deed dated 25 Mar 1724 and recorded in Book A, Vol 2, pg 300-301, conveyed to Jeremiah Langhorne of Bucks Co., gent., who sold it to Joseph Kirkbride by lease and release dated 15 May 1729 and recorded in Book A, Vol 2, pgs 314-315. Made 12 Oct 1731. Wit: Thomas James, Ja. Holcombe, John Kirkbride. Ackn: 13 Oct 1731. JP: Simon Butler. Rec: 6 Jan 1731/2.

P. 7   Deed. David Stevens of New Britain, yeoman, and his wife Mary, for £73, to David Morgan of the same place, mason, 100 acres of land in New Britain bounded by said Stevens land and by the lands of Jeremiah Langhorne, John Davis and Simon Mathews [part of the same land as described in above two entries.] Made 22 Oct 1731. Wit: Thomas James, Griffith Owen, Evan Jones. Ackn: 25 Nov 1731. JP: Simon Butler.

P. 8   Mortgage. Joseph Hembury of Makefield conveys to Joseph Higginbotham of the same place, cordwinder [sic], the tract of land Joseph Hembury lives on except the room he lives in and his orchard and bare plot on the south side of the orchard and the garden behind the house with Joseph Higginbotham to have the east end of the house and Higginbotham is to build Hembury a "lintoo" at his end of the house (the west end.) It is further agreed that Joseph Hembury and his wife Elinor will have all the above privileges as long as they both live. And if they both live another 4 years, then Hembury is to put new shingles on the part of the house he now lives in. Made 6 Sep 1720. Wit: Samuel Coombe, Hannah Coombe, Benjamin Coombe. Ackn: 9 Mar 1731/2. JP: Thomas Yardley.

P. 9   Mortgage. John Baldwin of Bucks Co., yeoman, and his wife Ann, for £100, to William Carter of Philadelphia, gent., 2 tracts of land in

Makefield. The first is 100 acres bounded by the lands of Richard Hough, Samuel Baker, the heirs of Ralph Miller and John Baldwin and is part of land patented to Samuel Baker who sold it to John Baldwin. The other tract is bounded by lands of Samuel Baker and Ralph Miller and contains 139 acres and was patented to John Baldwin. Made 31 Mar 1732. Wit: Chas. Read, Jas. Lawrence, Gael Burkerdike, Joseph Richardson. Ackn: 4 Apr 1732. JP: William Paxson.

P. 11   Lease.   John Rodman, Jr. of Burlington Co., NJ, gent., for 5 shillings, to John Bissonet of Bensalem, Bucks Co., mason, 133 and 1/3 acres of land in Middletown by Neshaminy Creek bounded by the lands of Bartholomew Jacobs, Francis White, and by the lands late of John Johnson (and now Harris Praul) and Samuel Carpenter. Made 6 Jan 1729. Wit: Jno. Hall, Nathan Watson, Jeremiah Langhorne.

P. 11   Release. John Rodman, Jr., for £133.4s.8p, to John Bissonet [same parties and land as in above entry.] Said land part of 500 acres which was patented 8 Feb 1685 to Robert Hall of Bristol, cooper, whose demise placed the land in the hands of his eldest son John Hall who by deed dated 13 Jun 1711 conveyed the land to Charles Levally of Middletown, cooper. Charles Levally conveyed the land to Thomas Stevenson of Bensalem, gent., by deed dated 1 Oct 1711 and recorded in Book A, Vol 2, pg 222. After Thomas Stevenson's death, Sheriff Thomas Biles, in order to pay Stevenson's debts, sold the land at public auction to Samuel Bayard of New York City, merchant, by deed dated 20 Jan 1723 and recorded in Book A, Vol 2, pg 224. Samuel Bayard then sold the land to John Rodman, Jr. by deed dated 2 Mar 1723. Made 7 Jan 1729. Wit: Jno. Hall, Nathan Watson, Jer. Langhorne. Ackn: 22 Mar 1731/2. JP: John Hall. Wit: Nathan Watson.

P. 14   Lease.   Bartholomew Jacobs of Bucks Co., for 5 shillings, to Mathew Rew of Middletown, one full sixth part of 2 water grist mills and boulting mills and 4 tracts of land containing 61¼ acres and 53 perches. Made 2 Jun 1731. Wit: Garrat Vandine, Jer. Langhorne.

P. 14   Release. Bartholomew Jacobs, for £100, to Mathew Rew [same parties and land as in above entry.] The first tract of 50 acres is by Neshaminy Creek and bounded by the land late of George Vansandt and by Joseph Growden's land. The second tract, also by Neshaminy Creek, contains 2½ acres and 11 perches. The third tract of 5 acres and 30 perches is bounded by the lands of Johannes Praul and John Plumbly. The fourth tract by the said creek contains 3¾ acres and 12 perches. This land was that which Jeremiah Langhorne, Stophel Vansandt, John Plumbly and Bartholomew

Jacobs by deed dated 25 Sep 1727 conveyed to Thomas Biles who sold the land to Bartholomew Jacobs by deed dated 30 Sep 1727. The deed is recorded in Book A, Vol 2, pgs 261-262. Made 3 Jun 1731. Wit: Garrat Vandine, Jer. Langhorne.

P. 16   Deed. Joseph Thorne of Flushing, Queens Co., NY, yeoman, for £30, to Thomas Stevenson of Bensalem, yeoman, 500 acres of land in Bucks Co., part of 5,000 acres laid out to Thomas Hudson and conveyed by William Biles, attorney for Hudson, to William Lawrence, John Talman, Joseph Thorne, Samuel Thorn and Benjamin Field by deed dated 1st da 3rd mo 1698 and each man given his share by Division dated 21 Jan 1705, the said 500 acres being Joseph Thorne's share. Made 25 Jul 1718. Wit: James Clement, Francis Yates. JP: William Bloodgood.

P. 17   Deed. Joseph Thorne of Flushing, Queens Co., NY, yeoman, for £60, to Thomas Stevenson of Bensalem, yeoman, 500 acres, part of the moiety of 5,000 acres conveyed to William Lawrence, John Talman, Samuel Thorne, Joseph Thorne and Benjamin Field by William Biles, deceased, by deed dated 1st da 3rd mo 1698. Said 5,000 acres was the original land of Thomas Hudson and sold to these men, each man having a moiety of 1,000 acres, by power of attorney from Thomas Hudson. Made 11 Jun 1719. Wit: Will. Doughty, John Talman, Samuel Thorne, Jno. Stevenson. Ackn: 3 Jun 1720. JP: Joseph Kirkbride.

P. 18   Deed. John Talman of Flushing, Queens Co., NY, yeoman, for £200, to Thomas Stevenson of Bensalem, Bucks Co., yeoman, 1,000 acres derived from the right of John Talman's father, John Talman, deceased. Also 500 acres which the seller purchased from Samuel Thorne, Jr. by deed dated 13 May 1718 which Samuel Thorne had by the right of his father and was part of 5,000 acres granted to William Lawrance, John Talman, Samuel Thorne, Joseph Thorne and Benjamin Field jointly from William Biles of Bucks Co., deceased, by deed dated 1 Mar 1698. The said 5,000 acres was originally purchased by Thomas Hudson and was sold by William Biles by power of attorney from Thomas Hudson. Made 11 June 1719. Wit: Wm. Doughty, Jno. Stevenson, Samuel Thorne, Joseph Kirkbride, Thomas Thorne.

P. 19   Deed. William Lawrance of Flushing, Queens Co., NY, gent., for £57.10s, to Thomas Stevenson of Bensalem, Bucks Co., yeoman, 500 acres in Bucks Co., being the moiety of Lawrance's share of 5,000 acres [same land as described in above entry.] Made 11 Jun 1719. Wit: Wm. Doughty, Jno. Stevenson, Samuel Thorne, John Talman. Ackn: 4th da 4th mo 1720 by Samuel

Thorne and Thomas Stevenson by personal appearance before JP Joseph Kirkbride.

P. 19   Deed. Sarah Stevenson of Bensalem, widow of Thomas Stevenson, deceased, and Joseph Kirkbride of Falls Township, yeoman, for £507.10s, to John Sotcher of Falls Township, yeoman, 4,000 acres, part of a larger tract of 5,000 acres (except 1,150 acres conveyed to John James, Thomas Edward and Evan Reese, all of Bucks Co.)

William Penn, now deceased, by indenture of lease and release dated 23 and 24 Apr 1683 conveyed to Thomas Hudson of Maxfield, Chester Co., England, gent., 5,000 acres in Pennsylvania. William Penn also conveyed by indenture dated 25 Apr 1683 to Thomas Hudson the yearly rents of the 5,000 acres, recorded in Bucks Co. Book A, Vol 1, pgs 240-249. It was surveyed and laid out to Thomas Hudson in Bucks Co. adjoining the boundary line of Philadelphia Co. by warrant dated 6th da 12th mo 1684. Hudson, by power of attorney dated 16 Aug 1697 proved in open court 14th da 2nd mo 1698 and recorded in Book B, Vol 4, pg 183-184, appointed William Biles, late of Falls Township, his attorney who sold the land by deed dated 1st da 3rd mo 1698 and recorded in Book B, Vol 2, pg 285 to William Lawrence, John Talman, Joseph Thorne, Samuel Thorne and Benjamin Field, all of Flushing, NY. William Lawrance sold 500 acres of the land to Thomas Stevenson by deed dated 11 Jun 1719. John Talman sold 1,500 acres by deed dated 11 Jun 1719 to Thomas Stevenson. Joseph Thorne by two deeds dated 25 Jul 1718 and 11 Jun 1719 sold to Thomas Stevenson 1,000 acres. Benjamin Field by deed dated 11 Jun 1719 conveyed to Thomas Stevenson 1,000 acres. All these lands are part of Thomas Hudson original 5,000 acres.

By mistake of the surveyor of the original survey, about 3,000 acres were run into a tract then surveyed for Denis Rochford whose heirs hold the land. Sarah Stevenson obtained a warrant dated 14 Oct 1720 to have it resurveyed and entered in the Surveyor General's Office, pg. 112. Made 28 Sep 1721. Wit: Tho. Watson, John Hutchinson, Jos. Kirkbride, Jr.

P. 22   Power of Attorney. John Linter, late of Warminster, Bucks Co., now of NY, yeoman, made Thomas Davids of Northampton, Bucks Co., yeoman, his attorney. Made 2 May 1732. Wit: Edmd. Perks, Thos. Skelton. Ackn: 25 May 1732 when Thomas Skelton, a Quaker, appeared before JP Thomas Greene and affirmed his witnessing of the document.

P. 22   Deed. John Sotcher of Falls Township, yeoman, for £507.10s, to Joseph Kirkbride of the same place, yeoman, 2 tracts of land. [For a description and history of ownership of this land, see the above entries for pgs 16 through 19 concerning Thomas Hudson's 5,000 acres which ended up in the hands of William Lawrance, John Talman, Joseph Thorne, Samuel Thorne, Benjamin Field and Thomas Stevenson and his wife Sarah.] Made 29 Sep 1721. Wit: Tho. Watson, John Hutchinson, Jos. Kirkbride, Jr.

P. 26   Deed. Humphrey Morrey of Philadelphia, distiller, for £68.16s to Ely Welding of Bucks Co., blacksmith, 172½ acres of land near Neshaminy Creek by Benjamin Armitage's corner and by John Beale's and Alexander Beale's land. Nathaniel Bromley of London, England, soapmaker, by lease and release received from William Penn 2,000 acres in PA, and by warrant 1,960 acres in Bucks Co. was surveyed and laid out to him. He conveyed the land to his three daughters Katherine, Elizabeth and Hannah Bromley who by indentures of lease and release dated 13 Sep 1717 conveyed the land to Richard Morrey and Humphrey Morrey. The Morrey's, by indenture dated 26 Sep 1722, divided the land equally between them. Made 14 Aug 1723. Wit: John Carver, Edw. Lightwood, Jno. Budd.

P. 28   Lease. Jonathan Woolston of Middletown, yeoman, and his wife Sarah, for 5 shillings, to Joseph Walker of Southampton, yeoman, 319 acres of land in Middletown by Neshaminy Creek and bounded by the lands late of Henry Hudleston and by Joseph Lupton's and Thomas Gill's land. Made 20 Aug 1722. Wit: Jeremiah Dungan, Jeremiah Croasdale, Robert Heaton.

P. 28   Release. Jonathan Woolston and Sarah his wife, for £354, to Joseph Walker [same parties and land as described in above entry.] Said land is part of 384 acres which Robert Heaton, late of Middletown, deceased, and Robert Heaton, Jr. conveyed to Jonathan Woolston by deed recorded in Book A, Vol 2, pgs 74-75. Made 21 Aug 1722. Wit: Jeremiah Dungan, Jeremiah Croasdale, Robert Heaton. Ackn: 6 Mar 1731 when Jonathan Woolston affirmed the deed before JP Jeremiah Langhorne.

P. 30   Deed. Daniel Ashcraft of Wrightstown, for £200, to William Allen of Philadelphia, gent., 220 acres of land in Wrightstown by Neshaminy Creek and Randall Run and bounded by the land of Godfrie Kirk. Made 10 May 1732. Wit: Peter Pursel, Denis Pursel, Abra Chapman

P. 31   Deed. Margaret Dunkan of Bucks Co., widow, for 5 shillings and for care during the rest of her natural life conveys to William Dunkan of the same place, yeoman, the land left to her by her late husband, John Dunkan, and father of said William Dunkan. Said land, 209 acres in Bensalem and bordering the lands of Edmund Dunkan, was left to Margaret by his Last Will and Testament. Made 20 Apr 1732. Wit: William Carver, Margaret

MacKelon. Ackn: 31 Aug 1732 Margaret Dunkan appeared before Justice of the Peace Jeremiah Langhorne and acknowledged her deed.

P. 32   Deed. William Dunkan of Bucks Co., yeoman, for 5 shillings, to his mother Margaret Dunkan and Edmund Dunkan and John Dunkan, his brothers for the term of his mother Margaret's natural life and the remainder to the said Edmund and John Dunkan, the land his father John Dunkan died seized of. [Same land as in above entry.] Made 21 Apr 1732. Wit: William Carver, Margaret MacKelon. Ackn: 31 Aug 1732 William Dunkan appeared before JP Jeremiah Langhorne and acknowledged his deed.

P. 33   Lease. Lawrence Growdon the Elder of the Parish of St. Mervyn, Cornwall, England, gent., for natural love and affection and for 5 shillings, to Lawrence Growdon the Younger of Pennsylvania, gent. and grandson of the Elder Lawrence Growdon, all his land in Pennsylvania now in the possession of Lawrence Growdon, his son. Made 25 Jun 1707. Wit: Peter Kekewich, Thomas Leverton, Mary Growdon, Tho. Symons.

P. 34   Release. Lawrence Growdon the Elder, for 10 shillings, to Lawrence Growdon the Younger. [Same parties and land as above entry. No boundaries or acreage given.] Made 26 Jun 1707. Wit: Peter Kekewich, Thomas Leverton, Mary Growdon, Tho. Symons. Memo: 26 Jun 1707 received 10 shillings from Lawrence Growdon the Younger by the hands of Roger Robins of Ruan Langhorne.

P. 36   Affidavit. Thomas Symons of St. Austell, Cornwall, England, gent., appeared before Henry Spiller, Mayor of the Burrough of Bodanyn (Cornwall, England) on 1 Jul 1731 and swore oath to his presence at the signing of the lease and release agreement between Lawrence Growdon the Elder and Lawrence Growdon the Younger. Wit: William Peters, John Tredwen, Hen. Dagge.

P. 36   Mortgage. Thomas Maybury of Middletown, blacksmith, for £100, to William Carter of Philadelphia, gent., 400 acres in Newtown bounded on the south by the land of John Walley, on the north by Thomas Hill's land and on the east by the lands of Thomas Stradlin. By indenture of lease and release dated 3 Jul 1731 James Goold of Boston, Suffolk Co., MA, mariner, conveyed to Thomas Maybury 400 acres. Made 9 Oct 1732. Wit: Mary Sutton, Josa. Lawrence.

P. 38   Deed. Francis Knowles, surviving executor of Elizabeth Teague of Philadelphia, deceased, for 5 shillings, to Joseph Drinker and William

Fisher of the same place, carpenters. Joseph Drinker and his wife Mary and William Fisher and his wife Tabitha by indenture dated 6 Jan 1729 conveyed to Henry Hodge, late of Philadelphia, deceased, and Francis Knowles land in Philadelphia on the north side of Mulbury Street and bounded by a lot owned by Widow Heart and by a house of Peter Tilley's, part of a larger lot formerly purchased by Pentecost Teague from Andrew Robinson and also 150 acres by John Otter's corner and Jeffrey Pollard's land, by John Clauson's land, by the lands of the Widow Blagden and William Crosdal. Elizabeth Teague bequeathed £150 to Constance Dusting which Drinker and Fisher have paid. Made 10 Oct 1732. Wit: John Kingey, Edmund Kearny.

P. 39   Deed. Thomas Biles, Sheriff of Bucks Co., for £360, to Thomas Winder. Samson Cary was granted the recovery of a debt of £106.12s and 65s.2p from Ralph Brock of Makefield at the Court of Common Pleas held at Bristol in December 1725. By writ dated 18 Mar 1725, Thomas Biles as Sheriff was to levy the debt against Brock's property in time for the next court to be held at Newtown 16 Jun 1725. Sheriff Biles took 341 acres in Makefield but the property remained unsold by the time of the Court. An inquisition dated 14 Jun 1726 affirmed that Samson Cary held the property which was bounded by lands of Nathaniel Hair, Thomas Janney, and John Clowes. Said land part of 600 acres which descended to the eldest son, John Brock, by the death of his father, John Brock and thence by the death of the younger John Brock to his brother Ralph Brock. A public auction was held 13 Jun 1727 and the land was purchased by Thomas Winder of Hopewell, Hunterdon Co., NJ, yeoman. Made 14 Sep 1728. Wit: William Biles, Wm. Saterthwate, Elizabeth Saterthwate, James Gould, James Neilson. Rec'd. 28 Jun 1729 £360 in full payment. Wit: James Gould, James Neilson.

P. 41   Mortgage. John Baker of Bensalem, yeoman, to secure a debt of £100, to Clement Plumstead of Philadelphia, merchant, 2 tracts of land in Bensalem. One tract of 21¼ acres is bounded by the lands of Abel Hinkston. The other tract, 142½ acres, is also bounded by Abel Hinkston's land and by the lands of Claus Johnson, Thomas Walmsley, Tobias Dymock, Nehemiah Allen and Thomas Knight. Said land was granted to William Baker, father of said John Baker, from Joseph Growdon, late of Bensalem, deceased. Made 30 May 1732. Wit: John Roberts, Jn. Durborow.

P. 43   Deed. Thomas Knight of Bristol, Philadelphia Co., yeoman, who is moving, for £60 formerly paid by Thomas Scott, late of Bensalem, deceased, and for 5 shillings paid by Samuel Scott, son and heir of Thomas Scott, 80 acres of land in Bensalem by the River Poquessin and by the lands of William Duncan, Francis Searle and late of Thomas Scott. Made 4 Dec 1729. Wit:

George Bringhurst, Henry Pastonus. Ackn: 3 Apr 1733 when Thomas Knight appeared before JP Jeremiah Langhorne.

P. 44 Lease. Thomas Lambert of Nottingham, Burlington Co., NJ, yeoman, for 5 shillings, to Thomas Yardley of Makefield, yeoman, 223 acres of land in Makefield by the River Delaware by the lands of Samuel Overton, Ralph Brock and late of Joseph Clows, deceased. Also another tract of 250 acres of land joining the first one and bounded by lands of Ralph Brock and James Tunclife. Made 29 Jan 1733. Wit: Wm. Biles, Is. Penington, Jos. Kirkbride, Jr. Ackn: 31 Jan 1732/3. JP: Joseph Kirkbride, Jr.

P. 46 Release. Thomas Lambert, for £700, to Thomas Yardley [same parties and land as in above entry.] Ralph Brock, late of Makefield, millwright, by deed recorded in Bucks Co. Book A, Vol 2, pg 21 conveyed 223 acres in Makefield to John Lambert. The other tract of land was conveyed to John Lambert by indentures of lease and release dated 8 and 9 Apr 1715 from Samuel Overton and Hannah his wife and their sons Constantine and Joseph Overton. When John Lambert died, the land descended to his eldest brother Thomas Lambert. Made 30 Jan 1732/3. Wm. Biles, Is. Penington, Jos. Kirkbride, Jr. Ackn: 31 Jan 1732/3. JP: Joseph Kirkbride, Jr.

P. 49 Mortgage. Thomas Yardley, for £400, to Thomas Lambert [same parties and property as in two previous entries.] Payment of £24 to be made on 31 Jan 1733 and the remainder to be paid 31 Jan 1734. Made 31 Jan 1732. Wit: Wm. Biles, Is. Penington, Jos. Kirkbride, Jr. Memo: By power of attorney by Achfah Lambert, one of the heirs of Thomas Lambert, full satisfaction is made on this mortgage 17 Jun 1739 acknowledged before Dan Martin, Samuel Gibbs.

P. 52 Deed. William Allen of Philadelphia, esq., for £37.8s, to Bernardus Swarthout of Menessing, Bucks Co., yeoman, 54 acres of land by the Delaware River by Nicholas Schoonhoven's Island called Wall Park, part of 10,000 acres which were conveyed to William Allen by William Penn, grandson and devisee named in the Last Will and Testament of William Penn, esq., deceased, by deeds of lease and release made in 1728. Made 16 Jun 1733. Wit: Jer. Langhorne, Wm. Fry, Jai. Sebering.

P. 55 Release. John Linter, late of Warminster, Bucks Co., now of NY, yeoman, and Thomas Davids of Northampton, Bucks Co., yeoman, for £260, to Joseph Howell of Philadelphia, shopkeeper, and Jane his wife, lately Jane Roberts, widow and one of the executors of the estate of John Roberts, late of Philadelphia, shopkeeper, deceased, 100 acres in Warminster bounded by the lands of George Harris, John Cadwallader and Nicholas Gilbert. By letter of attorney dated 2 May 1732 and recorded in Book B, Vol 2, pgs 22-23, John Linter authorized Thomas David to sell his land. Made 30 Jun 1732. Wit: Pet Evans, Jno. Ross.

P. 57   Mortgage. Francis Hague of Newtown, Bucks Co., yeoman, and his wife Jeane, for £240, to John Shalcross of Oxford, Philadelphia Co., yeoman, 600 acres in Newtown bounded by John Walley's land and the land late of John Hough except for 37½ acres which Francis Hague sold to William Ashburnet. Made 27 Apr 1733. Wit: Martha Milnor, John Milnor. Ackn: 15 May 1733. JP: Abraham Chapman.

P. 59   Lease. Samuel Swift of Bucks Co., blacksmith and executor of John Swift, late of Bensalem, deceased, for 5 shillings, to Lambert Vandike of Southampton, yeoman, 125 acres in Southampton by Jackman's line, Kirl's line, Richard Latham's corner and by land late of John Gregory. Made 18 Apr 1733. Wit: David Wilson, John Besonet, Tho. Worrall.

P. 59   Release. Samuel Swift, for £180, to Lambert Vandike [same parties and land as in previous entry.] By patent dated 8 Jul 1685 and recorded at Philadelphia in Patent Book A, pg 79, William Penn granted to Robert Presmall, late of Bucks Co., laborer, 250 acres in Southampton. Robert Presmall conveyed 125 acres of the 250 acres of land to John Baldwin, then of Philadelphia Co., by deed recorded in Bucks Co. Book A, Vol 1, pg 98. John Baldwin sold the land to John Swift by deed recorded in Book C, Vol 1, pg 327. Robert Presmall then sold to John Swift the other 125 acres of his tract by deed dated 1 Dec 1687. John Swift's Last Will and Testament dated 17 Feb 1732 bequeathed the land to his grandson Samuel Swift. Made 19 Apr 1733. Wit: David Wilson, John Besonet, Tho. Worrall. Ackn: May 1733. JP: John Hall, Esq.

P. 62   Lease. William Penn of Worminghurst, Sussex Co., esq., for 5 shillings, to Leonard Fell of Beakely in Furnis, Lancaster Co., yeoman, 500 acres in Pennsylvania. Made 8 Nov 1681. Wit: Js. [Is.?] Swinton, Tho. Coxe, Ben Griffith.

P. 63   Release. William Penn, for £10, to Leonard Fell [same parties and land as in preceding entry.] Made 9 Nov 1681. Wit: Js. [Is.?] Swinton, Tho. Coxe, Ben Griffith.

P. 65   Deed. Leonard Fell of Beackelife in Turnesse, Lancaster Co., yeoman, for tender love and affection for my friend William Norcross of

Alson, Lancaster Co., husbandman, 500 acres in Pennsylvania. Made 6 Apr 1699. Wit: Christopher Atkinson, Elijah Salthouse, Elizabeth Holme.

P. 66   Deed. William Ginne of London, refiner, and Ann his wife, for natural love and affection and for 5 shillings, to Mary Sheppard of New York City, single woman, their moiety of 500 acres. Barbara Blackden, late of Bristol, deceased, owned 500 acres in Pennsylvania and died without making distribution of her property. Her only child, Mary Blackden, had two daughters: Ann (wife of William Ginne) and Mary, the mother of the said Mary Sheppard. Made 20 Sep 1726. Wit: Andrew Hamilton, James Hamilton, both of Philadelphia. Ackn: 7 Jul 1731. JP: Jeremiah Langhorne.

P. 68   Release. William Penn of Worminghurst, Sussex Co., esq., for £10, to Leonard Fell of Beakley in Furniss, Lancaster Co., yeoman, for the purchase of 500 acres. Made 9 Nov 1681. Wit: Tho. Coxe, Bn. Griffith, Js. [Is.?] Swinton.

P. 68   Lease. James Corrie of Northampton, Bucks Co., yeoman, for 5 shillings, to Benjamin Walton of Bybury, Philadelphia Co., yeoman, 56¾ acres of land in Northampton by Joseph Hill's land and by the lands of Joseph Tod, John Jones and Robert Heaton. Made 30 Apr 1733. Wit: Wm. Fry, Jer. Langhorne.

P. 69   Release. James Corrie, for £115, to Benjamin Walton [same parties and land as preceding entry.] Made 1 May 1733. Wit: Wm. Fry, Jer. Langhorne. Ackn: 13 Jun 1733. JP: William Biles. [The name within these two documents is spelled "Corrie", but the name at the end of each deed is spelled "Currie".]

P. 71   Mortgage. Abel Janney of Makefield, blacksmith, for £163.16s.4p, to Joseph Kirkbride of Falls Township, yeoman, 242 acres in Makefield by the land belonging late to Samuel Overton and by the lands of Joseph Janney, Richard Hough and Amos Janney. This land Abel Janney by indenture of lease and release conveyed to Mahlon Stacy of Chester, Burlington Co., NJ, gent., who sold it back to Abel Janney by deed dated 24 Feb 1726. To be paid in 4 annual installments on the 1st of each November and final payment in 1737. Made 1 Nov 1733. Wit: James Hunter, Robert Buckles, Mathew Kirkbride. Ackn: 24 Dec 1733. JP: Thomas Yardley.

P. 74   Mortgage. Robert Ellis of Philadelphia, merchant, and Katherine his wife, for £330, to Samuel Powell, Jr. of Philadelphia, merchant, one full sixteenth part of a partnership. Robert Ellis, Jeremiah Langhorne, Anthony

Morris, James Logan, Charles Reed, George Fitzwater, Clement Plumstead, William Allen, Andrew Bradford, John Hopkins, Thomas Lindley and Joseph Turner hold in common tenancy a partnership in furnace and iron works on 6,000 acres of land on the River Delaware called Durham which was divided into equal shares, and by deed dated 4 Mar 1727 shares were conveyed to Griffith Owen (since deceased) and Samuel Powell for their use for 51 years. Robert Ellis, with consent of a majority of the partners, mortgages his share to Samuel Powell, Jr. Full payment to be made 1 Dec 1734. Made 1 Dec 1733. Wit: C. Brockden, Wm. Parsons, Joseph Breintnall. Ackn: 7 Feb 1733/4 before JP Jeremiah Langhorne by Charles Brockden and William Parsons, both of Philadelphia.

P. 78   Lease. Arthur Searle of Middletown, yeoman, for 5 shillings, to Henry Brise [Brice] of Bensalem, 400 acres in Bensalem beginning at William Duncan's line and by the lands of King Orphan, Joseph Growdon and by Searle's, Scot's and Knight's lands. Made 4 Jun 1733. Wit: Wm. Fry, John Hough.

P. 79   Release. Arthur Searle, for £675, to Henry Brise [same parties and land as preceding entry.] Joseph Growdon of Bensalem by deed dated 1st da 6th mo 1697 and recorded in Bucks Co. Book B, Vol 1, pg 45 sold the land to Francis Searle, late of Bensalem and by his Last Will and Testament bequeathed the land to his son Arthur Searle. Made 5 Jun 1733. Wit: Wm. Fry, John Hough.

P. 81   Deed. Stophel Vansandt of Middletown, yeoman, for £45, conveys to Johanes Praul of the same place, yeoman, one-sixth part of 2 grist mills and 4 tracts of land in Middletown. The first tract of 50 acres is bounded by land late of George Vansandt and by Joseph Growdon's land. The second tract is 2½ acres and 11 perches. The third tract by Johanes Praul's line is bounded by the land of John Plumbly and contains 5 acres and 30 perches. The fourth tract contains 3¾ acres and 12 perches and also borders John Plumbly's land. Made 24 Dec 1733. Wit: Wm. Fry, Jer. Langhorne. [Name also spelled "Stoffel".]

P. 83   Mortgage. Nicholas Dupue of Bucks Co., yeoman, to secure a debt of £800, to William Allen of Philadelphia Co., merchant, the same land which by indentures of lease and release dated 9 and 10 Sep 1733, William Allen sold to Nicholas Dupue, 3 islands in the River Delaware, the first called Maw Wallamink containing 126 acres and lying opposite where said Nicholas now lives. The second island called The Great Shawna Island is 146 acres near Shawna Town. The third tract is between creeks and small runs of the river and the adjacent land southward, the land lately held by John Smith, and is 31 acres. By means of another lease and release dated 10 Sep 1733 William Allen sold Nicholas Dupue 3 other tracts of land, all by the Delaware River. The first is sometimes called Shawna Town and contains 89 acres. The second is 112 acres and the third, 20½ acres. Full payment to be made by 13 Sep 1735. Made 13 Sep 1733. Wit: Jer. Langhorne, An. Hamilton, Jr. [Name also spelled "Dupui".]

P. 85 Lease. William Allen for 5 shillings paid by Nicholas Dupue [same parties as preceding entry.] The 3 islands in the Delaware [as described in above entry.] Made 9 Sep 1733. Wit: Jer. Langhorne, And. Hamilton, Jr. [Name is signed Will Allen.]

P. 86 Release. William Allen, for £400, to Nicholas Dupue [same parties as entry for P. 83 and 85.] 3 islands on the Delaware. These 3 island tracts of land are part of 10,000 acres which William Penn, deceased, by his Last Will and Testament, left to his grandson William Penn to be set out by his trustees, who sold the land to William Allen by indenture dated 20 Aug 1728 and recorded at Philadelphia in Book F, Vol 5, pg 92. The trustees, Richard Hill, Isaac Norris, Samuel Preston and James Logan, on 16 Nov 1727, directed Jacob Taylor to survey the islands as part of the 10,000 acres. Made 10 Sep 1733. Wit: Jere. Langhorne, And. Hamilton, Jr. Ackn: 7 Apr 1735 by William Allen before JP Jeremiah Langhorne.

P. 88 Lease. William Allen, for 5 shillings, to Nicholas Dupue [same parties as preceding entries for pgs 83-86.] 3 tracts of land on the Delaware River [for description see entry for P. 83.] Made 9 Sep 1733. Wit: Jer. Langhorne, And. Hamilton, Jr.

P. 88 Release. William Allen, for £350, to Nicholas Dupue [same parties and 3 tracts of land as preceding entry.] The third tract is part of 431 acres surveyed for William Allen, and the 3 tracts are part of 10,000 acres which William Penn bequeathed to his grandson, William Penn, who sold the land to William Allen by indenture dated 29 Aug 1728 and recorded at Philadelphia in Book F, Vol 5, pg 92. The first tract, and the 431 acre tract (of which the third tract is part of) was surveyed by Jacob Taylor by warrant dated 16 Nov 1727 at the request of William Penn's trustees Richard Hill, Isaac Norris, Samuel Preston and James Logan. Made 10 Sep 1733. Wit: Jer. Langhorne, And. Hamilton, Jr. Ackn: 7 Apr 1735. JP: Jeremiah Langhorne.

P. 91 Lease. William Allen, for 5 shillings, to Nicholas Dupue [see preceding entries for pgs 83-88.] 3 tracts of land by the Delaware River. The first tract contains 300 acres. The second tract contains 86 acres. The third tract contains 40 acres and borders William Allen's other land. Made 25 Sep 1733. Wit: Jer. Langhorne, Wm. Coleman.

P. 91   Release. William Allen, for £350, to Nicholas Dupue [see entries for pgs 83-91.] 3 tracts of land on the Delaware River, which are part of the 10,000 acres which William Penn bequeathed to his grandson William Penn. Made 26 Sep 1733. Wit: Jer. Langhorne, Wm. Coleman. Ackn: 7 Apr 1735. JP: Jeremiah Langhorne.

P. 94   Mortgage. Daniel Ashcraft of Wrightstown, Bucks Co., yeoman, for £160 paid by William Allen of Philadelphia, merchant, a plantation and 120 acres of land in Wrightstown by Neshaminy Creek and bounded by the lands of Richard Mitchel and Jonathan Cooper. Ashcraft to repay £160 plus interest on or before 14 June 1736. Made 14 Jun 1734. Wit: John Morris, Samuel Brock. JP: Abraham Chapman.

P. 96   Lease. Jacob Johnson, Yanica Johnson, John Johnson, Grace Johnson, Catherine Johnson, Lawrence Johnson and Abraham Johnson, all of Middletown, children of Hendricky Johnson, late of Middletown, deceased, for 5 shillings, to Johanes Praul of the same place, yeoman, 100 acres of land in Middletown by Neshaminy Creek and bounded by the land of John Plumly [Plumbly] and by land formerly George White's. Made 1 Jun 1720. Wit: Jer. Langhorne, Jonathan Woolston, Stoffel Vansand, Joseph Thornton.

P. 97   Release. Jacob Johnson, et al, for £106, to Johanes Praul, 100 acres of land in Middletown [same parties and land as preceding entry.] Abraham Vandine, late of Bucks Co., by deed recorded in Book D, Vol 1, pg [?] conveyed to Henricky Johnson, who died intestate, the land descending to her children. Made 2 Jun 1720. Wit: Jer. Langhorne, Jonathan Woolston, Stoffel Vansand, Joseph Thornton. Ackn: 25 May 1734 by Stophel Vansand before JP Jeremiah Langhorne.

P. 99   Deed. Bartholomew Jacobs of Middletown, yeoman, for £12, to Johannes Praul, 6 acres in Middletown by Neshaminy Creek, part of 500 acres which John White, deceased, conveyed to Bartholomew Jacobs by deed recorded in Book C, Vol 1, pg 164. Made 13 May 1723. Wit: Stoffel Vansand, Henry Mitchell. Ackn: 25 May 1734 by Stophell Vansand before JP Jeremiah Langhorne.

P. 101   Lease. Jeremiah Langhorne of Middletown, gent., for 5 shillings, to Johannes Praul of the same place, yeoman, 100 acres of land in

Middletown beginning at a corner between Bartholomew Jacob's and Francis White's land, then by the lands of John Hall and the lands late of Charles Levally. Made 11 May 1723. Wit: Stoffel Vansand, Cha. Read.

P. 101   Release.   Jeremiah Langhorne, for £40.7s, to Johannes Praul [same parties and land as preceding entry.] John Hall of Bristol, cooper, by deed recorded in Book D, Vol 1, pg 61, conveyed the land to John Johnson, late of Bristol, deceased. John Johnson's Last Will and Testament made his wife Margaret Johnson his executor and empowered her to sell the land to pay his debts. By deed dated 14 Dec 1722, Margaret sold the land to Jeremiah Langhorne. Made 12 May 1723. Wit: Stoffel Vansand, Cha. Read. Ackn: 13 Dec 1734 by Jeremiah Langhorne before JP Mathew Hughes.

P. 103   Deed. James Dyre of Little Compton, Bristol Co., New England, yeoman, for £5, to Joseph Dyre, his son of the same place, husbandman, 214 acres in Southampton, Bucks Co. by Neshaminy Creek and by the lands of John Hayhurst, Robert Heaton and the Widow Blagden. Said land that which Joseph Packcom by deed dated 2 Feb 1725/6 sold to James Dyre. Made 27 Apr 1726. Wit: William Cuthbert, Jonathan Head. Ackn: 6 May 1726. JP: Silvester Richmond at Little Compton, Bristol Co., NE.

P. 104   Deed. Joseph Kirkbride of Falls Township, gent., survivor of two executors named in the Last Will and Testament of Thomas Stevenson, of Bensalem, gent., deceased, for 5 shillings, to Benjamin Field of Middletown, yeoman, land in New Jersey which Thomas Stevenson and his wife Sarah, William Stevenson and wife Ann, and John Stevenson and wife Mercy, legatees named in the Last Will and Testament of Samuel Jennings (the said Sarah, Ann, and Mercy being daughters and only issue of Samuel Jennings, late of Burlington, NJ, merchant, deceased) by indenture dated 1 Nov 1709 recorded at Burlington Lib A, folio 274-276, granted to Thomas Gardiner, who by indenture dated 2 Nov 1709 granted the land to Thomas Stevenson.
Samuel Jennings owned one-eighth part of a property in New Jersey which Thomas Ellwood and Mary his wife by indenture of release dated 19 Feb 1703 granted to Samuel Jennings and another part of a property in New Jersey which Samuel Coles by indenture dated 16 Sep 1682 and recorded at Burlington in Book B, pg 19 granted to Samuel Jennings. Also to Benjamin Field a ¼ part of a 19th part of the property in New Jersey which George Hutchinson by indenture dated 17 Sep 1678 granted to Samuel Jennings. And also a tract of 1,200 acres of land in Hunterdon Co., NJ on the River Rockaway by the lands of Uriah Roe, Samuel Barker, Amos Strettle, William Biddle, and James Bollen, this being part of the land which Joseph Helby of London, England, brewer, authorized the sale of by his attorney

John Hamilton of New York City, who conveyed a moiety of the land to Thomas Stevenson.

Also to Benjamin Field 3 tracts of land by Neshaminy Creek in Bensalem, Bucks Co., PA. The first tract is 100 acres and lies by the land formerly belonging to Francis Walker and by the lands of Samuel Allen and John Rodman. The second tract borders Rodman's land and contains 122 acres. The third tract also bordering Rodman's land as well as the land of James Rue measures 100 acres. These last three tracts of land are part of 482 acres which William Penn's Commissioners patented 13 Jul 1688 to John Grey (also called John Tatham) and by his Last Will and Testament was bequeathed to his widow Elizabeth Tatham who died and left it to her son John Tatham, who died and left it to his widow Mary Tatham who later married George Emott of New York City, gent., who by indenture dated 22 Mar 1717 sold the land to Thomas Stevenson.

Benjamin Field is to sell these properties and return the funds raised by the sale to the administrator of Thomas Stevenson's estate.

At the time of his death, Thomas Stevenson owned these properties in New Jersey. His Will dated 10 Nov 1717 directed his assets be sold by his executors (naming his wife Sarah and Joseph Kirkbride) to pay his debts. He wished his estate to be divided into three parts; the first part to go to his wife. To his children Samuel, Edward, Ann, Sarah, Elizabeth and Olive several money legacies and the remaining part of his estate equally divided among the six children. If all his children should die, then the estate be divided among the children of his brothers William and John after his wife Sarah's death. A codicil to his Will dated 29 Apr 1719 bequeathed his property in New Jersey to his wife Sarah and Joseph Kirkbride and their heirs. Thomas Stevenson died shortly after the codicil was made. Joseph Kirkbride declined the executorship of Stevenson's Will, leaving Sarah to administer the Will. Then Sarah Stevenson herself died. Joseph Kirkbride, being aged and infirm and wishing to discharge the trust in him, now administers the Will of Thomas Stevenson. Made 15 Oct 1733. Wit: James Hunter, Robert Kirkbride, Mathew Kirkbride. Memo dated 7 Aug 1734 Joseph Kirkbride appeared before Thomas Yardley, JP, and acknowledged the deed as his own.

P. 109 Mortgage. Richard Hough of Makefield, yeoman, for £200, to John Shallcross of Oxford, Philadelphia Co., yeoman, 416 acres and 135 perches of land by the River Delaware bordering the lands of Abel Janney, Thomas Janney, Joshua Hoops, Thomas Kirl, Peter Worrel and Andrew Ellets. Annual payments to be made each November with final payment in 1739. Deborah Hough, wife of Richard, agrees to the contract. Made 28 Nov 1734. Wit: Jonathan Woollston, John Woollston. Acknowledged by Richard

Hough 31 Dec 1734. JP: Jeremiah Langhorne. Memo: 11 May 1749 John Shallcross appeared and stated full satisfaction of the mortgage. Lawr. Growdon, Recorder.

P. 111   Deed. Joseph Kirll of Philadelphia, merchant, for £100, to Francis, Jeremiah, Alexander, Lewis and Henrieta Gandovet, all of Bucks Co. 200 acres of land on the Delaware River. This land is part of 400 acres of land in Bucks Co. on the Delaware River bounded by Nehemiah Allen's land that was sold to Joseph Kirll by Elenor Allen (deceased widow of Nathaniel Allen of Philadelphia, cooper, deceased); Nehemiah Allen, son and heir of Nathaniel Allen; Lydia Smart, widowed daughter of Nathaniel Allen; Thomas Bradford and Thomas Pascall, two executors (along with son Nehemiah) of the estate of Nathaniel Allen by deed dated 13th da 8th mo 1694 and recorded in Bucks Co. Book B, Vol 1, pg 40-41. William Biles, Jr. attorney for Joseph Kirll. Made 2 Apr 1702. Wit: Cesar Ghiselin, Da'd. Lloyd, Richard Heath.

P. 113   Lease.   John Abraham Denormandie of Bristol, merchant, and his wife Henryeta, for 5 shillings, to Francis Gandovet of Philadelphia, practitioner in phisick, a one-third part of 200 acres by the Delaware River and bordering Nehemiah Allen's land. Made 10 May 1717. Wit: Jo'n. Hall, Cesar Godeffroy, Wm. Atkinson.

P. 114   Release.   John Abraham Denormandie and Henryeta his wife, for £50, to Francis Gandovet. [Same parties as preceding entry. For a description and genealogy of the land see entry for P. 111.] The share of the land held by Jeremiah Gandovet and Lewis Gandovet, who are now deceased, became vested in Francis Gandovet the son; Alexander Gandovet; and the said Henryeta Gandovet by right of survivorship. Made 11 May 1717. Wit: Jo'n.Hall, Cesar Godeffroy, Wm. Atkinson.

P. 115   Deed. Alexander Gandovet of Philadelphia, gent., for £40, to Francis Gandovet of the same place, practitioner of phisick, his share and interest in 201 [sic] acres on the River Delaware. [See entry for P. 111.] Made 6 Apr 1722. Wit: Evan Williams, Cha. Osborne. Memo: 6 May 1723 the land was turned over to Francis Gandovet by John Evans, attorney for Alexander Gandovet. Wit: John Baker, Daniel Banksen, John Williamson.

P. 116.   Power of Attorney. Alexander Gandovet appoints as his attorney John Evans of Petty France to take possession of 201 acres and its premises and to deliver the property to "my honored father the within named Francis Gandovet." Made 6 Apr 1723. Wit: Evan Williams, Cha. Osborne.

P. 116   Deed. Francis Gandovet, Jr. of Salem Co., NJ, gent., for the consideration of a tract of land containing 468 acres in NJ and because he is moving, to Francis Gandovet, Sr. of Philadelphia, Doctor, his one-third part of 201 acres of land in Bucks Co. known by the name of Petty France purchased from Joseph Kirl. [See the preceding 5 entries.] Made 15 Oct 1717. Wit: Tho. Mawd, Wm. Grahame. On 24 Feb 1721 Francis Gandovet appointed John Evans of Petty France his attorney. Wit: John Abra. Denormandie, Elizabeth Denormandie. Memo: 6 May 1723 possession of the property was delivered to Francis Gandovet, Sr. by John Evans. Wit: John Baker, Daniel Banksen, John Williamson.

P. 118   Deed. Robert Presmall of Bucks Co., laborer, for £20, to John Swift of the same place, 100 acres in Southampton bounded by the lands of John Martin and John Baldwin. Also 25 acres more in the village. This land granted by William Penn's Commissioners James Claypoole and Robert Turner to Robert Presmall by patent dated 8th da 5th mo 1685. Made 1st da 10th mo 1687. Wit: Walker Forrest, Nicholas Randall. Acknowledged by Nicholas Randall before JP Jeremiah Langhorne 28 May 1735.

P. 119   Deed. Anthony Burton, carpenter, and his wife Elizabeth, for £200, to Thomas Watson of Moreyhill, Bucks Co., planter, 130 acres of land bounded easterly by John Burgis' land, southerly by Israel Pemberton's land, northerly by the land of William Biles and on the west by the land of Thomas Watson. This land was part of land granted by William Penn to Thomas Woolf by patent dated 27th da 11th mo 1684. Woolf sold the land by deed dated 8th da 1st mo 1685 to Elizabeth Gibbs, who is now the wife of Anthony Burton. Made 5th da 11th mo 1703. Wit: Jacob Janney, Jos. Janney, Tho. Watson. Ackn: 10 Mar 1703/4. Jeremiah Langhorne attorney for Thomas Watson. Wit: William Atkinson, John Culler [Cutter?] Ackn: 14 Jun 1705.

P. 121   Deed. Joseph Growdon of Travose in Bensalem, esq., for £75, to Benjamin Scott of Bensalem, carpenter, 100 acres in or near Southampton on the west side of Neshaminy Creek and near the corner of Bensalem Township by the lands of Joseph Growdon, Stephen Sands, Henry Walmsley, Joseph Tomlinson and John Sands, part of a tract bought from James Plumley which was formerly laid out to Margery Plumley. Made 1st da 11th mo 1719. Wit: Samuel Bulkley, Gustavas Clawson. Acknowledged By Samuel Bulkley on 6 Jan 1734 before JP Jeremiah Langhorne.

P. 122   Deed. Hendrick Johnson Vandike of Middletown, yeoman, for £190, to Thomas Thwaits of the same place, yeoman, 183¾ acres of land in Middletown bounded by the lands of Thomas Thwaits, John Lucas and

William Paxson. Said land was conveyed to Hendrick Johnson Vandike by Robert Heaton by deed dated 5 Jun 1705 and recorded in Bucks Co. Book C, Vol 1, pg 224, and was part of 500 acres granted to James Dilworth from William Penn by lease and release dated 14 and 15 Apr 1682 and was sold by James Dilworth to Robert Heaton by deed dated 12 Oct 1697. Made 3 May 1710. Wit: Adam Harker, Mathew Wildman, John Cutter. Delivered in presence of Robert Heaton and Daniel Doane, Jr. Memo: Acknowledged by Adam Harker on 8 Nov 1735 before JP Charles Read, Esq.

P. 124   Mortgage. Philip Dracot of Southampton, yeoman, for £200, to Mathias Aspden of Philadelphia, merchant, and William Clare of Philadelphia, cordwainer, executors of Ralph Sandeford, deceased, a plantation and 178 acres of land bounded by the lands of Joseph Tomlinson, Robert Heaton, _____ Carter, Thomas Stackhouse and John Sands. This land was conveyed to Philip Dracot by William Biles, Sheriff of Bucks Co., by deed dated 18 Jun 1713 and recorded in Book A, Vol 2, pg 309. To be paid by or on 1 Apr 1738. Made 19 Mar 1734. Wit: Sam'll. Swift, Jos'a. Lawrence. Mathias Aspen acknowledged full satisfaction of the mortgage in Mar 1771. Ackn: 19 Mar 1734 before JP Abraham Chapman, Esq.

P. 125   Mortgage. Francis Hague of Newtown, yeoman, and his wife Jane, for £386, to John Shallcross of Oxford, Philadelphia Co., yeoman, a plantation and 600 acres of land in Newtown bounded by John Walley's land and the land late of John Hough. The 37½ acres, part of the 600 acres, which Francis Hague lately granted to William Ashburne, excepted. To be paid 13 Jan 1736/7. Made 13 Jan 1735/6. Wit: Patrick Cook, John Cridland. Ackn: 19 Jan 1735. JP: Thomas Yardley. John Shallcross acknowledged full satisfaction of the mortgage 13 May 1742.

P. 127   Mortgage. Nathan Watson of Bristol, cordwainer, for £145.8s.9p to Joseph Kirkbride, Jr. of Falls Township, yeoman, the land which Thomas Watson of Bristol, yeoman, by indenture of lease and release dated 8 and 9 October 1735 conveyed to Nathan Watson: a messuage, two tenements and a lot in Bristol by Mill Creek at a corner of Farewell Alley and extending to Mill Street and down to the River Delaware. Nathan Watson, by indenture of lease dated 10 Oct 1735 conveyed to Thomas Watson and Rebeckaw his wife the messuage, tenement and brick house bounded on the south by a fence which divides the lot from the other tenement of Nathan Watson's. Annual payments to be made with final payment made 1 Nov 1739. Made 1 Nov 1735. Wit: George Jones, John Langdale. Ackn: 29 Nov 1735. JP Wm. Biles.

P. 130   Lease. Joseph Shaw of Northampton, yeoman, and William Atkinson of Bristol, yeoman, executors of George Clough, late of Bristol, yeoman, deceased, for 5 shillings, to Joseph Peace of Trenton, Hunterdon Co., NJ, miller, a lot in Bristol near the mill formerly belonging to Samuel Carpenter. Made 24 Jun 1731. Wit: Nathan Watson, Tho's. Marriott, Sam'l. Harker.

P. 131   Release. Joseph Shaw et al, for £60, to Joseph Peace [same parties as preceding entry.] By indenture dated 1 Nov 1714 and recorded in Bucks Co. Book A, Vol 2, pgs 26-28 John Burgis conveyed part of this land to George Clough. The remainder of the land was granted by lease and release dated 15 and 16 Aug 1718 from Hannah Carpenter, widow of Samuel Carpenter, to George Clough. George Clough's Will named Joseph Shaw and William Atkinson his executors. Made 25 Jun 1731. Wit: Nathan Watson, Tho. Marriott, Saml. Harker. Ackn: 2nd da 7^{ber} 1731. JP: William Paxson.

P. 133   Deed. Thomas Biles, Sheriff, for £305, to Joseph Peace, milnor. James Parrock at a Court of Common Pleas held at Newtown on 14 Dec 1727 recovered from John Dickinson, surviving executor of the estate of John Willson, deceased, a debt of £253.3s.9p and 64s.4p. By writ of execution dated 15 Dec last, the Sheriff was commanded to seize the property of John Willson, a ¼ part of several mills and 5 tracts of land in Bristol, to sell in order to have the money at the next court on 14 Mar. The property remained unsold. An inquisition was held and the Sheriff was ordered to expose the land to public sale before the next court to be held 12 Sep.
   The first tract of land, 6¾ acres, begins at a corner of the intersection of Mill Street and Pond Street and goes by Joseph Bond's line.
   The second tract of 1,697 acres begins by William Atkinson's land by the Delaware River and by the lands of Anthony Burton, George Clough, John Large, Henry Tomlinson, John Hall, the Widow Large, William Fishbourn, the Widow Blackden, Clause Johnson, Benjamin Town, Peter Wood, Samuel Brelsford, William Baldwin, Thomas Sison, Thomas Stackhouse and by the lands late of John White, William Croasdale, and Henry Mitchell, all three now deceased.
   The third tract begins at a corner of the Radclif and Market Street intersection. The fourth tract begins at the Radclif Street corner and goes to Cedar Street then to Market Street and contains 1 acre 9 perches. The last parcel begins at Israel Pemberton's corner and goes to Wood Street, then to Market Street and is 1 acre 74 perches. The exception of this land is that which was sold by Samuel Carpenter, Sr. in his lifetime to Joseph White and is now in the possession of John Hall. Made 20 Sep 1728. Wit: William Biles, Joseph Furniss, Mathew Hughes, Jr.

P. 137   Lease.   Mathias Aspdin of Philadelphia, shopkeeper, Edward Horne of the same place, merchant, and William Stockdell of Warminster, Bucks Co., yeoman, trustees in the Last Will and Ttestament of George Harris, late of Warminster, deceased, for 5 shillings, to Charles Inyard of Warminster, husbandman, 100 acres in Warminster by John Linter's land. Made 14 Mar 1728. Wit: Steph'n. Ward, Jonas N. Smith, John Gilbert, John Hart.

P. 138   Release.   Mathias Aspdin, et al, for £130, to Charles Inyard [same parties and land as preceding entry.] By indenture of lease and release dated 23 and 24 June 1727 James Steel, gent., and his wife Martha conveyed to George Harris 100 acres, who made his Last Will and Testament on or about 9 Nov 1727, directing his land be sold by the appointed trustees and divide the money among his three children. Made 15 Mar 1728. Wit: Stephen Ward, Jonas N. Smith, John Gilbert, John Hart. Acknowledged 7 Jan 1734/5 when William Stockdell appeared before JP Benjamin Jones and 16 May 1735 when Mathias Aspdin and Edward Horne appeared before JP Benjamin Jones.

P. 140   Deed.   Joseph Waite of Philadelphia, bricklayer, and his wife Martha, administratrix of the estate of George Biles, late of Falls Township, Bucks Co., deceased, for £205, to Nehemiah Blackshaw of Falls Township, yeoman, two tracts of land by the Delaware River, the one by Samuel Beak's land and by land formerly Daniel Brinson's and containing 213 acres. The other tract of 102½ acres adjoining the first is bounded by the lands of Geoffrey Hawkins and Joseph Woods. John Harrison, late of Falls Township, gent., and his wife Elizabeth and Hannah Acreman of the same place, spinster, by indenture conveyed the two tracts of land to George Biles. George Biles died intestate, leaving his widow Martha with 5 small children. Joseph Waite and his wife Hannah exhibited a petition to the Orphans Court held 15 Mar 1713 and the court ordered the land be sold. Made 16 Sep 1715. Wit: Robert Fletcher, John Burgis, Joseph Kirkbride, Tho. Watson, Jer. Langhorne, Tho. Stevenson. Acknowledged 7 May 1735 when John Burgis appeared before JP Thomas Yardley and 29 May 1735 when Thomas Watson appeared before JP Emmon Williams.

P. 142   Lease.   Nehemiah Blackshaw, for 5 shillings, to Joseph Waite and his wife Martha [same parties and land as in preceding entry.] Made 16 Dec 1715. Wit: Robert Fletcher, John Burgis, Joseph Kirkbride. Ackn: 17 Dec 1715. JP: Joseph Kirkbride.

P. 144   Release. Nehemiah Blackshaw, for £205, to Joseph Waite and his wife Martha [same parties and land as in preceding two entries.] Made 17 Dec 1715. Wit: Robert Fletcher, John Burgis, Joseph Kirkbride. Ackn. same day before JP Joseph Kirkbride.

P. 146   Lease. Joseph Waite of Philadelphia and his wife Martha, for 5 shillings, to Joseph Kirkbride of Falls Township, [same land as in the three preceding entries.] Made 12 Dec 1717. Wit: Tho. Watson, Jer. Langhorne, Tho. Stevenson. Acknowledged by Thomas Watson before JP Emon Williams 29 May 1735.

P. 147   Release. Joseph Waite, et al, for £180, to Joseph Kirkbride [same parties and land as preceding entry.] Made 13 Dec 1717. Wit: Tho. Watson, Jer. Langhorne, Tho. Stevenson. Acknowledged by Thomas Watson before JP Em Williams 29 May 1735.

P. 150   Lease. Francis Borden of Shrosbury, Monmouth Co., NJ, yeoman, for 5 shillings, to Ebenezer Large of Burlington, NJ, merchant, 200 acres in Plumsted, Bucks Co., by the lands of Alexander Brown, Thomas Brown, Ephraim Fenton and Francis Hough. Made 14 Dec 1735. Wit: Samuel Woodward, Isaac DeCew, Tho's. Scattergood.

P. 151   Release. Francis Borden, for £125, to Ebenezer Large [same parties and land as in preceding entry.] William Penn by indenture dated 18 Oct 1681 granted the land to William Kent who on 11 Sep 1685 conveyed it to Walter Hill who sold it to Thomas Milnor on 29 Sep 1685 who sold it to John Davis 8 Apr 1721. John Davis died, his Will dated 7 Dec 1720, leaving £200 each to his daughters and to his wife Mary the residue of his estate as long as she remained a widow. Made 15 Dec 1735. Wit: Samuel Woodward, Is. DeCew, Tho. Scattergood. Ackn. 16 May 1836. JP: Emon Williams.

P. 153   Mortgage. Jacob Chamberlin of Penuel Plantation, Philadelphia Co., yeoman, conveys to George Emlen of Philadelphia, brewer, the land called Penuel situated partly in Philadelphia Co. and partly in Bucks Co. bordered by the road leading from Honsham to Bybury and by the lands of David Marple, Jacob Chamberlin, William Noble, James Craven, Avie Schout, Bartholomew Longstreth, Thomas Lasey and by the Manor of Moorland containing 466 acres. Jacob Chamberlin is bound by bond to George Emblen for £672. This indenture for the payment of £336 and to secure the payment of the debt. Final payment to be made by April 1738. Made 8 Apr 1736. Wit: Sep. Robinson, Jno. Webbe, Joseph Breinlnall, Wm. Biddle.

P. 155   Deed. Timothy Smith, Sheriff of Bucks Co., for £1,450, to Joseph Kirkbride, Jr., esq., of Falls Township. Samuel Siver, executor of the estate of Roger Coates, deceased, and who was executor of the estate of John Coats, late of London, merchant, deceased, at a Court of Common Pleas held at Newtown 12 Mar 1729, recovered against Ann Pidgeon, executrix of the estate of Joseph Pidgeon, late of Bucks Co., merchant, deceased, a debt of £964.15s.8p and 65s.10p. By writ dated 13 Jun 1730, the Sheriff was ordered to seize the property which Joseph Pidgeon died owning which was 2 messuages and 2 tracts of land of 504 acres in Falls Township. One tract by the River Delaware and by the land of Solomon Warder is 200 acres and the other adjoining the first borders Welcome Creek and the River Delaware and is 304 acres. Made 19 Jun 1731. Wit: Jonathan Woolston, John Winner, Tho. Wathel. Ackn. Same day. JP: Jer. Langhorne.

P. 157   Lease. Joseph Kirkbride of Falls Township, yeoman, for 5 shillings, to his son Joseph Kirkbride, Jr. of the same place, yeoman, 4 tracts of land in Falls Township. Joseph Waite of Philadelphia, bricklayer, deceased, and his wife Martha, by indentures of lease and release dated 12 and 13 Dec 1717 conveyed to Joseph Kirkbride, Sr. 2 tracts of land in Falls Township containing 315 acres. Thomas Kirkbride, late of Makefield, yeoman, deceased, by indentures of lease and release dated 15th and 16th das 12th mo 1717 conveyed to Joseph Kirkbride, Sr. 2 other tracts of land in Falls Township containing 154 acres. Made 1st da 3rd mo 1735. Wit: Tho's. Yeardley, John Burgis.

P. 158   Release. Joseph Kirkbride to Joseph Kirkbride, Jr. for 5 shillings and the love and natural affection he has for his son and also because he (the father) is moving. [Same parties and land as previous entry.] The first of the four tracts of land is 213 acres and begins by the River Delaware, bordering the lands of Samuel Beake and the land formerly Daniel Brinson's. The second tract, 102½ acres adjoining the first, by the River Delaware and by land formerly Jeffry Harvelans, and by lands of Joseph Woods; these two tracts were conveyed to George Biles of Falls Township by deed dated 29th da 1st mo 1707 from John Harrison, late of Rocky Hill, Middlesex Co., in the "Eastern Division of Nova Cessaria," gent., and Elizabeth his wife and Hannah Acreman of Bucks Co., spinster, deceased. It was granted to John Harrison and his wife and Hannah Acreman after the decease of George Biles. The two tracts, by order of an Orphans Court held at Bristol, was granted to Nehemiah Blackshaw of Falls Township by Joseph Waite, late of Philadelphia, bricklayer, and Martha his wife, administratrix of the estate of George Biles, by deed dated 16 Sep 1715. Nehemiah Blackshaw by deed dated

16 and 17 Dec 1715 sold the land to Joseph Waite and his wife Martha, who by deed dated 12 and 13 Dec 1717 sold the land to Joseph Kirkbride, Sr.
    Thomas Kirkbride of Makefield, deceased, by indenture of lease and release dated 15th and 16th das 12th mo 1717/8, sold 2 tracts of land in Falls Township to Joseph Kirkbride, Sr. The first is 54 acres and begins at Samuel Darke's corner and goes by land formerly Hawkins and George Biles. The second tract of 100 acres adjoins the first. Joseph Kirkbride, Sr. conveyed by deed dated 25 Mar 1731 to Richard Armstrong, late of Falls Township, turner, deceased, a lot of 1 acre and 47 feet in said township by Wood Street, King Street and Front Street, which lot was part of one of the two aforesaid tracts. Made 2nd da 3rd mo 1735. Wit: Tho's. Yeardley, John Burgis. Ackn: 7 May 1735. JP: Thomas Yeardley.

P. 161   Mortgage. John Shaw, yeoman, and his wife Susanah, for the consideration that John and Joseph Shaw have assumed the debt to the trustees of the General Loan Office, convey to their sons John Shaw and Joseph Shaw the land which their father John Shaw by indenture dated 19 Mar 1723 and recorded in Bucks Co. Book A, Vol 1, which was his plantation and 200 acres bordering land formerly George Williard's and by lands of Isaac Pennington and James Heaton conveyed to Samuel Carpenter, Jeremiah Langhorne, William Fishbourn and Nathaniel Newlin, appointed trustees of the General Loan Office. John Shaw was to pay to the trustees £125 to void the indenture. Made 18 May 1724. Wit: Jos. Watson, Cha. Brockden, George Shaw, John Hart. Acknowledged by Charles Brockden of Philadelphia on 12 Jan 1735 before JP Benjamin Jones.

P. 163   Mortgage. William Williamson of Philadelphia, shipwright, and his wife Sarah, for £12, to John Parrott of Petquesson, Bucks Co., miller, 100 acres in Bensalem bordering land of John Williamson (which was devised to him by the Will of William Williamson) and land late in the possession of Abraham Vandergrift, Jacob Vandergrift and the Widow Baker. William Williamson, late of Bensalem, deceased, father of the said William Williamson by his Last Will and Testament dated 15 Dec 1721 bequeathed to his son William Williamson 100 acres in Bensalem. To be paid by or on next 15 Dec. Made 9 Jun 1736. Wit: Humphrey Garland, William Ballard. Ackn: 15 Oct 1736 before JP Benjamin Jones by William Ballard of Philadelphia, sadler, and Humphrey Garland of said city, merchant.

P. 165   Deed. James Shaw of Southampton and his wife Mary, for £200, to Daniel Pritchard of Philadelphia Co., yeoman. George Willard owned 2 tracts of land in Southampton, the first of 246 acres lies by the land of John Parsons and lands late of Arthur Cook, Job Howell, and Phillip Conway and the second tract of 100 acres begins at a corner of George Willard's other land and runs by the land of John Shaw. By his Last Will and Testament dated 24 Jan 1705/6, George Willard appointed John Shaw and George Willard his executors who by indentures of lease and release dated 2 Apr 1718 conveyed the 2 tracts of land to William Carter. William Carter sold the land to James Shaw by deed dated 24 May 1718. Made 4 Feb 1723. Wit: Moses Wells, Jno. Cadwalader, John Brooks, James Parry. Ackn: 1 Oct 1736 before JP Abraham Chapman by James Shaw.

P. 167   Lease. Charles Plumley of Middletown, and his wife Ann, for 5 shillings, to Johannes Praul of the same place, yeoman, 100 acres of land in Middletown beginning at a corner of Peter Vanhorn's land and by Mathew Rue's land and by lands late of John Plumley. Made 8 Feb 1736/7. Wit: Jos. Rockhill, Is. Penington.

P. 168   Release. Charles Plumley and Ann his wife, for £205, to Johannes Praul [same parties and land as preceding entry.] This land is part of one moiety of 600 acres which the deceased John Plumley lived on and by his Last Will and Testament dated 24 Mar 1731/2 bequeathed to his son the said Charles Plumley. Made 9 Feb 1736/7. Wit: Jos. Rockhill, Is. Penington. Ackn: 9 Feb 1736/7. JP: Emon Williams.

P. 170   Deed. John Roberts of Makefield, yeoman, "for love, good will, favour, and affection I have and bear towards my loving sons Jonathan and Edmund Roberts" give "fully freely clearly and absolutely" land and buildings in Makefield and all household goods and chattels and personal goods to be divided between them after "payment of all my just and lawful debts." Except "I give and grant unto my beloved wife Deliverance Roberts the sum of £6" to be paid to her yearly while she remains a widow. "I give unto my beloved son Thomas Roberts" 5 shillings. To beloved daughter Susanna Roberts £5. Made 4 Jan 1734/5. Wit: Richard Hough, Edw. Tuckett, Cha. Henderson. Ackn: 19th da 8[ber] 1735 by John Roberts before JP Jeremiah Langhorne.

P. 171   Lease. Stephen Jenkins of Philadelphia Co. and Abigail his wife and Isaac Waterman of the same place and Priscilla his wife, for 5 shillings, to John Wilkinson of Wrightstown, a 307 acre tract in Wrightstown on Neshaminy Creek. Made 27 May 1713. Wit: Thomas Watson, Elizabeth Mather, Rachel Pemberton, Humphrey Bates, Samuel Hughes, Hugh Pugh.

P. 172   Release. Stephen Jenkins of Philadelphia Co., yeoman, and Abigail his wife, eldest daughter of Phineas Pemberton, late of Bristol, Bucks Co., deceased, and Isaac Waterman of Philadelphia Co., yeoman and Priscilla his wife, another of the daughters of Phineas Pemberton, for £115, to John Wilkinson of Wrightstown [same land as preceding entry.] This land is part of 400 acres which Phineas Pemberton by his Last Will and Testament dated 26th da 10th mo 1701 bequeathed to his daughters Abigail and Priscilla. The 400 acres is part of 1,500 acres William Penn warranted 26th da 11th mo 1682 to James Harrison, father of Phebe, late wife of Phineas Pemberton and mother of said Abigail and Priscilla. 500 of these acres were laid out by warrant dated 29th da 10th mo 1685 to James Harrison, who sold 200 of the acres, died seized of the remaining 800 acres and Phebe, his daughter and heir, became owner of the land. Made 28 May 1713. Wit: Thomas Watson, Elizabeth Mather, Rachel Pemberton, Humphrey Bates, Samuel Hughes, Hugh Pugh. Ackn: 8 Sep 1731 before JP Jeremiah Langhorne by Israel Pemberton of Philadelphia, merchant, he being the brother of Abigail and Priscilla and well acquainted with their handwritings.

P. 174   Release.   Israel Pemberton of Philadelphia, merchant, son of Phineas Pemberton and his wife Phebe, for 1 shilling and the regard he has for fulfilling his father's Will and because he is moving, quit claims to John Wilkinson 307 acres of land in Wrightstown on Neshaminy Creek north of Randall's Run which was lately conveyed to John Wilkinson from Stephen Jenkins and his wife Abigail, daughter of Phineas Pemberton, late of Bristol, deceased, and Isaac Waterman and his wife Priscilla, another of Phineas Pemberton's daughters by indentures of lease and release dated 27 and 28 May 1713 and was part of 400 acres which Phineas Pemberton bequeathed to his daughters. The 400 acres was part of James Harrison's purchase of 1,000 acres in Wrightstown, 800 acres being unsold after the decease of James Harrison and descended to Harrison's only daughter Phebe, the wife of Phineas Pemberton. Made 24 Dec 1717. Wit: Edward Haddon, Wm. Monington, Agnes Hall. Ackn: 8 Sep 1731 before JP Jeremiah Langhorne by Israel Pemberton.

P. 175   Lease.   Amos Janney of Makefield, yeoman, and his wife Mary, for 5 shillings, to Thomas Bayley of Falls Township, yeoman, a plantation and 264 acres of land in Makefield by the River Delaware and by the lands of Richard Hough, Mahlon Stacey and Thomas Tunicklief. Made 5 Sep 1732. Wit: C. Brockden, Wm. Parsons, Wm. Fry, Jer. Langhorne.

P. 176   Release.   Amos Janney, for £380, to Thomas Bayley [same parties and land as preceding entry.] This land part of 365 acres and 12 perches which by patent recorded at Philadelphia in Book A, Vol 2, pg 184 was granted to Abel Janney who by indenture dated 10 May 1720 sold it to

Mahlon Stacey who by indenture dated 27 Mar 1724 granted the land to Amos Janney and his wife Mary. Made 6 Sep 1732. Wit: C. Brockden, Wm. Parsons, Wm. Fry, Jer. Langhorne. Ackn: same day before JP Jeremiah Langhorne.

P. 178   Lease. Thomas Maybury of Newtown, blacksmith, for 5 shillings, to James Arbuckle of Southampton, 150 acres of land in Newtown by the road leading to Samuel Baker's place. Made 12 Apr 1736. Wit: Mathew Rue, Wm. Fry, John Jervis.

P. 179   Release. Thomas Maybury, for £150, to James Arbuckle [same parties and land as preceding entry] 150 acres which is part of a 400 acre tract which John Frost of Newtown died seized of in Newtown bordered southerly by the land of John Wally; westerly by Thomas Maybury's land; northerly by Thomas Hillburn's land and easterly by the land of Thomas Stradlin containing 400 acres and by his Last Will and Testament dated 20th da 8th mo 1716, he said to sell the land and divide the proceeds between his two brothers, Joseph and Edmund Frost and his sister Elizabeth Francis. Edmund Frost of Billerica and John Francis and Elizabeth his wife of Medford in Middlesex Co., MA, by deed dated 14 Aug 1717 conveyed their share of the land to their brother Joseph Frost of Charlestown, same county and province. Joseph Frost and his wife Hannah by deed dated 10 Mar 1718/9 and recorded in Bucks Co. Book A, Vol 2, pg 134 conveyed the 400 acres to James Gold of Boston, Suffolk Co., MA, mariner. James Gold by indenture of lease and release dated 2 and 3 Jul 1732 sold the land to Thomas Maybury. Made 13 Apr 1736. Wit: Mathew Rue, Wm. Fry, John Jarvis. Ackn: 1 May 1736 before JP Jeremiah Langhorne by Thomas Maybury.

P. 182   Lease. Thomas Maybury, for 5 shillings, to James Arbuckle [same parties as the previous entry] 133 acres and 155 perches of land in Newtown by the land of Benjamin Taylor, James Arbuckle and Thomas Stradlin. Made 16 Dec 1736. Wit: Wm. Fry, John Mitchell.

P. 183   Release. Thomas Maybury, for £100, to James Arbuckle [same parties and land as preceding entry.] This land is part of John Frost's original 400 acres [see entry P. 179 for description of John Frost's land.] Made 16 Dec 1736. Wit: Wm. Fry, John Mitchell. Ackn same day. JP: Jeremiah Langhorne.

P. 186   Lease. William Allen of Philadelphia, merchant, and Margaret his wife, for 5 shillings, to Barnardus Swarthoot of Bucks Co., yeoman, an island of 47½ acres on the River Delaware, opposite Nalpeck, NJ on one side and lands now held by Christopher Denmark and said Swarthoot in Bucks Co. on the other side of the river. Made 2 Oct 1735. Wit: Wm. Coleman, James Bingham, Jr.

P. 186   Release. William Allen, et al, for £40, to Barnardus Swarthoot [same parties and land as preceding entry.] This island part of 10,000 acres which William Penn by his Last Will and Testament bequeathed to his grandson William Penn who conveyed the land to William Allen by indenture dated 29 Aug 1728 and recorded at Philadelphia in Book F, Vol 5, pg 92 and a warrant by the trustees (Richard Hill, Isaac Norris, Samuel Preston and James Logan) dated 16 Nov 1727 directed Jacob Taylor to survey and lay out the island as part of the 10,000 acres. Made 3 Oct 1735. Wit: Wm. Coleman, James Bingham, Jr., Nicolas DuPui. Ackn: 24th da 7ber 1737 before JP Jeremiah Langhorne by William Allen.

P. 188   Sheriff's deed. Timothy Smith, Sheriff of Bucks Co., for £355, to Robert Edwards of Falls Township, 250 acres in Makefield. Joseph Kirkbride of Falls Township in the Court of Common Pleas held at Newtown 11 Jun 1733 recovered against Thomas Jones of Makefield £78.89s.1p. By writ 14 Sep the Sheriff was commanded to levy the goods of Thomas Jones to make good the debt and to have the money at the Court of Common Pleas to be held 12 Dec. Sheriff Smith seized from Thomas Jones 2 messuages and 2 tracts of land in Makefield, the first tract of 150 acres borders the land of Thomas Hilbourn, Ezra Croasdale, Thomas Stackhouse, Timothy Smith, Thomas Stradling. The second tract of 100 acres adjoins the first. After the land remained unsold, the Sheriff was ordered to sell the land to the highest bidder at public auction and to present the money at the next court to be held 12 Mar 1735. Made 12 Dec 1735. Wit: Is. Pennington, Jno. Horohock [Frohock?] and Wm. Fry. Ackn: 12 Dec 1735. JP: Jeremiah Langhorne.

P. 189   Deed (Lease). William Hibbs of Northampton, yeoman, for 5 shillings, to Christian Vanhorn of the same place, yeoman, 2 tracts of land in Northampton, the first of 109 acres and the second of 10 acres. Made 12 Jul 1731. Wit: Jos. Ogden, Abra Chapman, David Ogden, Jr.

P. 190   Release. William Hibbs, for £157, to Christian Vanhorn [same parties and land as above entry.] The 119 acres is part of the 500 acres near Neshaminy Creek which William Penn patented 4th da 2nd mo 1686 to Christopher Taylor. Christopher Taylor died intestate and the land descended to his children Israel Taylor, Joseph Taylor and Mary, the wife of John Busby, who by deed dated 18 Nov 1697 and recorded in Bucks Co. Book B, Vol 1, pg 219 conveyed the land to Robert Heaton who by deed recorded in Book C, Vol 1, pg 152 sold the 500 acres to Bernard Christian and Peter Laurence of Bergin, NJ. Bernard Christian by deed recorded in Book C, Vol 1, pg 396 conveyed 286 acres to Peter Laurence who by deed dated 19 Jun 1731 sold 285 acres to Josiah Ogden who by deed dated 19 Jun 1731 conveyed the 285 acres to William Hibbs. The first 109 acres borders the land of Isaac Pennington and also William Hibbs' and Christian Vanhorn's other lands as does the second 10 acres. Made 13 Jul 1731. Wit: Jos. Ogden, Abra Chapman, David Ogden, Jr. Ackn: 16 Jul 1731. JP: Abraham Chapman.

P. 193   Deed. Thomas Watson of Bristol and his wife Rebecca, for £15, to Mark Watson of Falls Township, 2 parcels of land in Falls Township excepting one graveyard and access to the graveyard which has been laid out and fenced and used for diverse years and lies near the dwelling house. One bounded by the land of Robert Solcher and containing 300 acres is the land which John Hiet of Falls Township conveyed to Thomas Watson by deed dated 2 Jun 1702 and recorded in Book C, Vol 1, pgs 88-89. The second parcel of 1½ acres adjoins the first and is the land which Thomas Terry of Falls Township conveyed to Thomas Watson by indenture dated 14 Oct 1712. The £15 to be paid to Thomas and Rebecca on 1 Apr yearly for the rest of their natural life. Made 30 Jul 1737. Wit: Tho. Hunloke, Jos. Bockhill, Wm. Atkinson. Signed Tho. Watson and Rebecca K. Watson. Ackn: 22 Aug 1737. JP: Joseph Kirkbride, Jr.

p. 195   Deed. Ruben Pownall of Makefield, yeoman, for £280, to John Harvey of Falls Township, yeoman, 274 acres and 56 perches of land in Makefield. William Penn by lease and release dated 21 and 22 Mar 1681 granted to George Pownall, father of Ruben Pownall, 1,000 acres. At the time of his death, George Pownall held 500 acres, part of the aforesaid 1,000 acres, and the land descended to his two sons, Ruben and George Pownall and two daughters, Rachel, afterwards the wife of Thomas Janney and Abigail, the wife of William Paxson. George Pownall (the son), Rachel Janney and Abigail Paxson by deed dated 10 Mar 1712 conveyed their share of their father's estate to Ruben Pownall. The tract of land in Makefield which is part of the 500 acres begins by the road leading from Thomas Yardley's to Wrightstown, then by Charles Read's land and by land late of Thomas Ashton. Made 1 Mar 1734. Wit: Thos. Yearley, James Downey. Ackn: 21 Oct 1737 before JP Jeremiah Langhorne by James Downey.

P. 197   Deed. James Logan of Philadelphia, merchant, for £320, to Joseph Gilbert of Philadelphia Co., yeoman, 2 tracts of land which William Penn by deeds of lease and release dated 14 and 15 Sep 1681 conveyed to Hugh Lamb of St. Martins in the Fields of the County of Middx Hosier [sic] containing

2,500 acres of land to be laid out in PA. By his Last Will and Testament dated 20th da 8th mo 1686, Hugh Lamb left his land to his brother Daniel Lamb. Daniel Lamb later died intestate and without issue and his estate descended to his surviving brother Joseph Lamb of Oxford, Hosier. Joseph Lamb by deeds of lease and release dated 30th and 31st das 8th mo 1711 conveyed the 2,500 acres to James Logan. By a warrant dated 25 Jun 1712 the land was surveyed and laid out near the Manor of Richland in Bucks Co. to James Logan. The first tract lays by the land of Joseph Jones and is 1,000 acres. The other tract adjoins the first tract and is bounded by the land of Robert Ashton and Joseph Pyke and contains 1,000 acres plus allowances of 6 acres to each hundred for roads and highways. Made 15 May 1714. Wit: William Beal, Abel Hinkston, James Steel, Tho. Stevenson. Ackn: 17 Oct 1737 before JP Jeremiah Langhorne by Abel Hinkston.

P. 199   Deed. Thomas Hillborn of Newtown, yeoman, and his wife Elizabeth, to Samuel Hillborn, son of Samuel Hillborn, deceased, and grandchild of the said Thomas Hillborn, paid by Margaret Hillborn, mother of Samuel Hillborn (the younger) as guardian for him, and for the natural affection they have for their grandchild and because they are moving, convey a piece of land in Newtown by the land formerly belonging to Israel Morris containing 229 acres. Said land part of 2 tracts of land, one conveyed from Edmund Cowgill and Israel Morris by deed dated 13th da 6th mo 1702 and recorded in Book C, Vol 1, pgs 94–95 and conveyed to Cowgill and Morris from Richard Burgess and his wife Elizabeth and conveyed to Burgess from Henry Pawlin as part of 1,000 acres. The other tract conveyed from Margaret Cooke and John Cooke by indenture tripartite dated 7th da 9ber 1701 and recorded in Book C, Vol 1, pgs 61–63, and was conveyed to Margaret Cooke by patent from William Penn dated 21st da 8ber 1701. Made 7th da 6th mo 1717. Wit: John Rutledge, John Stackhous, John Cutler. Ackn: 30 Apr 1736 before JP Abraham Chapman by John Stackhouse.

P. 201   Deed. Benjamin Field of Flushing, Queens Co., Long Island, NY, yeoman, for £89, to Thomas Stevenson of Bensalem, Bucks Co., yeoman, 1,000 acres, Benjamin Field's full proportion of 5,000 acres granted to William Lawrence, John Tallman, Samuel Thorne, Joseph Thorne and Benjamin Field jointly from William Biles, deceased, by deed dated 1st da 3rd mo 1698. The 5,000 acres was the original purchase of Thomas Hudson and was conveyed from Hudson to William Biles by deed in 1683. Made 10 Jun 1719. Wit: Francis Doughty, Jr., Thomas Thorne, Thomas Ford. Ackn: 3rd da 4th mo 1720. JP: Joseph Kirkbride.

P. 202   Deed. Christian Barnson, alias Vanhorn, of Northampton, Bucks Co., yeoman, and Williamkee his wife, Henry Vanhorn and Susanna his wife, lately called Susan Vandlecy of Middletown, for £500 to Jeremiah Langhorne of Middletown, gent., three tracts of land in Middletown, the first of 280 acres lies by Neshaminy Creek and is bounded by the land of William Hayhurst, William Paxton, Adam Harker, Henry Hudlestone, Thomas Baynes and John Stackhouse. The second tract of 66¼ acres is bounded by the land of Robert Heaton, Jr., William Darke and Giles Lucas. Said land that which Robert Heaton of Middletown conveyed to Henry Johnson Vandike, late of Middletown, by deed dated 5 Jun 1705 and recorded in Bucks Co. Book C, Vol 1, pg 226. The third tract of 81 acres of land bounded by the land of Thomas Baynes and by land formerly Thatcher's is land which William Cooper of Bucks Co. by deed recorded in Book C, Vol 1, pg 298 conveyed to Henry Johnson Vandike. Henry Johnson Vandike's Last Will and Testament bequeathed the land to his wife Yanica Vandike (now deceased) during her life and after her death the land was to go to his son-in-law Christian Barnson and his granddaughter Susanna Vandlecy. Made 3 Aug 1737. Wit: Joseph Pool, Wm. Fry. Ackn: 6 Nov 1737. JP: Lawrence Growdon, esq.

P. 204   Deed. Jeremiah Langhorne of Middletown, gent., for £250, to Christian Barnson Vanhorne, a plantation and two tracts of land in Middletown, the first of 170 acres begins by William Huddlestone's land and runs by the lands of Thomas Baynes, Thomas Stackhouse, Adam Harker and William Paxson. The other tract of 30½ acres is bounded by the lands of Edward Lucas, ___ Darke and Jonathan Woolstone. Said land part of 3 tracts which Christian Barnson, called Vanhorne, and wife WilliamKee, and Henry Vanhorne and his wife Susanna conveyed to Langhorne. Made 3 Aug 1737. Wit: Joseph Poole, Wm. Fry. Ackn: 7 Nov 1737. JP: Lawrance Growdon, esq.

P. 206   Deed. Jeremiah Langhorne of Middletown, for £250, to Henry Vanhorne of Middletown, a plantation and two tracts of land in Middletown. The first is 170 acres on Neshaminy Creek and bounded by the lands of Cuthbert Hayhurst, John Stackhouse, Adam Harker, William Hudleston and Benjamin Cutler. The other tract is 30½ acres of land bounded by the lands of Benjamin Fields, Edward Lucas and Jonathan Woolstone. These tracts are part of 3 tracts which Christian Barnson Vanhorne and his wife WilliamKee and Henry Vanhorne and his wife Susanna conveyed to Langhorne. Made 3 Aug 1737. Wit: Joseph Poole, Wm. Fry. Ackn: 7 Nov 1737. JP: Lawrance Growdon, esq.

P. 208   Deed.   Christian Barnson, otherwise called Vanhorne, of Middletown, and WilliamKee, his wife, for £15, to Joseph Richardson of Middletown, shopkeeper, a 1 acre lot in Attlebury in Middletown by the road that leads from the Falls to Philadelphia and by the Bristol road. This lot is part of 280 acres that Edward Shippen, Griffith Owen and James Logan conveyed to Robert Heaton, late of Middletown, by patent dated 20 May 1705. Robert Heaton conveyed the land to Henry Johnson Vandike by deed recorded in Book C, Vol 1, pg 224, who by his Last Will and Testament left the land to his wife Yanica during her lifetime and after her death to his son-in-law Christian Barnson and his granddaughter Susanna Vandlecy. Susanna, who married Henry Vanhorne, and Christian Barnson nee Vanhorne and his wife WilliamKee conveyed the land to Jeremiah Langhorne who conveyed the land back to Christian Barnson alias Vanhorne. Made 7 Nov 1737. Wit: Lawrance Growdon, Jr., Jno. Duncan. Ackn. Same day. JP: Jeremiah Langhorne.

P. 210   Lease.   Johannes Zuber of Bensalem, yeoman, for 5 shillings, to William Fry of Middletown, 215 acres in Bensalem by the road from Trevose to Philadelphia and by land late of Francis Searle, deceased. Made 28 Aug 1737. Wit: Henderick Breese, Hannah Breas.

P. 211   Release.   Johannes Zuber, for £176.10s, to William Fry [same parties and land as preceding entry.] This land is that which William Penn by lease and release dated 24 and 25 Oct 1681 conveyed to Joseph Growdon who, along with his wife Ann, conveyed the land to Johannes Zuber by lease and release dated 19 and 20 Oct 1722. Made 29 Aug 1737. Wit: Henderick Brees, Hannah Breas. Ackn. Same day. JP: Lawrance Growdon.

P. 214   Mortgage.   Nathan Watson of Bristol, cordwiner [sic], for £22.15s.10p, to Joseph Kirkbride, Jr. of Falls Township, yeoman, a lot in Bristol. Nathan Watson by mortgage dated 1 Nov 1735 and recorded in Book B, Vol 2, pg 127, conveyed to Joseph Kirkbride this same property in Bristol bounded by Mill Creek and Farewell Alley to Mill Street to the River Delaware, subject to be redeemed if Watson pays to Kirkbride £142.8s.9p plus interest. The property is subject to covenants mentioned in an indenture of lease and release dated 10 Oct 1735 between Nathan Watson and Thomas Watson and his wife Rebecca. Made 20 Aug 1737. Wit: Wm. Atkinson, Jno. Hall. Ackn: 1 Oct 1737. JP: Em Williams. Rec: 24 Nov 1737.

P. 216   Release.   Joseph Bond of Bristol, yeoman, and his wife Ann, for £625, to William Fishbourn of Philadelphia, merchant, all Burdens Little Island and adjacent land (151 acres and 27¼ acres), a part of the land which by indentures tripartite of lease and release dated 1 and 2 May 1716, Hannah Carpenter of said city (widow and executrix of Samuel Carpenter, Sr., merchant, deceased,) Samuel Carpenter, Jr., and John Carpenter, merchants and sons of Samuel Carpenter, Sr., Hannah Fishbourn, wife of said William Fishbourn and daughter of Samuel Carpenter, Sr., conveyed to Joseph Bond containing 815¼ acres: two islands, one called Burdens Little Island, the other Burdens Great Island, which with adjacent lands lie in Bristol by the Delaware River near the floodgates of the old mill and alongside Hog Run, the Green Swamp, by the lands of Daniel Peggs, Henry Tomlinson, Jeffry Pollard, Richard Mountaine and John Baldwin, by the road leading from Buckingham and the road to Neshaminy Ferry and by Otter Creek and Mill Creek. Excepting only a plot by Neshaminy Road reserved for a burying place and access plus a cartway from the island to Mill Street. Made 4 May 1716. Wit: Cha. Brockden, Nath'l. French, Geo. Shiers, Jos. Fox. Ackn: 24 Nov 1737 before JP Abraham Chapman by Samuel Baxter.

P. 220   Release. Joseph Bond of Bristol, yeoman, for £130, to Adam Harker of Middletown, mason, 4 tracts of land containing a total of 74 acres. The first tract of 26 acres in Bristol begins by the road leading to Otter's Bridge and runs by the land of Josiah Langdale. Another parcel is that of 14 acres lying by the same road and by Mill Creek. A third tract of 5 acres lies by Mill Creek and Josiah Langdale's land. A fourth parcel of 29 acres by the Delaware River adjoins Joseph Bond's land, all part of the land which Hannah Carpenter, et al, conveyed to Joseph Bond [see preceding entry for details.] Made 12 Apr 1718. Wit: Timothy Smith, Peter Hastings, Jer. Langhorne. Ackn: 30 Nov 1737. JP: Abraham Chapman.

P. 223   Release. Adam Harker of Middletown, mason, for good will and natural affection and for 5 shillings, to Samuel Harker, mason and son of Adam Harker, 3 tracts of land in Bristol. The first of 10 acres is bounded by Adam Harker's land and by the land of Josiah Langdale and Joseph Bond. The second of 13 acres is bounded by the lands of Adam Harker, William Fishbourn and Josiah Langdale. The third tract is 10 acres and bounded by Mill Creek and the lands of Adam Harker and Josiah Langdale. This land is part of 74 acres which Joseph Bond of Bristol sold to Adam Harker by lease and release dated 11 and 12 Apr 1718 [see entry for P. 220 above.] 5 Mar 1722/3. Wit: Wm. Biles, Jer. Langhorne. Ackn: 30 Nov 1737. JP: Abraham Chapman.

P. 225   Mortgage. Benjamin Armitage of Bristol, Philadelphia Co. [sic], joyner, and his wife Jane, to secure a debt of £100, to George Jones of Philadelphia, inn holder, a plantation and 212¾ acres in Buckingham by the land of Rodman & Co. and by Maley's land. This land is that which Humphrey Morry by indenture dated 22 Apr 1723 conveyed to Benjamin Armitage by the name of Benjamin Armitage the Younger. George Jones permits Benjamin Armitage to continue to live on the plantation. Made 19 Nov 1737. Wit: C. Brockden, Sam'l. Gifford, John Ord. Ackn. 25 Nov 1737 before JP Jeremiah Langhorne by Charles Brockden and John Ord, both of Philadelphia.

P. 227   Deed. John Chapman of Wrightstown, bachelor, for £15 and because he is moving, to Abraham Chapman, his brother, 268 acres of land in Wrightstown by the town square and by William Smith's land and this land is part of 536 acres granted to John Chapman by patent dated 9th da 5th mo 1705 and recorded at Philadelphia in Patent Book A, Vol 3, pg 176. Made 20th da 11th mo 1707. Wit: John Wildman, John Cutler. Ackn: 30 Aug 1733 before JP William Paxson by John Chapman.

P. 228   Release. James Streator of Buckingham, practitioner in phisick, for £190, to Edmund Kensey of Buckingham, yeoman, 500 acres and 87½ perches of land in Buckingham by the lands of Richard Lunday, William Say, Robert Wheeler, Margaret Atkinson, Thomas Parsons and Thomas Bye. Said land that which William Penn patented 5 Mar 1701 to James Streator. Made 11 Dec 1714. Wit: Jos. Thatcher, Daniel May, Jer. Langhorne. Memo: 10 acres of the above mentioned tract have already been sold to John Scarborough, John Rye, Tobias Dymocke, Samuel Baker and Nehemiah Blackshaw and that 10 acres is excepted out of the above mentioned 500 acres and 87½ perches of land. Ackn: 12 Jan 1737 before Abraham Chapman, JP, by oath of Jeremiah Langhorne.

P. 231   Deed (Indenture Tripartite.) Mary Knowles of Makefield, widow, Peter Taylor of the same place, yeoman, for the natural love and affection for her son John, her only son and heir whom she had by her former husband John Knowles, late of Makefield, deceased, and for 10 shillings paid by Joseph Kirkbride, Jr., Robert Satcher and John Kirkbride, all of Falls Township, yeomen, a messuage and 200 acres of land on the Delaware River bordering Samuel Baker's land except for Mary Knowles to use the land during the minority of her son John Knowles until he comes of age of 21. By indenture of release dated 30 Sep 1730 Mary Warder, executrix of Willoughby Warder, deceased, conveyed to Mary Knowles 200 acres of land in Makefield. And now Mary Knowles and the said Peter Taylor intend to marry soon. Made 28 Sep 1731. Wit: J. Growdon, C. Brockden. Ackn: 10 May 1732 before JP Thomas Yardley, Joseph Growdon and Charles Brockden, both of Philadelphia, gave their oath of witness.

P. 234   Deed. John Stackhouse of Middletown, yeoman, for 10 shillings, for his care in time to come and for natural love and affection to his eldest lawful son Thomas Stackhouse, of Bristol, yeoman, 160 acres of land in Bristol bounded by the land of Israel Pemberton, John Smith, John Lanings, and by the Manor of Pennsbury. Said land that which Robert Smith of Bristol, cooper, by deed dated 8 Mar 1714 conveyed to John Stackhouse. Made 11 Oct 1737. Wit: Jer. Langhorne, Jno. Duncan. Ackn: 11 Feb 1737. JP: Jeremiah Langhorne.

P. 235   Sheriff's Deed. Timothy Smith, Sheriff, for £135, to Ebenezer Large, one moiety of 2 tracts of land and a mill in Solebury. Richard Smith of Burlington, NJ, merchant, at the Court of Common Pleas held at Newtown, Bucks Co., 15 Jun 1736 recovered from John Hough of Bucks Co., yeoman, £103.12s and 66s.2p for his damages received by the detention of a debt, which recovery to be achieved by levying lands of John Hough, by writ dated 17 Sep 1736, the Sheriff to have the money at the next court to be held at Newtown 16 Dec 1736. The Sheriff seized from John Hough one full equal moiety of two tracts of land and a water grist mill in Solebury. The land begins at a corner of John Hough's land by Joseph Pike's line and by the land of Nehemiah Blackshaw, containing 8 acres and 50 perches. The other tract begins by the line between John Hough and Nehemiah Blackshaw's lands and by Pike's land and contains 9 acres and 37 perches. The land and mill remained unsold by the time of the next seating of the court. By another writ dated 19 Mar 1837 the Sheriff was ordered to sell the property at public auction to the highest bidder and to have the money for the next court to be held at Newtown 16 Jun 1837. The land was thus sold to Ebenezer Large of Burlington, NJ, merchant, for £135. Made 16 Sep 1737. Wit: Jos. Growdon, Wm. Atkinson. Ackn. same day before JP Jeremiah Langhorne. Is. Penington and Richard Smith, Jr. witnessed the payment in full from Ebenezer Large 15 Oct 1737. Rec: 21 Mar 1737/8.

P. 237   Deed. Jeremiah Bartholomew of Northampton, yeoman, and his wife Ellen, for £215, to Joseph Linton of Falls Township, cordwainer, 162 acres in Northampton by Neshaminy Creek and bounded by the lands of William Shrieve and Edward Glover. This land part of 284 acres which Bartholomew Thatcher and Joseph Thatcher by deed recorded in Bucks Co. Book D, Vol 1, pg 58 conveyed to William Cutler of Northampton, deceased. In his Last Will and Testament, William Cutler appointed his sister Ellen Cutler executrix, giving her authority to sell the land for payment of his debts. Ellen Cutler later married Jeremiah Bartholomew. Jeremiah and Ellen by deed dated 27 Feb 1733 conveyed the plantation and 162 acres to Thomas

Stackhouse of Middletown, who by deed dated 4 Mar 1733 conveyed it back to Jeremiah Bartholomew. Made 21 Feb 1736. Wit: Jonathan Woollston, Wm. Fry. Ackn: 25 Feb 1736. JP: Thomas Yeardley.

P. 240   Deed.   Stephen Townsend of Solebury, yeoman, for £80, to William Ridge of Bensalem, yeoman, 56¼ acres of land in Bensalem beginning by the Southampton line and Stephen Sands' corner, part of 2,957 acres which by patent 31 Oct 1736 was conveyed to Lawrance Growdon, esq., of Trevose. The yearly payment of one English silver shilling to be paid to Lawrance Growdon on the 1st of March each year forever. Made 23 Nov 1737. Wit: Jno. Duncan, Amos Shaw. Ackn: 24 Apr 1738. JP: Jeremiah Langhorne. Rec: 25 Apr 1738.

P. 242   Deed. Robert Heaton of Southampton, yeoman, for 10 shillings and the intent a meeting house for public worship and a schoolhouse for the education of the youth may be built on the ground herein described, to Richard Sands, David Wilson, William Carter and Cuthbert Hayhurst, all of Bucks Co., yeomen, land in Southampton beginning at the corner of the late John Naylor, deceased, on the north side of the road leading from the Falls to Philadelphia, and by Robert Heaton's land. Made 2 Mar 1737. Wit: Robert Heaton, Jr., Jno. Duncan. Ackn: 6 Mar 1737. JP: Jeremiah Langhorne. Rec: 25 Apr 1738.

P. 243   Letter of Attorney. John Orr of Rapho Parish, County Donegal in Ireland, labourer, make my trusty and well-beloved friend Andrew Henderson, merchant, my attorney to recover legacies by the Last Will and Testament bequeathed to me, the only son and heir of Humphrey Orr, late of Bucks Co., my deceased father. Made 20 Jun 1737. Wit: Alex'r. Rogers, Thomas Rogers, John Mackay. Memo: Andrew Colhoun of Rapho, Donegal, Ireland, notary publik & tabellion, witnessed John Orr's signing of the document and saw Alexander Rogers, Thomas Rogers and John Mackay witness the document and further certifies that James Finley and Zachias Finley, both of Tillydonnell in said county and kingdom, farmers, swore oaths that they know John Orr to be the son of Humphrey Orr and Elizabeth Orr alias Simrell, his wife, late of Artikelly in Rapho, who left his kingdom and went to Pennsylvania in America and died there. Dated at Rapho 13 Jun 1737. 10 Apr 1738 Alexander Rogers appeared before Henry Hayes, Justice of the Peace for the County of Chester, PA and declared he saw John Orr seal and deliver the Power of Attorney.

P. 245   Sheriff's Deed. Timothy Smith, Sheriff of Bucks Co., for £101, to Stephen Townsend of Bensalem. Benjamin Jennings, late of Solebury, yeoman, deceased, for securing the payment of £60 in bills of credit conveyed to Samuel Carpenter, Jeremiah Langhorne, William Fishbourne and Philip Taylor, the trustees of the General Loan Office of Pennsylvania on 29 Oct 1729 his plantation and 2 tracts of 150 acres in Solebury bounded by the lands of Ezra Croasdale and George Brown. Benjamin Jennings by his indenture on that date obliged himself bound to these men in the sum of £120. Andrew Hamilton, Jeremiah Langhorne, Charles Read and Richard Hays, the now trustees of the General Loan Office, at a Court of Common Pleas held at Newtown 13 Jun 1735 by default of payment of the £60 and interest recovered from Abraham Jennings, administrator of the estate of Benjamin Jennings. The trustees requested the land be sold to recover the debt. By writ dated 14 Jun 1735, the Sheriff was commanded to levy the land and have the money for the next court at Newtown on 11 Sep 1735. The land was exposed to public auction and sold 17 Sep 1735 to Stephen Townsend. Made 17 Sep 1736. Wit: Is. Penington, Wm. Fry, Nathan Watson. Ackn: 17 Sep 1736. JP: Jeremiah Langhorne.

P. 247   Deed. Adrian Bennet nee Ader John Bennet of Somerset, NJ, yeoman, for £270, to John Ogilby of Bensalem, yeoman, 2 tracts of 257 acres. The first of 57 acres is by Neshaminy Creek and bounded by the lands of Peter Buskirk and Jeremiah Bartholomew. The other tract of 200 acres, also by Neshaminy Creek, is bounded by the land of Robert Heaton, Jr. and Hudlestone and the land late of John Cutler. Bernard Christian of Bergin, NJ, yeoman, by deed dated 20 Sep 1707 and recorded in Bucks Co. Book C, Vol 1, pg 402 conveyed 257 acres in Bucks Co. to Peter Barnson Vanhorne. Christian Barnson, late of Middletown, yeoman, by indenture dated 24 May 1715 conveyed 200 acres in Middletown to Peter Barnson Vanhorn, who by indentures of lease and release dated 13 and 14 April 1727 conveyed 257 acres to Ader John Bennet. Made 23 May 1727. Wit: Tho. Clifford, Pieter Barson Vanhorne, Wm. Atkinson. Signed Adrian Bennet. Ackn: 9 Mar 1731 before JP Jeremiah Langhorne by Adrian Bennet.

P. 250   Deed. Peter Barnson Vanhorne of Middletown, yeoman, for £300 to Adrian nee Ader John Bennet of Somerset Co., NJ, yeoman, 2 tracts of land in Bucks Co. One tract of 57 acres stands by Neshaminy Creek and borders the lands of Jeremiah Bartholomew. The other tract of 200 acres is also on Neshaminy Creek and borders the lands late of Robert Heaton, Jr. and John Cutler and by Hudlestone's land. Barnard Christian of Bergen, NJ, yeoman by deed dated 20 Sep 1707 and recorded in Bucks Co. Book C, Vol 1, pg 402 conveyed 257 acres in Bucks Co. to Peter Barnson Vanhorne. Christian Barnson, late of Middletown, yeoman, by deed dated 24 May 1715 conveyed 200 acres in Middletown to Peter Barnson Vanhorne. Made 14 Apr 1727.

Wit: Abraham Stevese, Bernard Vanhorne. Ackn: 26 May 1738 before JP Jeremiah Langhorne by Peter Barnson Vanhorne. Rec: 30 May 1738.

P. 252   Deed. John Ogilby of Bensalem, yeoman, for £218.15s and the residue of a debt, conveys to William Carter of Middletown, yeoman, a plantation and 2 tracts of land. By deed dated 17 Jul 1727 John Ogilby, for £99.15s, conveyed to Samuel Carpenter, Jeremiah Langhorne, William Fishbourne and Nathaniel Newlin, trustees of the General Loan Office of Pennsylvania, a plantation and 2 tracts of land in Bucks Co., the first of 57 acres of land by Neshaminy Creek is bounded by the lands of Peter Buskirk and Jeremiah Bartholomew. The other tract contained 200 acres. A proviso in this deed said that if John Ogilby should repay the trustees then the deed is null and void. John Ogilby has paid part of the debt and William Carter has agreed to pay the remainder of the debt. By some mistake the description of the last recited tract of land is erroneous and should be described as beginning by the road by Hudlestone's line and by the land late of John Cutler. Made 30 Sep 1728. Wit: Jos. Lupton, John Carter. Ackn: 9 Mar 1731. JP: Jeremiah Langhorne. Rec: 30 May 1738. Memo: 9 Jul 1941 [sic] the mortgage is cleared by Virtue of Decree of the Court of Common Pleas and recorded in Misc. Book 78, pg 386, signed by Frederick W. Randall, Recorder of Deeds and John W. Cooper, Dep. Recorder.

P. 255   Deed. William Carter of Southampton, yeoman, and his wife Sarah, for £130, to Joseph Richardson of Middletown, shopkeeper, 57 acres in Northampton. John Ogilby of Bensalem, yeoman, by deed dated 30 Sep 1728 conveyed to William Carter this land which lies by Neshaminy Creek and is bounded by the lands of Peter Buskirk and Jeremiah Bartholomew. Made 12 Jun 1738. Wit: Jno. Dunkan, Benj'a. Field. Signed Wm. Cartar and Sarah Cartar. Ackn: 12 Jun 1738. JP: Jeremiah Langhorne.

P. 256   Lease. Jeremiah Bartholomew of Northampton, yeoman, and his wife Ellin, for 5 shillings, to Joseph Linton of Falls Township, cordwainer, 162 acres of land in Northampton by Neshaminy Creek bounded by the lands of William Shrieve and Edward Glover. Made 21 Feb 1736. Wit: Jonathan Woolston, Wm. Fry.

P. 257   Lease. Thomas Hillbourn of Newtown, cordwainer, for 5 shillings to James Arbuckle of Southampton, yeoman, 55 acres and 60 perches of land in Newtown by Newtown Creek. Made 8 May 1738. Wit: Wm. Fry, Henry Tuckney.

P. 258   Release. Thomas Hillbourn, for £50, to James Arbuckle [same parties and land as in preceding entry.] Robert Hillbourn, late of Newtown, deceased, owned 250 acres in Newtown when he made his Last Will and Testament dated 4 Mar 1719/20 and bequeathed the land to his son Thomas Hillbourn after he reaches the age of 21. Thomas Hillbourn has now reached the age of 21 and his father Robert Hillbourn soon after died. Made 8 May 1738. Wit: Wm. Fry, Henry Tuckney. Ackn: same day. JP: Emon Williams. Rec: 3 Sep 1738.

P. 261   Lease. James Arbuckle, for 5 shillings, to Thomas Hillbourn [same parties, reversed, and land as in previous entries for pgs 257 and 258.] 55 acres and 60 perches of land in Newtown bounded by the lands of Thomas Stradlin, Benjamin Taylor and Thomas Hillbourn. Made 8 May 1738. Wit: Wm. Fry, Henry Tuckney.

P. 261   Release. James Arbuckle, for £50, to Thomas Hillbourn [same parties and land as previous 3 entries.] 55 acres and 60 perches of land, part of 133 acres and 155 perches in Newtown which Thomas Maybury of Newtown, blacksmith, by indentures of lease and release dated 15 and 16 Dec 1736 and recorded in Book B, Vol 2, pg 183 conveyed to James Arbuckle. Made 8 May 1738. Wit: Wm. Fry, Henry Tuckney. Ackn: 8 May 1738. JP: Emon Williams. Rec: 4th da 7^{ber} 1738.

P. 264   Mortgage. Robert Cuming of Northampton, yeoman, for £111, to Thomas Lacey of Philadelphia, 240 acres of land in Northampton bounded by the land of James Worth and George Dungan, agreement void if and when Robert Cumming makes the last payment due 17 Jul 1742. Made 15 Jul 1738. Wit: Abra Chapman, Jr., Abra Chapman. Ackn: 15 Jul 1738. JP: Abraham Chapman. Rec: 19 Sep 1738. Memo: On 13 Sep 1941 [sic] the mortgage is satisfied by Virtue of Decree of Court of Common Pleas and recorded in Misc. Book 78, pg 480. Frederick W. Randall, Recorder of Deeds. John W. Cooper, Dep. Recorder.

P. 266   Lease. Jeremiah Langhorne of Middletown, esq., for 5 shillings, to Mathew Rue of the same place, yeoman, a lot in Bristol on the southwest side of Mill Street, by the lot late of John Rowland, by Israel Pemberton's lot, by Mill Creek. Made 1 Aug 1738. Wit: Jno. Duncan, Wm. Saterthwait.

P. 266   Release. Jeremiah Langhorne, for £75, to Mathew Rue [same parties and land as preceding entry.] This lot is that which Thomas Rogers, Jr., executor of the Last Will and Testament of John Rowland, late of Bristol, yeoman, deceased, by indenture of release dated 13 Dec 1717 conveyed to

Jeremiah Langhorne. Made 2 Aug 1738. Wit: Jno. Duncan, Wm Saterthwait. Ackn: 16 Sep 1738. JP: Lawrance Growden, esq.

P. 267   Lease. Abel Janney of Middletown, yeoman, for 5 shillings, to Peter LaRow of Hopewell, NJ, yeoman, a plantation and 258 acres of land in Makefield and bounded by the lands of Thomas Yardley, Abel Janney, Jr., Richard Hough and Edward Bailey. Made 11 Sep 1738. Wit: Jer. Langhorne, Jno. Duncan.

P. 268   Release. Abel Janney to Peter LaRow, for £350, [same parties and land as preceding entry.] This 258 acres is the residue of 640 acres which Mahlon Stacey of Chester, Burlington Co., NJ conveyed by deed dated 24 Feb 1726 to Abel Janney. Made 12 Sep 1738. Wit: Jer. Langhorne. Jno. Duncan. Ackn: 12 Sep 1738. JP: Jeremiah Langhorne.

P. 271   Deed. Lawrance Growdon of Trevose in Bensalem, esq., for £98.12s, to Joseph Rodman of New Rochel, West Chester Co., NY, gent., 98½ acres of land in Bensalem bounded by the land of James Rue, James Keen, Henry Enoch, Hannah Vanzandt and Joseph Rodman. This land part of 2,957 acres which was patented 31 Oct 1737 to Lawrance Growdon. Made 21 Sep 1738. Wit: Is. Penington, Joseph Severens. Ackn: 29 Sep 1738 before JP Jeremiah Langhorne.

P. 272   Lease. William Penn, late of Warminghurst, Sussex Co., esq., for 5 shillings, to Joseph Baynes of Stangerford, Westmoreland Co., yeoman, 500 acres in Pennsylvania. Made 24 May 1683. Wit: Harb't. Springett, Sell Craske, Tho. Coxe.

P. 273   Release. William Penn, for £10, to Joseph Baynes [same parties and land as preceding entry.] The 500 acres yet to be laid out.
      "*King Charles the Second by his letters under the Great Seal of England bearing date the fourth day of March in the three and thirtieth year of his reign for the considerations therein mentioned Hath given and granted unto the said William Penn his heirs and assigns All that Tract or parcel of Land in America with the Islands therein Contained and thereunto belonging as the Same is bounded on the East by Delaware River from twelve miles Distance Northward of Newcastle Town to the three and fortieth Degree of Northern Latitude and Extendeth Westward five Degrees in Longitude and is bounded on the South by a Circle drawn at Twelve miles Distance from Newcastle a---- Northward and Westwards to the Beginning of the fortieth Degree of Northern Latitude and then by a Strait Line Westwards to the limit of Longitutde above mentioned Together with Divers Great Powers Preheminonces Authorities Royalties Franchises and Immunities and hath Erected*

the Said Tract of Land into a Province or Signiory by the Name of Pennsylvania in order to the reestablishing of a Colony and plantation in the Same and hath hereby also further granted to the Said William Penn his heirs and assigns from Time to Time Power and Licence to assign alien grant Devise or Enfeoff Such Parts & Parcels of the Said Province or Tract of Land as he or they Shall think fitt to Such Person or Persons as Shall be Willing to purchase the Same in Fee Simple Fee Tayle or for Term of Life or Years to be holden of the Said William Penn his heirs and assigns as of the Signiory of Windsor by such Services Customs and Rents as Shall Seem fit to the Said William Penn his heirs or assigns and not immediately of the Said King his heirs & Successors Notwithstanding the Statue Quia Emptores Terrarum made in the Reign of King Edward the first."
 Made 25 May 1683. Wit: Harb't. Springett, Tho. Cox, Sell Craske.

P. 275   Deed.   Joseph Baines of Stangerwhaite in Killington, Westmoreland Co., yeoman, for the natural love and affection which he has for his son-in-law Daniel Jackson of Lamplagh, Cumberland Co., fuller, and Hannah, Daniel's wife and daughter to the said Joseph Baines, and John Jackson and Joseph Jackson, the children of the said Daniel and Hannah and all such other children whether male or female hereafter to be begotten by Daniel and Hannah, all of his 500 acres (not yet laid out) in Pennsylvania which was sold to him by William Penn 11 Jul 1681. All children to have fair and equal part of the land except the eldest male child a double part. The gift of this land is free and clear of the dower or widow's rights of Barbury, now wife of Joseph Baines. Made 16 Sep 1699. Wit: Thomas Cain, James Baines, Anah More, Richard Eglin. Memo: Joseph Baines makes Jeremiah Langhorne and Robert Heaton his attorneys. Wit: Thomas Cain, James Baines, Richard Eglin.

P. 278   Deed.   Derrick Kroesen (Crusen) and Henry Kroewsen (Crusen), both of Southampton, Bucks Co., yeomen, for 5 shillings and because they are moving, to Henry Brees, Jacobus VanSandt, Derrick Howgland and John Crusen, all of the said County, yeomen, a ½ acre lot in Southampton. Made 1 Jul 1738. Signed Derricke Kroesen and Henry Kroewsen Wit: Jno. Duncan, James C.H. Dougan, Jer. Langhorne. Rec: 23 Oct 1738.

P. 280   Deed.   Bernard Verkerck of Bensalem, yeoman, for 5 shillings, because he is moving, and for love and affection to his son John Verkerck, 106 acres in Bensalem by the Delaware River bounded by land formerly Jacob Grosebick's and by Barnard Berkerk's other land. This land part of 271 acres sold to Johannes Vandergrift of Bensalem by deed dated 1st da 5th mo 1697 by Joseph Growdon. Johannes Vandergrift conveyed the land to Bernard Vankerck [sic] by deed dated 5 Feb 1711. Made 29 May 1736. Wit: Benj'a.

Harris, Wm. Atkinson, Margaret Atkinson. Possession of the property delivered to John Verkerck by Bernard Verkerck 3 Jun 1736 before John Johnston and John Ingels. Ackn: 23 Oct 1738 before John Hall, Chief Burgess of Bristol by William Atkinson and Benjamin Harris.

P. 281   Deed. Stophel Vansandt of Middletown, yeoman, for natural love and affection and for £75, to John Vansandt of the same place, yeoman and son of Stophel Vansandt, 100 acres of land in Middletown bounded by the lands of Charles Plumly, William Paxson and Jeremiah Langhorne. Said land part of 500 acres granted by James Claypool and Robert Turner, two of William Penn's Commissioners, by patent dated 17th da 3rd mo 1686 to Henry Paulin, who conveyed the land to Stophel Vansandt by deed recorded in Bucks Co. Book A, Vol 1, pg 72. Made 8 Oct 1738. Wit: Jer. Langhorne, Jno. Duncan. Ackn: same day. JP: Jeremiah Langhorne.

P. 282   Deed. Jeremiah Langhorne of Bucks Co., gent., for £88, to William Thomas of North Philadelphia, cooper, 440 acres in Hilltown. By indenture dated 16 Nov 1713 Robert Brock (or Ralph Brock) of Bucks Co., millwright, conveyed to Jeremiah Langhorne 440 acres and by warrant dated 13 Aug 1714 the land was surveyed and laid out on the 18th day to Jeremiah Langhorne as follows: 440 acres in Hilltown bounded by the Philadelphia County line at a corner of Samuel Carts land. Made 12 Feb 1718. Wit: Cha. Brockden, Abraham Watkins, Wm. Strutt. Memo: This land was confirmed to Jeremiah Langhorne by patent dated 7 Dec 1714 and recorded at Philadelphia in Patent Book A, Vol 5, pg 112. Ackn: 24 May 1738 by Jeremiah Langhorne before James Hamilton, a Justice of the City and County of Philadelphia.

P. 284   Deed. James Logan of Philadelphia, merchant, and his wife Sarah, for £90, to William Thomas of Hilltown, Bucks Co., cooper, 300 acres of land in Hilltown beginning by Andrew Buskirk's line and bounded by the land of John Penn, part of 2,000 acres which William Penn by patent dated 1 Oct 1716 and recorded in Philadelphia Patent Book A, Vol 5, pg 235 conveyed to Israel Pemberton. By indenture dated 26 Sep 1723 Israel Pemberton sold the 2,000 acres to James Logan. Made 28 Sep 1723. Wit: Thomas Griffits, Cha. Osborne. Ackn: 29 Apr 1738 by the Honorable James Logan, esq. and Sarah his wife before William Allen, Justice of the Peace for the City and County of Philadelphia.

P. 286   Deed. James Logan, for £100, to William Thomas [same parties and part of the same 2,000 acres described in preceding entry.] 212 acres in Hilltown bounded by the land of Evan Griffith and James Logan's and

William Thomas' other lands, being part of an original tract of 2,000 acres. Made 10 Apr 1728. Wit: Andrew Cornish, Isaac Brown, Morr. Lloyd. Ackn: 29 Apr 1738 by the Honorable James Logan, esq. and Sarah his wife before William Allen, Justice of the Peace for the City and County of Philadelphia. Rec: 28 Nov 1738.

P. 289   Deed. Benjamin Philips of Hilltown, yeoman and Sage his wife, for £25, to William Thomas of the same place, cooper, 50 acres of land in Hilltown bounded by the lands of Benjamin Philips, William Thomas and John Morris, part of a 150 acre tract. Jeremiah Langhorne by deed dated 12 Oct 1713 conveyed to Andreas VanBuskirk 1,100 acres of land in Hilltown, who by deed dated 26 Nov 1726 conveyed 304 acres of the land to John Vanbuskek [sic] and his wife Mary who by deed dated 29 Nov 1726 sold 150 acres of the land to Benjamin Philips.   Made 30 Apr 1728. Wit: Tho. Cadwalader, Jno. Cadwalader, Thomas Harrys, Sarah Harrys, Thomas Thomas, Benjamin Philips, John Thomas. Ackn: 12 Aug 1738 before JP Simon Butler by Benjamin Phillips who acknowledged the document was his and his former wife's, Sage.

P. 291   Deed. Rowland Ellis, Jr. of Philadelphia, merchant, for £56, to William Thomas of Hilltown, Bucks Co., yeoman, 2 tracts of land, one 150 acres in Hilltown bounded by the land of William Thomas, Evan Griffiths, and Benjamin Philips and the other 106 acres near Perkesy, Bucks Co., bounded by the lands of Buskirk and John Humphrey. These 2 tracts part of 3,000 acres of land which William Penn by deeds of lease and release dated 3 and 4 Apr 1695 conveyed to Daniel Wharley of London, woollen draper. By indentures of lease and release dated 2 and 3 Apr 1724 Daniel Wharley, eldest son and heir of the said Daniel Wharley, deceased, sold the land to Rowland Ellis. By a warrant dated 21 May 1725 the land was surveyed and laid out on 22 Nov 1725. Made 18 Dec 1725. Wit: Cha. Osborne, Js. Watson. Ackn: 25 May 1738 before JP Clement Plumstead, esq., by Charles Brockden of Philadelphia, gent., who, when presented with this indented writing, swore oath that he believes the document is authentic, that Charles Osborne and Joseph Watson were both late of Philadelphia and that he, Charles Brockden, was well acquainted with their handwriting.

P. 294   Mortgage. John Bond of Richland, Bucks Co., weaver, and Sarah his wife, for £55, to Morris Morris of Abington, Philadelphia Co., yeoman, a plantation and 150 acres of land in the Great Swamp by the lands of Joseph Gilbert, John Lester and Wm. Tidmarsh, part of 250 acres in Richland which William Mountjoy of the County of Wilts, Great Britain, gent., conveyed to John Bond by indentures of lease and release dated 28 and 29 Jul 1723 and the land was surveyed and laid out for John Bond by warrant dated 20 Dec 1727 and patented to him 30 Dec 1737. Payments to be made yearly to Morris Morris with the final payment due 22 Jun 1744. Made 22 Jun 1738. Wit: Benj. Jones, Catharine Jones. Ackn: same day. JP: Benjamin Jones.

P. 296   Deed.   William Fry of Middletown, gent., for £126.10s, to Lawrance Growdon of Trevose, esq., 3 messuages and 215 acres of land in Bensalem by the road leading from Trevose to Philadelphia and by land late of Francis Searle, deceased. Said land part of 5,000 acres which William Penn by deeds of lease and release dated 24 and 25 Oct 1681 conveyed to Joseph Growdon, who, with his wife Ann, sold 215 acres of the land by indentures of lease and release dated 19 and 20 Oct 1722 to Johannes Zuber, who by indentures of lease and release dated 29 and 30 Aug 1737 sold it to William Fry. Made 11 Nov 1737. Wit: Richard Mitchell, Jno. Duncan. Ackn: same day. JP: Jeremiah Langhorne. Rec: 30 Dec 1738.

P. 299   Release. Jeremiah Langhorne of Middletown, yeoman, for £60, to Henry Paxson of the same place, yeoman, 2 tracts of 1,000 acres of land, part of 3,000 acres which William Penn by indentures of lease and release dated 17 and 18 Feb 1701 conveyed to George Beale of Guildford, County of Surrey, Great Britain, who by indentures of lease and release dated 17 and 18 Oct 1718 conveyed the land to Jeremiah Langhorne. Part of the land was surveyed and laid out near Perkesing in Bucks Co. by the County line and bordering James Logan's land and Jeremiah Langhorne's other land and contains 650 acres as well as another tract near Conestogoe, Chester Co. by James Hendrick's land containing 350 acres. Made 16 Sep 1720. Wit: Garrat Vandine, Tho. Watson. Ackn: 15 Jun 1732. JP: Abraham Chapman.

P. 300   Lease. Charles Read, esq., of Burlington, NJ, and Alice his wife, for 5 shillings, to George Logan of Makefield, Bucks Co., yeoman, 372 acres of land in Makefield by the Delaware River at John Deiver's corner, thence to James Read's corner and by Reuben Pownal's land. Made 4 Aug 1738. Wit: Jno. Robinson, Hum. Garland.

P. 301   Release. Charles Read, for £400, to George Logan [same parties and land as preceding entry.] Made 5 Aug 1738. Wit: Jno. Robinson, Hum. Garland. Memo: this tract of land is mortgaged in the General Loan Office of Pennsylvania for £100 which is now due and part of the consideration money here. George Logan has agreed that Charles Read may cut and carry away all the timber trees fit for shipbuilding. Ackn: 25 Jan 1738 before JP Joseph Kirkbride by John Robinson and Humphrey Garland, both of Philadelphia, gent.

P. 304　　Mortgage. George Logan of Makefield, yeoman, and his wife Jane, to Charles Read of Burlington, NJ, esq. George Logan stands bound to Charles Read for £484.18s conditioned for the payment of £242.9s plus interest. For the consideration of this debt, George and Jane Logan convey to Charles Read land in Makefield by the Delaware River at a corner of John Deiver's land [same land and parties as above two entries.] Made 7 Aug 1738. Wit: Jno. Robinson, Hum. Garland. Ackn: 25 Jan 1738 before JP Joseph Kirkbride by John Robinson and Humphrey Garland, both of the City of Philadelphia. Rec: 26 Jan 1738. Memo: by power of attorney recorded in Book D, Vol 2, pg 611 given to him from William Logan, executor for James Logan, deceased, Richard Gibbs acknowledges full satisfaction of the debt on 14 Jun 1766 before Law. Growdon, Recorder of Deeds. Indenture void when George Logan pays off the mortgage to Charles Read. Last payment to be made 25 Jun 1741.

P. 307　　Mortgage. Nicholas Parker of Plumstead, yeoman, for £86.3s.6p, to Baltes Peckel of Reading, Hunterdon Co., NJ, yeoman, 100 acres of land in Plumstead beginning by Lawrance Pearson's land which Joseph Kirkbride, late of Falls Township, deceased, by indentures of lease and release dated 1735 conveyed to Nicholas Parker. Payment to be made to Baltes Peckel by 15 Mar 1739. Made 15 Mar 1738. Wit: Michael Hutchinson, Jos. Kirkbride. Ackn. same day. Rec. 19 Mar 1738/9.

P. 309　　Mortgage. Elizabeth Archbald of Bucks Co., widow, to The Honorable Thomas Penn, esq., one of the Proprietors of Pennsylvania, for the consideration of a debt which Elizabeth Archbald is bound to Thomas Penn for £254.18s conditioned for the payment of £122.19s (payments to be made on 5 Nov annually through the year 1741) 476 acres and 74 perches of land bounded by the land of Uriah Hughes, Joseph Linton, Joseph Fell, Thomas Maleigh, John Watson and the heirs of Thomas Watson, deceased. Made 5 Apr 1739. Wit: Richard Peters, John Callahan (both of Philadelphia). Ackn: 7 Apr 1739. JP: Lawrance Growdon, esq. Rec: 14 Apr 1739. Memo: By decree of the Court of Common Pleas recorded in Misc. Book 2, No. 49, pg 357, full satisfaction of mortgage is acknowledged by Roland Hack, Recorder of Deeds, 8 Mar 1920.

P. 311　　Lease. Jeremiah Langhorne of Middletown, gent., for 5 shillings, to Richard Leadame of Southampton, yeoman, 242 acres and 76 perches of land in Southampton by the lands of Richard Leadam, William Wait and Thomas Harding. Made 21 Oct 1734. Wit: Wm. Fry, David Wilson.

P. 312   Release. Jeremiah Langhorne to Richard Leadame, for £242.10s, 242 acres and 76 perches of land [same parties and land as preceding entry.] Said land part of 500 acres which William Penn by indentures of lease and release dated 7 and 8 Feb 1681 conveyed to John Kirton of Kensington, England to be laid out in PA. By deeds of lease and release dated 13 and 14 Jan 1731, John Kirton, son and heir of John Kirton, conveyed the land to Joseph Turner of Philadelphia, merchant. John Penn, Thomas Penn and Richard Penn, the present Proprietors of Pennsylvania, by patent recorded in Philadelphia Patent Book A, Vol 6, pg 287 confirmed 465¾ acres of this 500 acres to Joseph Turner who conveyed it to Jeremiah Langhorne by deeds dated 19 and 20 Aug 1734. Made 22 Oct 1734. Wit: Wm. Fry, David Wilson. Ackn: 2 Apr 1739. JP: Lawrance Growdon.

P. 314   Mortgage. John McGlauglin of Bucks Co., to secure a debt of £140.2s to be paid 16 Nov annually through 1743, to Thomas Penn, one of the Proprietors of Pennsylvania, 399 acres of land in Bucks Co. which is part of a tract commonly known as Strepors Tract bound by lands of William Colter, James Kelley and Moses Marshall. Made 28 Mar 1739. Wit: Richard Peters, John Callahan (both of Philadelphia.) Ackn: 7 Apr 1739. JP: Lawrance Growdon. Memo: 5 Apr 1937 Release of Mortgage by Decree of Court of Common Pleas, Misc. Book 74, pg 15.

P. 316   Mortgage. James Brooks of Bucks Co., yeoman, to secure a debt of £61.14s.3p to be paid on 16 Nov annually through 1743, to Thomas Penn, one of the Proprietors of Pennsylvania, 175 and 1/3 acres of land, part of the tract known as the Streipors Tract and bounded by the lands of William Goodin and Joseph Combs. Made 28 Mar 1739. Wit: Richard Peters, John Callahan (both of Philadelphia.) Ackn: 7 Apr 1739. JP: Lawrance Growdon.

P. 319   Mortgage. John Sample of Bucks Co., yeoman, to secure a debt of £61.14s.3p to be paid annually on 16 Nov through 1743, to Thomas Penn, one of the Proprietors of Pennsylvania, 175 and 1/3 acres of land, part of a tract called Streipers Tract and bounded by the land of William Goodin. Made 28 Mar 1739. Wit: Richard Peters, John Callahan (both of Philadelphia.) Ackn: 7 Apr 1739. JP: Lawrance Growdon.

P. 321.   Mortgage. George Cope of Bucks Co., yeoman, to secure a debt of £67.10s.9p to be paid annually on 16 Nov through 1743, to Thomas Penn, one of the Proprietors of Pennsylvania, 191 acres and 100 perches of land, part of the Streipers Tract and bounded by the land of Samuel Dyer. Made 28 Mar 1739. Wit: Richard Peters, John Callahan (both of Philadelphia.) Ackn: 7 Apr 1739. JP: Lawrance Growdon. Rec: 18 Apr 1739.

P. 324   Lease. Thomas Tomlinson of Southampton, yeoman, and his wife Elizabeth, for 5 shillings, to Johannes Praul of Middletown, yeoman, 120 acres of land in Southampton bounded by the lands of Joseph Lynn, Benjamin Scott, Henry Walmsley, Benjamin Tomlinson and Philip Dracor. Made 20 Apr 1739. Wit: Joseph Poole, Jer. Langhorne.

P. 324   Release. Thomas Tomlinson, for £175, to Johannes Praul [same parties and land as preceding entry.] Said land that which Joseph Tomlinson, late of Southampton, deceased, father of Thomas Tomlinson, by his Last Will and Testament made about 30 Oct 1722, bequeathed to his son. Made 21 Apr 1739. Wit: Joseph Poole, Jer. Langhorne, Wm. Atkinson, Rebeckah Dunker. Ackn: 21 Apr 1739. JP: Jeremiah Langhorne. Rec: 24 Apr 1739.

P. 327   Release. Christian Barnson Vanhorne of Northampton, yeoman, and WilliamKee his wife, for £15, to Joseph Richardson of Middletown, shopkeeper, 2 acres of land in Attlebury in Middletown and by Christian Vanhorn's other land, by the lands of Henry Vanhorne, Joseph Richardson, Jonathan Woolston and by the Philadelphia Road. Said land part of 280 acres which Jeremiah Langhorne sold to Christian Vanhorne alias Barnson by deed recorded in Book B, Vol 2, pg 204. Made 6 Jul 1739. Wit: Jeremiah Croasdale, Jno. Duncan. Ackn: 6 Jul 1739. JP: Jeremiah Langhorne.

P. 329   Release. Christian Barnson Vanhorne of Northampton, yeoman, and WilliamKee, his wife, for £14, to Jeremiah Croasdale of Middletown, yeoman, 2 acres of land in Attlebury in Middletown by the land of Joseph Richardson, Henry Vanhorne and Christian Vanhorne, part of 280 acres which Jeremiah Langhorne sold to Christian Barnson alias Vanhorne by deed recorded in Book B, Vol 2, pg 204. Made 6 Jul 1739. Wit: Joseph Richardson, Jno. Duncan. Ackn: 6 Jul 1739. JP: Jeremiah Langhorne.

P. 332   Release. Christian Barnson Vanhorne and his wife WilliamKee, for £10, to Jonathan Woolston of Middletown, blacksmith, a 1 acre lot in Attlebury in Middletown by the Bristol Road and bordering the lands of Christian Vanhorne and Joseph Richardson, part of 280 acres which Jeremiah Langhorne sold to Christian Vanhorne by deed recorded in Book B, Vol 2, page 204. Made 6 Jul 1739. Wit: Joseph Richardson, Jno. Duncan. Ackn: 6 Jul 1739. JP: Jeremiah Langhorne.

P. 334   Deed.   Thomas Tomlinson of Bensalem, yeoman, for £50, to Lawrance Growdon of Trevose in the same township, esq., 2 parcels of land in Bensalem. The first parcel is 12¾ acres and bounded by Thomas

Tomlinson's land and Poquesink Creek. The other tract is 12¼ acres and is also bounded by Tomlinson's land. Made 28 Dec 1737. Wit: Peter Bleker, Jno. Duncan. Ackn. same day. JP: Jeremiah Langhorne. Rec: 24 Aug 1739.

P. 336   Deed (Indenture Tripartite.) Charles Mutell of Potterne, County Wilts, clerke, and John Childs of Barton Regis, Gloucester Co. near Bristoll, yeoman of the first part; Solomon Gandovett, Alexander Gandovett, Jeremiah Gandovett, Francis Gandovett the Younger, Mary Gandovett, Henrietta Gandovett, all children of Francis Gandovett the Elder of Bristol, Doctor, of the second part, to Samuel Perry of Barton Regis, gent., and Abraham Alley of the third part, 500 acres which William Penn conveyed Sep 1681 to Anne Cawley, Spinster, since deceased, which she bequeathed to Richard Webb. Charles Mutell and John Childs, by lease and release dated 29 and 30 Oct last past bought the 500 acres from Richard Webb of Rowde, Wilts Co., gent. One moiety of this land belonged to Solomon Gandovett. Made 4 Nov 1707. Wit: Sol Pages, N. Bland, Jo'n. Locke, Thomas Farr, Daniel B. Londeau.

P. 340   Release and Quit Claim. Alexander Gandovett, Mary Gandovett, Francis Gandovett the Younger, Henrietta Gandovett (now Henrietta Denormandie wife of John Abraham Denormandie,) and John Abraham Denormandie, surviving heirs of Francis Gandovett the Elder, for £140, and because they are moving, to Francis Gandovett the Elder, quit claim the one moity of 500 acres. Made 12 Dec 1730. Wit: Peter Carmick, Sarah Carmick, Tho. Watson, Cesar Godfrey, Nathan Watson. Rec: 18th da 8ber 1739.

P. 341   Release. Samuel Carpenter and William Fishbourn, both of the City of Philadelphia, merchants and surviving executors of the estate of Samuel Carpenter, late merchant of said city, deceased, and James Moon of Bristol, Bucks Co., innkeeper, for £12, to John Abraham Denormandie of Bristol, merchant, a 1 acre lot in Bristol bounded by Wood Street and Pond Street. Before his death Samuel Carpenter had agreed to sell the lot to James Moon, for which Moon paid Carpenter £10, but did not actually convey the land. By his Last Will and Testament dated 6 Apr 1714 Samuel Carpenter appointed his wife Hannah executrix and after her death his children Samuel Carpenter, John Carpenter, William Fishbourn and Hannah his wife to be his executors. Samuel's widow Hannah and his son John Carpenter and daughter Hannah, wife of William Fishbourn are now also deceased. James Moon has agreed to sell the land to John Abraham Denormandie. Made 30 Apr 1733. Wit: Swan Warner, C. Brockden, Richard Jones, Jno. Sison. Ackn: 6 Jul 1730. JP: Joseph Kirkbride, esq.

P. 343　　Release. Caleb Offley of Dutch Creek in the County of New Castle on Delaware, yeoman, and his wife Elizabeth, for £60, to John Abraham Denormandie of Bristol, Bucks Co., shopkeeper, 2 lots in Bristol, the first bounded by the land late of Samuel Carpenter, deceased, Market Street, George Clough's lot and Mill Street and the other 2-acre lot in Bristol bounded by the land late of Thomas Bills, Henry Tomlinson's land, John Hall's land, and James Allen's land. George Clough of Bristol sold these 2 lots to Elizabeth, now the wife of Caleb Offley, by deed dated 1 Nov 1714. Made 21 Mar 1718. Wit: George Clough, Jos. Bond, John Hall. Ackn: 29 Apr 1736 before JP Joseph Kirkbride, Jr., by John Hall.

P. 347　　Deed. George Clough of Bristol, boulter, for £60, to Elizabeth Collins of Bristol, widow, 2 lots in Bristol, the first bounded by the land late of Samuel Carpenter, deceased, Market Street, George Clough's lot and Mill Street, and the other lot of 2 acres bounded by the lands of Thomas Bill, Henry Tomlinson, John Hall and James Allen. Elizabeth Collins sold the lots to George Clough by deed recorded in Bucks Co. Book D, Vol 1, pg 512 [the #322 written above the #512.] Made 1 Nov 1714. Wit: Samuel Baker, Will'm. Watson, Thomas Biddle.

P. 348　　Release. Michael Huff of Bristol, yeoman, and his wife Jennet, for £80, to John Abraham Denormandie of Bristol, merchant, a lot in Bristol at the intersection of Mill and Pond Streets and bounded by George Clough's lot and Jacobus Clough Tillico's lot. Samuel Carpenter sold this lot to Thomas Brock by deed dated 26th da 7^{ber} 1705. Thomas Brock in his Last Will and Testament bequeathed the lot to Michael Huff and soon after died, the Will proved and recorded at Philadelphia. Made 7 Nov 1723. Wit: Thos. Waitrell, Jno. Sisom, Wm. Atkinson. Rec'vd. from John Abraham Denormandie £80 27 Jan 1723/4. Wit: Jno. Sisom, Wm. Atkinson. Ackn: 29 Apr 1736 before JP Joseph Kirkbride, Jr. by William Atkinson and John Sisom.

P. 350　　Release. John Hall of Bristol, cooper, and his wife Sarah, for £68, to John Abraham Denormandie of Bristol, merchant, a lot in Bristol by land formerly Samuel Carpenter's on Mill Street and a corner of John Hall's lot and by Mill Creek. Charles Lavally of Bristol, cooper, sold the lot to John Hall by deed dated 10 Dec 1707 and recorded in Book C, Vol 4, pgs 333-334. Made 27 Dec 1720. Wit: Jos. Bond, George Clough, Wm. Atkinson. Rec'vd. from Denormandie £68 5 Jan 1720. Ackn: 29 Apr 1736 before JP Joseph Kirkbride, Jr. by John Hall.

P. 352   Lease. William Jolliffe of Northampton, yeoman, and his wife Mary, for 5 shillings, to Joseph Dyer of the same place, yeoman, a plantation and 2 tracts of land, the first of 102 acres of land in Northampton by Neshaminy Creek and the lands of Joseph Dyer, John Baxter, William Jolliffe and Jeremiah Bartholomew. The other tract of 55 acres is bounded by the land of Joseph Dyer, Cuthbert Hayhurst, John Baxter and William Jolliffe. Made 2 Jul 1736. Wit: Is. Penington, Jo. Jackson, Edward Glover.

P. 353   Release. William and Mary Jolliffe, for £157, to Joseph Dyer [same parties and land as preceding entry.] The first tract of 102 acres is part of a moity of 500 acres which William Ginn of London, England, refiner, and his wife Ann sold to Mary Sheppard of New York City, now the wife of William Jolliffe, by deed dated 27 Sep 1726. The other tract was sold to William Jolliffe by John Mitchell, late of Northampton. Made 3 Jul 1736. Wit: Is. Penington, Jo. Jackson, Edward Glover. Proved to Lawrance Growdon before Jn. Ab. Denormandie by Jo. Jackson 30 May 1743. Rec: 4 Jun 1743.

P. 355   Lease. William Jolliffe of Northampton and his wife Mary, for 5 shillings, to Thomas Evans of the same place, yeoman, 46 acres of land in Northampton bounded by the land of John Baxter, James Logan, Thomas Evans and William Jolliffe. Made 2 Jul 1736. Wit: Is. Penington, Jo. Jackson, Edward Glover.

P. 356   Release. William and Mary Jolliffe, for £62, to Thomas Evans [same parties and land as preceding entry.] Said land part of a moity of 500 acres which William Ginn of London, England and Ann his wife sold to Mary Sheppard, then of New York City, single woman but now wife of William Jolliffe, by deed dated 27 Sep 1726. Made 3 Jul 1736. Wit: Is. Penington, Jo. Jackson, Edward Glover. Ackn: 6 Jul 1736. JP: Jeremiah Langhorne.

P. 359   Mortgage. Archibald Anderson of Philadelphia, brewer, and his wife Mary, to secure a debt of £300 to be paid in one payment on 5 Dec 1742, to Thomas Annis of the same place, mariner, a plantation and 391 acres of land in Bristol by Neshaminy Creek near John Clauson's land and bounded by the lands of Pentecost Teague, John Otter and Samuel Allen. Made 5 Dec 1739. Wit: Jno. Ord, Da. Edwards. Ackn: same day. JP: Joseph Kirkbride. Rec: 1 Jan 1739/40.

P. 361   Commission. John Penn, Thomas Penn, Richard Penn, esqs., Proprietors and Governors in Chief of Pennsylvania and the Counties of Newcastle, Kent and Sussex on Delaware, appoint James Steel of Philadelphia to be Receiver General of all rents, quit rents, issues, fines, forfeitures, debts, sums of money, etc. Made 15 Oct 1734.

P. 362 Mortgage. John Eastburn of Southampton, yeoman, to secure a debt of £110 due on 1 Feb 1740, to John Danby of Philadelphia, distiller, 206 acres of land in Southampton by land formerly Isabel Cutler's but now John Naylor's, other land formerly Peter Swift's, by lands of Thomas Harding and Thomas Eastburn, and by land late of John Naylor's, deceased, now Charles Biles'. Made 6 Feb 1739. Wit: A. Hamilton, Joseph Chatham. Memo: On 12 Oct 1747 full satisfaction of the mortgage acknowledged by Sarah Danby, widow and executrix of John Danby to Lawrance Growdon, Recorder.

P. 364 Deed. John Hall of Bristol, for £100, to Joseph Peace of West Jersey, miller, a lot in Bristol bounded by Pond and Market Streets and by a lot of John Abraham Denormandie's. Made 1 Oct 1739. Wit: Is. Penington, David Murray. Ackn: 25 Mar 1740. JP: Joseph Kirkbride.

P. 366 Mortgage. Anthony Wilson of Middletown, mason, and his wife Ann, to secure a debt of £200 due in a single payment 16 Apr 1741, to George Jones of Philadelphia, innholder, a plantation and 218 acres and 109 perches of land in Middletown bounded by the lands of Joseph Yates, Henry Nelson, E. Longshore, John Watson, John Woolston and Thomas Jenks. Made 16 Apr 1740. Wit: C. Brockden, Saml. Gifford. Ackn: same day. JP: Mathew Hughes. Rec: 24 May 1740. Memo: Mortgage declared satisfied by Decree of the Court of Common Pleas dated 18 Apr 1904 by Harry J. Molloy, Recorder of Deeds, 27 Apr 1904.

P. 368 Release. Samuel Oldale of Bristol, cooper, and his wife Ann, for £160, to Sampson Cary of Bristol, merchant, 200 acres of land in Bristol in the middle of the Pigeon Swamp by land formerly belonging to William Hage and Thomas Bowman. Samuel Smith sold the land to Samuel Oldale by deed recorded in Bucks Co. Book C, Vol 1, pgs 223-224. Made 27 Nov 1733. Wit: Em. Williams, Samuel Cary, Wm. Atkinson. Full payment rec'vd. from Sampson Cary 30th da 9^{ber} 1733.

P. 371 Release. Samson Cary of Bristol, merchant, and his wife Mary, for £200, to Andrew Wright and Daniel Wright, cooper, both of Bristol, 200 acres of land in Bristol in the middle of the Pigeon Swamp by lands formerly belonging to Wm. Hage and Thomas Bowman. Samuel Smith sold the land to Samuel Oldale who by lease and release dated 26 and 27 Nov 1733 sold it to Sampson Cary. Made 8 May 1739. Wit: Em. Williams, Samson Cary, Jr., Wm. Atkinson. Ackn: 9 May 1739. JP: Emmon Williams.

P. 373   Release.   John Hamilton of Amboy, NJ, attorney for Robert Sandilands, late of Aberdeen but now of Great Britain, clerk, for £50, to Jeremiah Langhorne of Bucks Co., gent., 500 acres of land not yet laid out which William Penn conveyed to Robert Sandilands by lease and release dated 15 and 16 Aug 1682 who made John Hamilton his attorney to sell the land by letter of attorney dated 5 Jun 1725 and recorded in Book A, Vol 2, pg 341. Made 21 Jul 1730. Wit: Evan Drummond, John Barclay. Ackn: 22 Dec 1739 before Abraham Chapman by John Kensey who on oath swore he recognized the handwriting of John Hamilton, Evan Drummond and John Barclay. Rec. 7 Jun 1740.

P. 375   Mortgage.   George Whitefield of Savannah, Georgia but now residing in Philadelphia, clerk, in consideration of a debt of £400 owed to William Seward of London, Great Britain, gent., for the payment of £200 due 30 Apr 1742 (and also a Set of Bills on Mr. Benjamin Seward at Mr. John Brays, brazier in Little Britain for £2,000,) 5,000 acres of land. William Allen of Philadelphia, merchant, and Margaret his wife by indenture dated 30 Apr last for £2,200 sold to George Whitefield 5,000 acres of land on the Forks of the Delaware River in Bucks Co. bounded by the lands of William Allen and Jeremiah Langhorne. This indenture was signed by William and Margaret Allen and delivered to John Stephen Benezet of Philadelphia, merchant, who was to deliver it to George Whitefield. Made 6 May 1740. Wit: J. Stephen Benezet, C. Brockden. Ackn: 10 May 1740. JP: Joseph Kirkbride. Rec: 5 Jul 1740.

P. 379   Mortgage.   John Duer of Makefield, yeoman, to James Reed of Philadelphia, gent., for the consideration of debts which John Duer and Joseph Duer stand jointly indebted to James Read for £200 conditioned for the payment of £100 on 25 Mar 1741 and another debt for £200 conditioned for the payment of £100 on 25 Mar 1742, 260 acres of land in Makefield bounded by the land of Charles Read, Neal Grant, Sarah Read and Ruben Pownal. Made 24 Nov 1739. Wit: Caleb Bansted, Jno. Webbe. Ackn: 11 Jun 1740. JP: Thomas Yardley.

P. 380   Mortgage.   John Burk of Bristol, gent., to William Whitaker of the Island of Barbados, merchant, for £931.17s, 900 acres of land in Bristol by the Delaware River bounded by the land of William Atkinson, Thomas Marriott, Thomas Stackhouse, Emmon Williams, John Abraham Denormandie, John White, Benjamin Canby, George Clough, John Large, Henry Tomlinson, Ebenezer Large, John Hall, William Hill, John Sisom, by land late of John Underwood and by the Quaker Burying Ground and Wood,

Market and Mill Streets and by Newtown Road and also 2 islands and the land adjacent at the flood gates on the creek by the mill to the Delaware River and bounded by Normandies land and Neshaminy Road and by Otters Creek near the bridge, 416 acres in all, plus the grist mills, furling mills, saw mills, boulting houses, dye houses etc. on the premises. The mortgage payment of £55.18s to be paid 3 Jan annually through the year 1748 and the principle sum of £931.17s to be paid in 1748. Made 3 Jan 1739. Wit: Timothy Griffith, John Webbe, both of Philadelphia. Attorney for Whitaker: Alexander Graydon. Ackn: 12 Jan 1739. JP: Benjamin Jones.

P. 389   Release. William Fishbourne of Philadelphia, merchant, and his wife Jane, for £2,600, to John Burk, late of the Island of Barbados but now of Bristol, gent., 1,634 acres of land in Bristol by the Delaware River and bounded by the lands of William Atkinson, Thomas Marriott, Thomas Stackhouse, Emmon Williams, John Abraham Denormandie, by land late of John White and Benjamin Canby, George Clough, John Large, Henry Tomlinson, Ebenezer Large, John Hall, William Hill, Joshua Wright, by land late of Henry Mitchell, John Besonet, Francis White, Samuel Brelsford, Joseph Healey, Henry Neilson, John Sisom, by land late of John Underwood and by the Quaker Burying Ground and Newtown Road. Plus 2 islands and the land adjacent at the flood gates on the creek by the mill to the Delaware River and bounded by Normandies land and Neshaminy Road and by Otters Creek near the bridge, 416 acres in all. Made 2 Jan 1739. Wit: Timothy Griffith, Jno. Webbe. Memo: It was agreed William Hope, John Alfreth, Robert Smith and Emmon Williams have a right to several parcels of woodland not exceeding 20 acres. Ackn: 12 Jan 1739. JP: Benjamin Jones.

P. 395   Release. Thomas Banes of Middletown, taylor, for £14, to James Welch of Attlebury, joyner, a lot by the road from Bristol to Newtown and by the land of Christian Vanhorn containing 1 acre and 2½ perches. Said lot is part of 60 acres which John Scarborough of Middletown, deceased, sold to Thomas Banes by deed dated 9th da 1st mo 1698 and recorded in Book B, Vol 1, pg 174. Made 12 Jul 1740. Wit: John Duncan, Alexr. Moore, Daniel Doan, Jr. Ackn: 24 Jul 1740. JP: Jeremiah Langhorne.

P. 398   Release. Henry Vanhorne of Middletown, yeoman, and his wife Susannah, for £114.5s, to John Mitchell of the same place, carpenter, 67½ acres of land in Middletown by Neshaminy Creek. Said land part of 170 acres which Jeremiah Langhorne of Middletown conveyed to Henry Vanhorne by deed dated 3 Aug 1737 and recorded in Book B, Vol 2, pg 206. Made 8 Apr 1740. Wit: John Vaughan, Jer. Langhorne, William Huddleston, Jno. Duncan. Ackn: 8 Apr 1740. JP: Jeremiah Langhorne.

P. 401 Deed. Nicholas Penquite of Northampton, yeoman, for £118, to William Atwood of Philadelphia, merchant, 200 acres. By indenture dated 13th da 1st mo 1688 William Pickering of Neshaminy Creek, yeoman, sold to John Penquite of Bucks Co., husbandman, who was the father of Nicholas Penquite, 200 acres of land by Neshaminy Creek, being 1 moity of a tract of land patented to William Pickering by James Claypoole and Robert Turner, Commissioners, on 1st da 5th mo 1686 and recorded in Bucks Co. Book A, Vol 1, pg 156. By his Last Will and Testament, John Penquite bequeathed the land to his son, Nicholas Penquite, who mortgaged the land to Andrew Hamilton 4 Sep 1734 to secure the payment of £90.15s, which remains unpaid and William Atwood has agreed to undertake the debt. Made 24 Sep 1740. Wit: M. Walton, Mary Walton. Ackn: 24 Sep 1740. JP: Emmon Williams.

P. 403 Mortgage. Nathan Watson of Bristol, yeoman, for £50, to Mary Andrews of Philadelphia, spinster, a lot in Bristol by Mill Creek with the shop, slaughterhouse and stable on the lot. Made 26 Dec 1740. Wit: Owen Joseph Breintnall. Ackn: 2 Mar 1740. Jeremiah Langhorne. Rec: 3 Mar 1740.

P. 405 Mortgage. Thomas Treame of Philadelphia, esq., and his wife Margaret (the only daughter of the Honorable William Penn, esq., deceased, by Hannah his wife, also deceased) to The Honorable Thomas Penn, esq., one of the Proprietors of the Province of Pennsylvania, and Richard Hockley, of Philadelphia, merchant, because they are moving and in consideration of the debt which Thomas Treame and his wife Margaret owe to John Penn, Thomas Penn, and Richard Penn for £2,066 conditioned for the payment of £1,033 on 20 Sep., two tracts of land in Bucks Co. By indenture dated 6 Aug 1735 Isaac Norris, son and heir of Isaac Norris, late of Fairhill in North Philadelphia, merchant, deceased, conveyed to John Penn, Thomas Penn, Richard Penn, sons of William and Hannah Penn; and Thomas Treame and his wife Margaret, a tract of 10,000 acres of land in Bucks Co. which was 1 moity of the Manor of Perkasie, which they partitioned, Thomas Treame and Margaret his wife's share called the Second Lott bounded by Richard Penn's part called No. 1, and by Thomas Penn's part called No. 3 containing 2,500 acres and recorded in Book F, Vol 8, pg 338. By patent dated 30 Jul 1735 and recorded in Philadelphia Patent Book A, Vol 7, pg 221, John Penn, Thomas Penn and Richard Penn conveyed to Thomas Treame 2,780 acres of land on Perkeamming Creek near the Manor and bounded by land of William Briggs in the line dividing Bucks Co. from Philadelphia Co., by land of William Allen and James Logan. Made 22 Sep 1740. Wit: Ann Hockley, Lynford Lardner. Ackn: 22 Sep 1740. JP: Thomas Greene. Rec: 3 Mar 1740/1.

P. 409   Release. Samuel Darke of Falls Township, yeoman, and his wife Martha, for £200, to Thomas Warrell of Bristol, schoolmaster, 3 tracts of land in Makefield. The first of 116 acres of land is bounded by the lands of Richard Hough, Andrew and William Elliott and Thomas Kirle. The other of 232 acres is bounded by the lands of Henry Marjorum, John Snowdon and Richard Hough. Another tract of 400 acres of land in Buckingham is bounded by the lands of Richard Tucker, William Gibson and Nancy Phillips. Made 6 Aug 1715. Wit: Edward Burke, Nicholas Nut, Ann Turner. Ackn: 27 Feb 1739 by Ann Prickett, formerly Ann Turner, before JP Joseph Kirkbride.

P. 411   Deed. John Kinsey, Jonathan Robeson, Joseph Kirkbride, Caleb Coupland and John Wright (Trustees of the General Loan Office) for £500, to Thomas Clarke of Bucks Co., gent., two tracts of land. Samuel Beakes, late of Bucks Co., yeoman, deceased, by indenture dated 15 Apr 1724 for £100 paid by Jeremiah Langhorne, William Fishbourne and Nathaniel Newlin (former Trustees of the General Loan Office) conveyed to them 173 acres of land by the River Delaware bounded by the land of Joshua Boare and by land formerly in the possession of Richard Ridgeway now Samuel Beakes. By another indenture dated 3 Jun 1731 for the consideration of £98 paid by Andrew Hamilton, Charles Read, Jeremiah Langhorne, Richard Hayes and John Wright (then Trustees of the General Loan Office) Samuel Beakes conveyed to them a plantation and 120 acres of land in Falls Township by the River Delaware and bounded by the lands of William Biles and John Ackerman. After executing this last indenture, Samuel Beakes died intestate. Administration of his estate was granted to John Axford and Josiah Appleton, who have not paid these two debts, which are now in default. The two tracts of land were put up for public auction and sold to the highest bidder, Thomas Clarke. Made 4 Apr 1739. Wit: Joanna Kearney, R. Hartshorne. Ackn: 7 May 1740. JP: Benjamin Jones.

P. 414   Mortgage. William Hudleston of Middletown, cordwainer, and his wife Dorothy, to secure a debt of £300 due on 17 Mar 1743/4, to Joseph Richardson of Middletown, merchant, a plantation and two tracts of land in Middletown. One tract of 100 acres is bounded by the lands of James Dilworth, Richard Thatcher and William Hayhurst. The other of 12½ acres is bounded by the lands of Huddleston, Robert Heaton and by lands formerly Thatcher's. Made 17 Mar 1740/1. Wit: Wm. Huddleston, C. Brockden, Benjamin Field, Henry Vanhorne. Memo: ½ acre of this land is excluded as it was formerly sold to James Welch. Ackn: 21 Mar 1740/1. JP: Jeremiah Langhorne. Rec: same day. Memo: 3 Apr 1744 before Lawrance Growdon, Recorder of Deeds, Joseph Richardson acknowledged full satisfaction of the mortgage.

P. 415 Deed. Andreas Vanbuskirk of Bergen, NJ, for £126, to Bernard Young of Perkesy, Bucks Co., husbandman, 300 acres of land near Perkesy bounded by Vanbuskirk's own land and by land formerly William Baldwin's, deceased, and by land of Evan Thomas. Said land part of 1,250 acres which was patented to Andreas Vanbuskirk 15 Oct 1713 and was recorded in Philadelphia Patent Book A, Vol 4, pg 370. Made 12 Nov 1724. Wit: Isaac Vanhorne, Yoost Vanbuskirk. Ackn: 24 Apr 1741. JP: Jeremiah Langhorne.

P. 417 Mortgage. Joseph Thornton of Newtown, innholder, and his wife Margaret, to secure a debt of £70 due on 23 Apr 1746, to Joseph Richardson of Middletown, merchant, a lot in Newtown. Made 23 Apr 1741. Wit: Jno. Frohock, Nich Tompson. Ackn: 24 Apr 1741. JP: Jeremiah Langhorne.

P. 419 Release. John Burrowes and Roger Burrowes, both of Kilwarlin, County Downe, gents., and Robert Barnett of Belfast, County Antrium, merchant, and Elizabeth Barnett alias Burrowes, his wife, for £26.2s.9p, to John Beaumont of Falls Township, Bucks Co., 100 acres of land in Falls bounded by the plantation of Mahlon Kirkbride and by the plantation lately belonging to Thomas Kirkbride, deceased. John Burrowes, late of Falls Township, deceased, owned 100 acres of land in said township and died intestate without issue. Francis Burrowes, late of Kilwarlin, County Downe, Ireland, his eldest brother and heir, has since died, his surviving children being John Burrowes, Roger Burrowes and Elizabeth Barnett alias Burrowes, who now own the land. Made 20 Mar 1738. Wit: Moses Morice, James Hunter, Isaac Haddock, James Wilson, James James, Jacob Mark. Ackn: 11 May 1741 by James Wilson, Mariner, before Clem Plumsted, JP for the County of Philadelphia.

P. 421 Deed. Henry Walmsley of Bucks Co., yeoman, and his wife Mary, for £150, to The Rev. John Philip Streiter, Minister of the Dutch Lutheran Church at Rockhill, Bucks Co., 200 acres of land bounded by the land of William Briggs and Andrew Hamilton. Said land that which by patent dated 25 Feb 1735 and recorded in Philadelphia Patent Book A, Vol 7, pg 456, was granted to Henry Walmsley. Made 31 Dec 1740. Wit: William Ridge, Andres Prompoor, Jacob Carl Wittanam. Ackn: 20 May 1741 by William Ridge of Bensalem before JP Lawrance Growdon.

P. 422 Deed. Andreas Vanbuskirk of Bergin, NJ, yeoman, and his wife Antie, for £44, to William Britain of Hilltown, Bucks Co., husbandman, 100 acres bounded by the lands of John Penn, Bernard Young, Bartholomew Young and Mary Lewis, part of 500 acres which by indentures of lease and release dated 7 and 8 Nov 1681, William Penn conveyed to Thomas Langhorne of Hiltondale, Westmoreland County, yeoman. After Thomas Langhorne's death, the land descended to his only son Jeremiah Langhorne of Bucks Co., who by warrant dated 28 May 1707 had the land surveyed and laid out in Bucks Co., and by deed dated 12 Oct 1713 sold the 500 acres plus other lands which totaled 1,221 acres to Andreas Buskirk. Made 29 Apr 1730. Wit: G. Schutt, John VanBuskirk. Ackn: 17 Dec 1742 before JP Lawrance Growdon.

P. 425   Deed. Thomas Maybury of Newtown, yeoman, for £16.10s, to Joseph Thornton of Newtown, yeoman, a 2-acre lot in Newtown. Thomas Penn, by powers granted to him by John Penn and Richard Penn, patented 24 Jun 1736 to Agnes Yeales of Newtown, widow, 20 acres of land in Newtown, who by deed dated 14 Aug 1736 sold 2 of the 20 acres of land to Thomas Maybury, said 2 acres bounded by the road leading to Bristol by Samuel Carry's lot. Made 24 Aug 1736. Wit: John Frohock, Richard Iliff, Jonas Moon. Ackn: 2 Feb 1737/8. JP: Abraham Chapman.

P. 427   Deed. Jeremiah Langhorne, William Biles, Joseph Kirkbride, Jr., Abraham Chapman, all of Bucks Co., esqrs., for 5 shillings, to Joseph Thornton of Newtown, innkeeper, part of 5 acres of County land. Rent of 9 shillings to be paid on 25 Mar yearly. An Act of the General Assembly allowed Jeremiah Langhorne, William Biles, Joseph Kirkbride, Jr., Thomas Watson, practitioner in physick, and Abraham Chapman to purchase land to build a new courthouse and prison in Bucks Co. They purchased 5 acres of land in Newtown from John Waley of Newtown, yeoman, bounded by James Yates' land and by Newtown Street, and divided the land into 6 equal parts of which the courthouse and prison will be built on one part and the other parts to be rented out. Made 16 Mar 1733. Wit: Mathew Rue, Jno. Frohock. Ackn: 13 Jun 1741. JP: Lawrance Growdon.

P. 429   Deed. William Baldwin of Appecon Settlement, Orange Co., VA, for £101, to William Ashbourn of Newtown, Bucks Co., weaver, 2 lots in Newtown, the first of 20¾ acres and 24 perches of land bounded by land formerly Ezra Croasdale's, and by lands late of Israel Morris and Thomas Hilbourn. The other is 10 acres and bounded by the first and by William Croasdale's land. Said land was conveyed by Thomas Maybury to William Baldwin by deed dated 16 Aug 1736. Made 25 May 1741. Wit: John Scott, Joseph Smith, Abra Chapman, James Yates, Chas. Bryan. Ackn: 5 May 1741. JP: Abraham Chapman.

P. 431 Deed. Joseph Burgess of Makefield, yeoman, Daniel Burgess of Falls Township, yeoman, and Dorothy his wife, for £50, to John Burgess of Falls Township, yeoman, 13 acres of land in Falls by the road leading from the Falls to Philadelphia where the meeting house and graveyard is and by John Burgess' land and by the land of Anthony Burton. John Rowland and Thomas Rowland by deed recorded in Bucks Co. 10th da 12th mo 1685 sold the land to Samuel Burgess of Falls Township, yeoman, deceased, and by his Last Will and Testament dated 14 Oct 1713 left the land to his son Daniel Burgess. Made 5 Jul 1740. Wit: Nehemiah Blackshaw, Sarah Hutchinson, Wm. Atkinson. Ackn: 17 Aug 1740. JP: Joseph Kirkbride.

P. 434 Mortgage. Joseph Thornton of Newtown, innholder, and his wife Margaret, to secure a debt of £30 due 23 Apr 1746, to Joseph Richardson of Middletown, merchant, a 2-acre lot in Newtown by Samuel Cary's lot and by the road to Bristol. Made 23 Apr 1741. Wit: Jno. Frohock, Nick Thompson. Ackn: next day. JP: Jeremiah Langhorne.

P. 435 Mortgage. William Ramsey of Warwick, Bucks Co., yeoman, to secure a debt of £425.15s to be paid by 3 Jul 1742, to Richard Ashfield of New York City, gent., 2 full third parts of 638 acres and 44 perches of land in Warwick bounded by Henry Baily's land, by land late of James Claypoole, deceased, and by land late of George Willard. Said land that which William Penn's Commissioners patented 31 Jan 1703 and recorded in Philadelphia Patent Book A, Vol 2, pg 649 to Isaac Norris and David Lloyd, executors of the estate of Thomas Lloyd, deceased, who sold the two third parts to Richard Ashfield who lately conveyed it to William Ramsey. Made 3 Jul 1741. Wit: C. Brockden, J. Reily, J. Ord. Ackn: 3 Jul 1741. JP: Thomas Griffitts. Memo: 8 Oct 1748 before Lawrance Growdon, Recorder of Deeds, a power of attorney made by Robert Huntor Morris, esq., administrator for Richard Ashfield, discharges mortgage but a bond remains in force for recovery of the money.

P. 437 Deed. William Allen of Philadelphia, esq., and Margaret his wife, for £200, to Jeremiah Best of Bucks Co., yeoman, 213 acres of land on the west branch of the Delaware River. Said land part of 10,000 acres which was surveyed and laid out to William Penn, grandson of William Penn, deceased, by warrant dated 16 Nov 1727, and by indenture dated 29 Aug 1728 and recorded at Philadelphia in Book F, Vol 5, pg 92. William Penn sold the land to William Allen. Made 1 Jul 1741. Wit: Nathaniel Allen, James Bingham. Ackn: 1 Jul 1741. JP: Thomas Lawrance for the City of Philadelphia. Rec: 4 Oct 1741.

P. 439   Deed. Lawrance Growdon of Trevose in Bensalem, and his wife Sarah, for £320.17s, to John Townsend of Bybury, Philadelphia Co., yeoman, 102½ acres of land in Bensalem bounded by the land of Samuel Scott, Thomas Townsend, Thomas Tomlinson and by Lawrance Growdon's other land. Said land part of 2,957 acres which was patented 31 Oct 1737 to Lawrance Growdon and recorded in Philadelphia Book A, Vol 1, pg 81....
....by him the said Lawrance Growdon or by Lawrance Growdon his grandfather. Made 22 Jun 1741. Wit: Benjamin Scott, Jeremiah Woolston. Ackn: 14 Sep 1741. JP: Jeremiah Langhorne.

P. 441   Deed. Mathias Keen of Bristol, carpenter, for £50, to John Kirl of Bristol, yeoman, a lot in Bristol bounded by Samuel Cary's lot on Mill Street and by Anthony Burton's lot and by Thomas Stackhouse's garden. Thomas Jenney, son and heir of Jacob Jenney, late of Bristol, deceased, by indentures of lease and release dated 21 and 22 Jun 1732, sold the lot to Mathias Keen. Made 29 Apr 1741. Wit: William Atkinson, Margaret Atkinson, Joseph Atkinson. Ackn: 24 Jun 1741. JP: Emon Williams.

P. 443   Power of Attorney. James Read of Philadelphia, gent., for £60, to William Allen of Philadelphia, merchant, the mortgage held on 261 acres of land in Makefield which John Duer and Joseph Duer, both of Bucks Co., yeomen, became bound to James Read for several sums of money, particularly one debt of 22 Nov 1739 for £200 conditioned for the payment of £100 on 5 Mar 1742. John Duer, by indenture dated 24 Nov 1739 conveyed to James Read 261 acres of land in Makefield bounded by the lands of Charles Read, Neal Grant, Sarah Read and Reuben Pownall. James Read appoints William Allen his attorney to receive the money owed him. Made 15 Oct 1741. Wit: Jno. Ord, G. Reily. Ackn: 15 Oct 1741. JP: Joseph Kirkbride.

P. 444   Mortgage. The Rev. John Philip Streiter, Minister of the Dutch Lutheran Church at Rockhill, and Juliana, his wife, for £75, to William Allen of Philadelphia, esq., 200 acres of land bounded by the lands of William Briggs and late of Andrew Hamilton. Said land was patented 25 Feb 1735 and recorded in Philadelphia Patent Book A, Vol 7, pg 456 to Henry Walmsly of Bucks Co., yeoman, and his wife Mary, who conveyed the land to John Philip Streiter by indentures of lease and release dated 30 and 31 Dec 1741. Payment to be made 10 Feb next. Made 10 Feb 1741. Wit: Wm. Peters, James Bingham. Signed Johann Philip Streiter. Ackn: 26 Mar 1742. JP: Lawrance Growdon. Memo: 20 Dec 1748 William Allen acknowledged full satisfaction of the mortgage.

P. 446   Power of Attorney. Joseph Cary, taylor, Richard Williams and Jane his wife of the out parish of Saint Philip & Jacob, Gloucester Co., and Richard James of the parish of Saint George, Middlesex Co., taylor, and Abigail his wife, because we are moving, appoint Sampson Cary of Bristol, weaver, our attorney, to demand and receive from Samuel Cary of Bristol, merchant, all money due us for any legacy left to us by the Last Will and Testament of Samson Cary, late of Bristol, merchant, deceased. Made 18 Apr 1740. Wit: Thomas Richardson, John Evans, Wm. Tecck [sic]. Sworn to 4 Dec 1740 before Samuel Hasell, Mayor of Philadelphia by John Evans of Philadelphia, mariner. Sworn to 21 Dec 1741 before. JP Mathew Rue by William Tresck [Treeck?] of Bucks Co., weaver.

P. 447   Receipt. Samson Cary received from Samuel Cary 21 Apr 1742 by power of attorney £151.16s, the balance of 3 legacies left by Samson Cary to Joseph Cary, Richard Williams and Jane Williams late Jane Cary, Richard James and Abigail James late Abigail Cary. Each to receive £50.12s. Wit: Jno. Frohock. Wm. Snowdon. Thomas Hilbourn.

P. 447   Deed. Thomas Maybury of Newtown, blacksmith, for £100 paid by John Scott of Makefield for William Baldwin, nephew of John Scott and son of John Baldwin of Makefield, conveys to William Baldwin two tracts of land in Newtown, the first by land formerly Ezra Croasdales and by lands late of Israel Morris and Thomas Hillbourn containing 20¾ acres and 24 perches, and the other by the land late of Thomas Hillbourn and by William Croasdale's land and is 10 acres. Made 16 Aug 1736. Wit: John Chapman, John Chapman, Jr., Ralph Lee. Ackn. same day before JP Abraham Chapman.

P. 450   Mortgage. Thomas Yardley of Makefield, yeoman, and Ann his wife, to secure a debt of £400 due on 15 Apr 1743, to John Shallcross of Oxford, Philadelphia Co., yeoman, 600 acres of land in Newtown by John Wally's land and by land late of John Hough's except 37½ acres of this 600 acres, that which Francis Hague granted to William Ashburnett. Made 15 Apr 1742. Wit: Evan B. Evan, Benj'a. Taylor. Ackn: 3 May 1742. JP: Joseph Kirkbride. Memo: On 7 Oct 1784 Leonard Shallcross, executor of the estate of John Shallcross, acknowledged before John Hart, D. Recorder, that he had received from Thomas Yardley and Samuel Yardley, assignees of Thomas Yardley, full satisfaction of the mortgage.

P. 451   Mortgage. Timothy Roberts of Middletown, cooper, for £200, to Robert Edwards of Falls Township, yeoman, 3 full equal and undivided fourth parts of 2 water grist mills in Middletown and 4 tracts of land. The first parcel of 50 acres is bounded by Neshaminy Creek, by land late of John

Vansant and by land of Joseph Growdon. The second parcel of 2½ acres and 11 perches also lies by Neshaminy Creek. The third parcel of 5 acres and 34 perches, also by Neshaminy Creek, is bounded by the land of John Praul and John Plumley. The last lot is 3¾ acres and 12 perches by Neshaminy Creek and bounded by land of John Plumley. Made 1 Jan 1741/2. Wit: Wm. Atkinson, Joseph Atkinson. Ackn: 25 Mar 1741. JP: Mathew Rue. Memo: Robert Edwards appeared before Lawrance Growdon, Recorder of Deeds, and acknowledged full satisfaction of the mortgage on 3 Jan 1742.

P. 453   Mortgage. Isaac Vanhorn of Northampton, yeoman, for £66.12s, to William Allen of Philadelphia, esq., a plantation and 276 acres of land in Northampton by the lands of Johannes Blaker, Anthony Tomkin, late of Edward Penington and Bernard Vanhorn. Payments to be made 26 Mar annually, final payment in 1747. Made 26 Mar 1742. Wit: Wm. Atkinson, Jno. Frohock. Ackn: 28 Aug 1742. JP: Benjamin Jones.

P. 455   Deed. Jeremiah Langhorne of Middletown, esq., for £101, to Michael Dowd of Newtown, weaver, 61 acres of land in Newtown by the road by Newtown Common and by land of William Buckman. Said land part of 250 acres which Joseph Jackson, Sheriff of Bucks Co., by deed dated 12 Mar 1740 sold to Jeremiah Langhorne. Made 8 Dec 1741. Wit: Sarah Biles, John Duncan. Ackn: 16 Jan 1741. JP: Lawrance Growdon.

P. 456   Recorder's Office, Doylestown, PA, January 24, 1902:
"I hereby certify that the foregoing records, which have been recopied and transcribed into this book from the original Deed Book B, Vol 2, which is dilapidated and worn, are true and correct copies of instruments of writing therein recorded. In testimony whereof, I have hereunto set my hand and seal of office, the day and year aforesaid." Burroughs Michener, Recorder of Deeds.

1742-1749
Deed Book A, Vol. 3

P. 1   Deed. Timothy Roberts of Middletown, cooper, for £100, grants to Joseph Kinderdine of Horsham, Philadelphia Co., millwright, 1 full and equal fourth part of 2 water grist mills with bolting mills and 4 tracts of land in Middletown. All four tracts are bounded by Neshaminy Creek and the first tract of 50 acres lies at a corner of land late of George Vansant and by Joseph Growdon's land. The second tract contains 2½ acres and 11 perches. The third tract of 5 acres and 30 perches lies by the lands of John Praul and John Plumley. The fourth tract also lies by John Plumley's land and contains 3¾ acres and 12 perches. Made 4 Jan 1742. Wit: Thos. Whitton, William Atkinson, Margaret Hamson. Ackn: 27 Jan 1742 before Justice of the Peace John Abraham Denormandie. Rec: 25 Feb 1742.

P. 2   Mortgage.   Peter Taylor of Bristol, carpenter, and Rebecca, his wife, to secure a debt of £20 due on 29 Dec 1743, to Jonathan Livezey of Lower Dublin, Philadelphia Co., yeoman, a plantation and 115 acres in Bristol by a corner of Joseph Shaw's land, by land late of William Croasdale's and by James Boyles' land. Made 29 Dec 1742. Wit: Joseph Jackson, Tho. Hutchinson. Ackn: 30 Dec 1742. JP: Lawrence Growdon, Esq. Rec: 25 Feb 1742.

P. 3   Deed. William Penn's Commissioners William Markham, Robert Turner, John Goodson and Samuel Carpenter to John White 250 acres in Bucks Co. by Neshaminy Creek and bounded by the land of William Carter and John White. Said land granted by warrant dated 15th da 6th mo 1682 and laid out 22nd da 6th mo 1682 to Richard and William Amos by a former patent dated 20th da 4th mo 1689 [sic.] John White's petition claims the 250 acres were signed over to his father George White, deceased, by William Amos, land which John White laid out and paid on behalf of Richard Amos in the time of his sickness and for his burial. He was to be granted a new patent in his own name for the 250 acres. Petitioned 16th da 10th mo 1689. Made 10th da 12th mo (Feb) 1690/91. Rec. 5 Mar 1742.

P. 4   Patent.   William Penn's Commissioners William Markham, Thomas Ellis and John Goodson to John White 500 acres in Bucks Co. by Neshaminy Creek and bounded by the lands of Richard and William Amos and George White, not including 1 equal half of a meadow granted to John Clawson by warrant from William Markham dated 15th da 6th mo 1682 and laid out 22nd da 6th mo 1682 to John White in right of his father George White. John White requested the land be confirmed by patent. Made at Philadelphia 12th da 4th mo 1689. Rec. 1 Mar 1742.

P. 5   Release.   John Rowland of Bristol, merchant and executor of the estate of John White, deceased, late of the same place, and husband of Elizabeth, daughter of the said John White, also deceased, for £5 paid by George White of New Bristol, eldest son of John White, and other considerations especially that we are moving, quit claim to George White all of my part of the estate of John White. Made 4 Jun 1715. Wit: Henry Tomlinson, Unity Bushill, Mary Tomlinson. Ackn: 10 Nov 1741 before Emon Williams, JP. Rec: 1 Mar 1742.

P. 5   Deed.   Samuel Bushill of Burlington, NJ, attorney for Unity White, late of Bristol, Bucks Co., deceased widow, and executor of the Last Will and Testament of Unity White, for £150, to Anthony Wright of Middletown, yeoman, a plantation and 200 acres of land in Middletown by land formerly William Carter's and by land of Peter White. Said land part of 2 tracts which William Penn's Commissioners patented 12th da 4th mo 1689 and 10th da 12th mo 1690/91 to John White, late of Bristol, and Joan his wife, who by their deed dated 29th da 4th mo 1698 granted the land to John White of Middletown, yeoman, who by deed dated 10th da 4th mo 1701 granted the 200 acres to Benjamin White of Kent Co., PA, yeoman, who by deed dated 20 May 1703 granted the land to the aforesaid John White who made his Last Will and Testament dated 16 Dec 1703 leaving all his estate to his son George and his daughter Elizabeth, making John Rowland and John Baldwin, both of Bucks Co., yeomen, executors, to dispose of his lands in Pennsylvania and west New Jersey, and died soon after making the will. Elizabeth White then died, leaving no lawful issue, and her part of her father's estate descended to her brother George White. John Rowland by release dated 4 Jun 1715 quit claimed his interest to George White. George White by his Last Will and Testament dated 19 Dec 1716 bequeathed to his well beloved wife Unity White his house and lots of land in Bristol and his lot in Middletown adjoining the land of Joseph Headley. Unity White, before her death, made her Will dated 18 Jul 1731, leaving the bulk of her estate to Samuel Bushill. Made 23 Oct 1741. Wit: John Frohock, Nathan Watson. Ackn: 29 Oct 1741. JP: Mathew Rue. Rec: Mar 1742.

P. 8   Lease.   Margery Hough of Makefield, widow, John Bainbridge of Maidenhead, Burlington Co., NJ, yeoman, and Sarah his wife, Neel Grant of Makefield, yeoman, and Elizabeth his wife, Hannah Lambert and Sarah Lambert, daughters of John Lambert, late of NJ, deceased, for 5 shillings, to

John Chapman of Wrightstown, Bucks Co., yeoman, 400 acres, part of a 500 acre grant from William Penn dated 23 and 24 Apr 1683 to John Clowes, late of Bucks Co., deceased, and bequeathed from him to his daughters Margary Hough, Sarah Bainbridge and Rebeckah Clowes, who is the mother of the said Lambert's daughters Elizabeth Grant, Hannah Lambert and Sarah Lambert. Made 24 Jul 1713. Wit: Johannes Lawrance, Elizabeth Bainbridge, John Hough, James Arnett, Thomas Ashton, Nicholas Noot, Joseph Chapman.

P. 9   Release. Margery Hough of Makefield, widow, John Bainbridge of Maidenhead, Burlington Co., NJ, yeoman, and Sarah Bainbridge, his wife, Neel Grant of Makefield, yeoman and Elizabeth Grant, his wife and one of the daughters of Rebecca Clowes, who died, Hannah Lambert and Sarah Lambert, daughters of John and Rebecca (Clowes) Lambert, late of NJ, deceased and sisters of said Elizabeth Grant, for £26, to John Chapman of Wrightstown, Bucks Co., yeoman, 400 acres of land to be allotted in Bucks Co. and a warrant from the Surveyor General's office dated 22 Oct 1712 pursuant to another warrant dated 10 Sep 1712. Said land part of 500 acres which William Penn by indentures of lease and release dated 23 and 24 Apr 1683 granted to John Clowes then of Chester Co., yeoman. By his Last Will and Testament dated 29th da 11th mo 1686, John Clowes bequeathed the land to his 3 daughters Margary Hough, Sarah Bainbridge and Rebecca Clowes. Made 25 Jul 1713. Wit: Johannes Lawrance, Elizabeth Bainbridge, John Hough, James Arnett, Thomas Ashton, Nicholas Noot, Joseph Chapman. Ackn: 10 Nov 1739 before JP Abraham Chapman by Neel Grant and Elizabeth his wife and Joseph Chapman.

P. 11   Lease. Henry Nelson of Middletown, yeoman and Alice his wife, for 5 shillings, to Thomas Dowdney of Bristol, yeoman, 53 acres and 139 perches of land in Bristol by the River Delaware bounded by Thomas Dowdney's other land. Made 25 Jun 1741. Wit: Daniel Palmer, Joseph Simcock, Wm. Atkinson.

P. 12   Release. Henry Nelson of Middletown, yeoman and Alice his wife, for £79.10s, to Thomas Dowdney of Bristol, yeoman, 53 acres and 139 perches of land in Bristol by the River Delaware bounded by Thomas Dowdney's other land. Joseph Bond of Bristol by indentures of lease and release dated 12 and 13 May 1721 granted the said land with other land to Henry Nelson. Made 26 Jun 1741. Wit: Daniel Palmer, Joseph Simcock, Wm. Atkinson. Dowdney paid in full 3 Jul 1741. Ackn: 17 Jun 1742 before JP Emmon Williams by Henry and Alice Nelson. Rec: 5 Mar 1742.

P. 14   Mortgage. Thomas Banks of Lower Milford, Bucks Co., yeoman, for £40, to Richard Peters of Philadelphia, gent., 102 acres of land in the Great Swamp bounded by the lands of James Course, Thomas Perry, Henry Taylor, Samuel Mickle [Nickle?] Said land part of 2,000 acres granted to Joseph Growdon, esq., the Elder, by warrant dated 20 Mar 1715 and granted to Thomas Banks by patent dated 6 Oct and recorded in Philadelphia Patent Book A, Vol. ?, pg 494. Made 24 Nov 1742. Wit: Wm. Peters, John Callahan. Ackn: 17 Dec 1742 before Lawrance Growdon, esq., JP, by William Peters. Rec: 8 Mar 1742.

P. 15   Deed. Lawrance Growdon of Bensalem, gent., and Sarah his wife, for £302, to Henry Poynter of the same township, yeoman, 151 acres and 20 perches of land bounded by the Southampton Township line and by the lands of Edmund Dunkan, William Dunkan, William Rodgers, and by Lawrence Growdon's other land. This land part of that which John Penn, Thomas Penn and Richard Penn patented to Lawrence Growdon 31 Oct 1737 and recorded at Philadelphia in Book A, Vol. 1, pg 87. Free of all claims, etc., by him the said Lawrence Growdon or by Lawrence Growdon his grandfather. Made 1 Nov 1742. Wit: John Conley, Thomas Tomlinson. Ackn: 21 Feb 1742 before Benjamin Jones, esq., JP. Rec: 8 Mar 1742/43.

P. 17   Mortgage. Henry Poynter of Bensalem, yeoman, and Mary his wife, for £135.18s.2p, to Lawrence Growdon of Trevose in Bensalem, gent., 151 acres and 20 perches [see previous entry for P. 15.] Made 2 Nov 1742. Wit: John Conley, Thomas Tomlinson. Ackn: 15 Nov 1742 before Mathew Rue, JP. Rec: 8 Mar 1742.

P. 18   Release. William Fishbourn of Philadelphia, merchant, and Jane his wife; Joseph Peace of Trenton, Hunterdon Co., NJ, miller, and Mary his wife, for £17, to Ennion Williams of Bristol, Bucks Co., cooper, 4 acres and 43 perches of land in Bristol bounded by the land of Anthony Burton, by the church yard and the Quaker burying ground, by Thomas Marriot's line, and by the land of Ennion Williams which formerly belonged to Robert Smith.
    Hannah Carpenter, Samuel Carpenter and the said William Fishbourn and Hannah his wife by indentures of lease and release dated 29 and 30 Jun 1720 conveyed this land to Joseph Bond of Bristol. By indentures of lease and release Joseph Bond and his wife Ann conveyed a one-third share of the mill houses and messages to William Fishbourn 1 and 2 Jul 1720 and a one-fourth part to John Wilson of Philadelphia, merchant, on the same day, and to William Fishbourn a sixth part on 9 and 10 Apr 1722 and an eighth part on 25 and 26 Mar 1729 and to Joseph Peace an eighth part 20 and 21 Aug 1729.

By writ Thomas Biles, Sheriff, was directed to sell the said John Wilson's fourth part of the premises to satisfy a debt and it was conveyed to Joseph Peace. By virtue of these transactions William Fishbourn and Joseph Peace became seized of all the premises. Made 22 May 1734. Wit: Thomas Barnes, Jr., Simon Bakin. Ackn: 27 Jul 1734 before Edward Roberts, JP for the County of Philadelphia by William and Jane Fishbourn. Ackn: 4 Oct 1736 before William Morris, JP of the County of Hunterdon in NJ, by Joseph and Mary Peace. Rec. 10 Mar 1742/43.

P. 21   Release. William Hope of Bensalem, carpenter, and Rebecca his wife, for £140, to Ennion Williams of Bristol, cooper, a lot in Bristol by the River Delaware and by William Fishbourn's Company land. William Fishbourn of Philadelphia, merchant and Hannah his wife and Joseph Peace of Trenton, Hunterdon Co., NJ, miller, and Mary his wife, and John Wilson, also of Philadelphia, merchant, conveyed the land to Robert Smith of Bristol by lease and release dated 17 and 18 Jun 1724. Robert Smith and Mary his wife sold it to William Hope by lease and release dated 12 and 13 May 1728. Made 24 Jul 1733. Wit: Thomas Marriot, Joseph Jackson, Wm. Atkinson, John Cross. Ackn: 12 Aug 1734. JP: Thomas Yeardley. Rec: 11 Mar. 1742/3.

P. 23   Release. Benjamin Canby of Solebury, yeoman, and Sarah his wife, for £60, to Ennion Williams of Bristol, yeoman, 17¼ acres land in Bristol by land formerly William Fishbourn & Company's and by land lately belonging to George Clough, deceased. Said land Joseph Shaw and Mary his wife conveyed by indentures of lease and release to Benjamin Canby on 23 and 24 Jun 1732. Made 2 Jun 1742. Wit: Isaiah Quimby, Sarah Ritcher. Ackn: 15 Jul 1742 before John Wells, JP. Rec: 11 Mar 1742/3.

P. 24   Deed. Thomas Dungan of Northampton, yeoman, for 5 shillings and natural love and affection and because I am moving, to Jacob Dungan and Jonathan Dungan (my grandsons, two of the sons of my son Jonathan Dungan, deceased, and when the said Jonathan Dungan the younger of them shall attain his full age of 21 years) my plantation and 120 acres in Warwick Township beginning in the middle of the SW branch of Neshaminy Creek and by Samuel Dungan's land, by John Cart's line, by David Lantry's line, by Samuel Fairies. Said land part of 400 acres conveyed to Thomas Dungan by indentures of lease and release dated 31 May and 1 Jun 1734 by Nicholas Hellings and Elizabeth his wife. Made 30 Oct 1741. Wit: Bartholomew Longstrett, John Dungan, John Huings, John Hart. Ackn: 8 Jan 1741/2 before Benjamin Jones, JP. Rec: 26 Mar 1743.

P. 25   Mortgage. William Fry of Middletown, gent., to secure a debt of £41.2s.9p due on 3 Jun 1743, to Lawrence Growdon of Trevose, 200 acres of land on the Delaware River. Said land Thomas Penn patented 26 Jan 1740 and recorded at Philadelphia in Patent Book A, Vol 9, pg 260 to William Fry. Made 3 Jan 1742/3. Wit: Joseph Poole, John Duncan. Ackn: 19 Mar 1742/3 before JP Benjamin Jones. Rec: 19 May 1743.

P. 26   Mortgage. John Stackhouse, Jr. of Middletown, yeoman, to secure a debt of £110 due on 22 Apr 1747, to William Allen of Philadelphia, 100 acres of land in Middletown by the lands of John Stackhouse, Thomas Stackhouse, Adam Marker and Henry Vanhorne. Said land part of 200 acres which Nicholas Waln conveyed by deed dated 10th da 1st mo 1695 and recorded in Book B, Vol 1, pg 55 to John Stackhouse, father of said John Stackhouse, Jr. Made 22 Apr 1743. Wit: John Duncan, James Bingham. Ackn: 26 Apr 1743. JP: Mathew Rue. Rec: 4 Jun 1743. Note: mortgage acknowledged satisfied by William Allen on 28 Jul 1748 before Lawrence Growdon, Rec.

P. 27   Mortgage. Alexander Tippenderver of Bucks Co., for securing payment of £20 due to John Penn, Thomas Penn and Richard Penn, to Richard Peters and Lynford Lardnor, both of Philadelphia, gents., convey a plantation and 150 acres in Bucks Co. by the lands of George Welver, George Shoemaker and Jacob Buttons. A series of annual payments to be made; final payment 1747. Attorney William Peters of Philadelphia. Made 18 Feb 1742. Wit: Wm. Peters, John Callahan. Ackn: 21 Jun 1743 before JP Lawrence Growdon by John Callahan of Philadelphia. Rec: 8 Jul 1743.

P. 29   Deed.   John Abraham Denormandie, merchant, and John Anthony Denormandie, mariner, both of Bristol, for £230, to Ann Amos of Bensalem, widow. On 12 Jun 1684 William Penn granted to John Gilbert of Bucks Co. 100 acres of land on Poquessin Creek. John Gilbert sold the land (but did not actually convey it) to Nicholas Vandergrift. By indenture dated 15 Oct 1709 Nicholas Vandergrift sold the land to Robert Caille of London, merchant. By deed dated 4 May 1710, Robert Caille conveyed the land to John Abraham Denormandie and John Anthony Denormandie. Said land bounded by the lands late of Walter Harris and Joseph Growdon. 26 Apr 1742. Wit: Jn. Frohock, Elizabeth Elfreth. Ackn: 16 Jun 1743. JP: Enion Williams. Rec: 18 Jul 1743.

P. 31   Release. Thomas Cary of Wootton Underidge, Gloucester Co., to Samuel Cary. Sampson Cary, late of Bristol, by his Last Will and Testament bequeathed to Thomas Cary £50 and made Samuel Cary of Newtown his executor. Sampson Cary in his lifetime paid to Thomas Cary £27, part of his legacy. John White, late of Philadelphia but now of London, merchant, on behalf of Samuel Cary, paid Thomas Cary £23, the remainder of his legacy. Thomas Cary herewith acknowledges having received these sums of money as his legacy and releases Samuel Cary from further obligation to him. Made 4 Oct 1742. Wit: Samuel Martyn, Edward Faulkener. Edward Faulkener, clerk for Samuel Martyn of Birchim Lane, London, Notary Publick, makes an oath he did see Thomas Cary, who was at that time in London, sign and seal the document before George Heathcote, Lord Mayor of London. Rec. 22 Jul 1743.

P. 32   Receipt.   William Baily, Hannah Baily, Mary Cary, William Cary, Samson Cary, each received 25 and 28 Sep 1742 and 4 Oct 1742 from Samuel Cary of Bucks Co., executor of the estate of Sampson Cary, deceased, £23 paid by John White of Croydon, Surry Co., full legacy left them by their deceased Uncle Sampson Cary, and they release Samuel Cary from further obligation. Wit: Thomas Cary, Sampson Cary, Edward Faulkener.
Thomas Cary of Wooton Underidge, Gloucester Co., cordwainer, at present in London ackn. he saw William Cary, Samson Cary, William Baily and Hannah his wife, and Mary Cary, all of Wooton Underidge sign their names to the receipt and that he (Thomas Cary) with his brother Samson Cary subscribed their names as witnesses. Made 4 Oct 1742 before George Heathcote, Lord Mayor of London. Rec: 22 Jul 1743.

P. 34   Mortgage. John Hall of Bristol, cooper, and Hannah his wife, to secure a debt of £100 due on 5 Sep 1743, to George Jones of Philadelphia, gent., 3 tracts of land in Bristol. The first of 27¼ acres bounded by land of Joseph Bonds, Jeffry Pollard, and Samuel Carpenter (deceased.) The second of 11¼ acres bounded by Underwood's land, Watson's land, Daniel Jackson's land, Fishbourn's land, and the mill. The last of 2¼ acres is bounded by the lands of James Allen, Harry Tomlinson and Thomas Bitts. Also a lot in Bristol by the garden late of Thomas Brooks and Market Street, it being part of a lot which Samuel Carpenter granted to Thomas Brooks. Made 25 Sep 1742. Wit: John Frohock, Mary Atkinson.

P. 36   Mortgage. Ambrose Barcroft of Solebury, yeoman, and Hannah his wife, to Clement Plumstead of Philadelphia, merchant, for £118, a share of a 450 acre tract of land bounded by the lands of Jedediah Allen and Randal Black. Ambrose Barcroft, late father of the said Ambrose Barcroft, died some years ago intestate leaving Elizabeth his widow (still living) and William his eldest son, Ambrose, and John his youngest son still a minor, 450 acres of land. William Barcroft by deed 5 May 1727 quit claimed his share to his brother the said Ambrose Barcroft, entitling said Ambrose to 3 parts of the land. Made 1 Apr 1743. Wit: Nicholas Penquite, Wm. Peters, Mathew Hughs, Henry Hudleston. Rec: 1 Sep 1743. (Mortgage released by Court of Common Pleas. See Misc. Book No. 72, pg 181. Rec. 17 Mar. 1937.)

P. 37   Power of Attorney. Amos Janney of Fairfax County, VA, yeoman, because I am moving, make my loving brother Thomas Janney of Falls Township, Bucks Co., PA, carpenter, my attorney to sell my property and lands. Mahlon Stacy, late of Burlington Co., NJ, gent., died intestate, and owned an iron works, furnace and land located in NJ which descended to Amos Janney, the eldest son of Elizabeth Janney, deceased, who was one of the sisters and heirs of Mahlon Stacey, Mary Pownal, another sister and heir, Mahlon Kirkbride, the only son of Sarah Kirkbride (also deceased, a sister and heir of Mahlon Stacey,) Rebeckah, late wife of [illegible] and another sister of Mahlon Stacey, Ruth Atkinson, sister and heir. Made 5 Apr 1743. Wit: Langhorne Biles, Elias Hughs, William Biles. JP: Joseph Kirkbride. Rec: 26 Sep 1743.

P. 38   Mortgage. Thomas Rawlings of Richland Township, Bucks Co., yeoman, for £55, to William Allen of Philadelphia, merchant, 102 acres of land in Richland bounded by the land of Walter McCool. Made 1 Aug 1743. Wit: Abraham Griffith, Joseph Breintnall. Ackn: 2 Aug 1743 before Abram Denormandie, JP. Rec: 26 Sep 1743.

P. 39   Mortgage. Peter Lerew of Marshfield, Bucks Co., yeoman, for £170, to Richard Hockley of Philadelphia, merchant, 216 acres and 150 perches of land bounded by the land of James Turniclofts, Baker's line, Peter Lerew's other land, Abel Janney's corner and Thomas Yardley's land. Said land was conveyed to Peter Lerew by Thomas Bishop Vickeris of Chew Magna, Somerset Co., England and his attorney Richard Hockley. Made 14 Sep 1743. Wit: Richard Hough, Wm. Peters. Full satisfaction of mortgage ackn. 23 May 1749 by Langhorne Biles, attorney for Richard Hockley before Lawrance Growdon.

P. 40   Deed. Joseph Growdon of Trevose, for £100, to Henry Mitchel of Bristol, carpenter, 125 acres of land in Bristol by land late of John Towns. Said land part of 135 acres purchased from John Jones of Philadelphia, merchant, who sold it to Joseph Growdon by deed recorded in Bucks Co. Book C, Vol [8?] pgs 81-82. Made 25 Dec 1714. Wit: Richard Scott, Jer. Langhorne. Ackn: 10 Aug 1743 by Richard Scott before JP Thomas Edwards. Rec: 29 Sep 1743.

P. 41   Deed. Hannah Carpenter, widow and sole executrix of the estate of Samuel Carpenter, late of Philadelphia, merchant, deceased, for £105, to Henry Mitchel of Bristol, Bucks Co., 106¼ acres of land in Bristol by Neshaminy Creek and by land of Robert Hall. Said land part of 660 acres which Henry Johnson, Silas Crispen and Joseph Sidon conveyed by indenture dated 5 Dec 1702 to Samuel Carpenter. Samuel Carpenter made his Last Will and Testament dated 6 Apr 1714 duly proved and recorded in the Register General's Office in Philadelphia. Made 13 Oct 1716. Wit: Joseph Bond, Jer. Langhorne, Wm. Fishbourn. Ackn: 25 Aug 1743 before JP Mathew Rue by John Duncan of Middletown, gent., who swears the signature of Jeremiah Langhorne, late of Middletown, deceased, is authentic as he served Jeremiah Langhorne as his clerk for several years and is familiar with his handwriting. Rec: 29 Sep 1743.

P. 43   Deed. John Rowledge of Southampton, yeoman, and Margaret his wife, for £520, to John Peckom of Bristol Co., MA, yeoman, 214 acres of land in Southampton by Neshaminy Creek and bounded by the lands of John Hayhurst, Robert Heaton and Widow Blagdon. Robert Heaton and Grace his wife sold the land to John Rowledge by deed recorded in Bucks Co. Book D, Vol [?], pgs 376-377. Also another tract of 150 acres in Southampton bounded by the land of Jeremiah Bartholomew. Robert Fletcher of Abington, Philadelphia Co., and Elizabeth his wife, sold the land to John Rowledge by deed dated 13 Sep 1722. [Name within body of deed is also spelled John Rootledge.] Made 16 Oct 1722. Wit: Robert Heaton, Henry Mitchel, Jer. Langhorne. Ackn: 15 Sep 1732 before Jeremiah Langhorne by Robert Heaton. Rec. 3 Oct 1743.

P. 46   Sheriff's Deed. Joseph Jackson, Sheriff of Bucks Co., to Thomas Clark, 742 acres of land in Bristol bounded by the lands of Joshua Wright, _____ Mitchell, John Bossenett, Francis White, Samuel Brelsford and _____ Headley. Said land was the land of John Burk at the time of his death.

Joseph Turner, at a Court of Common Pleas held at Philadelphia in September 1740, was awarded recovery of a debt of £24.1s.2p and £3.7s against Joseph Peace and John Abraham Denormandie, administrators of the estate of John Burk, late of Bristol, deceased. By writ issued by the Court, the then Sheriff of Philadelphia Co. was directed to levy the debt against the goods of John Burk's estate. On 25 Aug 1742, the Sheriff exposed Burk's land for public auction. It was purchased by the highest bidder, Thomas Clarke of Bucks Co., gent., for £537.19s. Made 17 Mar 1742. Wit: John Duncan, William Fry, John Ross. Acknowledged at Newtown 17 Mar 1742 before Lawrence Growdon. Rec: 4 Oct 1743.

P. 48   Mortgage. John Cawley of Middletown, tanner, for £52, to William Allen of Philadelphia, merchant, a plantation and 2 tracts of land in Makefield, the first bounded by Thomas Winder's land containing 45 acres; the second bounded by Abraham Woods' land, by Cawley's other land, and by John Johnson's land containing 41 acres. Final payment to be made on 14 May 1745. Made 14 May 1743. Wit: Joseph Breintnal, Jo. Pritcherd, Jr. Ackn: 1 Oct 1743 before JP Lawrence Growdon by John Cawley. Rec: 4 Oct 1743.

P. 49   Mortgage. James Gregg of Middletown, yeoman, for £42, to William Allen of Philadelphia, merchant, a plantation and 162½ acres of land in Makefield bounded by the lands of John Hough, Thomas Scott, and John Whitacre. To be paid in full on 14 May 1745. Made 14 May 1743. Wit: Joseph Breintnall, Jo. Pritcherd, Jr. JP: Thomas Lawrence. Rec: 10 Oct 1743.

P. 50   Mortgage. Robert Heaton of Northampton, yeoman, for £200, to William Clymer of Philadelphia, merchant, a dwelling house and 340 acres of land bounded by John Naylor's line on the north side of the road leading from the Falls to Philadelphia, by Thomas Harding's land, by land laid out to Samuel Allen, by lands belonging to Christopher Wetherill, James Carter and Ralph Draker. One entire payment due on 14 Sep 1744. Made 14 Sep 1743. Wit: Sept. Robinson, Rob. Greenway. Ackn: 26 Sep 1743. JP: Lawrence Growdon. Rec: 10 Oct 1743. William Clymer acknowledges full satisfaction of the mortgage on 14 March 1744/5 before Lawrence Growdon.

P. 52   Deed. Isaac Pennington, Sheriff of Bucks Co., for £31, to Stephen Twining, one moiety of 128 acres in Newtown. John Frohock, at a Court of Common Pleas held at Newtown 15 Jun 1732, recovered against John Pearson of Newtown a debt of £13.4s4p and 67s.6p. By writ dated at Newtown 17 Jun 1732, the Sheriff was directed to levy the debt against the lands of John Pearson. The Sheriff took into his custody one moiety or half-part of a tenement and 128 acres of land in Newtown bounded by the lands of Ezra Croasdale and Jeremiah Bowman. Said land descended from Aaron Pearson to his eldest son John Pearson. The property was sold at public auction to the highest bidder, Stephen Twining of Wrightstown on 8 Mar 1732/3. Made 4 Jun 1733. Wit: John Frohock, Christian Vanhooten. Certified by Jeremiah Langhorne on 14 Mar 1733. Rec: 12 Oct 1743.

P. 54   Lease. Nathaniel Irish of Bucks Co., for 5 shillings, to George Cruickshanks of the Island of Montserrat in the West Indies, gent., 75 acres of 150 acres of land on the Delaware River by Nathaniel Irish's other land and by land of William Allen. Nathaniel Irish sold to Isaac Islestein 75 acres of this land plus another tract of 500 acres bounded by land surveyed to

William Allen. Made 12 Oct 1743. Wit: Wm. Peters, James Bingham. Rec: 15 Oct 1743.

P. 55   Release.   Nathaniel Irish of Bucks Co., for £800, to George Cruickshanks of the Island of Montserrat in the West Indies, gent., 75 acres of a 150 acre tract [see entry P.54 above.] This land was patented to Caspar Wistar 18 Mar 1738 and recorded in Philadelphia Patent Book A, Vol 8, pg 351. Caspar Wistar and his wife Katherine by deeds of lease and release dated 11 and 12 Apr 1738 sold the 150 acres of land to Nathaniel Irish. Also 500 acres which was patented to Nathaniel Irish 10 Oct this instant and is recorded in Philadelphia. Made 13 Oct 1743. Wit: Wm. Peters, James Bingham. Ackn: 14 Oct 1743. JP: Lawrence Growdon. Rec: 15 Oct 1743.

P. 57   Sheriff's Deed.   Joseph Jackson, Sheriff of Bucks Co., for £4.5s. to Eucledus Longshore, a lot in Middletown. Mathias Keen recovered £30.14s and 82s.1p against Thomas Taylor, late of Bucks Co., innkeeper, at a Court of Common Pleas held at Newtown in Dec 1742. By writ the Sheriff was directed to levy the debt against the land and goods of Thomas Taylor and seized from Taylor a lot in Middletown by the road leading from the Falls to Philadelphia containing one-sixth part of an acre. In Aug 1743, the Sheriff put the lot up for public auction and sold it to the highest bidder, Eucledus Longshore of Middletown, tanner. Made Sep 1743. Wit: John Wells, Richard Mitchell. Ackn: at Newtown 16 Sep 1743 before Lawrence Growdon. Rec: 15 Oct 1743.

P. 59   Mortgage. Anthony Wright of Middletown, yeoman, along with Charles Wright and Thomas Wright, his sons, became indebted to Thomas Clarke of Falls Township, gent., for several sums of money and for the consideration of these debts grants to Thomas Clarke a plantation and 200 acres of land in Middletown by land formerly William Carter's and by land belonging to Peter White. Made 15 Oct 1743. Wit: John Frohock, John Abraham Denormandie. Ackn: 19 Oct 1743. JP: John Abraham Denormandie. Rec: 20 Oct 1743.

P. 60   Lease.   William Allen of Philadelphia, for 5 shillings, to George Cruickshanks of the Island of Montserrat in the West Indies, gent., 290 acres of land on Saucong Creek and the River Delaware. Made 12 Oct 1743. Wit: Wm. Peters, James Bingham. Rec: 20 Oct 1743.

P. 61   Release. William Allen of Philadelphia, and Margaret his wife, for £400, to George Cruickshanks of the Island of Montserrat in the West Indies, gent., 290 acres of land on Saucong Creek and the River Delaware.

Said land part of 10,000 acres which he purchased 29 Aug 1728 from William Penn, esq., who was bequeathed it from his grandfather the Honorable William Penn. Made 13 Oct 1743. Wit: Wm. Peters, James Bingham. Ackn: 13 Oct 1743. JP: Nat Irish. Rec: 20 Oct 1743.

P. 63   Lease. Edward Glover of Middletown, sadler, for 5 shillings, to Joseph Richardson of Middletown, merchant, a plantation and 232 acres of land in Middletown by Neshaminy Creek by Robert Holgates lands and by the line of Thomas Constable, Walker Bridgman and John Croasdell. Made 3 Mar 1740. Wit: Benj. Field, Henry Vanhorn, Jno. Duncan. Rec: 25 Oct 1743.

P. 63   Release. Edward Glover of Middletown, sadler, for £325, to Joseph Richardson of Middletown, merchant, a plantation and 232 acres of land [see previous entry.] Said land part of 1,000 acres which William Penn by indentures of lease and release dated 20 and 21 Apr 1682 granted to Thomas Croasdale of Newhay, York Co., and a tract of 620 acres was patented to Thomas Croasdale on 28 Jun 1692. After Thomas Croasdale's death, his sons William and John by deed dated 20th da 12th mo 1798 sold 197 acres of the land to John Cowgill of Bucks Co. William Penn by patent dated 14th da 4th mo 1712 executed by his Commissioners James Logan, Isaac Norris and Edward Shippen, conveyed to John Cowgill 232 acres, who along with his wife Rachell, on 16 Jun 1712 conveyed the 232 acres to Nicholas Barnson, which is recorded in Book D, Vol 1, pg 284. Nicholas and Rebeckah Barnson by indentures of lease and release dated 3 and 4 May 1725 conveyed the land to Edward Glover. Made 4 Mar 1740. Wit: Benj Field, Henry Vanhorn, Jno. Duncan. Ackn: 11 Jun 1740. JP: Joseph Kirkbride. Rec: 25 Oct 1743.

P. 66   Sheriff's Deed. Joseph Jackson, Sheriff of Bucks Co., for £1,940, to Alexander Grayson of Philadelphia, merchant, 1,000 acres of land in Bristol bounded by the lands of William Atkinson, Thomas Marriott, Thomas Stackhouse, Ennion Williams, John Abraham Denormandie, John White, Benjamin Canby, John Large, Henry Tomlinson, Ebenezer Large, John Hall, William Hill, Joshua Wright, John Sisom, by the lands late of George Clough and John Underwood and by the Quaker Burying Ground. Also 2 islands by the River Delaware adjacent to Bristol and bounded by Normandy's land and containing 416 acres. Also a 5-acre tract in Bristol bounded by Mill Street and Pond Street and Nathan Watson's land. Also a small lot in Bristol excepting what belongs to Joseph Kirkbride. And a 1 acre lot at the corner of Market and Ratcliff Streets. Also a lot in Bristol lately belonging to Israel Pemberton and now Malachi Walton.

William Whitaker of London, merchant, at a Court of Common Pleas held at Newtown 16 Sep last past recovered £1,863.14s and 79s.9p against John Abraham Denormandie and Joseph Peace, administrators of the estate of John Burke, late of Bristol, merchant, deceased. By writ dated 19 Mar 1743, Sheriff seized a tract of 1,000 acres of land in Bensalem, part of land known as the Mill Land, and also the 200-acre Great Island, a 100-acre Little Island, and a 70-acre tract of land. Also an 80-acre tract adjoining lands belonging to John Abraham Denormandie and land lately belonging to Nathan Watson and another tract of land containing 5½ acres. Also a lot in Bristol by Ratcliff and Market Streets; another 1-acre lot in Bristol sold by Israel Pemberton, which is the lot where the Quaker Meeting House stands. By a writ dated 18 Jun last past and executed 29 Jul the several tracts of land were sold at public auction to the highest bidder. Made 16 Sep 1743. Wit: Tench (?) Francis, Wm. Peters. Ackn: 16 Sep 1743 before Lawrence Growdon. Rec: 27 Oct 1743.

P. 71   Sheriff's Deed. Joseph Jackson, Sheriff of Bucks Co., for £136, to Jeremiah Langhorne of Middletown. By writ the Sheriff was commanded to seize the goods and lands of Thomas Story, late of Bucks Co., yeoman, to levy a debt of £198 on behalf of the Trustees of the General Loan Office of Pennsylvania. The Sheriff seized Story's 250 acres of land in Newtown bounded by the lands of Christopher Taylor and by Elizabeth Barber which were sold at public auction to the highest bidder. Made 12 Mar 1741. Wit: Michael Dowd, Jno. Duncan. Ackn: 16 Sep 1743 before Lawrence Growdon. Rec: 31 Oct 1743.

P. 72   Mortgage. Christian Shook of Bucks Co., farmer, for £30, to William Allen of Philadelphia, merchant, 270 acres of land on a branch of Cook's Creek near Durham bounded by the lands of Theobald Leatherman and John Griffith. To be repaid in two payments by 30 Sep 1745. Made 30 Sep 1743. Wit: James Bingham. Ackn: 25 Nov 1743 before Lawrence Growdon. Rec: 1 Dec 1743.

P. 74   Release. Christian Barnson (aka Vanhorne) of Northampton, yeoman, and Williamkee his wife, for £18, to Joseph Richardson of Middletown, merchant, 2 acres and 30 perches of land in Attlebury in the township of Middletown by land late of Jonathan Woolston and Joseph Richardson's and Christian Vanhorne's other lands, and by the road leading from Bristol to Newtown. Said land part of 280 acres which Jeremiah Langhorne, late of Middletown, deceased, conveyed to Christian Vanhorne The deed is recorded in Bucks Co. Book B, Vol 2, pg 204. Made 4 Nov 1743.

Wit: Barnard Vanhorne, Jno. Duncan. Ackn: 4 Nov 1743. JP: Mathew Rue. Rec: 2 Dec 1743.

P. 75   Mortgage. Lewis Evan of Hilltown, yeoman, and Alice his wife, to secure a debt of £100, to William Thomas of the same place, yeoman, a plantation and 300 acres of land in Hilltown by land of Jenkin Williams, by land laid out to Adam Harker and by Jeremiah Langhorne's land. Made 15 Nov 1743. Wit: Matt Hughes, George Hughes. Ackn: 16 Nov 1743. JP: Matt Hughes. Rec: 5 Dec 1743. William Thomas acknowledged full satisfaction of the mortgage on 13 Sep 1748 before Lawrence Growdon, Recorder.

P. 77   Release. Richard Peters of Philadelphia, gent., for £67.10s, to William Thomas of Bucks Co., yeoman, 150 acres of land on Deep Run and bounded by the lands of Nicholas Dillon, John Kennard and Lawrence Growdon. Made 14 Dec 1743. Wit: William Peters, John Callahan. Ackn: 17 Dec 1743. JP: Lawrence Growdon. Rec: 23 Dec 1743.

P. 78   Release. Edward Shippen of Philadelphia, merchant, for £50 and because he is moving, to Richard Peters of the same place, gent., 300 acres of land on Deep Run bounded by the lands of Nicholas Dillon, Joseph Townsend, John Kennard, Joseph Growdon, and by land formerly called the Dutch Tract. Said land was granted to Edward Shippen by patent dated 26 Dec last past and is recorded at Philadelphia in Patent Book A, Vol 9, pg 542. Made 1 Jan 1742. Wit: Wm. Peters, John Callahan. Ackn: 17 Dec 1743. JP: Lawrence Growdon. Rec: 23 Dec 1743.

P. 80   Release. Jacob Vandegrift, yeoman, Cornelius King, Jr., Katherine King, William Williams, yeoman, and Christian his wife, all of Appequiming Hundred in New Castle Co., and Francis King, yeoman, and Christian his wife, Francis Crewson, yeoman, and Elizabeth his wife, Albert Vansant, yeoman, Leonard Vandegrift, yeoman, and Mary his wife, Jacob Vandegrift, yeoman, and Mary his wife, John Lea, yeoman, and Hannah his wife and Sarah Vandegrift, all of St. Georges Hundred in New Castle Co., and Jacob Haughhead, yeoman, and Hannah his wife of Makefield, Bucks Co., (children and grandchildren of Leonard Vandegrift, deceased) for 5 shillings and because they are moving, quit claim to Abraham Vandegrift of Bensalem, yeoman, 107 acres of land in Bensalem on the Delaware River and bounded by Lawrence Growdon's land. Said land formerly belonged to Leonard Vandegrift of Bensalem, deceased. Made 7 Dec 1743. Wit: Thomas Evan, Leo. Vandegrift King. Ackn: 23 Dec 1743. JP: Lawrence Growdon. Rec: 25 Dec 1743.

P. 82　　Release. Joseph Claypoole of Philadelphia, joiner, for £95.19s, to Jonathan Bavington of Northampton, cordwainer, 137 acres of land in Northampton by another parcel sold by Joseph Claypoole to Joseph Dungan, part of 1,000 acres formerly belonging to James Claypoole. William Penn, now deceased, had obtained a writ against Francis Cook, administrator of the estate of James Claypoole, merchant, deceased, which estate was to have been administered by Helena, his widow. The writ directed William Biles, Sheriff of Bucks Co. to expose to public sale 1000 acres of James Claypoole's estate. By deed dated 23 Nov 1719, Sheriff Biles sold the land to Joseph Claypoole. Made 27 Sep 1738. Wit: Jno. Jones, Jos. Lawrence. JP: Jeremiah Langhorne. Rec: 2 Feb 1743.

P. 84　　Lease. Jacob Bennet of Northampton, for 5 shillings, to Jonathan Abbot of the same place, cordwainer, a plantation and 100 acres of land in said town by Neshaminy Creek bounded by the lands of Samuel Blaker. Made 11 Dec 1739. Wit: Abra. Chapman, Jr., Richard Haire.

P. 84　　Release. Jacob Bennet of Northampton, yeoman, for £105, to Jonathan Abbot of the same place, cordwainer, a plantation and 100 acres of land in said town by Neshaminy Creek bounded by the lands of Samuel Blaker. Said land was granted to Jacob Bennet by Abraham Bennet and Annace his wife and is part of 500 acres granted to Abraham Bennet from Samuel Bown 1 May 1731. Made 12 Dec 1739. Wit: Abra. Chapman, Jr., Richard Haire. Ackn: 12 Dec 1739. JP: Abraham Chapman. Rec: 4 Feb 1743.

P. 86　　Mortgage. Abel Noble of Warminster, cooper, for £166.6s.11p, to Peter Turner of Philadelphia, merchant, 100 acres of land in Warminster bounded by the lands of William Noble, James Cravens, Abel Noble (his other land) and Thomas Dungan, land which Abel Noble acquired through an inheritance. To be repaid in 5 annual payments with final payment 9 Nov 1748. Made 10 Nov 1743. Wit: Charles Brockden, John Reily, both of Philadelphia. Ackn: 15 Dec 1743 before JP Benjamin Shoemaker and again 11 Feb 1743/4 before Lawrence Growdon, JP. Rec: 15 Feb 1743.

P. 89　　Release. Caspar Wistar of Philadelphia, brass button maker, and Catherine his wife, for £52.10s, to Nathaniel Irish of Bucks Co., 150 acres of land on the south side of the west branch of the Delaware River adjoining Nathaniel Irish's other land and by William Allen's land. Said land one of two tracts which were patented 28 Mar last past (recorded at Philadelphia in Patent Book A, Vol 8, pg 351) to Caspar Wistar. Made 20 Apr 1738. Wit: Jacob Shoemaker, William Parsons of Philadelphia (surveyor), Jos. Yeats,

James Bingham. Ackn: 11 Feb 1743. JP: Lawrence Growdon. Rec: 15 Feb 1743.

P. 90   Mortgage. John Hill of Buckingham, yeoman, and Sarah his wife, for a debt of £150, to George Emlen of Philadelphia, brewer, a plantation and 107 acres of land in Buckingham bounded by the lands of John Large, Margaret Atkinson and James Streeter. Made 5 Aug 1743. Wit: Paul Isaac Voto, John Reily. Ackn: 15 Aug 1749. JP: Lawrence Growdon. Rec: 15 Feb 1749. Mortgage released by decree of Court 16 Nov 1922 (see Misc. Book 3, pg 405.)

P. 92   Release. William Allen of Philadelphia, esq., and Margaret his wife, for £113, to Jacob Mussleman of Bucks Co., yeoman, 126 acres of land in Richland bounded by the lands of John Landus, Morris Morris and Abraham Heastand. Said land part of 772 acres which is part of 10,000 acres which William Penn, esq. bequeathed by his Last Will and Testament to his grandson Springet Penn who granted the 10,000 acres to his youngest brother, William Penn by indenture dated 10 Apr 1729 and recorded at Philadelphia in Book F, Vol 5, pg 562. William Penn the brother sold the land to William Allen by indenture dated 16 Apr 1729 and recorded at Philadelphia in Book F, Vol 6, pg 1. The said 772 acres, by warrant from the Trustees Isaac Norris, Samuel Preston and James Logan dated 5 Mar 1729/30 directed to Jacob Taylor, Surveyor General, was surveyed and laid out in part of the said 10,000 acres. Made 21 Dec 1743. Wit: Wm. Parsons, surveyor, and James Bingham, merchant, both of Philadelphia. Ackn: 11 Feb 1743. JP: Lawrence Growdon. Rec: 20 Feb 1743.

P. 94   Release. William Allen of Philadelphia, and Margaret his wife, for £100, to John Landus of Bucks Co., yeoman, 125 acres of land in Richland by Jacob Mussleman's land. Said land part of 772 acres [see description of land in above entry for P. 92.] Made 21 Dec 1743. Wit: Wm. Parsons, surveyor, and James Bingham, merchant, both of Philadelphia. Ackn: 11 Feb 1743. JP: Lawrence Growdon. Rec: 20 Feb 1743.

P. 96   Release. Robert Smith of Bristol, cooper, for £112, to John Stackhouse of Middletown, yeoman, 160 acres of land in Bristol bounded by the lands of Israel Pemberton, John Smith, Jr., John Lanins, and by the Manor of Pensberry. Said land part of 268 acres and 18 perches granted to Robert Smith from John Smith, Jr., by deed dated 4 Apr 1713 and recorded in Book D, Vol 1, pgs 433-434 and was granted to John Smith, Jr. by William Atkinson by deed dated 26 May 1710 and recorded in Book D, Vol 1, pgs 426-427. Made 8 Mar 1714. Wit: John Smith, John Cutler. On 20 Dec 1743,

JP Joseph Kirkbride certified he was well acquainted with Robert Smith, now deceased, and his handwriting for many years before his decease and also was well acquainted with John Cutler, also now deceased, and his handwriting. Rec: 25 Feb 1743.

P. 97   Agreement between George Brown of Buckingham, carpenter, and James Evans of the same place, yeoman, that George Brown, for £50, has sold to James Evans 100 acres of land in Buckingham bounded by the land of _____ Dyer, Alexander Brown, Daniel Jackson and George Brown. Made 20 Oct 1733. Wit: Jonah Carlile, Sarah Brown. Ackn: 25 Oct 1743 before Matt Hughes by George Brown, Elecksander Brown, James Evans.

P. 98   Mortgage. Jacob Walton of Bucks Co., for £32 (due to Hon. John Penn, Thomas Penn and Richard Penn, esqs., Proprietors of PA) to Richard Peters and Lynford Lardnor, both of Philadelphia, gents., a plantation and 150 acres of land by Three Mile Run (creek branch) and bounded by the lands of James Dickens, Adam Sheiffer and Peter Patridge. Final payment of 6 annual payments to be made 16 Jan 1749 in Philadelphia. Made 16 Jan 1743. Wit: William Peters, John Callahan, both of Philadelphia. Ackn: 10 Mar 1743. JP: John Moland. [Lynford Lardnor's name is also spelled Leardner in body of deed.] Rec: 13 Mar 1743. Mortgage released on 30 Jan 1939 by Decree of the Court of Common Pleas (see Misc. Book 76, pg 26.) Rec. 1 Feb 1939.

P. 101   Mortgage. James Kilpatrick of Bucks Co., to secure a debt of £52.3s (due to the Hon. John Penn, Thomas Penn and Richard Penn, esqs., Proprietors of PA,) to Richard Peters and Lynford Lardner, both of Philadelphia, gents., a plantation and 200 acres of land on a branch of Tohickon Creek called Three Mile Run and by the lands of Isaac Walton, Michael Frylick, and by land late of Adam Shaffer, dec'd. Seven payments due 16 Jan annually with final payment made in 1750. Made 16 Jan 1743. Wit: William Peters, John Callahan, both of Philadelphia. Ackn: 10 Mar 1743. JP: John Moland. Rec: 13 Mar 1743.

P. 103   Mortgage. Peter Gruber of Bucks Co., for a debt of £40 (due to the Hon. John Penn, Thomas Penn and Richard Penn, esqs., Proprietors of PA,) to Richard Peters and Lynford Lardner, both of Philadelphia, gents., a plantation and 150 acres of land on a branch of Tohickon Creek called Three Mile Run bounded by land laid out for Jacob Herman, _____ Dicken and Peter Patridge. To be repaid in 6 annual payments with final payment due 16 Jan 1749. Made 16 Jan 1743. Wit: William Peters, John Callahan, both of Philadelphia. Ackn: 10 Mar 1743. JP: John Moland. Rec: 13 Mar 1743.

P. 105   Mortgage. John Hutchinson of Bucks Co., for a debt of £35 (due to the Hon. John Penn, Thomas Penn and Richard Penn, esqs., Proprietors of PA,) to Richard Peters and Lynford Lardner, both of Philadelphia, gents., a plantation and 166 acres of land bounded by the lands of Andrew Gatohels [sp?] and Thomas Lancaster. To be repaid in 7 annual payments, final payment due 31 Jan 1750. Made 31 Jan 1743. Wit: William Peters, John Callahan, both of Philadelphia. Ackn: 10 Mar 1743. JP: John Moland. Rec: 14 Mar 1743. On 16 Jun 1750 Lynford Lardner acknowledged full satisfaction of the mortgage before Lawrence Growdon, Recorder of Deeds.

P. 107   Mortgage. Solomon Leibkap of Bucks Co., for a debt of £50 (due to the Hon. John Penn, Thomas Penn and Richard Penn, esqs., Proprietors of PA,) to Richard Peters and Lynford Lardner, both of Philadelphia, gents., a plantation and 207 acres of land in Rockhill by land of Jacob Herman, Francis Lewis and Adam Shaffer. To be repaid in 7 annual payments, final payment due 18 Feb 1750. Made 18 Feb 1743. Wit: Edwd. Reily, John Callahan, both of Philadelphia. Ackn: 10 Mar 1743. JP: John Moland. Rec: 14 Mar 1743.

P. 109   Mortgage. Jacob Frelly of Bucks Co., for a debt of £22.6s.8p (due to the Hon. John Penn, Thomas Penn and Richard Penn, esqs., Proprietors of PA,) to Richard Peters and Lynford Lardner, both of Philadelphia, gents., a plantation and 101 acres of land adjoining the Darkan Tract. To be repaid in 5 annual payments, final payment due 18 Feb 1748. Made 18 Feb 1743. Wit: Edwd. Reily, John Callahan, both of Philadelphia. Ackn: 10 Mar 1743. JP: John Moland. Rec: 14 Mar 1743. Acknowledged by Richard Peters on 10 Sep 1750 that full satisfaction of the mortgage had been made before Lawrence Growdon, Recorder.

P. 111   Mortgage. Michael Wisel of Bucks Co., for a debt of £70 (due to the Hon. John Penn, Thomas Penn and Richard Penn, esqs., Proprietors of PA,) to Richard Peters and Lynford Lardner, both of Philadelphia, gents., 131 acres of land in Bedmister by Michael Frelick's, James Kilpatrick's and John Wootman's lands. Also a tract of 150 acres on Perkconey Creek by William Allen's land. To be repaid in 7 annual payments, final payment due 18 Feb 1750. Made 18 Feb 1743. Wit: Edwd. Reily, John Callahan, both of Philadelphia. Ackn: 10 Mar 1743. JP: John Moland. On 7 Aug 1773, by power of attorney recorded in Book E, Vol 3, pg 100 granted to Richard Gibbs by the said Richard Peters and Lynford Lardner, full satisfaction of the mortgage is acknowledged before ____ Hicks, Recorder.

P. 113 Mortgage. William Graham of Bucks Co., for a debt of £67.10s (due to the Hon. John Penn, Thomas Penn and Richard Penn, esqs., Proprietors of PA,) to Richard Peters and Lynford Lardner, both of Philadelphia, gents., 131 acres of land on Tohickon Creek by land laid out for James Dicken and David Camron and by David Griffiths land. Also another tract of 175 acres on said Creek by James Sloams land and David Griffiths land. Final payment of 7 annual payments due 20 Feb 1750. Made 20 Feb 1743. Wit: Edwd. Reily, John Callahan, both of Philadelphia. Ackn: 10 Mar 1743. JP: John Moland. Rec: 19 Mar 1743. By Decree of Court of Common Pleas before Judge Harman Jenks mortgage declared satisfied 6 Dec 1889 and recorded by Timothy Cadwallader, Rec. of Deeds.

P. 115 Mortgage. George Newburne of Buckingham, yeoman, to secure a debt of £60 to be paid by 1746, to William Hinton of Philadelphia, yeoman, a plantation and 100 acres of land in Buckingham by lands of Jacob Heston [Heaton?], Robert Smith, Robert Strettell and Edward West. Said land that which Robert Strettell of Philadelphia, merchant, and his wife deeded 2 Jul 1743 to George Newburne. Made 4 May 1744. Wit: Paul Isaac Voto, J. Okely. Ackn: 4 May 1744 before Richard Mitchell, JP. Rec: 12 May 1744. Debt declared satisfied Jan 1747/8 by William Hinton before Rebekah Eyre and Richard Hayes.

P. 116 Mortgage. Rudolph Serbor of Bucks Co., for a debt of £42 (due to the Hon. John Penn, Thomas Penn and Richard Penn, esqs., Proprietors of PA,) to Richard Peters and Lynford Lardner, both of Philadelphia, gents., a plantation and 200 acres of land by the land of William Allen. Final payment of 6 annual payments due 31 Jan 1750. Made 31 Jan 1743. Wit: William Peters, John Callahan, both of Philadelphia. Ackn: 10 Mar 1743 before JP John Moland.

P. 119 Mortgage. James Vansant [also spelled Vanzant, Vansandt] of Bucks Co., for a debt of £52.17s (due to the Hon. John Penn, Thomas Penn and Richard Penn, esqs., Proprietors of PA,) to Richard Peters and Lynford Lardner, both of Philadelphia, gents., a plantation and 188¾ acres of land bounded by the lands of George Benbow and Solomon Lightcap. 7 annual payments. Final payment due 31 Jan 1750. Made 31 Jan 1743. Wit: William Peters, John Callahan, both of Philadelphia. Ackn: 10 Mar 1743. JP: John Moland. Rec: 12 May 1744.

P. 120 Release. William Hudleston of Middletown, cordwainer, and his wife Dorothy, for £183.18s.6p, to Joseph Richardson of the same place, merchant, 59 acres and 94 perches of land in Middletown by the road from

Philadelphia to Trenton by the lands of Joseph Walker, Christian Vanhorne, and by Hudleston's land. Said land part of 100 acres which William Hayhurst deeded 3 Feb 1688 to Henry Hudleston, the father of said William Hudleston and is recorded in Book A, Vol 1, pgs 218-219. Henry Hudleston by his Last Will and Testament dated 14 Apr 1706 bequeathed the land to his son William. Made 3 Apr 1744. Wit: John Smith, Jno. Duncan. JP: Lawrence Growdon. Rec: 14 May 1744.

P. 123   Release. William Hudleston of Middletown, cordwainer, and his wife Dorothy, for £3.16s.6p, to John Mitchel of the same place, carpenter, a ½ acre lot by the road from Bristol to Newtown and bounded by the lands of Thomas Tomlinson and William Wildman, part of 100 acres of land in said town by the lands of James Dilworth and Richard Thatcher. Said land that which William Hayhurst, eldest son of Cuthbert Hayhurst, deeded to Henry Hudleston, late father of said William Hudleston, and is recorded in Book A, Vol 1, pg 218. Henry Hudleston, in his Will dated 14 May 1706, devised to his wife Elizabeth all his estate to maintain it for his children until his said son William comes of age and then William is to have two-thirds part of the land and his wife Elizabeth to have the other third during her natural life. After her death, William is to have the whole of the land. The said Elizabeth has since married Thomas Davis and by deed dated 19 Nov 1729 conveyed Elizabeth's one-third share of the land to William. Made 3 Mar 1744. Wit: Wm. Fry, Benjamin Tomlinson, William Wildman. Ackn: 3 Apr 1744. JP: Lawrence Growdon. Rec: 14 May 1744.

P. 124   Mortgage. Mathias Keen of Bristol, carpenter, and Susannah his wife, to secure a debt of £150 to be paid 9 Jun 1750, to David Murray of Philadelphia, gent., a lot in Bristol bounded by the land of Samuel Cary, by Mill Street, by a lot lately belonging to Anthony Burton and by Thomas Stackhouse's garden. Made 9 Jun 1743. Wit: Sarah Burton, John Frohock. Ackn: 31 Jun 1743. JP: Enion Williams. Rec: 14 May 1744.

P. 125   Mortgage. Richard Glover of Bristol, weaver, for £37, to David Murray of Philadelphia, merchant, a lot in Bristol by Mill Street and bounded by a lot formerly John Rowland's and by Israel Pemberton's lot. To be paid on or by 7 Jun 1747. Made 7 Jun 1743. Wit: Benjamin Harris, Simon Sacket, Wm. Atkinson. Ackn: 31 Jan 1743. JP: Enion Williams. Rec: 14 May 1744.

P. 127   Release. Deborah Conoly of Philadelphia, widow, for £120, to John Abraham Denormandie of Bristol, merchant, a lot in Bristol. Joseph Bond of Bristol, yeoman, and his wife Ann; William Fishbourn of Philadelphia, merchant and his wife Hannah; and John Wilson, merchant of

Philadelphia, by indenture dated 26 Jun 1723 conveyed to Mathew Durham of Bristol, malster, a lot with a malthouse and brewhouse in said burrough at the intersection of Mill Street and Pond Street and by John Abraham Denormandie's lot. Mathew Durham made his Last Will and Testament 2 Sep 1723 and nominated Thomas Wathel of Bristol, malster, his executor and bequeathed to said Wathel all of his estate. Thomas Wathel made his Last Will and Testament 13 May 1733 and made Joseph Peace, sometimes of Trenton, Hunterdon Co., NJ, miller, his executor to sell his property to pay his debts. Joseph Peace, by indenture dated 29 Jul 1737 sold the lot to Deborah Conoly [also spelled Connoly and Conolly.] Made 14 Apr 1739. Wit: Rice Peters, Saml. Gifford. Ackn: 5 Jun 1740 before Ennion Williams, JP, by Deborah Conolly. Rec: 14 May 1744.

P. 129   Mortgage. Samuel Wilkins of Orange Co., VA, yeoman, and his wife Sarah, for £100, to Nathaniel Irish of NJ, gent., 250 acres of land in the great swamp in Bucks Co. by the Manor of Richland and by James Logan's land. To be repaid on or by 13 Jun 1745. Made 13 Jun 1744. Wit: Thomas Bonde, James Bingham, William Allen. Ackn: 13 Jun 1744. JP: Joseph Kirkbride. Rec: 18 Jun 1744.

P. 131   Lease. Thomas Marple of Abington, Philadelphia Co., yeoman, and Susannah his wife, for 10 shillings, to Bernard Young of Hilltown, Bucks Co., yeoman, 379 acres of land in Hilltown by the lands of Jeremiah Langhorne, Joseph Kirkbride and David George. Made 24 Dec 1741. Wit: William Brittin, Abraham Stephens.

P. 132.   Release. Thomas Marple of Abington, Philadelphia Co., yeoman, and Susannah his wife, for £359, to Bernard Young of Hilltown, yeoman, 379 acres of land in Hilltown by the lands of Jeremiah Langhorn, Joseph Kirkbride, and David George. Jeremiah Langhorne, gent., by indentures of lease and release dated 18 and 19 Dec 1723 conveyed to John Chapman of Bucks Co., yeoman, 400 acres of land in Hilltown. Said 400 acres is part of 3,000 acres which William Penn, esq., deceased, by deeds dated 17 and 18 Feb 1701 conveyed to George Beal of or near Guildford in Surrey Co., Great Britain, who by deeds dated 17 and 18 Oct 1718 sold the land to Jeremiah Langhorne.

John Chapman by deeds dated 29 and 30 Dec 1723 sold 200 acres of the said 400 acres of land to Thomas Marple. John Chapman by deed dated 5 Jun 1724 conveyed to David Marple, father of said Thomas Marple, 100 acres, part of the said 400 acres. John Chapman by another set of deeds dated 17 and 18 Nov 1730 conveyed to said David Marple another 79 acres, also part of the 400 acres. David Marple and Jane his wife by deeds dated 1 and 2

Nov 1733 granted the said 79 acres to Thomas Marple. David Marple made his Last Will and Testament dated 5 Aug 1736 and bequeathed to his son Thomas the other 100 acres, to be his after the death of his mother, Jane. Said Will recorded in Philadelphia. By the death of his parents, Thomas Marple became owner of 379 acres in Hilltown, part of the said 400 acres which Jeremiah Langhorne sold to John Chapman. Made 25 Dec 1741. Wit: William Britton, Abraham Stevens. Ackn: 29 Dec 1741. JP: Benjamin Jones. Rec: 21 Jun 1744.

P. 135 Release. Richard Glover of Bristol, weaver, and his wife Rachel, one of the daughters of John Clarke by Martha his wife, both deceased, the said Martha being the daughter and heir at large of Gilbert White, late of said County, yeoman, also deceased, for £30 and because they are moving, to John Clarke of Falls Township, yeoman, only son and heir at law of the said John Clarke and Martha his wife, deceased, 3 tracts of land. The first tract containing 180 acres lies by the River Delaware bounded by the lands of William Biles and Robert Harvey. The next tract contains 300 acres and lies next to the first, bounded by land late of Thomas and John Rowland and by Robert Harvey's land. The third parcel contains 400 acres, lies by the River Delaware, and is bounded by the land belonging to the London Company and by land late of John Pedcock. Made 16 Aug 1731. Wit: Wm. Eaton, Mary Jenkins. Ackn: 16 Aug 1731. JP: Thomas Watson. Rec: 10 Sep 1744.

P. 137 Mortgage. Robert Heaton borrowed from William Clymer £100 and secures the payment with his dwelling house, grist mill, and 340 acres of land (not described.) Made 28 Feb 1743. Wit: Wm. Whitehead, Rob Greenway. Ackn: 12 Apr 1744. JP: John Moland. Rec: 25 Sep 1744. William Clymer acknowledged full satisfaction of the mortgage 20 Mar 1744/5 before Lawrence Growdon.

P. 138 Deed. Mathew Rue of Middletown, yeoman, for 5 shillings, to his son Lewis Rue, 150 acres of land in Middletown by Newtown Road bounded by the lands of John Goslin, Francis White, Peter Vanhorn and John Praul. Bartholomew Jacobs by deed dated 27 May 1730 recorded in Bucks Co. Book E, Vol 1, pg 4, sold the said land to Mathew Rue. [A side note says there was then no Book E, that the deed is recorded in Book B, Vol 2, pg 3.] Not dated. Wit: Benj. Harris, Giles Lawrence, Wm. Atkinson. Ackn: 24 Oct 1744. JP: John Abraham Denormandie. Rec: 29 Nov 1744.

P. 139 Mortgage. Nathan Watson of Bristol, butcher, to secure a debt of £55 due 10 Jan next, to William Atkinson, of the same place, yeoman, a meadow in Bristol by a burying ground containing 9 acres. Made 10 Jul

1744. Wit: Thomas Clifford, William Atkinson, Jr. of Philadelphia, Jacob Gambley. Ackn: 27 Nov 1744. JP: Emon Williams. Rec: 20 Dec 1744.

P. 141 Mortgage. Joseph Warder of Falls Township, yeoman, and his wife Elizabeth, to secure a debt of £200 payable in 3 annual payments, to Rachel Baker of Makefield, widow, a plantation and 100 acres of land in Falls Township by the River Delaware by the lands of Samuel Brown and Joseph Kirkbride. Also all Joseph Warder's 2 fifth parts in 200 acres adjoining the first tract and bounded by Samuel Brown's land. Both tracts of said land are part of that which Samuel Carpenter of Philadelphia, merchant, by deed dated 16 Feb 1702 recorded in Book C, Vol 1, pg 114, conveyed to Willoughby Warder, the grandfather of said Joseph Warder. Made 2 Dec 1741. Wit: Wm. Yeardley, Thos. Yeardley, Jr. Ackn: 15 Dec 1741, JP: Joseph Kirkbride. Rec: 28 Jan 1744. On 3 Aug 1767 Thomas Pryor, assignee of Rachel Baker, appeared and acknowledged full satisfaction of the mortgage. Lawrence Growdon. Recorder.

P. 143 Mortgage. Johanne Philip De Berholt, chemist, of Germantown, Philadelphia Co., and Catherine his wife, to secure a debt of £190, to Richard Peters of Philadelphia, esq., 379 acres of land in Bucks Co. on the Delaware River bounded by the lands of William Allen and Thomas Craig. Made 29 Sep 1744. Wit: Joseph Crellins, John Callahan of Philadelphia. Ackn: 7 Nov 1744 before JP Lawrence Growdon. Rec: 28 Jan 1744. Richard Peters acknowledged full satisfaction before Lawrence Growdon 11 May 1745.

P. 145 Mortgage. Robert Heaton of Northampton, yeoman, to secure a debt of £500, to William Clymer of Philadelphia, merchant, a dwelling house with grist mill and 340 acres of land in Northampton by the Falls to Philadelphia road and bounded by the land of John Naylor, Thomas Harding, Samuel Allen, Christian Weatheril, James Carter and Ralph Draycot. Made 13 Mar 1744. Wit: John Plumly, Robt. Greenway. Ackn: 20 Mar 1744. JP: Lawrence Growdon. Rec: 25 Mar 1744. William Clymer acknowledged full satisfaction 19 Oct 1747 before Lawrence Growdon, Recorder.

P. 147 Mortgage. Archibald Anderson of Philadelphia, brewer, and his wife Mary, to secure a debt of £150, to George Emlen of the same place, brewer, a plantation and 391 acres of land situated in Bristol by Neshaminy Creek and bounded by the lands of John Clauson, _____ Teague, John Peters and Samuel Allen. Made 22 Mar 1744/5. Wit: Jacob Shoemaker, Jr., Arthur _____. Ackn: 22 Mar 1744/5. JP: John Kinsey. Rec: 24 Mar 1744. On 7 Oct 1752, George Emlen acknowledged full satisfaction of the mortgage before Lawrence Growdon, Recorder.

P. 149   Mortgage. Mathias Keene of Bristol, carpenter, for £75, to John Abraham Denormandie of the same place, merchant, 2 lots in Bristol. The first lot is at the intersection of Market and Pond Streets. The other lot lies by Pond Street adjoining the first lot and is bounded by the lot of John Large and land formerly belonging to George Clough. To be paid in full on or by 9 Jul 1750. Made 9 Jul 1743. Wit: John Futham, John Frohock. Ackn: 31 Jan 1743. JP: Ennion Williams. Rec: 24 Mar 1744.

P. 151   Mortgage. Timothy Baynes of Solebury, yeoman, for £80, to John Abraham Denormandie and John Snowdon, tanner, both of Pennsylvania, and Joseph Peace of Trenton, NJ, gent., a plantation and 400 acres of land in Solebury bounded by land late of Edward Corns, by the lands of Samuel Beaks, Henry Seams (sp?) and James Hamilton. To be paid annually on 16 Jan, final payment 1747. Made 16 Jan 1743. Wit: John Frohock, John Denormandie, Jr. Ackn: 16 Jan 1743. JP: Ennion Williams. Rec: 24 Mar 1744.

P. 153   Mortgage. Hendrick Forst of Bensalem, yeoman, for £50, to John Abraham Denormandie, esq., and John Snowdon, tanner, a plantation and land in Bensalem bounded by the lands of John Williams and Peter Williams, by Rodman's land and by Richard Johnson's land. Made 14 May 1744. Wit: John Frohock, Thomas Hutchinson. Ackn: 14 May 1744. JP: Mathew Rue. Rec: 24 Mar 1744. On 25 May 1759 John Denormandie, administrator of John Abraham Denormandie, deceased, acknowledged that Henry Forst had paid the mortgage before Lawrence Growdon, Recorder.

P. 155   Lease. Owen Roberts of Philadelphia, esq., for 5 shillings paid by William Blakey, Jr., of Pensbury, Bucks Co., yeoman, 500 acres of land in Soulbury by the River Delaware and bounded by George Pownal's land. Made 12 Feb 1724. Wit: John Cadwalader, Thomas Leech [Luck?], Nicholas Seull.

P. 156   Release. Owen Roberts of Philadelphia, esq., for £155, to William Blakey, Jr. of Pensbury, yeoman, 500 acres of land in Soulbury [same parties and land as set out in previous entry for P. 155.] Daniel Smith, late of Philadelphia County, distiller, formerly of Malbrough, Wiltshire, England, deceased, in his lifetime had rights to land in Pennsylvania which he bought from the Proprietors in England by deeds of lease and release. Randall Spakeman of Philadelphia, administrator of the estate of Daniel Smith obtained a warrant dated 6 Apr 1702 in order to survey and lay out 500 acres of land for the use of said Smith's estate. John Smith of London, England, eldest son and heir of Daniel Smith, by power of attorney dated 5 Jan 1719 and recorded in Philadelphia Book D3, Vol 5, pg 215 on 17 Aug 1721, empowered Thomas Chalkley of Philadelphia to sell the 500 acres. Thomas Chalkley by lease and release dated 16 and 17 May 1722 sold the land to Owen Roberts. Made 13 Feb 1724. Wit: John Cadwalader, Thomas Leech [Luck?], Nicholas Seull. Rec'd. full monetary amount 9 Mar 1724/5 and witnessed by Thomas Leech [Luck?], John Cadwalader. Ackn: at Philadelphia 17 Oct 1744 before JP Joshua Madox by Thomas Leech or Luck and Nicholas Seull, both of Philadelphia.

P. 159   Deed.   William Huddleston of Middletown, cordwainer, and Dorothy his wife, for £12.2s, to William Blakey of the same township, yeoman, 2 acres of land in Middletown lying by William Blakey's land, by Paxon's land and by Huddleston's other land. Said land part of 100 acres of land bounded by the land of James Dilworth and Richard Thatcher which William Hayhurst, eldest son of Cuthbert Hayhurst, by deed recorded in Bucks Co. Book A, Vol 1, pg 210 sold to Henry Huddleston (late father of said William Huddleston) who by his Last Will and Testament dated 17 May 1706 devised to his wife Elizabeth all his estate for payments of debts in consideration of maintaining his children until his said son William reached the age of 21, at which time William should enjoy two-thirds of the above mentioned parcel of land and his wife Elizabeth the other third during her lifetime. After her decease, William to have the whole of the land. Henry Huddleston died soon after writing the Will and his wife Elizabeth has since married Thomas Davis. Thomas Davis and Elizabeth his wife by deed dated 19 Nov 1729 released Elizabeth's share of the land to her son William Huddleston. 3 Apr 1744. Wit: John Cawley, Euclydus Longshore. Ackn: 3 Apr 1744 before JP Lawrence Growdon.

P. 162   Deed.   Ezra Croasdell of Middletown, yeoman, and Thomas Stackhouse of the same place, yeoman, for 5 shillings (and because they are moving) to Jeremiah Croasdell, Joseph Walker, Joseph Stackhouse, Cuthbert Hayhurst, Benjamin Cutler and William Paxon, all of Bucks Co., 3 acres of land in Middletown by a corner of William Huddleston's land and by the lands of Christian Vanhorn and Benjamin Cutler. One acre is that which William Hayhurst sold to Joseph Growdon, Ezra Croasdell, William Paxon, Thomas Hillbourn, John Cutler and Thomas Stackhouse by deed recorded in Book C, Vol 1, pgs 238-240. The other two acres were sold by Robert Heaton to Joseph Growdon, Ezra Croasdell, William Paxon, Thomas Hilbourn, John Cutler and Thomas Stackhouse by deed recorded in Book C, Vol 1, pgs 236-238. Since the said Joseph Growdon, Thomas Hilbourn, William Paxon and John Cutler are all deceased, the rights to the land fall to Ezra Croasdell and Thomas Stackhouse. Made 2 Jul 1739. Wit: David Willson, James Thackrey,

Robert Collison. Ackn. 10th da 4th mo 1742 when Robert Collison appeared before JP Joseph Kirkbride.

P. 165   Release. John Ingals of Philadelphia, sawyer, and Rebecca his wife, for £160, to Ann Amos [also spelled Ames in body of deed] of Bensalem, widow, 100 acres of land in Bensalem by the Delaware River and by Samuel Swift's land. Samuel Swift of Bensalem, blacksmith, and Elizabeth his wife, he being the eldest surviving grandson and heir of John Swift, late of Bensalem, yeoman, deceased, by deed dated 14 Jul 1738 granted to John Ingals 100 acres of land. Made 20 Mar 1743. Wit: Benjamin Hoster, Joseph Bush. Witnesses to the transfer of money are John Ashmead and James Shillingford. Ackn: 17 Apr 1745 before JP Ennion Williams by John Ingals and wife Rebecca.

P. 167   Release. Lawrence Growdon, gent., and Sarah his wife, and Thomas Janney, carpenter, and Hannah his wife, all of Bucks Co. (said Sarah and Hannah are nieces of Jeremiah Langhorne, deceased) for £1,000, to Langhorne Biles of the same place, gent., 1,000 acres of land in Hilltown (already in his possession by virtue of a lease.) William Penn by lease and release dated 13th and 14th da 8th mo 1601 granted to Edward Belms of Oxford, England, chirurgeon, 2,000 acres of land in Pennsylvania. The rights to this land, by various means, came to be vested in James Logan of Philadelphia, merchant, who by deed dated 10 Oct 1713 sold 1,000 acres of the land to Jeremiah Langhorne of Bucks Co.

By other indentures of lease and release dated 16 and 17 Sep 1605, William Penn granted to Isaac Decow of York County in England, yeoman, 2,500 acres of Pennsylvania land, who by his Last Will and Testament did devise 2,050 acres of the land to his daughter Susannah Decow. Susannah later married Ambrose Field and then by deed dated 17 Oct 1709 sold the 2,050 acres to Isaac Decow, son of the first mentioned Isaac Decow. Isaac Decow the son, by deed dated 17 Nov 1709 sold 150 acres of the land to Jeremiah Langhorne.

William Penn by several indentures of lease and release on record in Bucks Co. granted to John Rowland 4,500 acres of PA land. Rowland, by deed dated 26 May 1711 sold 500 of the 4,500 acres to Jeremiah Langhorne. Jeremiah Langhorne later obtained 3 warrants, the first dated 13th da 1st mo 1712 for laying out 320 acres; the second warrant dated 17th da 8th mo 1713 for laying out 150 acres; the third warrant dated 13th da 6th mo 1714 for laying out 500 acres, all three of which were laid out to Jeremiah Langhorne in one entire tract of 970 acres on 18th da 6th mo 1714 in Hilltown by the lands of Coll. Mildmay, Edward Kemp and by John Penn's Manor. This land was confirmed by patent dated 17 Dec 1714 and is recorded at Philadelphia in Book A, Vol 5, pg 112.

Jeremiah Langhorne made his Last Will and Testament dated 16 May 1742 and bequeathed to his nieces Sarah Growdon and Hannah Janney to be equally divided between them the Hilltown tract of 1,000 acres. He died soon after and his Will was proved and recorded in Bucks Co. Will Book B, pg 19. Made 11 Feb 1744. Wit: Saml. Cary, Wm. Yeardley. Ackn: 19 Feb 1744. JP: John Abraham Denormandie. Rec: 1 May 1745.

P. 173   Mortgage. Thomas Scott of the Manor of Highlands in Bucks Co., yeoman, to secure a debt of £100 due 2 Apr 1746, to James Logan of Stinton, Philadelphia Co., gent., 137½ acres of land in the Manor of Highlands by Peter Johnson's land. Said land part of 300 acres which Tobias Collet, Daniel Quare and Henry Goldney, late of London, Great Britain, by indenture of release dated 14 Mar 1722 granted to Thomas Scott. Made 2 Apr 1745. Wit: Peter Haig, Christian Lehman. Ackn: 13 Apr 1745. JP: John Kinsey. Rec: 28 May 1745.

P. 176   Mortgage. John Hutchinson of Bucks Co., for securing a debt of £38.9s.5p (due the proprietors of PA, John Penn, Thomas Penn and Richard Penn,) to Richard Peters and Lynford Lardner, both of Philadelphia, gents., 158¼ acres of land on Gallows Hill and bounded by the lands of John Hayes, John Simples, William Wares and John Young. To be repaid in 7 annual payments, final payment due 14 Mar 1751. John Moland, attorney. Made 14 Mar 1744/5. Wit: James Aiskill, John Callahan, both of Philadelphia. Ackn: 12 Apr 1745. JP: Lawrence Growdon. Rec: 1 Jun 1745.

P. 179   Mortgage. Benjamin Collins of Bucks Co., for securing a debt of £38.15s (due to John Penn, Thomas Penn and Richard Penn, Proprietors of PA,) to Richard Peters and Lynford Lardner, both of Philadelphia, gents., a plantation and tract of 150 acres of land in Plumstead bounded by the lands of John Norcross and William Freams. 5 annual payments; final payment due 21 Feb 1750. Made 21 Feb 1744. Wit: William Norcross, John Callahan of Philadelphia. Ackn: 12 Apr 1745. JP: Lawrence Growdon. Rec: 1 Jun 1745.

P. 181   Deed. Robert Caille of London, merchant, bequeaths after his death to John Abraham Denormandie and John Anthony Denormandie, both sons of Andrew Denormandie, all his lands in Pennsylvania providing that Andrew Denormandie their father shall have the revenue and benefit of the lands during his natural lifetime. Made 10 May 1710. Wit: Martha Andrews, Peter Ripert, Jane Dufay, Marie Dufay [Dussay?] Ackn: 12 Apr 1745 before JP Lawrence Growdon by Anna Kearsley, wife of John Kearsley of

Philadelphia, chirurgeon, who swore on oath that she was well acquainted with the handwriting of Robert Caille, late of London as she had formerly exchanged many letters with him. Rec: 13 Jul 1745.

P. 182   Release. Langhorne Biles of Falls Township, for £500, to Thomas Janney of the same place, carpenter, 550 acres of land in Hilltown bounded by the lands of John Lewis, Lawrence Growdon, James Andrew Hamilton and lands late of Mathew Hughes. A tract of 970 acres of land in Hilltown was surveyed and laid out to Jeremiah Langhorne, late of Bucks Co., on 18th da 6th mo 1714 and bounded by the lands of Coll. Mildmay, Edward Kemp and by John Penn's Manor. This land is part of what had originally been purchased by Edward Bettris, Isaac Decow and John Rowland. The land was confirmed to Jeremiah Langhorne by patent dated 7 Dec 1714 and recorded at Philadelphia in Book A, Vol 5, pg 112. By his Last Will and Testament dated 16 May 1742 and recorded in Will Book B, pg 19, Jeremiah Langhorne gave 1,000 acres of the land to his nieces Sarah Growdon and Hannah Janney. By indentures of lease and release dated 10 and 11 Feb 1744 and recorded in Book B, Vol 3, pg 167, Lawrence Growdon of Bucks Co., gent., and Sarah his wife and Thomas Janney of Falls Township and Hannah his wife (the two nieces of Jeremiah Langhorne) sold it to Langhorne Biles. A recent survey shows the land contains 1,100 acres. Made 14 Feb 1744. Wit: Saml. Cary, W. Yeardley. Ackn: 13 Jun 1745. JP: Enion Williams. Rec: 16 Jul 1745.

P. 184   Release. Langhorne Biles of Falls Township, for £530, to Lawrence Growdon of Trevose, gent., 550 acres of land in Hilltown bounded by the lands of John Lewis, Thomas Janney, Barnet Young, Thomas Jones and by land late of Joseph Kirkbride. Said land part of 1,000 acres of land which was owned by Jeremiah Langhorne [for history of this land see above entry for P. 182.] Made 14 Feb 1744. Wit: Saml. Cary, Wm. Yeardley. Ackn: 13 Jun 1745. JP: Enion Williams. Rec: 13 Jul 1745.

P. 187   Lease. Joseph Burgess of Makefield, yeoman, and Hannah his wife, for 5 shillings, lease for one year to Mahlon Kirkbride of the same place, yeoman, 103 acres of land in Makefield by the River Delaware and bounded by Henry Marjorum's land, and by lands late of Joseph Kirkbride and William Beakes. Made 13 May 1741. Wit: Sarah Kirkbride, John Burgess, Joseph Kirkbride.

P. 187   Release. Joseph Burgess of Makefield, yeoman, and Hannah his wife, for £155, to Mahlon Kirkbride of the same place, yeoman, 103 acres of land in Makefield [see preceding entry.] William Penn by patent dated 16th da 7th mo 1701 granted to John Parsons of Bucks Co., yeoman, 103 acres of land in Makefield by the River Delaware by lands late of Henry Marjorum's, Joseph Kirkbride's and William Beaks'. By indenture dated 1 Dec 1701, John Parsons sold the land to Joseph Kirkbride of Falls Township, who by deed dated 7th da 9th mo 1702 and recorded in Book C, Vol 1, pg 133 granted the land to Mathew Kirkbride. Jean Kirkbride and Thomas Kirkbride, executors of the Last Will and Testament of Mathew Kirkbride, deceased, by deed dated 5 Nov 1709 granted the land to George Slater of Makefield. Slater sold the land to Samuel Burgess of Bristol by deed dated 7 Jun 1714 and recorded in Book A, Vol 2, pg 25. Ann Burgess and John Burgess, executors of the said Samuel Burgess, deceased, by indentures of lease and release dated 2 and 3 May 1716, granted the land to the said Joseph Burgess. Made 14 May 1741. Wit: Sarah Kirkbride, John Burgess, Joseph Kirkbride. Ackn: 4 Jun 1741. JP: Joseph Kirkbride. Rec: 6 Aug 1745.

P. 189   Lease. Samuel Smith of Burlington, NJ, and Jane his wife, for 5 shillings, to Mahlon Kirkbride of Makefield, Bucks Co., yeoman, 292 acres and 116½ perches of land in Hilltown bounded by the lands of George Fishwater, John Mark, Clement Doyle and Jeremiah Langhorne. Said land part of 2,580 acres that Jeremiah Langhorne, deceased, by deed dated 15 May 1729 granted to Joseph Kirkbride, also deceased. Made 11 Oct 1744. Wit: Thos. Marriott, Jos. Rockhill, Henry Scott.

P. 190   Release. Samuel Smith of Burlington, NJ, merchant, and Jane his wife, for £270, to Mahlon Kirkbride of Makefield, Bucks Co., yeoman, 292 acres and 116½ perches of land in Hilltown [see description of land in previous entry.] Charles Read, Job Goodson, Evan Owen, George Fishwater and Joseph Pidgion, late of Philadelphia Co., gent., land agents for the Free Society of Traders, by deed dated 29 Mar 1724 and recorded in Bucks Co. Book A, Vol 2, pgs 300-301, granted to Jeremiah Langhorne, late of Middletown, 5,200 acres of land in Hilltown. By indentures of lease and release dated 15 and 16 May 1729 and recorded in Book A, Vol 1, pgs 315-316 [written above it is 314-315], Jeremiah Langhorne sold 2,580 acres of the land to Joseph Kirkbride, late of Falls Township. Joseph Kirkbride made his Last Will and Testament dated 1 Jun 1736 and devised to his daughter Jane Kirkbride 440 acres of land bounded by the land of Edward Doyle. Made 12 Oct 1744. Wit: Thos. Marriott, Jos. Rockhill, Henry Scott. Ackn: 12 May 1745. JP: Joseph Kirkbride. Rec: 12 Aug 1745.

P. 192   Deed. Thomas Bishop Vickris of Chew Magna, Somerset Co., Great Britain, esq., and Richard Hockley of Philadelphia, PA, merchant and attorney for Thomas Bishop Vickris, for £200, to James Turniclift of Makefield, Bucks Co., yeoman, 266 acres of land on the Delaware River bounded by the lands of _____ Baker, Peter Lerner and _____ Yeardley. Said land part of a tract of 483 acres. By order of William Penn, since deceased, in Apr 1683, for Richard Vickris, then of Bristol in Great Britain, now deceased, a survey was made of 483 acres of land on the River Delaware in Bucks Co., which was part of 2,000 acres purchased by Richard Vickris, and was confirmed to him by warrant dated 16 Aug 1700. Thomas Bishop Vickris, only surviving son of said Richard Vickris, by letter of attorney dated 24 Apr 1740 made Thomas Penn his attorney and said letter is on record at Philadelphia in Book G, Vol 1, pg 186. Thomas Penn by letter of substitution dated 8 Dec 1740 made Richard Hockley attorney for Vickris. Made 13 Sep 1743. Wit: Wm. Peters, Richard Peters. Ackn: 11 Jan 1744. JP: Thomas Lawrence, a Justice of the Peace for the City of Philadelphia. Rec: 23 Oct 1745.

P. 195   Mortgage. Thomas Dungan of Warminster, carpenter, to secure a debt of £100, to Stephen Anthony, skinner, Robert Showel, bolter, John Breezely, blockmaker, Augustine Stillman, cordwainer, all of Philadelphia, William Marshall of Bybury, Philadelphia Co., taylor, and Stephen Watts of Southampton, Bucks Co., yeoman, a plantation and 100 acres of land in Warminster bounded by the lands of Bartholomew Longstreth, James Craven, Abel Noble, Thomas Rush, and by Thomas Dungan's other land. To be repaid in 10 annual payments, final payment due 21 Jun 1755. Made 21 Jun 1745. Wit: Arthur Forster, Paul Isaac Voto. Ackn: 17 Oct 1745. JP: Benjamin Jones. Rec: 23 Oct 1745. Full satisfaction of mortgage acknowledged 9 Dec 1771 by Joseph Hant, attorney for John Bearley, before J. Hicks, recorder.

P. 196   Mortgage. Malachi Walton of Bristol, innholder, for £20, to William Sheals of Burlington, NJ, butcher, a lot in Bristol at the corner of Cedar and Market Streets bounded by the land of James Downey and by land formerly belonging to John Burk. [Name also spelled 'Sheels' in body of deed.] Made 25 Apr 1745. Wit: Jon. Frohock, Thos. Hutchinson. Ackn: 24 Oct 1745. JP: John Hall. Rec: 25 Oct 1745.

P. 198.   Mortgage. William Mead of Makefield, yeoman, to secure a debt of £354, to Samuel Parr of Philadelphia, merchant, a plantation and 220 acres of land in Makefield by the Delaware River and bounded by the lands of Henry Margerinus and Richard Hough. To be repaid in 5 payments; final payment due 23 Jul 1747. Made 4 May 1745. Wit: Edmund Keerny, John Kinsey. Ackn: 4 May 1745. JP: John Kinsey. Rec: 4 Nov 1745. Satisfaction of mortgage acknowledged before Lawrence Growdon 25 Sep 1759.

P. 200 Mortgage. Benjamin Tomlinson of Middletown, sadler, to secure a debt of £120, to Benjamin Scott of Southampton, carpenter, a plantation and 113 acres of land in Southampton bounded by Bristol Road. Said land is part of that which Joseph Tomlinson by his Last Will and Testament bequeathed to his son Joseph Tomlinson "the remaining part of my tract of land when he shall attain to the age of twenty-one years but if should not attain to that age then I give and bequeath his said share of land unto my son Benjamin Tomlinson." Joseph Tomlinson the father died soon after. Joseph Tomlinson the son did not attain the age of twenty-one years. Mortgage to be repaid in 6 annual payments; final payment due 5 Aug 1751. Made 5 Sep 1745. Wit: Joseph Richardson, Thos. Tomlinson, Wm. Fry. Ackn: 5 Sep 1745. JP: Mathew Rue. Rec: 12 Nov 1745. Benjamin Scott appeared before Lawrence Growdon, Recorder, and acknowledged full satisfaction of the mortgage 22 Jul 1746.

P. 201 Mortgage. Joseph Hinton of Northampton, yeoman, and his wife Mary, for £360, to William Bennet of the same place, blacksmith, a plantation and 226 acres of land in Northampton bounded by the lands of Paul Blake, Nicholas _____, Adrian Conel, Saffert Sefferts [sic] and Barnard Vanhorne. Made 1 Jun 1745. Wit: Garret Kroensen, Benj. Jones. Ackn: 21 Oct 1745. JP: Benjamin Jones. Rec: 15 Nov 1745. William Bennet acknowledged full satisfaction of the mortgage 28 Nov 1765.

P. 203 Lease. Morris Morris of Abington in Philadelphia County, yeoman, and his wife Susanna, Richard Walln of the northern reaches of the City of Philadelphia, yeoman, and his wife Ann, for 10 shillings, to John Wells of Lower Dublin in said County, carpenter, 500 acres of land in Solebury by the River Delaware and bounded by land late of Tobias Dymock and by the land of Jacob Holcombe. Made 25 Jun 1717. Wit: Cha. Brockden, Cha. Osborne.

P. 204 Release. Maurice Morris of Abington, Philadelphia Co., yeoman, and his wife Susanna, Richard Walln of northern Philadelphia, yeoman, and his wife Ann (Susanna and Ann being the sisters of Richard Heath, late of said City, gent., deceased) for £96, to John Wells of Lower Dublin in said County, carpenter, 500 acres of land in Solebury [see preceding entry.] William Penn by his Commissioners Edward Shippen, Griffith Owen and Thomas Story patented to Richard Heath 500 acres of land in Solebury as described above and another tract of 500 acres by the River Delaware and bounded by the first mentioned tract. Patent is dated 2nd da 11th mo 1700 and is recorded at Philadelphia in Patent Book A, Vol 4, pg 242. By indenture dated 27 Apr 1716 and recorded in Book E7, Vol 9, pg 372, Morris Morris and his wife Susanna; Richard Walln and his wife Ann; Thomas Levesley of Dublin in said County and his wife Elizabeth; Richard Worrell of Dublin and his wife Hannah; and Mary Heath of Abington, spinster, (Elizabeth, Hannah and Mary being the other sisters of the said Richard Heath) sold the 1,000 acres to Charles Brockden of Philadelphia (excepting the land formerly sold to Jacob Holcomb.) In another indenture dated 28 Apr 1716 (and recorded in same book as before, pg 374) Charles Brockden sold the 1,000 acres to Morris Morris and Richard Walln. Made 26 Jun 1717. Wit: Cha. Brockden, Cha. Osborne. Ackn: 6 Oct 1744 before JP Mathew Hughes by Morris Morris and Richard Walln. Rec: 30 Nov 1745.

P. 208   Deed. William Hooper of Bristol, shipwright, for £40, to Mary Martin of the same place, widow, 40 acres of land in Bristol by the Delaware River and bounded by Thomas Dowdney's land and by the land formerly belonging to William Bagley, excepting the east end of the old house to be reserved for Elizabeth Jones during her natural life. Said land part of 60 acres granted by George Guineys and Elizabeth his wife to Daniel Jones by indentures of lease and release dated 23 and 24 Nov 1726. Daniel Jones died intestate and the land fell to Elizabeth Jones, his widow and to Grace and Mary Jones, two of his daughters and to another of his daughters, Sarah, who is the wife of the said William Hooper. On 1 Feb 1743 Elizabeth, Grace and Mary Jones quit claimed their share of the land to William Hooper. Made 1 Jun 1745. Wit: Wm. Atkinson, Margaret Atkinson, Joseph Atkinson, Sarah Hooper. Ackn: 25 Sep 1745 before JP Emion Williams by William Atkinson of Bristol. Rec: 4 Dec 1745.

P. 209   Mortgage. Benjamin Canby of Solebury, yeoman, and his wife Sarah, in order to secure the payment of a debt of £300 due 2 Nov 1746, to William Attwood of Philadelphia, merchant, a messuage and 135 acres of land in Solebury on the River Delaware and bounded by the lands of Benjamin Canby, Anthony Morris, John Wells and by land late of William Kitchen, deceased. Also 2 other tracts of land in Solebury: one of 21¾ acres on the river bounded by the above described tract and by land late of Tobias Dymock, deceased, and the other of 100 acres bounded by the river and by the said Canby and Morris' lands. The 100 acres was granted to Benjamin Canby by John Wells of Solebury 29 Oct last. Made 2 Nov 1745. Wit: Thomas Phillips, Rachel Quinby. Ackn: 2 Nov 1745. JP: John Wells. Rec: 5 Dec 1745.

P. 211   Deed. John Smith of Bristol, husbandman, for £32, to Lancelot Martin of Bucks Co., husbandman, 13 acres of land in Bristol bounded by the lands of William Colonelly, deceased, John Clay, Israel Pemberton and

William Dongan. Said land is part of 100 acres granted by Elisabeth Large, Joseph Large and Ebeneser Large to Robert Smith by indenture dated 2 Jun 1710 and recorded in Book D, Vol 1, pg 430. On 24 Jun 1720 Robert Smith granted the land to John Smith. Made 12 Nov 1739. Signed by John Smith and Sarah Smith. Wit: Daniel Wright, Joseph Mountain, Charles Wright. Ackn: same day. JP: Emion Williams. Memo: 17 Jun 1740 Mary Martin paid £12, the balance of the consideration money. Wit: Jn. Abrah. Denormandie, Nich. Thompson. Rec: 6 Dec 1745.

P. 213   Lease. Benjamin Combe of Makefield, yeoman, and Ann his wife, for 5 shillings, to Randle Hutchinson of the same place, mason, 182 acres of land in Makefield by land formerly John Snowden's, and by land belonging to Joseph Warder and his wife Elisabeth and Martha Worrall and by land late of Henry Margerum's. Made 7 Jan 1742. Wit: Samuel Brown, James Carruthers.

P. 214   Release. Benjamin Combe of Makefield, yeoman, and Ann his wife, for £240, to Randle Hutchinson of the same place, mason, 182 acres of land in Makefield [described in previous entry.] Said land part of 232 acres of land in Makefield which Samuel Darke, late of Falls Township, yeoman, deceased, and Martha his wife by indentures of lease and release dated 6 Aug 1715 and recorded in Book B, Vol 2, pg 409, granted to Thomas Worrall, late of Bristol, schoolmaster, deceased. Thomas Worrall died intestate and the land descended to his daughters Elisabeth Warder (the wife of Joseph Warder) and Ellen Meed (the wife of William Meed) and Martha Worrall. Joseph Warder and Elisabeth his wife and Martha Worrall by indenture of release dated 29 Jan 1740 granted 182 acres of the land to William Meed and his wife Ellen. By indentures of lease and release dated 1 and 2 Feb 1741, William and Ellen Meed sold the land to Benjamin Combe.
   Benjamin Combe executed a mortgage dated 11 Feb 1740 for £76 and 10 shillings to the Trustees of the General Loan Office and Randle Hutchinson will pay off the mortgage. Made 8 Jan 1742. Wit: Samuel Brown, James Carruthers. Ackn: 7 Feb 1743. JP: Joseph Kirkbride. Rec: 23 Jan 1745/6.

P. 218   Mortgage. Thomas White of Baltimore Co., Maryland, merchant, for £1,500, to Richard Hill of Philadelphia, merchant, now residing in part beyond the seas, and Samuel Preston Moore, late of Londontown, Maryland, but now of Philadelphia, practitioner in physick, attorney for Richard Hill. Richard Hill and Hannah, the wife of said Samuel Preston Moore, named the heirs of Richard Hill the Elder, lately deceased, who was the uncle of Dr. Richard Hill who was the father of the said Richard Hill (the merchant), and

Hannah Moore, by the Last Will and Testament (dated 28 Aug 1729) of their uncle Richard Hill the Elder.

Richard Hill (the merchant) by letter of attorney dated 20 Oct 1743 and recorded at Philadelphia in Book D2, Vol 2, pg 358, made Samuel Preston Moore his attorney to sell his lands in Pennsylvania. Samuel Preston Moore conveyed numerous pieces of land on behalf of Richard Hill. Each conveyance of land had within a clause which stated that various sums of money received from the rents of each parcel of land was to be reserved for Richard Hill (the uncle.) He sold to Thomas White for £1,500 one full moiety of diverse lots of land in Philadelphia totaling 60½ acres and one part of 19 yearly ground rents of these Philadelphia city lots which were sold: 8 May 1719 to Abram Watkins; 30 Jul 1721 to George Campion; 18 Jun 1719 to John Hart; 7 Mar 1705/6 to Samuel Borden; 12 Mar 1708/9 to William Boulding; 31 Dec 1717 to Simon Edgell; 4 Mar 1722/3 to Abel Cotty; 1 Jul 1720 to Henry Frogley; 31 Dec 1717 to Daniel Harrison; 31 Dec 1717 to John Ingram; 7 Aug 1718 to Dennis Rockford; 1 Sep 1720 to John Williams; 1 Sep 1720 to Daniel Ridge.

Also the following several tracts of land in Bucks Co. were sold and each held a clause reserving for Richard Hill (the uncle) various sums of money from the yearly proceeds of the land: 250 acres of land sold 26 Mar 1723 to William Metchener; 26 Mar 1723 to John Dyer 300 acres of land; 26 Mar 1723 to James Hughes 150 acres of land; 26 Mar 1723 to John Earle 150 acres of land; 15 Dec 1727 to John Britain 375 acres of land; 26 Mar 1723 to Silas McCarty 150 acres of land.

Also, a moiety of 11 other ground rents received from city lots sold: 23 May 1743 to William Maugridge; 2 city lots sold 18 Oct 1744 to Thomas Boude; 19 Oct 1744 to John Bood; 18 Oct 1744 to John Coats; 18 Oct 1744 to John Gould; 20 Oct 1744 to Daniel Dawson

Also ground rents received from lands in Bucks Co. sold: 3 Oct 1744 to Mathew Grier 250 acres in Plumsted; 3 Oct 1744 to Samuel Ferguson 187½ acres in Plumsted; 20 Sep 1743 to James Caldwell 187½ acres in Plumsted; 20 Sep 1743 to Hugh Ferguson 250 acres in Plumsted.

Made 12 Oct 1745. Wit: Charles Brockden of Philadelphia, Paul Isaac Voto, Arthur Forster of Philadelphia. Ackn: 2 Nov 1745. JP: Lawrence Growdon. Rec: 7 Feb 1745/6. [See next entry.]

P. 223   Deed. Richard Hill of Philadelphia, merchant, now residing in parts beyond the seas, by his attorney Samuel Preston Moore, late of Londontown, Maryland but now of Philadelphia, practitioner of physick, for £1,500, to Thomas White of Baltimore Co., MD, merchant, a full moiety or equal half-part of a lot in Philadelphia, part of a lot which Humphrey Murry and Richard Murry by direction of Samuel Corker by indenture dated 13 Jun

1716 and recorded in Philadelphia Book F, pg 37 conveyed to Richard Hill the Uncle. And another lot which Thomas Sysom and wife by indenture dated 22 Jul 1717 granted to Richard Hill the Uncle. [See previous entry.]

Also 2 other lots bounded by a lot late of John Key, deceased, part of a lot laid out for Joan Dixon and George Whitehead and several lots granted to Evan Owen by patent dated 12 Apr 1718 and recorded at Philadelphia in Patent Book A, Vol 5, pg 289 and by deed dated 14 Apr 1718 and recorded at Philadelphia in Book E7, Vol 10, pg 460 was granted to Richard Hill the Uncle.

Also 2 lots bounded by Thomas Smith's lot which were conveyed to Richard Hill the Uncle by Mary Witchall, James Stewart and Rachel his wife (said Mary the widow of Thomas Witchall, deceased, the former owner, and the said Rachel his daughter) by indenture dated 5 Aug 1719 granted to Evan Owen who by indenture dated 12 Aug 1719, recorded at Philadelphia in Book F, Vol 3, pgs 53 and 57, conveyed it to Richard Hill. Also another lot bounded by the last mentioned lot, the burying ground, and lots late of Griffith Jones and John Day, which were surveyed and located for Evan Owen who by deed dated 1 Mar 1719 and recorded in Philadelphia Book F, Vol 4, pg 75, conveyed it to Richard Hill the Uncle.

Also a house and lot bounded on the east by the lots of Rawle and Pidgeon, which Frances Rawle and wife, by indenture dated 29 Sep 1722 granted to John Heap which was conveyed to Richard Hill the Uncle. Also another lot bounded by Thomas Barker's lot which Samuel Preston and Anthony Morris, Jr., and wife, by indenture dated 2 Jun 1720 granted to Richard Hill the Uncle.

Also to Evan Owen 60½ acres of land on the River Delaware in Philadelphia Co. were conveyed by warrant dated 24 Sep 1744, which Evan Owen and Mary his wife by deed dated 8 Mar 1719 and recorded at Philadelphia in Book F, Vol 4, pg 75, conveyed to Richard Hill the Uncle.

Also one full moiety of 19 yearly ground rents [as stated in the preceding entry] of lots in Philadelphia. The first one bounded by John Richard's lot and George Hatfield's ground. George Campion's lot bounded by land of Redman and Coyle. Borden's lot bounded by the lots of Thomas Martin, Letitia Penn and Samuel Harriott. Boulding's lot borders the lot late of William Clews. Edgell's lot bounded by the lot of John Read. Daniel Harrison's lot is bounded by the lot late of John Day's but then of John Durborow's. The lot of John Ingrams is bounded by the lot sold to Daniel Harrison. Dennis Rockford is bounded by George Harman. Also the yearly rents of several tracts of land in Bucks Co. [as named in previous entry.]

Also the yearly rents of land in Philadelphia conveyed by Richard Hill and his sister Hannah 23 May 1743 to William Maugridge bounded by the lots of George Fitzwater, Enoch Coats, James Parrock, William Tidmarsh and Samuel Cooper.

Richard Hill the Elder, late of Philadelphia, merchant, deceased, (who was the uncle of Doctor Richard Hill, the father of the first named Richard Hill, and thus his great uncle) in his lifetime became seized of diverse lands and rents. He made his Last Will and Testament (dated 28 Aug 1729 and recorded in Philadelphia) and devised his lands and rents to Richard Hill the merchant and his (Richard Hill the merchant's) sister Hannah Moore. Richard Hill the merchant, by his deed dated 20 Oct 1743, appointed his brother-in-law Samuel Preston Moore to be his attorney to dispose of his lands (recorded in Philadelphia in Book D2, Vol 2, pg 358.)

Made 12 Oct 1745. Wit: Charles Brockden, Arthur Forster, Paul Isaac Voto. Ackn: 2 Nov 1745. JP: Lawrence Growdon. Rec: 15 Feb 1745/6.

P. 236   Release. John Wilkinson, because he is moving, quit claims his 76 acres and 27 perches of land in Warwick to Jonathan Bavington. By indenture dated 6 Nov 1745, James Claypool of Philadelphia, painter, and Rebecca his wife, conveyed to Jonathan Bavington, cordwainer, of Warwick, Bucks Co., and John Wilkinson, Jr. of Wrightstown in same county, cooper, 150¾ acres and 32 perches of land in Warwick by Neshaminy Creek and bounded by the lands of William Shippen and by John Wilkinson's other land. Made 30 Dec 1745. Wit: Paul Penington, Richard Mitchell. Ackn: 17 Feb 1745. JP: Richard Mitchell. Rec: 22 Mar 1745/6.

P. 238   Mortgage. Jacob Wildman of Middletown, yeoman, and Elisabeth his wife, in order to secure a debt of £110 due 10 Jan 1749, convey to Joseph Richardson of the same place, merchant, two plantations and tracts of land in Middletown. The first tract of 177 acres is bounded by the lands of John Croasdale, George Hulms, John Wildman and by land late of Jonathan Woolstone. The other tract is 50 acres and bounded by the lands of Benjamin Fields, Joseph Walker, Jonathan Woolstone, John Wildman and land lately belonging to Joseph Wildman, deceased. Made 6 Jan 1745. Wit: John Denormandie, Jr., John Frohock, Adam Harker, Samuel Stackhouse. Ackn: 15 Mar 1745/6. JP: Abraham Chapman. Rec: 27 Mar 1746.

P. 239   Lease. James Goold of Boston, Suffolk Co., MA, mariner, for 5 shillings, to Thomas Maybury of Middletown, Bucks Co., blacksmith, 400 acres of land in Newtown bounded by the lands of John Wally, Thomas Hilburne, Thomas Maybury and Thomas Stradlin. Made 2 Jul 1732. Wit: Joseph Fithian, Ben Davis, Amos Strickland.

P. 240   Release. James Goold of Boston, Suffolk Co., MA, mariner, for £560, to Thomas Maybury of Middletown, Bucks Co., PA, blacksmith, 400 acres in Newtown [see previous entry.] Joseph Frost of Charlestown, Middlesex Co., MA. and Hannah his wife by deed recorded in Bucks Co. Book B, Vol 2, pg 134, conveyed the 400 acres to James Goold. Made 3 Jul 1732. Wit: Josiah Fithian, Ben Davis, Amos Strickland. Ackn: 1 Oct 1737. JP: Abraham Chapman. Rec: 8 Apr 1746.

P. 243   Deed. Alexander Graydon of Philadelphia, merchant, for £10, to Joseph Hough of Bristol, Bucks Co., miller, a lot in Bristol by Nathan Water's orchard, part of land formerly belonging to John Burke, deceased, and by the sheriff in a suit of William Whitacre was sold at public auction to Alexander Graydon. Made 12 Oct 1744. Wit: Jon. Frohock, Jo. Jackson. Ackn: 13 Oct 1744. JP: John Abraham Denormandie. Rec: 10 Mar 1746.

P. 244   Lease. Alice Heaton of Southampton, widow and executrix of Robert Heaton, late of Middletown, deceased, for 5 shillings, to Thomas Stackhouse of Middletown, yeoman, 60 acres and 32 perches of land in Middletown by Neshaminy Creek and a corner of Nicholas Vanhorn's land. Made 18 May 1721. Wit: Henry Comly, Thomas Thwailrs, Henry Comly, Jr.

P. 245   Release. Alice Heaton of Southampton, widow and executrix of Robert Heaton, late of Middletown, deceased, for £100, releases to Thomas Stackhouse of Middletown, yeoman, 60 acres and 32 perches of land in Middletown [see previous entry.] Said land is part of 818 acres which William Penn's Commissioners conveyed to Robert Heaton by patent dated 12 Mar 1714. In his Last Will and Testament, Robert Heaton devised the land to "my dear and well beloved wife Alice Heaton" whom he also made executrix. Made 19 May 1721. Wit: Henry Comly, Thomas Thwailrs, Henry Comly, Jr., Bartholomew Longstreth. Ackn: 7 Apr 1746 before JP Mark Watson by Euclydus Longshore and Isaac Stackhouse, executors of the Last Will and Testament of the within named Thomas Stackhouse and declared the above described land was bequeathed to his son Joseph Stackhouse. Memo: 9 Apr 1746 before JP Lawrence Growdon. Henry Comly, Jr. of Philadelphia Co., yeoman, affirmed his own signature and the signature of his father, now deceased, as witness. Rec: 24 Apr 1746.

P. 247   Release. George Jones, the mortgagee, and his attorney (Power of Attorney made 27 Sep 1742) Lawrence Anderson of Philadelphia, mariner, acknowledges full satisfaction of a mortgage to Anthony Wilson. Mortgage recorded in Book B, Vol 2, pg 226. Made 11 Apr 1746. Wit: Samuel Cary,

Charles Brockden. Ackn: 21 Apr 1746. JP: Lawrence Growdon. Rec: 25 Apr 1746.

P. 248 Deed of Gift. John Blaker of Southampton, yeoman, for 5 shillings and for natural affection and because he is moving, to Peter Blaker of the same place, his eldest son, 350 acres of land in Southampton on Neshaminy Creek and bounded by the land of Anthony Tompkins and by the said John Blaker's land. Said land part of 1,000 acres granted to Robert Turner 23 Aug 1690 who conveyed the land to Charles Brooks. Charles Brooks conveyed the land to John Blaker by deed dated 15 Mar 1699 and recorded in Bucks Co. Book C, Vol 1, pg 14. Made 1 Mar 1719. Signed with his mark: Johannes Blaker. Wit: William South, Daniel Falesner. Robert Heaton. Ackn: 6 May 1734. JP: Jeremiah Langhorne. Rec: 1 May 1746.

P. 250 Mortgage. Rowland Smith of Bucks Co., yeoman, for £35.15s, to Richard Peters of Philadelphia, a plantation and 68 acres of land above the forks of the Delaware River and bounded by William Peck's land. To be paid on or by 6 Feb 1746. Made 6 Feb 1745. Wit: James Aishelle of Philadelphia, John Callahan. Ackn: 7 May 1746. JP: Lawrence Growdon. Rec: 10 May 1746. Full satisfaction of the mortgage acknowledged 31 Aug 1767 before Lawrence Growdon.

P. 251 Mortgage. Daniel Wright of Bristol, cooper, for £50, to Mary Martin of Bristol, widow, a lot in Bristol by Samuel Cary's lot and by the road to Newtown. Also another 2-acre lot adjoining the first by the road and by John Large's land. John Mountaine of Bristol by indenture dated 10 Mar 1741/2 sold the 2 lots to Daniel Wright. To be paid on or by 13 May 1749. Made 13 May 1746. Wit: Robert Barnard, Joseph Smith, Wm. Atkinson. Ackn: 15 May 1746. JP: Emion Williams. Rec: 27 May 1746. On 15 Jul 1752 Mary Martin acknowledged full satisfaction of the mortgage before Lawrence Growdon, Recorder of Deeds.

P. 252 Mortgage. Cornelius Neefies of Somerset Co., NJ, carpenter, and John Neefies of Northampton, Bucks Co., weaver, executors of the estate of George Neefies, deceased, for £115 and because they are moving, to Nicolas Winecope of Northampton, blacksmith, a messuage and 194 acres and 69 perches of land in Northampton bounded by the lands of Ram Vanderbelts, Cornelus Corfons [Corsons?], Benjamin Joans, David Dunging, Jeremiah Dunging, James Adams and by land lately John Carts. To be paid 22 Apr 1756. Made 22 Apr 1746. Wit: Jacob Bennet, Andrew Patterson. Ackn: 22 Apr 1746. JP: Benjamin Jones. Rec: 28 May 1746. [The name "Neefies" is also spelled as "Nephew" in the acknowledgment.] On 11 May 1755 Nicholas

Winecope acknowledged full satisfaction of the mortgage before Lawrence Growdon.

P. 254   Lease. Garret Winekoop of Philadelphia Co., gent., for 5 shillings, to Nicholas Winekoop of Northampton, Bucks Co., blacksmith, 260 acres of land in Northampton bounded by the lands of Peter Blacot and Garret Winekoop the Younger. Made 30 Oct 1738. Wit: Richard Treat, Nathaniel Brittain, David Parry.

P. 255   Release. Garret Winekoop of Philadelphia Co., gent., for £250, to Nicholas Winekoop of Northampton, Bucks Co., blacksmith, 260 acres of land in Northampton. Two warrants issued by William Penn, lately deceased, dated 20th and 21st das 12th mo 1684 directing Thomas Home, then Surveyor General, to survey 500 acres of land for each survey in Philadelphia or Bucks Co. for Anthony Tomkins, late purchaser of 1,000 acres The 1,000 acres (located in Bucks Co.) was surveyed 2nd da 2nd mo 1685 on Neshaminy Creek and bounded by land belonging to Robert Turner. Anthony Tomkins conveyed 500 acres of the land to Griffith Jones. Tomkins then died intestate and the residue of the land descended to his only son Joshua Tomkins. Joshua Tomkins sold (but did not actually convey) the land to Margaret Rutlidge of Northampton, widow. Joshua Tomkins made his Last Will and Testament dated 12 Nov 1726 and recorded at Philadelphia, bequeathing to Joshua Hambly £5, and "I make Edward Weston of the City of Philadelphia, Bricklayer (who married my only sister Hannah) my Sole Executor and I hereby give devise and bequeath unto him the said Edward Weston all the Remainder of any Estat real and Personal whatsoever and wheresoever the same be." Edward Weston and Hannah his wife by indenture tripartite of lease and release dated 15 and 16 May 1727 (at the request of Margaret Rutlidge who witnessed the transaction) conveyed the land to Garret Winekoop. This 521 acres of land was by Neshaminy Creek and bounded by the lands of Isaac Vanhorn and Peter Blacot. Made 31 Oct 1738. Wit: Richard Treat, Nathaniel Britain, David Parry. Ackn: 8 May 1744 before JP Benjamin Jones by Garret Winekoop. Rec: 28 May 1746.

P. 258   Deed. Edmond Frost of Billerica and John Francis and his wife Elizabeth of Medford, all in Middlesex Co., MA, brothers and sisters to John Frost, late of Newtown, Bucks Co., PA, deceased, because they are moving, to their brother Joseph Frost of Charlestown, MA, yeoman, all their rights and claims to their deceased brother John Frost's estate, including his 400 acres of land in Newtown bounded by the land of Shadrack Walley. John Frost's Last Will and Testament was dated 20th da 8th mo 1716. Made 14 Aug 1717. Wit: Joseph Whittemore, Theophilus Ivory, Amos Merrell. Ackn: 21 Aug

1717. JP: Joseph Lynde. In Charlestown 11 Mar 1718/9, John Francis and his wife Elizabeth appeared before JP Henry Phillips and acknowledged their deed. Rec. in Cambridge, Middlesex Co., MA 14 Mar 1718/9 in Lib: 20, pgs 220-222 by Samuel Phipps, Reg. Rec. in Bucks Co., PA 2 Jun 1746.

P. 259 Deed. Joseph Kirkbride of Falls Township, gent., for £10, to Joseph Chapman of Wrightstown, yeoman, 2 tracts of land in Wrightstown, the first tract of 5 acres and 55 perches is bounded by the lands of William Smith, Joseph Chapman and James Harker. The second tract containing 6 acres and 38 perches is bounded by Joseph Chapman's land. Said land is part of 205 acres granted to Joseph Kirkbride by patent dated 19 Jun 1736 from John Penn, Thomas Penn and Richard Penn (recorded at Philadelphia in Book A, Vol. 6, pg 184.) Made 25 Aug 1736. Wit: Charles Reilles, John Beaumont. Ackn: 22 Dec 1737. JP: Abraham Chapman. Rec: 3 Jun 1746.

P. 261 Deed. Joseph Chapman of Wrightstown, yeoman, for £18, to Joseph Kirkbride of Falls Township, gent., 20 acres and 55 perches of land in Wrightstown bounded by both men's lands. Said land part of 125 acres which was granted to Joseph Chapman by patent dated 15 Jan 1736 from John Penn, Thomas Penn and Richard Penn (recorded in Patent Book A, Vol 1, pg 139.) Made 25 Aug 1736. Wit: Charles Reilles, John Beaumont, Thomas Lancaster, John Chapman, Jr. Ackn: 22 Dec 1737. JP: Abraham Chapman. Rec: 3 Jun 1746.

P. 263 Mortgage. Johannes Philip DeBertholt, chymist, of Germantown, Philadelphia Co., to secure a debt of £100 due 9 Dec 1746, to Silas Prior of Philadelphia, baker, 379 acres of land in the forks of the Delaware bounded by the lands of William Allen and Thomas Craig. Made 9 Dec 1745. Wit: Arthur Forster of Philadelphia, Paul Isaac Voto. Ackn: 9 May 1746. JP: Richard Mitchell. Rec: 4 Jun 1746.

P. 264 Release. John Rodman of Bensalem and Nealeha his wife, release to Henry Brees and John Brees, brothers of Nealeha, two cows, one feather bed and bedding, six pewter plates and three platters given to her by the Last Will and Testament of their father Henry Brees, deceased. Made 14 Aug 1745. The release is signed with his seal "John Rodeman, Junr.", and with her mark "Eleoner Rodeman." Wit: Thos. Homer, James Vansandt. Rec: 5 Jun 1746.

P. 265 Release. John Rodman of Bensalem and Nealeha his wife, one of the daughters of Henry Brees, late of the same place, yeoman, deceased. By his Last Will and Testament dated 2 Feb 1736, Henry Brees bequeathed to his said daughter Nealeha £100 and named to be his executors his loving wife Hannah Brees and friend Philip Tillyer of Bybury in Philadelphia County. John Rodeman and his wife Nealeha acknowledged having received the £100 legacy from the executors and release them from any further obligation. Made 14 Aug 1745. Closed with the seal of "John Rodman, Junr." and "Elenor Rodeman." Wit: Thos. Homer, James Vansandt. Rec: 5 Jun 1746.

P. 265   Release. Hannah Brees of Bensalem, widow, and Philip Tillyer of Bybury in Philadelphia County, were appointed by the Court guardian and next friend of Sarah Brees and Hannah Brees, the girls being under the age of 21 and the daughters of the first named Hannah Brees and her deceased husband Henry Brees. In his Will dated 2 Feb 1736, Henry Brees bequeathed to his two youngest daughters £100 each and that his two sons Henry and John should give each of the girls on the day of their marriage two cows, one bed and bedding, six pewter plates and three pewter platters. He devised the residue of his estate to his sons Henry and John. Hannah Brees and Philip Tillyer acknowledge receipt of the £200, cows, bedding and pewterware from the sons Henry and John and release them of further obligation to the estate. Made 14 Aug 1745. Wit: John Rodman, James Vansandt. Rec: 5 Jun 1746.

P. 266   Mortgage. Hugh Orlton of Bucks Co., yeoman, and Elizabeth his wife, for £31, to William Allen of Philadelphia, 163 acres of land. Said land is part of 321 acres of land which the Trustees of the General Loan Office John Penn, Thomas Penn and Richard Penn patented 12 Oct 1739 to Nicholas Hill of Bucks Co., yeoman, located on Cook Creek near Durham bounded by the lands of Casper Wistair, Peter Lester, John Lester and Thomas Blair. By indenture of mortgage dated 18 Oct 1739 for £72, Nicholas Hill conveyed the land to the said Trustees. Later Nicholas Hill by indentures of lease and release dated 21 and 22 Sep 1741 conveyed the land to Hugh Orlton, who, in order to pay off the loan, by indentures of lease and release dated 26 and 27 Feb 1745 conveyed to Isaac Kirk of Bucks Co., yeoman, 158½ acres of the land. Made 12 Mar 1745. Wit: Robert Ellis, Thomas Evans, William Peters. Ackn: 7 Apr 1746. JP: Robert Ellis. Rec: 27 Jun 1746. Satisfaction of the mortgage acknowledged 26 Mar 1747 by William Allen before Lawrence Growdon.

P. 268   Release. Thomas Eastburne of Southampton, yeoman, and Sarah his wife, Richard Studdam of Philadelphia, taylor, and Mary his wife and Thomas Walton of the Manor of Moreland, Philadelphia Co., yeoman, and Elizabeth his wife (Thomas Eastburne, Mary Studdam and Elizabeth Walton are the children of John Eastburne the Elder, late of Southampton, and his wife Margaret, both deceased) for the consideration that they are moving, release to John Eastburne of Southampton, clockmaker (eldest son of John Eastburne the Elder and Margaret his wife) all their share of 206 acres of land in Southampton formerly belonging to John Eastburne their father and their mother Margaret. Said land is bounded by land formerly Isabel Catlen's, now John Naylor's, by land formerly belonging to Peter Groome and John Swift, by the lands of Thomas Herding and Thomas Eastburne and by land late of John Naylor's, deceased, now Charles Biles. Made 24 May 1746. Wit: Horman Vansandt, John Agilly, Thomas Walton the Elder, Isaac Bolton, John Jones, Edwd. Pleadwell. Ackn: 29 May 1746. JP: Benjamin Jones. Rec: 1 Jul 1746.

P. 271   Release. John Eastburne of Southampton, clockmaker, Richard Studam of Philadelphia, taylor, and Mary his wife, and Thomas Walton of the Manor of Moreland in Philadelphia County, yeoman, and Elizabeth his wife (John Eastburne, Mary Studam and Elizabeth Walton are the son and daughters of John Eastburn the Elder, late of Southampton, and Margaret his wife, both deceased) because they are moving, quit claim to Thomas Eastburn of Southampton, yeoman (another son of John Eastburne the Elder and Margaret his wife) part of a parcel of land in Southampton formerly in the possession of John Eastburn the father and after his decease in the possession of his wife Margaret, their mother. Said land is bounded by lands of Thomas Harding and Charles Biles and is 100 acres. Made 24 May 1746. Wit: Thomas Walton, Elder, Isaac Bolton, John Jones, Edwd. Pleadwell. Ackn: 29 May 1746. JP: Benjamin Jones. Rec: 2 Jul 1746.

P. 272   Release. Thomas Tomlinson of Middletown, yeoman, eldest son and heir of Joseph Tomlinson, late of Southampton, yeoman, for 5 shillings and because he is moving, quit claims to Benjamin Tomlinson of Middletown, sadler, another son of said Joseph Tomlinson, a plantation and 113 acres of land in Southampton which formerly belonged to their father. Made 1 Jul 1746. Wit: Langhorne Biles, Lawrence Growdon. Ackn: 1 Jul 1746. JP: Lawrence Growdon. Rec: 18 Jul 1746.

P. 273   Deed. Johanes Vandergrift of Bensalem, yeoman, for love and goodwill, gives to his son Abraham Vandergrift of the same place, the land whereon he (the father) now lives. Made 31 Aug 1743. Wit: Tolehart Vandergrift, Garrat Vansant. Ackn: Jun 1746 by Tolehart Vandergrift and Garrat Vansant on oath that Johanes Vandergrift made this deed "in his lifetime" before JP Mathew Rue. Rec: 22 Jul 1746.

P. 274   Deed. Peter Vanhorn the Elder of Middletown, yeoman, and his wife Elisabeth, for £139, to their son Peter Vanhorn the Younger of the same place, 69½ acres of land in Middletown bounded by the lands of Anthony Wright, Thomas Walmsley, and the other land of Peter Vanhorn the Elder. Said land part of that purchased by Peter Vanhorn the Elder from Frances White. Made 21 Jul 1746. Wit: Wm. Rodman, Lawrence Growdon. Ackn: 21 Jul 1746. JP: Lawrence Growdon. Rec: 3 Jul 1746 [sic.]

P. 276   Mortgage. Samuel Faires of Warwick, clothier, to secure a debt of £80 due 4 Apr 1747, to Abraham Claypoole of Philadelphia, gent., 100 acres of land in Warwick bounded by Neshaminy Creek and by the lands of Hugh Mern, Henry Jamison, Abraham Claypoole, and by Samuel Faires' other land. Said land Abraham Claypoole sold to Samuel Faires 3 Apr 1747. Made 4 Apr 1746. Wit: Arthur Forster, Paul Isaac Voto. Ackn: 5 Apr 1746. JP: John Kinsey. Rec: 4 Aug 1746.

P. 277   Deed. David Oliphant of Warwick, weaver, and Ann his wife, for £50, to Abraham Claypoole of Philadelphia, gent., 42 (45?) acres of land in Warwick bounded by the lands of Jacob Beams, Abraham Claypoole and David Oliphant's other land. Said land part of 236 acres of land in Warwick which John Penn, Proprietor of PA, by patent dated 7 July 17[?] and recorded at Philadelphia in Patent Book A, Vol 8, pg 10, granted to Reuben Allen. Thomas Penn, by authority of said John Penn (to whom the premises were devised by his grandfather Thomas Callowhill by his Last Will and Testament) by deed endorsed on the said patent, confirmed the premises to Reuben Allen. Reuben Allen by indenture dated 22 May 1740 granted the land to John Lock and his wife, who sold the premises to David Oliphant. Made 17 May 1746. Wit: John Kinsey, Jr., Joseph Galloway, John Wilkinson, Jr., James Wood. Ackn: 6 Jun 1746. JP: Richard Mitchell. Rec: 12 Aug 1746.

P. 278   Bond. John Ross of Makefield, weaver, is bound to Robert Edwards, yeoman, for £30. Made 18th da 9th mo 1745. Wit: Joseph Woodford, John Harvey. Ackn: 27 Aug 1746. JP: Lawrence Growdon. Rec: 27 Aug 1746.

P. 279   Bill of Sale. John Ross of Makefield, weaver, for £19, to Robert Edwards of Makefield, yeoman, 2 beds and bed clothes, 3 gowns, 2 great coats, a loom and all tackling belonging to it, 2 iron pots, 2 pails, 3 chairs, a dough trough, a quill wheel, a little wheel, a side saddle, a mans saddle, a bay horse with a bobtail branded "H", 2 cows (one black, one red) and a black calf. Made 20 May 1746. Wit: Richard Plumer, John Monnington, William Thompson. Ackn: 27 Aug 1746. JP: Lawrence Growdon. Rec: 17 Aug 1746.

P. 279   Deed. Henry Kitchin of Amwell, Hunterdon County, New Jersey, husbandman, and Ann his wife, one of the daughters of Gilbert Wheeler, late of Bucks Co., PA, yeoman, deceased, for 300 acres of land in Hunterdon Co., NJ, conveyed to them by John Clarke of Falls Township in Bucks Co., yeoman (son and heir of the other daughter of Gilbert Wheeler) and because they are moving, quit claim to John Clarke their share of two tracts of land in Makefield. In his lifetime, Gilbert Wheeler had two tracts of land in Bucks Co., one of 400 acres in Makefield and the other, also in Makefield, bounded by the lands of William Biles and the River Delaware and containing 500 acres. Made 28 May 1726. Wit: Sarah Green, Samuel Green, James Richards. Ackn: 7 Aug 1731 before JP John Hough by James Richards. Rec: 20 Sep 1746.

P. 280   Deed. John Shaw of Bucks Co., yeoman, and George Willard of the same place, yeoman, executors of the estate of George Willard, deceased, for £130, to William Carter of Philadelphia 2 tracts of land in Southampton. George Willard, deceased, by deed from Joseph Paul dated 21 Aug 1697 and recorded in Book B, Vol 1, pg 141, acquired 246 acres of land in Southampton bounded by John Parsons land and by land late of Arthur Cook, Job Hunt and Philip Conway. George Willard also acquired by deed from John Shaw dated 17th da 12th mo 1698/9, recorded in Book B, Vol 1, pg 243, 100 acres of land in Southampton bounded by other lands of George Willard and John Shaw. By his Last Will and Testament dated 24 January 1705/6, George Willard made John Shaw and George Willard his executors. Made 26 Apr 1718. Wit: Jona. Cockshaw, Jno. Cadwalader, James Shaw. Ackn: 17 Sep 1746. JP: Simon Butler. Rec: 29 Sep 1746.

P. 283   Mortgage. James Baldwin of Philadelphia Co., joyner, for £120, to John Abraham Denormandie of Bristol, Bucks Co., merchant, a plantation and 120 acres of land in Bensalem by the Delaware River by lands formerly belonging to Dank Williams and John Abraham Denormandie. Money to be repaid on or by 17 Dec 1747. Made 4 Apr 1746. Wit: John Hall, John Frohock. Ackn: 12 May 1746. JP: John Hall. Rec: 1 Oct 1746.

P. 284   Release. John Kirkbride of Falls Township, yeoman, £100, to William James of New Brittain, Bucks Co., yeoman, 277 acres of land in New Brittain, part of 2,850 acres which John Sotcher by indenture dated 29 Sep 1722 and recorded in Book B, Vol 2, pg 23 sold to Joseph Kirkbride, lately deceased, father of the said John Kirkbride. In his Last Will and Testament dated 5 Jun 1736, Joseph Kirkbride devised the land to the said John Kirkbride. Made 15 Dec 1738. Wit: S. Butler, Pat Kelly, Arthur (Anthony?) Murphy. Ackn: 6 Dec 1738. JP: Simon Butler. Rec: 15 Nov 1746.

P. 286   Mortgage. John Buley of Warwick, yeoman, and Ann his wife, for £50, to William Gilbert of Warminster, yeoman, a plantation and 103 acres of land in Buckingham by the lands of Josiah Wilkinson, Barnet Vanhorn and Richard Murrey. To be repaid on or by 1 Aug 1748. Made 2 Aug 1746. Wit: Elizabeth Mitchell, Richard Mitchell. Ackn: 2 Aug 1746. JP: Richard Mitchell. Rec: 15 Nov 1746.

P. 288   Deed of Gift. Samuel Gilbert of Warminster, yeoman, for natural love and affection and for 5 shillings and because he is moving, to William Gilbert of the same place, yeoman, son of Samuel Gilbert, a stone messuage and 120 acres of land in Warminster near the road leading to Southampton and by the lands of Charles Bealy, William Miller, H[?] Gilbert, John Radcliff and by land late of Charles Inyard. Said land part of 250 acres granted to Samuel Gilbert by indenture of lease and release dated 24 and 25 May 1721 from James Steel and [?] his wife. Made 1 Jul 1746. Wit: Nicholas Gilbert, Esther Gilbert, John Hart. Ackn: 31 Jul 1746. JP: Benjamin Jones. Rec: 17 Nov 1746.

P. 289   Mortgage. Margaret Patterson of Bucks Co., widow, to Richard Peters and Lynford Lardner, both of Philadelphia, gents., to secure a debt of £23.6s due to John Penn, Thomas Penn and Richard Penn, Proprietors of PA, a plantation and 155 acres of land by the London Company's land. To be repaid in 5 annual payments on or by 12 Jun 1751. Made 12 Jun 1746. Wit: James Devies of Tohickon, John Callahan of Philadelphia. Ackn: 11 Nov 1746. JP: Robert Ellis. Rec: 2 Dec 1746. Mortgage released by court decree and recorded in Misc. Book 68, pg 601 on 29 May 1934 by Deputy Recorder Gertrude H. Gulick.

P. 291   Release. Daniel Wright of Bristol, cooper, for 5 shillings and because he is moving, to Andrew Wright of the same place, a moiety (or half-part) of 200 acres of land in Bristol in the Pigeon Swamp by lands formerly belonging to William Hage [Haye?] and Thomas Bowman. Said land part of 500 acres confirmed to Andrew Robertson by patent dated 10 Aug 1685 from James Claypoole and Robert Turner, William Penn's Commissioners. Andrew Robertson sold the land by deed dated 2 Aug 1686 to Daniel Jones, who by assignment on the back of the deed dated 11 Oct 1696, conveyed it to Daniel Smith. By indenture dated 12 May 1702, Daniel Smith sold it to Samuel Smith, who by deed dated 14 Jun 1704 conveyed it to Lemuel Hale. Hale sold the land to Samson Cary by indentures of lease and release dated 26 and 27 Nov 1733. By indentures of lease and release dated 7 and 8 May 1739 Samson Cary and his wife Mary sold the land to Daniel Wright and

Andrew Wright. Made 22 Jan 1746. Wit: Samuel Cary, Jno. Frohock. Ackn: Dec 1746. JP: En. Williams. Rec: Dec 1746.

P. 294   Release. Benjamin Canby of Solebury, yeoman, and Sarah his wife, for £445, to Geysbert Bogert (Boogaert) of the same place, yeoman, 2 pieces of land in Solebury. By indentures of lease and release dated 27 Apr 1731 Thomas Canby, Sr., of Buckingham, yeoman, and Jane his wife, sold to the said Benjamin Canby a plantation and 241 acres of land in Buckingham (now Solebury) bounded by the lands of John Byes, Thomas Canby, Jr. and John Scarbrough. The Canby's also sold to him another parcel of 8½ acres of land bounded by said Bye's land and by Thomas Canby, Jr.'s land together with the adjacent cart way and passage to the adjacent land of Thomas Canby, Sr. (intended to be granted to Thomas Canby, Jr., brother of the said Benjamin Canby.) Made 18 Feb 1745. Wit: Joseph Smith, Jonas Seely. Ackn: 9 Oct 1746. JP: John Wells. Rec: 15 Dec 1746.

P. 295   Mortgage. Jenkin Phillips of Rockhill, yeoman, for £330, to John Moland of Philadelphia (the northern part), gent., a plantation and 308 acres of land in Rockhill, the same place where John Moland lately dwelt and then conveyed to Jenkin Phillips. To be repaid on or by 16 Jun 1748. Made 5 Dec 1746. Wit: C. Brockden, Arthur Forster. Ackn: 5 Dec 1746. JP: John Kinsey. Rec: 22 Jan 1746/7.

P. 297   Release. Nathaniel Irish of Bucks Co., for £55, to Richard Peters of Philadelphia, 225 acres of land which the Proprietors patented 8 Jan 1744 to Nathaniel Irish. Made 12 Jan 1744. Wit: William Allen of Philadelphia, James Bingham. Ackn: 18 Nov 1746. JP: Lawrence Growdon. Rec: 28 Jan 1746.

P. 298   Deed. Henry Brees of Bensalem, yeoman (the eldest son and heir of Henry Brees, late of the same place, deceased) and Margaret his wife, Hannah Brees (widow of Henry Brees the father,) and John Brees (another son of Henry Brees,) for £265, to Isaac Larew of Bensalem, carpenter, the southern part of a moiety of 400 acres of land bounded by the lands of Edmund Durham, John Brees, Samuel Scott, Peter Statts, and David and Edmund Dunkan containing 200 acres.

By indentures of lease and release dated 24 and 25 Oct 1681, William Penn granted 5,000 acres of PA land to Lawrence Growdon and on the same day granted 5,000 acres to Joseph Growdon (son of said Lawrence Growdon.) A tract of 6,507 acres in Bensalem was laid out by warrant and by indentures of lease and release dated 25 and 26 Jun 1707, Lawrence Growdon granted his 5,000 acres to his grandson Lawrence Growdon, son of the said

Joseph Growdon. Upon a writ of partition at the Supreme Court in Philadelphia in Apr 1737, the younger Lawrence Growdon was awarded a moiety of the land (2,957 acres) by a proprietary patent dated 1 Oct 1737 that was recorded at Philadelphia in Commission Book A, Vol 8, pg 81. The other moiety of 6,507 acres was claimed by other persons, among whom was Henry Brees the Father who, on 5 Jun 1733 (recorded in Book B, Vol 2, pg 79) purchased part of it from Arthur Searl, who inherited the land from his father Frances Searl by his Last Will and Testament, who purchased 400 acres (part of the 6,507 acres) from the said Joseph Growdon 1st da 6th mo 1697 (recorded in Book B, Vol 1, pg 143.) By petition dated 17 Nov 1737, Lawrence Growdon the grandson released 200 acres of the land (part of the said 400 acres) to Henry Brees the Father. The other 200 acres he held and is the part intended to be granted here in this deed.

Henry Brees in his lifetime held the 400 acres, and made his Will dated 2 Feb 1736, leaving annuities for his wife Hannah, £100 to each of his four daughters and the rest of the estate to his two sons Henry and John, decreeing that the first of them to marry shall settle on the north part of his plantation. He died shortly after making the Will. John Brees was the first to marry and the northernmost 200 acres of land went to him. The southernmost part (being sold here) went to Henry Brees (the son.) The daughters Margaret with her husband Jacob Vansant and Nealiha with her husband John Rodman, each received their £100. The other daughters, Sarah and Hannah, who are underage, released the obligation through their guardians Hannah Brees and Phillip Tilleyer. Made 15 Aug 1745. Wit: Phillip Tilleyer, Tho. Homer, John Rodman, Jr., Garret Vansant, Garret Vansant, Jr. Ackn: 25 Apr 1745. JP: Benjamin Jones. Rec: 29 Jan 1746/7.

P. 301   Release.   William Paxson of Middletown, yeoman; Thomas Paxson of the same place, yeoman; Henry Paxson of Mount Holly, NJ, tanner; James Paxson of Middletown, yeoman; and William Wildman of the same place and Deborah his wife, for £340, to Joseph Richardson of the same place, merchant, five one-sixth parts of a plantation and 200 acres of land in Middletown bounded by the lands of William Plumbly, James Paxson, William Paxson, John Vansant and by land formerly belonging to Jeremiah Langhorne. Said land part of 3 tracts of 150 acres, 50 acres and 90 acres of which the 150 acres is part of a larger tract granted to Henry Paulin by patent from James Claypoole and Robert Turner and dated 17th da 3rd mo 1686. Henry Paulin sold it 1st da 7th mo 1686 (recorded in Book A, Vol 1, pg 60) to William Paxson the Elder.

The 50 acre tract was granted by Henry Paulin on 13th da 1st mo 1688 (recorded in Book A, Vol 1, pg 118) to John Taylor, who on 1st da 8th mo 1688 sold it to John Smith. It was then sold by John Smith on 3rd da 10th

mo 1692 (recorded in Book B, Vol 1, pg 47) to John Burling, who sold it on 9th da 8th mo 1695 (recorded in Book B, Vol 1, pg 48) to William Paxson the Elder.

The 90 acre tract is part of 800 acres which is part of a larger tract which William Penn patented to William Wigans, Frances Dove and Edward Lamways. They sold the 800 acres by indentures of lease and release dated 6 and 8 Sep 1687 to Thomas Langhorne. Thomas Langhorne died intestate and the 800 acres descended to his children Jeremiah Langhorne and Sarah Biles nee Langhorne. Then Jeremiah Langhorne, William Biles and his wife the said Sarah Biles by deed dated 9th da 4th mo 1697 and recorded in Book B, Vol 1, pg 133 granted the aforesaid 90 acres to William Paxson the Elder. In his Last Will and Testament, William Paxson the Elder left to his son William Paxson, father of the above named William Paxson, Thomas Paxson, etc., parties to this deed, all his land on the south side of the high road leading from Neshaminy to the Falls (including the said 200 acres.) William Paxson the Father made his Last Will and Testament and gave to his son John Paxson 200 acres of the land on the south side of the Kings Road leading from Neshaminy Creek to the Falls and further willed as follows: "if either my son Thomas, John, James or Henry die before they attain at twenty-one years of age then I do will that the said lands herein bequeathed to such son or sons so deceasing be equally divided amongst all my surviving children." He appointed Mark Watson and Nathan Watson to make a division of the lands bequeathed to his sons within one year after his death. The Watsons surveyed and laid out the 200 acres to John Paxson, but he died before he reached 21 years and the land descended to his siblings William Paxson, Thomas Paxson, Mary Richardson nee Paxson, Henry Paxson, James Paxson and Deborah Wildman nee Paxson. Made 8 Dec 1746. Wit: Nathan Watson, Jno. Frohock. Ackn: 8 Dec 1746. JP: Mark Watson. Rec: 10 Feb 1746/7.

P. 304   Release.   Lawrance Growdon of Trevose in Bensalem, and Langhorne Biles of Bucks Co., gent., two of the executors of the Last Will and Testament of Jeremiah Langhorne, lately deceased, for £200.8s, to William Davies of New Britain, yeoman, 167 acres of land in New Britain bounded by the lands of David Morgan, Robert Shewell, Walter Shewell and Thomas Barton. Said land part of a 5,200 acre tract formerly owned by Jeremiah Langhorne.

Free Society of Traders members Charles Read, Job Goodson, Evan Owen, George Fitzwater and Joseph Pidgeon, all merchants of Philadelphia, by their deed dated 25 Mar 1724 and recorded in Book A, Vol 2, pg 300, conveyed to Jeremiah Langhorne 5,200 acres of land in Bucks Co., who later sold off several parcels of the tract before he died. In his Last Will and Testament, he devised the remainder of his estate to Lawrence Growdon and Langhorne Biles, his nephews, to be divided between them equally. He named Lawrence Growdon, Langhorne Biles and Joseph Turner his executors. Jeremiah Langhorne's Will was dated 16 May 1742 and recorded in Will Book B, Pg 19. Made 14 Nov 1746. Wit: Aaron James, Elizabeth Votring, Thomas James. Ackn: 28 Jan 1746/7. JP: Simon Butler. Rec: 6 Feb 1746/7.

P. 307   Release. Lawrence Growdon of Bensalem and Langhorne Biles of Bucks Co., gents., two of the executors of the Last Will and Testament of Jeremiah Langhorne, deceased, for £327.10s, to Thomas Jones of Hilltown, taylor, 327½ acres of land in Hilltown bounded by the lands of Barnard Yong, John Williams, Lewis Evan, John Lewis, Lawrence Growdon and Thomas Jenney. Said land part of a 1,000 acre tract which itself is part of a larger tract of 3,000 acres.

William Penn, by indentures of lease and release dated 7 and 8 Jan 1701, granted to George Beal of Surrey in Great Britain, yeoman, 3,000 acres of land in Pennsylvania. George Beal of Warburrow, County Surrey, Great Britain conveyed by indentures of lease and release dated 17 and 18 Oct 1718 the 3,000 acres to Jeremiah Langhorne. By warrant obtained from the Proprietors Richard Hill, Isaac Norris and James Logan dated 15 Jul 1717, George Beal had 1,000 acres of the land surveyed and laid out for Jeremiah Langhorne in Hilltown. In his Last Will and Testament dated 16 May 1742, Jeremiah Langhorne empowered his executors Lawrence Growdon, Langhorne Biles and Joseph Turner to dispose of his lands. Made 26 Dec 1744. Wit: Thomas James, Benjamin Allman. Ackn: 11 Feb 1746. JP: Mathew Rue. Rec: 10 Mar 1746/7.

P. 310   Deed. Thomas Clarke of Falls Township, gent., for £729, to Anthony Wright, Charles Wright and Thomas Wright, all of Bucks Co., yeomen, 486 acres of land in Bristol bounded by the lands of Joshua Wright, Samuel Brelsford, _____ Headly, _____ Sysom and _____ Stackhouse. Said land part of 742 acres formerly belonging to John Bur[?,] deceased, and taken to satisfy a lawsuit filed by Joseph Turner. The land was sold at public auction to Thomas Clarke by deed acknowledged in open court 17 Mar 1742 (recorded in Book B, Vol 3, pg 46.) Made 15 Oct 1743. Wit: John Abraham Denormandie, John Frohock. Ackn: 19 Oct 1743 before JP John Abraham Denormandie. Rec: 21 Mar 1746/7.

P. 313   Release. John Morris of Southampton, yeoman, for 20 shillings and because he is moving, to Jeremiah Dungan of Northampton, yeoman, Robert Parsons of Northampton, weaver, John Hart of Warminster, yeoman and Thomas Dungan of Warminster, carpenter, 112½ acres of land in

Southampton bounded by the lands of Cornelius Wincope, Thomas Duffield, Thomas Kirk, _____ Shippen, and by the Widow Fletcher's land. Also a log house and an acre of land in Southampton bounded by the lands of Richard Letham and John Morris, part of a larger tract of 582 acres.

James Plumly, deceased, by deed dated 20 Jan 1698 and recorded in Book B, Vol 1, pgs 218-219, conveyed to John Morris land in Southampton reputed to contain 582 acres. The land was resurveyed and found to be 572 acres. The Proprietary Commissioners Edward Shippen, E. Owen, Thomas Story and James Logan, by patent dated 16 Jul 1705 and recorded at Philadelphia in Patent Book A, Vol 3, pg 148, confirmed the 572 acres to John Morris. By indentures of lease and release dated 17 and 18 Apr 1730, William Cooper and his wife Mary of Philadelphia, husbandman, sold to John Morris 112½ acres of land in Southampton. Made 11 Nov 1732. Wit: Benj. Griffith, Stephen Watts, Joseph Shaw. Ackn: 23 Aug 1746. JP: Benjamin Jones. Rec: 2 Apr 1747.

P. 317   Declaration of Trust. Jeremiah Dungan of Northampton, yeoman, Robert Parsons of the same place, weaver, John Hart of Warminster, yeoman, and Thomas Dungan of the same place, carpenter (members of the Christian Society or Congregation of People called Baptists who usually meet at their meeting house in Lower Dublin in Philadelphia Co., in Philadelphia or in Southampton) promise to John Morris of Southampton, yeoman (who is also a member of the aforesaid Society) to keep the land conveyed to them for the use of the Society for it's meetings, ministers, and burying ground. (John Morris previously conveyed to Jeremiah Dungan, Robert Parsons, John Hart and Thomas Dungan a log house on one acre of land and also 112½ acres in Southampton.) Made 11 Nov 1732. Wit: Stephen Watts, Joseph Banes. Ackn: 5 Feb 1746/7. JP: Benjamin Jones. Rec: Apr 1747.

P. 320   Mortgage. Robert Cumings of Northampton, yeoman, to secure a debt of £300, to William Attwood of Philadelphia, merchant, a plantation and 240 acres of land in Northampton bounded by the lands of James Worth, George Dungan and by Robert Cumings' other land. Said land that which Thomas Lay sold to Robert Cumings by indenture dated 15 Jul 1738. Also a plantation and 200 acres of land in Northampton by Neshaminy Creek. Said land that which William Attwood sold to Robert Cumings by indenture dated 5 Dec 1746. To be repaid in 9 annual payments, final payment due on or by 6 Dec 1756. Made 6 Dec 1746. Wit: Allwood Shute, Arthur Forster of Philadelphia. Ackn: 17 Dec 1746. JP: John Kinsey. Rec: 22 Apr 1747. Memo: Mortgage released by Decree of the Court of Common Pleas. See Misc. Book #66, pg 235. Rec. 2 Jul 1930 by John W. Cooper. Again by Decree of Court of

Common Pleas dated 13 Sep 1941 and recorded by Fredrick W. Randal. See Misc. Book #78, pg 480.

P. 323   Deed. Isaac Penington, Sheriff of Bucks Co., for £256, to John Watson, yeoman, a plantation and 250 acres of land in Middletown bounded by the lands of John Wildman, John Canby, Euclydus Longshore and Joseph Wildman. Said land descended to Thomas Croasdale from his father John Croasdale, who died intestate.
   Sheriff Penington was commanded to seize the land and goods of Thomas Croasdale, late of Newtown, yeoman, also called Thomas Croasdale of Middletown, to satisfy a debt of £69.5s.2p and 65s.11p due to Thomas Howard and James Hamilton, administrators of the estate of John Beaks, deceased, and to have the money at the Court of Common Pleas to be held at Newtown 15 Jun 1732. The Sheriff seized Thomas Croasdale's plantation and 250 acres of land in Middletown. The land remained unsold for a year and was ordered by the court on 16 Jun 1733 to be put up for public auction and the money to be ready for the Court of Common Pleas to be held 13 Sep 1733. Made 20 Sep 1733. Wit: Joseph Pearce, Nathan Watson, Thomas Watson. Ackn: 14 Mar 1733/4. JP: Jeremiah Langhorne. Rec: 23 Apr 1747.

P. 326   Release. William Shreve of Northampton, yeoman, and Freelove, his wife, for £200, to Joseph Linton of the same place, cordwainer, 151 acres of land in Northampton by Neshaminy Creek bounded by the lands of Christian Vanhorn, Benjamin Dyer and Joseph Linton's other land, part of 266 acres previously belonging to the children of James Dyer, deceased.
   James Dyer, late of Northampton, gent., deceased, owned a tract of 266 acres of land in Northampton by Neshaminy Creek and bounded by the lands of Christian Vanhorn, Jeremiah Bartholomew and William Carter. The land (and other lands of James Dyer) descended to Charles Dyer, James Dyer, Benjamin Dyer, Joseph Dyer, Samuel Dyer, Freelove Dyer, the wife of the said William Shreve, Martha Dyer, wife of John Algan, and Comfort Dyer, wife of Humphrey Stringer, all children of the said James Dyer, deceased.
   Charles Dyer and Elizabeth; John Algan and Martha; James Dyer and Hannah; Benjamin Dyer and Deborah; Samuel Dyer and Hannah; and Humphrey Stringer and Comfort by deed dated 12 Apr 1742 released their rights to their father's 266 acres of land to the said William Shreve. Made 3 May 1743. Wit: Wm. Carter, Jno. Duncan. Ackn: 1 May 1743. JP: Lawrence Growdon. Rec: 24 Apr 1747.

P. 329   Release. Benjamin Tomlinson of Middletown, sadler, and his wife Elizabeth, for £250, to Benjamin Scott of Southampton, carpenter, 113 acres of land in Southampton bounded by his brother Thomas Tomlinson's part, now Peter Praules, by the lands of Philip Dracott and by the road leading from the Falls to Philadelphia and the road leading to Bristol.

John Swift of Philadelphia Co., yeoman, by deed dated 13 Sep 1742 and recorded in Book D, Vol 2, pg 298, conveyed to Joseph Tomlinson of Southampton, weaver, late father of the said Benjamin Tomlinson, 8 acres of land in Southampton which is part of a tract of land conveyed to John Swift by Israel Taylor by deed dated 26th da 1st mo 1690. John Naylor, late of Southampton, yeoman, by deed dated 20 Dec 1709 and recorded in Book D, Vol 1, pg 150, sold 110 acres of land in Southampton to Joseph Tomlinson.

This land is part of a tract of land confirmed by patent dated 29th da 11th mo 168[3?] to Nicholas Avalon who, by deed dated 6th da 4th mo 1686 and recorded in Book A, Vol 1, pg 25, conveyed part of the land - 200 acres - to Edmund Cutler of Southampton. Edmund Cutler died intestate. His widow Isabel Cutler, administratrix, by deed dated 11th da 8th mo 1698 and recorded in Book B, Vol 1, pg 223, sold the 200 acres to William Paxson, Sr., who on 10th da 1st mo 1700 endorsed the backside of the deed over to Thomas Walmsley and it is recorded in Book C, Vol 1, pg 84. Thomas Walmsley sold it to Evan Griffith of Southampton, cordwainer, by deed dated 7th da 1st mo 1703/4 and recorded in Book C, Vol 1, pg 198. By deed dated 30 May 1706 and recorded in Book C, Vol 1, pg 263, Evan Griffith sold 110 acres of the 200 acres to John Naylor, who then sold it to Joseph Tomlinson, as stated above.

Joseph Tomlinson made his Last Will and Testament dated 30 Oct 1722 and left to his son Thomas Tomlinson when he reaches the age of 21 years 120 acres of land. The remainder of the land he gave to his son Joseph Tomlinson when he reaches the age of 21 years. He wished his sons Thomas and Joseph to each pay £25 to his son Benjamin when he reaches the age of 21 years. If Benjamin should survive either his son Thomas or Joseph then he shall have their legacy. This Will is recorded in Will Book A, folio 71. Joseph Tomlinson the Father died soon after. Joseph Tomlinson the son died under the age of 21 and his brother Benjamin Tomlinson survived him. Thus the remainder of the land descended to his brother Benjamin. By agreement between the two brothers, the plantation was surveyed and a full 120 acres on the southeast side was laid off to Thomas Tomlinson. The remainder of the plantation contained 113 acres. Thomas Tomlinson, by indentures of lease and release quit claimed his share of his father's land to his brother Benjamin (recorded in Book B, Vol 3, pg 272.) Made 19 Jul 1746. Wit: Langhorne Biles, Jno Frohock. Ackn: 21 Jul 1746. JP: Matthew Rue. Rec: 29 Apr 1747.

P. 334   Mortgage.   George Dun of Northampton, yeoman, to secure a debt of £80 due 23 Dec 1747, to John Petty of Philadelphia, merchant, a plantation and 159½ acres of land in Northampton bounded by the lands of Abraham Vanhorn, Ralph Dun, Christian Vanhorne, and by the road to Newtown. Made 23 Dec 1746. Wit: Paul Isaac Voto, Arthur Forster. Ackn: 23 Dec 1746. JP: John Kinsey. Rec: 30 Apr 1747. Memo: John Petty acknowledged full satisfaction of the mortgage from George Dunn on 23 Mar 1750/1. Wit: C. Brockden, Thos. Marsh, Nicholas Wynkoop. Ackn: 20 Apr 1751 before JP Lawrence Growdon by Nicholas Wyncoop.

P. 335   Mortgage. Nicholas Dupree of Bucks Co., yeoman, to secure the repayment of a debt, to William Allen of Philadelphia, 3 islands, one called Maw Wallamink in the River Delaware opposite the plantation where Nicholas Dupree lately dwelt, containing 126 acres. Also an island called the Great Shawna Island in the River Delaware containing 146 acres. The third island lying between small branches of the Delaware, adjacent to land lately held by John Smith, contains 31 acres. These islands are the same that William Allen sold by indentures of lease and release dated 9 and 10 Sep 1733 to Nicholas Dupree.

Also 3 other tracts of land in Bucks Co., one called Shawna Town which is beside the River Delaware and contains 89 acres. The second tract also lies by the River Delaware and contains 112 acres. The third parcel of land, also by the said river, contains 20½ acres. These parcels are the same which William Allen sold to Nicholas Dupree by indentures of lease and release dated 9 and 10 Sep 1733

To be repaid in 8 annual payments, final payment due 1 Jun 1754. Made 31 Dec 1746. Wit: Nathaniel Allen, Joseph Prichard. Ackn: 18 May 1747. JP: Lawrence Growdon. Rec: 27 May 1747. By power of attorney recorded in Book D, Vol 2, pg 659, William Allen acknowledged full satisfaction of the mortgage on 18 Oct 1766. Lawrence Growdon, Recorder.

P. 339   Release. Charles Plumley of Middletown, yeoman, and Ann his wife and Samuel Cary of Newtown, yeoman, and Sarah his wife (Ann and Sarah are two of the daughters of Thomas Stackhouse, late of Middletown, deceased, by his wife Ann, formerly Ann Mayos, widow and executrix of Edward Mayos formerly of Bristol) for 5 shillings and because they are moving, quit claim to Jacob Stackhouse of Middletown, yeoman, eldest son and heir of Ann Mayos (afterwards Ann Stackhouse) by the said Thomas Stackhouse, 2 lots of land. The first lot with a brick house in Bristol is on Redcliff and Cedar Streets and bounded by the lots of Samuel Cary (which formerly belonged to John Sotcher,) Mathias Keen, Henry Nelson and a lot lately belonging to Anthony Burton. The other lot in Bristol lies between Thomas Mariot's lot and the old mill pond. Made 3 Feb 1746. Wit: Edwd.

Roberts, Thomas Tomlinson, Sarah Inslee. Ackn: 9 Feb 1746. JP: Lawrence Growdon. Rec: 16 Jun 1747.

P. 341 Mortgage. Jacob Stackhouse of Middletown, yeoman, to secure a debt of £34.5s, to Arthur Murphy of Pensbury, yeoman, a lot in Bristol on Redcliff and Cedar Streets and bounded by the lots of Samuel Cary (which formerly belonged to John Sotcher,) Mathias Keen, Henry Nelson and a lot lately belonging to Anthony Burton. To be repaid 16 Jan 1747. Made 16 Jan 1746. Wit: Lawrence Growdon, Langhorne Biles. Ackn: 10 Feb 1746. JP: Lawrence Growdon. Rec: 17 Jun 1747.

P. 343 Deed. John Bringhurst of Philadelphia, merchant, and Mary his wife, for £400, to Samuel Sansom of the same place, merchant, land in Northampton. Said land that which by indentures of lease and release dated 7 and 8 Oct 1728, Job Goodson, John Warder, William Fishburn and Joseph Kirkbride, legatees and devisees in trust named in the Last Will and Testament of Samuel Cart, late of Abington, Philadelphia Co., merchant, deceased, and Sarah Cart, widow of Samuel Cart and one of his executors, conveyed to Joseph Trotter of Philadelphia, cutler, 420 acres of land in Bucks Co. by Neshaminy Creek by land laid out to Benjamin East, by land of John Burden, George Willard and James Claypoole. Joseph Trotter, by indentures of lease and release dated 16 and 17 Jan 1728, sold the land to Sarah Cart. Sarah Cart conveyed 210 acres of the land to Thomas Norris and by indentures of lease and release dated 6 and 7 May 1745 sold the rest to Ralph Loftus of the said city, mariner. Ralph Loftus and Jane his wife by deed dated 6 Mar 1746 sold it to John Bringhurst. Made 25 Mar 1746. Wit: Joseph Shippen, J. Reily. Ackn: 25 Mar 1746. JP: Charles Willing. Rec: 6 Jul 1747.

P. 345 Release. Joseph Stretch of Philadelphia, hatter, and Lydia his wife (she is the only issue and heir of Sarah Knight, formerly Sarah Cart, deceased, by John Knight, also deceased, Sarah being one of the children of Samuel Cart,) for 5 shillings and because they are moving, quit claim to Samuel Sansom, all the residue of 420 acres of land (Norris' part excepted.) Made 26 Mar 1746. Wit: Jonathan Zane, J. Reily. Ackn: 27 Mar 1746. JP: Edward Shippen. Rec: 6 Jul 1747. Note: This Release is endorsed on the back of the deed from John Bringhurst and Mary his wife to Samuel Sansom [see previous entry.]

P. 346 Mortgage. John Dougall of Philadelphia, merchant, for £46.15s, to Sarah Price of Northampton, widow, a messuage with 15 acres of land in Northampton by the lands of Benjamin Cotton, John Addis and Sarah Price's land. This is the same land which Sarah Price sold to John Dougall by her indenture dated 9 Jul 1745. To be repaid 24 Feb 1748 in one payment. Made 24 Feb 1746. Wit: Reese Peters, Jr., John [...?...], Jno. Reily. Ackn: 24 Feb 1746. JP: Thomas Greene. Rec: 7 Jul 1747.

P. 348   Lease. Henry Sell of Basingbourne, Cambridge Co., yeoman, for 5 shillings, to John Bangs of Braintree, Essex Co., draper and Benjamin Banges of Stockport, Chester Co., and Alderman of that town, 500 acres of land in Cheltingham near Germantown in Philadelphia Co., 500 acres of land near Buckingham in Bucks Co. and 500 acres of land near Warmester in Bucks Co. All of this land was known as Mary Philips' land.

Henry Sell is the eldest son and heir of Winifred Sell, his late mother, deceased. Winifred Sell was the sister and heir of Robert Jefferson, late of Basingbourne, farrier, deceased, who died intestate. Robert Jefferson was the nephew and heir of Edward Jefferson, late of Ashwell, Hertford Co., malster, who also died intestate. Edward Jefferson purchased from William Penn 1,500 acres of land by indentures of lease and release dated 10 and 11 Oct 1681. Made 11 Sep 1734. Wit: Mathew Day, Robert Lukin.

P. 350   Release. Henry Sell of Basingbourne, Cambridge Co., yeoman, for £5, to John Bangs of Braintree, Essex Co., draper, and Benjamin Banges of Stockport, Cheshire Co., and Alderman of that town, 1,500 acres of land in Pennsylvania. [See previous entry.] Made 12 Sep 1734. Wit: Mathew Day of Halsted in Essex Co., Robert Lukin of Braintree, Essex Co., both in old England. On 12 Oct 1734, Henry Sell appeared before William Chambers, Mayor of Cambridge in Cambridge Co., and acknowledged the two deeds as his. Wit: Guy Lindrey, Town Clerk. Rec: 3 Aug 1747.

P. 354   Lease. Joshua Bangs of Braintree, Essex Co., gent., and Thomas Hough of Stockport, Chester Co., gent., for 5 shillings, to Ebenezer Large of Burlington, NJ, gent., several tracts of land amounting to 1,500 acres of land in Philadelphia County and Bucks County. [See entry for P. 348 above.]

Joshua Bangs is the son and heir of John Banges, late of Braintree, deceased. Thomas Hough is the son and heir of Mary Hough, his mother, also deceased, and also heir of Elizabeth Clarridge, deceased, who died without issue. The said Mary Hough and Elizabeth Clarridge were daughters and heirs of Benjamin Bangs of Stockport, Alderman of that town, also now deceased. John Bangs and Benjamin Bangs purchased 1,500 acres from Henry Sell of Basingbourne, Cambridge Co., yeoman. Made 28 May 1746. Wit: John Hollis, Edmund Peekover.

P. 356   Release. Joshua Bangs of Braintree, Essex Co., gent., and Thomas Hough of Stockport, Chester Co., gent., for £200, to Ebenezer Large of

Burlington, NJ, gent., several tracts of land amounting to 1,500 acres of land. [See above entry.] Made 29 May 1746. Sworn to at Goldsmith Hall, London, on 30 May 1746 by Edmund Peekover of Wells in the County of Norfolk, gent., and John Hollis of Brownlow Street in the Parish of Saint Andrew Holborn in the County of Middlesex, before Richard Hoare, Lord Mayor of the City of London. Rec: 5 Aug 1747.

P. 360   Mortgage. William Hill of Bristol, sadler, and Elizabeth his wife, to secure a debt of £40, to Mary Martin, Jr., of Bucks Co., spinster, a lot of land in Bristol by Mill Creek fronting Farewell Alley to Mill Street. To be repaid in one payment on or by 8 Jun 1751. Made 8 Jun 1747. Wit: Abraham Bown, Jno. Frohock. Ackn: 8 Jun 1747. JP: John Hall. Rec: 10 Sep 1747.

P. 362   Lease. William Allen of Philadelphia, and Margaret his wife, for 5 shillings, to William Murray of Sawcong in Bucks Co., yeoman, 200 acres of land at Sawcong bounded by the land of Joseph Samuels. Made 20 Jan 1740/1. Wit: Wm. Parsons, James Bingham.

P. 362   Release. William Allen of Philadelphia, and Margaret his wife, for £100, to William Murray of Sawcong in Bucks Co., yeoman, 200 acres of land. [See above entry.] Said land is part of 10,000 acres which William Penn, by his Last Will and Testament, left to his grandson William Penn, to be set out in a proper place by his Trustees. William Penn the Grandson conveyed the land to William Allen by indenture dated 29 Aug 1728 and recorded at Philadelphia in Book F, Vol 5, pg 92. The said 200 acres being granted here was laid out on 6 Nov 1733 to William Allen by Benjamin Eastburn, Surveyor General, as part of the 10,000 acres. Made 21 Jan 1740/1. Wit: Wm. Parsons, James Bingham. Ackn: 2 Mar 1742/3. JP: Nathaniel Irish. Rec: 11 Sep 1747.

P. 364   Mortgage. Sebastian Henry Knaufs of Upper Milford, Bucks Co., wheelwright, to secure a debt of £54, to Joseph Spangenberg of Bethlehem, clerk, Charles Brockden of Philadelphia, gent., and Timothy Horsefield of Brookland of Kings County, Nassau Island in New York, butcher, a plantation with 200 acres of land in Upper Milford bounded by the lands of Jacob Ehrenhart. The money loaned is properly the money of Thomas Noble, Isaac Noble, James Noble and Mary Noble, infants under the age of 21 years, the surviving children of Thomas Noble, late of New York City, merchant, deceased. To be repaid on or by 1 Oct 1748. Made 1 Oct 1747. Wit: David Miller, J. Okely. Ackn: 2 Oct 1747. JP: Henry Antes. Rec: 13 Oct 1747.

P. 366   Mortgage.   Jacob Ehrenhart of Upper Milford, blacksmith, to secure a debt of £25, to Joseph Spanagenberg of Bethlehem, clerk, Charles Brockden of Philadelphia, gent., and Timothy Horsefield of Brookland, Kings Co., Nassau Island, New York, butcher, a plantation and 126 acres of land in Upper Milford bounded by the line of Henry Sebastian Knaufs, late of Geo. Hoffman. The money loaned is properly the money of Thomas Noble, Isaac Noble, James Noble and Mary Noble, infants under the age of 21 years, the surviving children of Thomas Noble, late of New York City, merchant, deceased. To be repaid on or by 1 Oct 1748. Made 5 Oct 1747. Wit: David Miller, J. Okely. Ackn: 2 Oct 1747. JP: Henry Antes. Rec: 13 Oct 1747.

P. 367   Mortgage.   John Eastburn of Southampton, yeoman, to secure a debt of £110, to Sarah Danby of Philadelphia, widow and executrix of John Danby, late of said city, distiller, deceased, a plantation and 102 acres of land in Southampton bounded by land formerly Isabel Cutler's, now or late John Naylor's, by land formerly Peter Groom's, by land lately sold to John Gilleylan by John Eastburn, and by land late of John Naylor's, deceased, now in the tenure of Charles Biles. To be repaid on or by 1 Oct 1748. Made 1 Oct 1747. Wit: George Okill, Rob. Greenway. Ackn: 12 Oct 1747 before JP Lawrence Growdon. Rec: 14 Oct 1747. Memo: Sarah Danby acknowledged full satisfaction of the mortgage Apr 1750. The money was paid to Richard Peters, assignee of Sara Danby. Rec: 25 May 1750 by Lawrence Growdon, Recorder of Deeds.

P. 369   Deed.   Daniel Burges, Joseph Burges and John Burges, yeoman, all of Bucks Co., for 5 shillings and because they are moving, to Daniel Burges, Jr., a son of the said Joseph Burges, 2 tracts of land in Falls Township, excepting the land granted to the Quakers and the 6 acres granted by their father Samuel Burges to Thomas Jenney. The first tract of land contains 76 acres and lies in Falls Township bounded on the north by the land of John Burges, on the west by John Burges' land and 6 acres granted to the Quakers for a graveyard and meetinghouse, on the south by John Hutchinson's land and on the east by land called the Common. This land is part of 200 acres granted to Samuel Burges, father of said Daniel, Joseph and John Burges, by deed dated 1st da 10th mo 1685 from John and Thomas Rowland. The other parcel is of 140 acres of land in Falls Township bounded on the south by Pensbury Manor, on the west by the Great Timber Swamp and on the north and east by William Allen's land. This land is part of 300 acres granted to the said Daniel Burges by deed dated 3rd da 10th mo 1697 from John Rowland.

Granted on the conditions that the first named Daniel Burges and Dorothy his wife shall have the whole use and benefits of the land during his and her natural life and the said Daniel Burges, Jr. shall live with him the said Daniel Burges his Uncle during his natural life. If he chooses to live else where then he shall pay his Uncle £20 a year for every year that he the said Uncle lives. After the decease of Daniel Burges the Uncle and his wife, the said Daniel Burges, Jr. shall have the property free and clear. If Daniel Burges, Jr. should die and leave no issue, then John Burges, another son of the said Joseph Burges, shall have the 2 tracts of land. Memo: If Dorothy Burges, wife of the first named Daniel Burges, should marry again, she shall surrender the premises and have no further right to the property. Made 7 May 1745. Wit: William Atkinson, Margaret Atkinson, Joseph Atkinson. Acknowledged on 20 Jun 1745 by Daniel Burges, Joseph Burges and John Burges before JP John Abraham Denormandie. Rec: 27 Oct 1747.

P. 371   Release. Isaac Penington of Bristol, gent., for £33, to Christian Vanhorn of Northampton, yeoman, 19¼ acres of land in Northampton by the road from Newtown to Robert Heaton's mill, by Nicholas Winecup's land and by Christian Vanhorn's land. Said land part of 651 acres which William Penn patented 21 Oct 1701 to Edward Penington, late of Philadelphia, gent., who died intestate leaving only one son, the said Isaac Penington. Made 24 May 1739. Wit: John Frohock, John Shaw. Ackn: 26 Oct 1747 by John Shaw before JP Benjamin Jones. Rec: 4 Nov 1747.

P. 374   Lease. Christian Vanhorn of Northampton, yeoman, for 5 shillings, to John Vanhorn of the same place, yeoman, son of the said Christian Vanhorn, 128¾ acres of land in Northampton by the Newtown road, by the land of Nicholas Winecope, and by Christian Vanhorne's other land. Made 5 Jun 1745. Wit: Josh Jones, Benj. Jones. Rec: 4 Nov 1747.

P. 375   Release. Christian Vanhorn, for 10 shillings and for natural love and affection and because he is moving, to his son John Vanhorn, 128¾ acres of land by the land of Nicholas Winecope and by Christian Vanhorn's other land [see previous entry.] William Penn by patent dated 6th da 2nd mo 1686 granted to Christopher Taylor 500 acres of land near Neshaminy Creek. William Hibbs of Northampton, who previously purchased 119 acres of the aforesaid 500 acres, by indentures of lease and release dated 12 and 13 Jul 1731, sold the 119 acres to Christian Vanhorn (recorded in Book B, Vol 2, pg 190.) William Penn by patent dated 21 Oct 1701 granted 651 acres of land in Northampton to Edward Penington. Edward Pennington died intestate, leaving the land to his only issue, one son, Isaac Penington, who by deed dated 24 May 1739 sold 19¼ of those acres to Christian Vanhorne. Made 5 Jun 1745. Wit: Josh Jones, Benj. Jones. Ackn: 8 Jun 1745. JP: Benjamin Jones. Rec: 4 Nov 1747.

P. 377   Mortgage. John Gilleylen of Philadelphia, merchant, to secure a debt of £200, to John Eastburn of Moorland, Philadelphia Co., glazier, 106 acres of land and plantation in Southampton bounded by the lands of John Thomas Harding and Charles Biles. This is the same land which the said John Eastburn conveyed to John Gilleylen. To be repaid 17 Oct 1748. Made 17 Oct 1747. Wit: Lawrence Growdon, Langhorne Biles. Ackn: 7 Oct 1747. JP: Lawrence Growdon. Rec: 5 Nov 1747. Memo: On 30 May 1751 John Eastburn acknowledged full satisfaction of the mortgage before Lawrence Growdon, Recorder.

P. 378   Mortgage. Robert Heaton of Northampton, yeoman, and Ann his wife, to secure a debt of £600, to William Clymer of Philadelphia, merchant, a dwelling house and grist mill with 340 acres of land in Northampton on Mill Creek by the road which leads from the Falls to Philadelphia and bounded by the lands of John Naylor, Thomas Harding, Samuel Allen, James Carter, Christopher Weatherel and Ralph Draycot. To be repaid on 13 Dec 1747. Made 13 Jun 1747. Wit: John Ross, George Ross, Jr. Ackn: 16 Oct 1747. JP: Abraham Chapman. Rec: 5 Nov 1747. On 6 Nov 1752, Margaret Climer, widow of William Clymer, lately deceased, and named executrix of his Last Will and Testament, acknowledged full satisfaction of the mortgage before Lawrence Growdon. Rec: 29 Dec 1753.

P. 380   Mortgage. John Hill of Buckingham, yeoman, and his wife Sarah, to secure a debt of £300, to George Emlen of Philadelphia, brewer, 107 acres of land in Buckingham bounded by the lands of John Large, Margaret Atkinson and James Streater. Also another 125 acres of land in Buckingham bounded by the lands of Thomas Gilbert, Matthew Hughes, Mary Gilbert, and by John Hill's other land. To be repaid by or on 1 Nov 1748. Made 1 Nov 1747. Wit: C. Brockden, Arthur Forster. Ackn: 7 Nov 1747. JP: Lawrence Growdon. Rec: 23 Nov 1747. Mortgage released by court decree. See Misc. Book No. 54, pg 405.

P. 382   Deed. Henry Paxson, Jr., of Masn [sic,] yeoman, for £45, to John Dark of Falls Township, yeoman, 100 acres of land in Falls Township bounded by the lands of William Paxson, Giles Lucas, William White, John Dark and the said Henry Paxson. Said land is part of 380¾ acres which James Paxson, father of the said Henry Paxson, conveyed to the said Henry Paxson, Jr., by deed which is recorded in Book B, Vol 1, pgs 123-124. Made 8 May 1717. Wit: John Parsons, Wm. Strutt, Jer. Langhorn. Ackn: 12 Oct 1747. JP: John Wells. Rec: 18 Dec 1747.

P. 385   Deed of Gift. Thomas Head of Plumstead, yeoman, for love and affection, give to my loving son John Head of Solebury, turner, 100 acres of land in Solebury bounded by the lands of Henry Paxson and John Dawson, which is part of 220 acres bought from John Dawson. Made 26 Apr 1743. Wit: John Wells, Mary Wells. Ackn: 29 Apr 1743. JP: John Wells. Rec: 13 Jan 1747/8.

P. 386   Deed. Henry Paxson of Mountholly, NJ, tanner, and Martha his wife, for £50, to Samuel Johnson of Bristol, carpenter, 2 lots in Bristol. The first lot by Mill Street and Wood Street is bounded by a lot formerly John Rowland's. The other lot lies by Wood Street and Market Street bounded by a lot that was John Rowland's and by the first described lot. Both lots formerly belonged to James Moon of Bristol and his wife Agnes who by indentures of lease and release dated 19 and 20 Sep 1719 conveyed the lots to William Watson of Bristol and his wife Hannah who sold the lots to Joseph Bond of Bristol by indentures of lease and release dated 25 and 26 Jan 1721. Joseph Bond and his wife Ann, by indentures of lease and release dated 7 and 8 Sep 1724, sold the lots to Joan Forrest of Philadelphia, widow, who sold them to William Paxson of Middletown by indentures of lease and release dated 19 and 20 Sep 1730. William Paxson made his Last Will and Testament dated 17 Jan 1734 and bequeathed the 2 lots to his son Henry Paxson. Made 31 Oct 1743. Wit: Wm. Ashburn, John Frohock, William Claypoole. Ackn: 11 Jul 1746. JP: John Abraham Denormandie. Rec: 19 Jan 1747/8.

P. 390   Mortgage. William Mitchel of Buckingham, taylor, to secure a debt of £20, to Mary Wilson, widow of James Wilson, late of Buckingham, deceased, a plantation and 21 acres of land in Buckingham bounded by the lands of Abraham Scott, Richard Church and lands lately William Cooper's. Said land that which Richard Church and his wife Sarah sold to William Mitchel by indentures of lease and release dated 6 and 7 Jan 1742/3. To be repaid on or by 28 Aug 1752. Made 28 Aug 1747. Wit: Thos. Butler, Mary Wilson, Jr., John Watson, Jr. Ackn: 31 Aug 1747. JP: Mathew Hughes. Rec: 20 Jan 1747/8. Memo: On 11 Sep 1757 before Lawrence Growdon, Recorder of Deeds, Daniel Knight of Byberry, Philadelphia Co., yeoman, for Mary Wilson, acknowledged full satisfaction of the mortgage money received from William Mitchel.

P. 392   Bond. Thomas Jones of Makefield, yeoman, is bound to Thomas Yeardley, Thomas Harvey, James Downey, all of the same place, yeomen, for £174.17s, and they are bound to John Shawcross of Oxford, Philadelphia Co., yeoman, for the same amount of money conditioned for the payment of £87.8s to be repaid in one year's time. Made 13 Oct 1729. Wit: Stephen Wilson, Benjamin Harvey. Ackn: 3 Mar 1747. JP: Lawrence Growdon. Rec: 4 Mar 1747.

P. 393   Mortgage. James Grigg of Middletown, yeoman, for £100, to William Allen of Philadelphia, merchant, a plantation with 162½ acres of land in Makefield and bounded by the lands of John Hough, Thomas Scott and John Whitacres. To be repaid on or by 10 Feb 1748/9. Made 10 Feb 1747/8. Wit: George Cremere. Alex. Shiart. Ackn: same day before JP Thomas Greene. Rec: 5 Apr 1748.

P. 395   Deed. John Hall and his wife Sarah of New Bristol, for £20, to Joseph Baldwin, cooper, a 1½ acre lot in New Bristol. John Baldwin of said Bucks Co., by his Last Will and Testament, bequeathed to his daughter Sarah, now wife of John Hall, one half part of 1½ acres of land adjoining a lot of Richard Mountain's and John Large's and is part of a corner lot adjoining Bristol. Said lot that which Samuel Carpenter by deed dated 19 Jun 1707 and recorded in Book D, Vol 1, pgs 30-33 sold to John Baldwin. Made 29 Oct 1728. Wit: Henry Tomlinson, Sarah Tomlinson, Hannah Atkinson. Ackn: 4 Apr 1748. JP: John Abraham Denormandie. Rec: 6 Apr 1748.

P. 396   Release. Joseph Baldwin of Bristol, cooper, and Ann his wife, for £30, to Samson Cary of Bristol, merchant, a ¾ acre lot in Bristol by the road to Newtown and at a corner of Richard Mountain's lot, and by the land of John Baldwin and John Large. Said ¾ acre is part of a lot containing 1½ acres that Samuel Carpenter sold to John Baldwin by deed recorded in Book D, Vol 1, pgs 30-33. By his Last Will and Testament dated 24 Aug 1711, John Baldwin bequeathed the lot to his three sons and daughter Sarah, now wife of John Hall. He gave Sarah a half acre, to Joseph Baldwin he gave one third part of an acre. Sarah and her husband John Hall conveyed Sarah's share to her brother Joseph Baldwin [see previous entry.] Made 27 May 1730. Wit: Samson Cary, Jr., Daniel Headly, William Atkinson. Receipt of money acknowledged 26 Nov 1730. Wit: Daniel Headly, Wm. Atkinson. Ackn: 4 Apr 1748. JP: John Abraham Denormandie. Rec: 6 Apr 1748.

P. 398   Deed. Samuel Cary of Retirement, for £50, to Daniel Wright of Bristol, cooper, a lot in Bristol by the road to Newtown by land formerly belonging to Richard Mountain, by the lots of John Baldwin and John Large, containing three-quarters of an acre and 13 and one-third perches. Said lot part of a 1½ acre lot which Samuel Carpenter conveyed to John Baldwin who died and left it to his children, including Sarah, wife of John Hall, and her brother Joseph Baldwin. Joseph Baldwin and his wife Ann sold the lot to

Samson Cary by indentures of lease and release dated 26 and 27 May 1730 [see previous entry.] Samson Cary made his Last Will and Testament dated 9 Feb 1732 and bequeathed the lot to his son the said Samuel Cary. Made 3 May 1746. Wit: James Welch, Charles Reeder. Ackn: 7 May 1746. JP: John Hall. Rec: 8 Apr 1748.

P. 401   Mortgage. Giles Lawrence of Philadelphia, joiner, to secure the payment of several debts, to William Allen and Robert Strettell of said city, one full one-third part of 530 acres of land in Bristol on Neshaminy Creek's northside. Said land lately the estate of John Johnson, deceased. The said third part Giles Lawrence and his wife Wilmeth, who is now deceased and was one of the daughters named in the Last Will and Testament of the said John Johnson, by indenture dated 4 Mar 1745, conveyed to Peter Bard, who with his wife Mary, by indenture dated 13 Mar 1745, conveyed it to Giles Lawrence. To be repaid on or by 16 Mar 1748. Giles Lawrence is also in debt for various sums of money to Joseph Turner, Samuel Cary of Newtown, gent., John Hopkins, Peter Bard and Emerson & Graydon, of said city, merchants. Made 16 Oct 1747. Wit: Anthony Adamson, Rob. Greenway. Ackn: 10 Mar 1747/8. JP: John Kinsey. Rec: 12 Apr 1748.

P. 403   Mortgage. Samuel Faires of Warwick, clothier, to secure a debt of £100, to John Harcomb of Philadelphia, tobacconist, 100 acres in Warwick bounded by the lands of Henry Jemison, Abraham Claypoole, Hugh Mein and by Samuel Faires other land. Said land that which Abraham Claypoole of Philadelphia, gent., by indenture dated 3 Apr 1746 conveyed to Samuel Faires. To be repaid by or on 9 Jan 1748/9. Made 9 Jan 1747/8. Wit: Paul Isaac Voto, Sarah Voto. Ackn: 11 Jan 1747/8. JP: William Till. Rec: 14 May 1748.

P. 404   Deed. Peter Vanhorn the Younger of Middletown, yeoman, and his wife Margaret, for £208.10s, to Peter Vanhorn the Elder of the same place, yeoman, a plantation and 69½ acres of land in Middletown bounded by the lands of Anthony Wright, Thomas Walmsley, and Peter Vanhorn the Elder's other land. Said land that which Peter Vanhorn the Elder and his wife Elizabeth by indentures of lease and release dated 24 Jul 1746 (recorded in Book B, Vol 3, pg 274) conveyed to Peter Vanhorn the Younger. Made 2 Apr 1748. Wit: Sarah Growdon, Mary Harris. Ackn: 4 Apr 1748. JP: Lawrence Growdon. Rec: 14 May 1748.

P. 406   Mortgage. Mathias Keen of Bristol, carpenter, for £80, to Jonathan Price of Philadelphia, carpenter, a house and lot in Bristol on Mill Street by Samuel Cary's lot, by Anthony Burton's lot and by the garden of

Thomas Stackhouse. David Murray, late of Bristol, deceased, had a mortgage on this property for a debt of £150 to Jonathan Price by indenture dated 9 Jun 1743. Alexander Graydon held a lease on the property for 5 years. To be repaid on or by 16 Nov next. Made 16 Nov 1747. Wit: John Frohock, John Frohock, Jr. Ackn: 14 May 1748. Lawrence Growdon. Rec: 15 May 1748.

P. 408   Deed. James Bingham of Philadelphia, merchant, and William Bingham of the same place, sadler (they are the two sons named in the Last Will and Testament dated 24 Aug 1707 of James Bingham, late of said city, sadler) for £550, to John Stephen Benezet of Philadelphia, merchant, 2 tracts of land, each of 500 acres, at the west branch of the Delaware River. The first tract is bounded by the lands of Jeremiah Langhorne and William Allen. The other tract, which adjoins the first, is also bounded by the lands of Jeremiah Langhorne. John Penn, Thomas Penn and Richard Penn, by patent dated 22 Jun 1797 and recorded in Patent Book A, Vol 8, pg 245, granted to James Bingham the Father 4 tracts of land of 500 acres each near the west branch of the River Delaware in Bucks County. James Bingham bequeathed to his sons James and William 500 acres each. Made 1 Jun 1741. Wit: Thomas Gramey, Joseph Pritchard, Jr., C. Brockden, J. Reily. James Bingham acknowledged the deed as his on 1 Jun 1741 before William Allen. William Bingham appeared before William Allen on 9 Dec 1743 and acknowledged the deed. On 1 Jun 1748 Charles Brockden of Philadelphia, gent., appeared before Henry Antis, Justice of the Peace, and acknowledged that he witnessed the signing of the deed. On 1 Jun 1748, John Okely of Bethlehem, gent., appeared before JP Henry Antis to verify the handwriting of the witness Joseph Pritchard, Jr. of Philadelphia, merchant, stating he was well acquainted with him and with his handwriting. Rec: 21 Jun 1748.

P. 412   Deed. William Allen of Philadelphia, merchant, and Margaret his wife, for £100, to Isaac Iselstein of Bucks Co., yeoman, 178 acres of land on the west branch of the Delaware River and an island containing about 10 acres lying opposite the first said tract. Said lands were laid out to William Allen under the right of John and Ann Sharlot Lowther. Made 5 Dec 1740. Wit: John Webb, James Bingham. Ackn: 5 Dec 1740. JP: Nathaniel Irish. Rec: 21 Jun 1748.

P. 413   Mortgage. John Tool of Upper Sacoon, Bucks Co., husbandman, to secure a debt of £120, to Dirck Keyser of Germantown, Philadelphia Co., cordwainer, Isaac Samuel of Bucks Co., yeoman and Thomas Owen of Bucks Co., gent., 200 acres of land in Bucks Co. bounded by the lands of Joseph Samuels, John Landis and William Murray. Said land was patented (dated 24 Sep 1747 and recorded at Philadelphia in Patent Book A, Vol 13, pg 309) to

John Tool. To be repaid on 22 Dec 1748. Made 27 Dec 1747. Wit: Barak Wright, Christian Lehman. Ackn: 28 May 1748. JP: John Jemison. Rec: 21 Jun 1748.

P. 415   Deed. Christian Barnson alias Vanhorn of Northampton, yeoman, and Williamkee his wife, for £100, to Joseph Richardson of Middletown, merchant, 40¾ acres of land which is part of a tract of 80 acres of land in Middletown by land formerly Thomas Baynes and by land formerly _____ Thatchers. The part being conveyed here lies by Newtown Road and is bounded by Christian Barnson alias Vanhorn's land and by the lands of Robert Collison and Joseph Stackhouse. The 80 acres of land is part of 250 acres which the late William Penn, by indenture dated 4 Jul 1682, granted to John Scarborough who, by letter of attorney dated 15 Oct 1696 and recorded in Book B, Vol 1, pgs 250-251, empowered his son John Scarborough to dispose of his lands. In that context, John Scarborough the Son, by deed dated 4 Sep 1699 and recorded in Book B, Vol 1, pg 247, sold the 80 acres to Henry Hudleston. Henry Hudleston made his Last Will and Testament dated 16 Apr 1706 and appointed his "trusty friend and father in law" William Cooper his executor, empowering him to sell the 80 acres, which Cooper, by deed dated 11 Dec 1706 and recorded in Book C, Vol 1, pgs 298-299, sold to Henry Johnson Vandike. By his Last Will and Testament dated 4 Apr 1717, Henry Johnson Vandike gave to his wife Yanica all his estate during her lifetime, and after her decease, to his son Christian Barnson and his granddaughter Susanna Vanvlieg, who later married Henry Vanhorn. Christian Barnson alias Vanhorn and Williamkee his wife and Henry Vanhorn and Susanna his wife by deed dated 3 Aug 1737 and recorded in Book B, Vol 2, pg 202 conveyed the 80 acres to Jeremiah Langhorne, who by deed dated 3 Aug 1737 and recorded in Book B, Vol 2, pg 204 conveyed the 80 acres to Christian Barnson alias Vanhorne. Made 9 Apr 1748. Wit: Adam Harker, Robert Collison, John Frohock. Ackn: 9 Apr 1748. JP: Mark Watson. Rec: 8 Jul 1748.

P. 419   Deed. Alexander Graydon of Philadelphia, merchant, and his wife Rachel, for £262, to Ennion Williams of Bristol, yeoman, 132 acres and 152 perches of land in Bristol by the mill pond and by the lands of Ennion Williams and Joseph Shaw. Said land is part of a tract of land formerly belonging to the estate of John Burke, deceased, and sold at public auction to satisfy a lawsuit filed by William Whitacre and Joseph Jackson, then Sheriff of Bucks County. Alexander Graydon was the highest bidder and purchased the land by deed dated 16th da 7th mo 1743 and recorded in Book B, Vol 3, pg 66. Made 30 Mar 1747. Wit: Francis White, Jr., Joseph Atkinson, John Abraham Denormandie. On 16 Nov 1747 the property was delivered to

Ennion Williams by Alexander Graydon. Wit: John Hutchinson, Joseph Church. The money exchanged hands 2 Apr 1747 and was witnessed by Francis White, Jr., and Joseph Atkinson. Ackn: 3 Apr 1747. JP: John Abraham Denormandie. Rec: 8 Jul 1748.

P. 424 Deed. Presly Raymon of Little Dutch Creek, Kent Co., yeoman, and Mary his wife, Rebecca Steel of Philadelphia, widow, William Shute of the northern liberties of said city, yeoman, and Elizabeth his wife, Richard Renshaw of the said city, baker, and Ann his wife, and James Thompson, under age twenty-one and the only child and heir of Ruth Thompson, late of said city, deceased (the said Mary, Rebecca, Elizabeth, Ann and Ruth are the only children named in the Last Will and Testament of James Steel, late of said city, gent., deceased) for £155, to Nicholas Walver of Upper Milford, Bucks Co., yeoman, 276 acres of land in Upper Milford by the land of Ulrich Reese.

By indenture of release made 21 Jan 1729 and recorded at Philadelphia in Book F, Vol 5, pg 310, Henry D'Avenant of the Parish of Saint Georges, Westminster, Middlesex Co., and Frances his wife, the only daughter and heir of Mary Bathurst, deceased, who was the only sister and heir of Theodore Colby, late of London, deceased, sold to James Steel 2,400 acres of land. Said land the same land which William Markham, late of Philadelphia, since deceased, devised to his wife Joanna Markham by his Last Will and Testament. Joanna Markham in her lifetime granted 2,400 acres of land to her nephew the said Theodore Colby, who died intestate and without issue so the land descended to Henry D'Avenant and his wife Frances.

By warrant dated 26 Mar 1733 the land was surveyed on 24 Apr 1734 to James Steel. James Steel agreed to sell (but did not actually convey) 276 acres of the land for £189 to Nicholas Walver for which Walver made a partial payment of £34. Then by his Last Will and Testament dated 21 Dec 1741, James Steel requested that his land (including the 276 acres) be equally divided between his 5 daughters, Mary Hilliard, Rebecca Steel, Elizabeth Shute, Ann Renshaw and Ruth Thompson. Made 2 Jun 1747. Wit: John Clifton, Adam Laster, Joseph Groves, Daniel Forest, Benjamin Jones, Thomas Renshaw, Stephen Sanders. Ackn: 18 Mar 1747. JP: Benjamin Jones. Rec: 11 Jul 1748.

P. 426 Mortgage. James Baldwin of Bensalem, joiner, to secure a debt of £150, to Mary Carter of Philadelphia, widow, a plantation with 120 acres of land in Bensalem by the Delaware River by land formerly Dunk Williams and by the land of John Abraham Denormandie. To be repaid by 18 Mar 1748/9. Made 18 Mar 1747/8. Wit: Arthur Forster, Paul Isaac Voto. Ackn: 19 Mar 1747. JP: William Buckley. Rec: 11 Jul 1748.

P. 428   Mortgage. Samuel Allen of Philadelphia but late of Bensalem, yeoman, for a debt of £100, to Henry Van Ahen of Philadelphia, merchant, 28½ acres of land in Bensalem by Neshaminy Creek and bounded by the lands of John Johnson, Richard Johnson and by Samuel Allen's other land. Also a 3 acre meadow in Bensalem by Neshaminy Creek adjoining the first tract and bounded by the meadows of John Johnson and Richard Johnson. Said land is that which Claus Johnson, Jacob Johnson, Lawrence Johnson, Robert Goodgeen [sp?] and Rebecca his wife, Joseph Kitchen and Gotha his wife, Peter Johnson, Benjamin Johnson, Jacob Vandergrift and Willmuth his wife, and Deborah Johnson (the said Claus, Jacob, Lawrence, Peter, Benjamin, Rebecca, Gotha, Willmuth and Deborah are the children of Lawrence Johnson, late of said Bensalem, deceased) by indenture dated 22 May 1747 sold to Samuel Allen. To be repaid by 12 May 1749. Made 12 May 1748. Wit: Paul Isaac Voto, Arthur Forster. Ackn: 12 May 1748. JP: William Till. Rec: 12 Jul 1748.

P. 430   Mortgage. Bartholomew Young of Bucks Co., yeoman, to secure a debt of £348.10s, to William Allen of Philadelphia, 3 tracts of land totaling 648½ acres. One tract bounded by lands intended to be granted to Edward Eaton, Thomas Christy, Joseph Thomas, James Halfpenny and Joseph Dempsy. The second tract adjoins the first. The third tract adjoining the other is bounded by land that is intended to be granted to Thomas Kid and Joseph Dempsey. These 3 tracts of land were sold by indentures of lease and release dated 19 and 20 Apr 1748 by Richard Penn by his attorney Lynford Lardner of Philadelphia, gent., to Bartholomew Young. To be repaid on or by 20 Apr 1749. Made 21 Apr 1748. Wit: Wm. Peters, Alex. Stuart. Ackn: 30 Apr 1748. JP: William Till. Rec: 15 Jul 1748.

P. 433   Deed. Joseph Jackson of Bristol, shopkeeper, for £50, to Ann Burgess of the same place, spinster, a 6 acre lot in Bristol by land formerly Joseph Bond's and by Otter Creek. Made 27 Mar 1744. Wit: John Frohock, Joseph White. Ackn: 23 Jun 1748. JP: Lawrence Growdon. Rec: 15 Jul 1748.

P. 435   Mortgage. Joseph Thomas of Hilltown, yeoman, to secure a debt of £188, to George Davis of Philadelphia, mariner, a plantation and 200 acres of land in Hilltown bounded by the lands of Abraham Ustine, William Britain and Evan Mathias. To be repaid on or by 10 Mar 1748. Made 10 Mar 1747. Wit: Evan Thomas, Arthur Forster. Ackn: 10 Mar 1747. JP: Simon Butler. Rec: 19 Jul 1748. Memo: By power of attorney dated 22 Feb 1765 and recorded in Book D, Vol 2, pg 343, William Allen, executor of the Last Will and Testament of Mary Plumstead, late of Philadelphia, widow, deceased, and executrix of George Davis, acknowledged satisfaction of this mortgage 30 Apr 1765. Recorded by Lawrence Growdon.

P. 436   Deed. Thomas Stevenson of Bensalem, gent., for £130, to Jonas Keen of Bensalem, yeoman, 150 acres of land in Bensalem by Neshaminy Creek and bounded by the lands of George Vansand and Henry Stevenson. Cornelius Vansand and his wife Derica by deed recorded in Book A, Vol 2, pg 43 sold the 150 acres to Thomas Stevenson. Made 13 Oct 1716. Wit: George James, Isaac Penington, Richard Scott. Ackn: 2 Feb 1739 by Isaac Penington before JP Ennion Williams. Rec: 31 Aug 1748.

P. 438   Mortgage. Jacob Maurer of Morris Co., NJ, yeoman, for £100, to William Allen of Philadelphia, 148 acres of land on Tohicton Creek on the north branch of the Delaware River and bounded by the lands of Philip Bartolet and Daniel Worms. Said land is part of 500 acres purchased by Daniel Worms from William Allen and Margaret his wife by indenture dated 14 May 1741. By indenture dated 17 May 1748 Daniel Worms sold it to Jacob Maurer. To be paid by or on 26 Jun 1749. Made 27 Jun 1748. Wit: Wm. Peters, Alex. Stuart. Ackn: 27 Jun 1748. JP: William Till. Rec: 31 Aug 1748. Memo: William Allen acknowledged full satisfaction of the mortgage on 20 Mar 1756. Rec: 20 Jun 1756 by Lawrence Growdon.

P. 440   Mortgage. John Fullerton of Warrington, yeoman, to secure a debt of £33 due to Thomas Penn and Richard Penn, to Richard Peters and Lynford Lardner of Philadelphia, gent., a plantation and 47½ acres of land in Warrington by John Fullerton's other land and by the lands of William Allen, William Walker and William Leech. To be paid in 7 annual payments with the final payment due on 1 Jun 1755. Made 1 Jun 1748. Wit: William Finney of Chester Co., John Callahan of Philadelphia. Ackn: 20 Aug 1748. JP: Lawrence Growdon. Rec: 1 Sep 1748. Richard Peters acknowledged full satisfaction of the mortgage on 19 Dec 1758. Rec: 7 Apr 1759.

P. 442   Mortgage. William Walker of Warrington, yeoman, to secure a debt of £56.16 due to Thomas Penn and Richard Penn, to Richard Peters and Lynford Lardner, both of Philadelphia, gents., a plantation and 110½ acres of land in Warrington by the land William Walker bought from Charles Tennant and bounded by James Huston's land. To be repaid in 7 annual payments with final payment due on 27 Apr 1755. Made 27 Apr 1748. Wit: James Aiskell, John Callahan of Philadelphia. Ackn: 20 Aug 1748. JP: Lawrence Growdon. Rec: 1 Sep 1748. By power of attorney from Richard Peters and Lynford Lardner recorded in Book C, Vol B, pg 265, full satisfaction of the mortgage was acknowledged 8 Jun 1761 by Lawrence Growdon.

P. 447   Mortgage. Ephraim Leech of Warrington, yeoman, to secure a debt of £50.7s.6p due to Thomas Penn and Richard Penn, to Richard Peters and Lynford Lardner, both of Philadelphia, gents., a plantation and 94¾ acres of land in Warrington by the county line and by Ephraim Leech's other land and bounded by the lands of William Leech and Charles Tennant. To be paid in 7 annual payments, final payment due 20 Apr 1755. 20 Apr 1748. Wit: John Callahan of Philadelphia, James Aiskell. Ackn: 20 Aug 48. JP: Lawrence Growdon. Rec: 2 Sep 1748. Satisfaction of mortgage acknowledged 27 Mar 1758.

P. 450   Mortgage. William Leech of Warrington, to secure a debt of £91 due to Thomas Penn and Richard Penn, to Richard Peters and Lynford Lardner, both of Philadelphia, gents., a plantation and 141¾ acres of land in Warrington bounded by the lands of William Walker, Ephraim Leech and John Fullerton. To be paid in 7 annual payments, final payment due 20 Apr 1755. Made 20 Apr 1748. Wit: John Callahan of Philadelphia, James Aiskell. Ackn: 20 Aug 1748. JP: Lawrence Growdon. Rec: 2 Sep 1748.

P. 454   Deed. Nathan Watson of Bristol, cordwainer, for £240, to Daniel Wright of the same place, cooper, 2 pieces of land, the first a meadow in Bristol by Mill Creek bounded by the land formerly belonging to Josiah Langdale and containing 5 acres. The meadow was sold to Nathan Watson by Adam Harker and his wife Grace by indentures of lease and release dated 30 and 31 Jan 1729. The second meadow of 9 acres, also in Bristol, adjoins the first and is bounded by a burying ground and Mill Creek. This meadow was sold to Nathan Watson by Samuel Helton Palsyunk of Philadelphia Co., merchant, and his wife Margaret who was formerly the widow of Josiah Langdale of Bridlington Hey in the County of York, Great Britain, yeoman, deceased, by indenture dated 5 May 1726. Made 25 Jul 1746. Wit: Mark Watson, James Doraugh, Wm. Atkinson, John Frohock, Wm. Buckley. Ackn: 28 Jul 1746. JP: Mark Watson. Rec: 3 Sep 1748.

P. 457   Mortgage. Daniel Wright of Bristol, cooper, and his wife Rebecca, to secure a debt of £200, to Robert Harvey of Falls Township, yeoman, two meadows in Bristol, the first is 5 acres by land formerly Josiah Langdale's and the second is 9 acres, adjoining the first meadow. To be paid on 14 Jun 1749. Made 11 Jul 1748. Wit: John Frohock, Elizabeth Frohock. Ackn: 16 Jul 1748. JP: Ennion Williams. Rec: 3 Sep 1748.

P. 459　　Mortgage. Lewis Evans of New Britain, yeoman, and Madlen his wife, to secure a debt of £100, to William Thomas of Hilltown, yeoman, a plantation and 200 acres of land in New Britain by the lands of Thomas Evans, William Wilson, John Williams, Philip Wood, John Grier, Thomas Steward and Thomas Rowland. To be repaid on or by 15 Nov 1749. Made 20 Jun 1748. Wit: Abel Griffith, Benjamin Griffith. Signed and sealed by Lewis Evans and Magdalen H. Evans. Ackn: 20 Jun 1748. JP: Simon Butler. Rec: 3 Sep 1748.

P. 461　　Deed. Lewis Evans of Hilltown, yeoman, for £100 and for love and affection, to Lewis Evans, Jr., of New Britain, yeoman and second son of the said Lewis Evans, 200 acres of land in New Britain bounded by the lands of Thomas Evans, William Wilson, John Williams, Philip Wood, John Grier, Thomas Steward and Thomas Rowland. Said land is part of 300 acres which John Penn, Thomas Penn and Richard Penn by patent dated 18 Apr 1734 and recorded at Philadelphia in Patent Book A, Vol 6, pg 277, conveyed to Lewis Evans the Father. Made 19 Jun 1748. Wit: Abel Griffith, Benjamin Griffith, William Thomas, Thomas Evan. Ackn: 21 Jun 1748. JP: Simon Butler. Rec: 4 Sep 1748.

P. 465　　Deed. Lewis Evans of Hilltown, yeoman, for £100 and for love and affection, to Thomas Evans of New Britain, yeoman and eldest son of the said Levis Evans, 200 acres of land in New Britain and bounded by the lands of Thomas Rowland, Owon Rowland, Thomas Jones, Thomas Jones Weaver, William Williams, Richard Williams, William Wilson and Lewis Evans, Jr. Part of said land (100 acres) is that which John Penn, Thomas Penn and Richard Penn by patent dated 16 Oct 1735 and recorded at Philadelphia in Patent Book A, Vol 7, pg 332, conveyed to Lewis Evans the Father. The other 100 acres is part of 300 acres which John Penn, Thomas Penn and Richard Penn by patent dated 18 Apr 1734 and recorded at Philadelphia in Patent Book A, Vol 6, pg 277, conveyed to Lewis Evans. Made 16 Jun 1748. Wit: Rachel Bartholomew, Benjamin Griffith, William Thomas, Edward Jones. Ackn: 21 Jun 1748. JP: Simon Butler. Rec: 5 Sep 1748.

P. 468　　Mortgage. Thomas Evans of New Britain, yeoman, to John Bartholomew of Montgomery, Philadelphia Co., yeoman, to secure a debt of £100, 200 acres in New Britain [for description of land see previous entry.] To be repaid in 7 payments due on or by 17 Jun yearly, final payment due 1755. Made 17 Jun 1748. Wit: Rachel Bartholomew, Benjamin Griffith. Ackn: 21 Jun 1748. JP: Simon Butler. Rec: 5 Sep 1748. Mary Bartholomew, executrix of John Bartholomew's Last Will and Testament acknowledged full satisfaction of the mortgage received from Thomas Evans in 1757 [full date not given] before Lawrence Growdon, recorder.

P. 470   Jacob Cadwallador of Warminster, yeoman and Magdalen his wife, for £150, to Oliver Hart of the same place, carpenter, 50 acres of land in Warminster bounded by the lands of Joseph Dolworth, Abel Noble, Job Noble and by the said Jacob Cadwallador's other part of a tract of 164¾ acres. John Cadwallador of Horsham, Philadelphia Co., mason, and Margaret his wife, by indentures of lease and release dated 1 Dec 1736, conveyed to Jacob Cadwallader, third son of the said John Cadwallador, 164¾ acres of land in Warminster. Jacob Cadwallador mortgaged the premises to John Hinsy and others of the General Loan Office of Pennsylvania to secure a debt of £88 in 1746, which is recorded at Philadelphia. Made 30 Jul 1748. Wit: Joseph Hart, John Hart. Received £150 from Oliver Hart 2 Aug 17468. Wit: Joseph Hart and John Hart. Ackn: 8 Aug 1748. JP: Benjamin Jones.

P. 474   Deed. Daniel Palmer of Makefield, yeoman, for £41, to John Palmer of the same place, yeoman, 42 acres of land in Makefield by John Palmer's other land, by Daniel Palmer's other land and by the lands of Jonathan Palmer and Amos Palmer. Said land is part of 250 acres which by indentures of lease and release dated 14 and 15 Mar 1728 was conveyed by Daniel Hoopes of Chester Co., yeoman, and his wife Jane, to Daniel Palmer. Made 2 Dec 1729. Wit: John Hoopes. Ackn: 5 Aug 1748. JP: Mark Watson.

P. 476   Deed. John Palmer, Sr. of Makefield, yeoman, for £50, to John Palmer, Jr. of the same place, yeoman, 2 tracts of land in Makefield, the first of 100 acres is bounded by the lands of Leonard Shawcross, John Neild and by land late of Joshua Hoopes. The second tract of 20 acres adjoins the first and is bounded by the land late of Joshua Hoopes, and by John Palmer's land. Made 16 Nov 1721. Wit: John Waln, Jonathan Palmer, Daniel Palmer. Ackn: 5 Aug 1748. JP: Mark Watson.

P. 479   Lease. Jonas Keen of Bensalem, yeoman, and his wife Frances, for 5 shillings, to Robert Brodnax of the same place, yeoman, a plantation and 68 acres of land in Bensalem bounded by the lands of James Russ, Lawrence Growdon, Timothy Roberts and by land formerly Joseph Growdon's. Made 2 Feb 1739. Wit: James Rue, John Howel, Mathew Rue.

P. 480   Release. Jonas Keen of Bensalem, yeoman, and his wife Frances, for £50, to Robert Brodnax of the same place, yeoman, a plantation and 68 acres of land in Bensalem [see previous entry.] Said land is part of 150 acres which Cornelius Vansant, late of Bensalem, yeoman, and Dorica his wife by deed recorded in Book A, Vol 2, pg 48, conveyed to Thomas Stevenson, late of Bensalem, gent., deceased, who conveyed the land to Jonas Keen by deeds of lease and release dated 12 and 13 Oct 1716. Made 2 Feb 1739. Wit: James Rue, John Howel, Mathew Rue. Ackn: 4 Feb 1739. JP: Lawrence Growdon.

P. 483   Lease. Robert Brodnax of Bensalem, yeoman, and Christian his wife, for 5 shillings, to Lawrence Growdon of the same place, gent., 68 acres of land and a house in Bensalem bounded by the lands of James Rue, Timothy Roberts, by land formerly Joseph Growdon's and by the said Lawrence Growdon's land. Signed Robert and Christian alias Catherine Brodnax. Made 3 Jun 1740. Wit: Jeremiah Langhorne, Torrence Dunn. Rec: 17 Sep 1748.

P. 484   Release. Robert Brodnax of Bensalem, yeoman, and Christian his wife, for £65, to Lawrence Growdon of the same place, gent., 68 acres of land and a house in Bensalem [see previous 2 entries.] Made 4 Jun 1740. Wit: Jeremiah Langhorne, Torrence Dunn. Ackn: 2 Jul 1740. JP: Jeremiah Langhorne. Rec: 17 Sep 1748.

P. 487   Mortgage. James Carrell of Northampton, yeoman, and Dinah his wife, to secure a debt of £150, to William Attwood of Philadelphia, merchant, a plantation with 100 acres of land in Northampton bounded by the lands of Abraham Bennet, Nicholas Cruson and Thomas Dungan. Said land part of 2 tracts of land which Samuel Gilbert and his wife Elizabeth, Silas McCarty and his wife Sarah, and Robert Tomkins and his wife Lydia (Elizabeth, Sarah and Lydia are the surviving daughters of James Carrell, late of Northampton, yeoman, deceased) by deed dated 8 May 1724 conveyed to said James Carrell. Also, a tract of 50 acres of land in Southampton (across the road from the first described land) bounded by the lands of _____ Morris, Bartholomew Longstreet and Abram Bennet. This land George Willard of Southampton, yeoman, and his wife Mary sold to the said James Carrell by deed dated 27 Mar 1736. To be repaid on or by 7 Apr 1749. Made 27 Apr 1748. Wit: Mary Stevenson, Paul Isaac Voto, Benjamin Jones, Barnard Carrell. Ackn: 2 May 1748. JP: Benjamin Jones. Rec: 22 Oct 1748.

P. 488   Mortgage. Edward Doyle of New Britain, yeoman, to secure a debt of £60, to Thomas Watson of Buckingham, yeoman, a plantation and 150 acres of land in New Britain bounded by lands late of Jeremiah Langhorne and Joseph Kirkbride, deceased. Said land Joseph Kirkbride and his wife Mary sold to Edward Doyle by indentures of lease and release dated 22 and 23 Mar 1730. To be repaid on or by 9 Aug 1753. Made 9 Aug 1748. Wit: Moses Crawford, Patrick Malone. Ackn: 29 Sep 1748. JP: Lawrence Growdon. Memo: On 27 Aug 1779 Jonathan Fell, one of the administrators of John Fell, deceased, who was assignee of Thomas Watson, acknowledged receiving full satisfaction of the mortgage from William Doyle and Edward Doyle, executors of Edward Doyle, deceased, before John Hart, Recorder of Deeds.

P. 490   Deed. Joseph Headley of Middletown, carpenter, and Hannah his wife, for natural love and affection they have for their son-in-law Andrew Moode of Middletown, weaver, give to him 12 acres and 112 perches of land in Middletown by the road to Bristol bounded by the lands of Francis White, Peter Vanhorn and by Joseph Headley's other land. Said land is part of 250 acres which John Headley, father of said Joseph Headley, purchased from Peter White. Made 10 Feb 1747. Wit: John Hall, En Williams. Premises delivered to Andrew Moode 4 Oct 1748. Wit: Randal Hutchinson, John Bates, Jr. Ackn: 26 Mar 1748. JP: Enion Williams. Rec: 27 Oct 1748.

P. 491   Deed. John Praul of Middletown, yeoman, for the consideration of several covenants and agreements to be performed and for £3, to Stephen Williams of the same place, gent., a lot in Middletown by Beaver Pond, by the road leading to Stephen Williams' mill and by the line which divides John Praul's land from the land of Charles Plumly, containing 1 acre. Said Stephen Williams agrees to make and maintain in good repair a fence sufficient to confine horses, cattle and hogs on the line beside Neshaminy Creek at the buttonwood tree and running between the mill land and John Praul's land. Made 1 Nov 1748. Wit: Lawrence Growdon, Mary Harris. Ackn: 1 Nov 1748. JP: Lawrence Growdon. Rec: 7 Nov 1748.

P. 493   Mortgage. David Owen of Bucks Co., yeoman, for £100, to William Coleman and James Pemberton of Philadelphia, merchants and executors of the Last Will and Testament of Samuel Powel the Younger, late of said city, merchant, deceased, 150 acres of land which Joseph Samuel and his wife Sarah, by deed dated 4 Jul 1743 sold to David Owen. To be repaid at the end of one year. Made 6 Sep 1748. Wit: Reiner Kuster, Joseph Galloway. Money received at Philadelphia 6 Sep 1748. Wit: Israel Pemberton, Samuel Emlon, Jr. Ackn: 6 Sep 1748. JP: John Kingsley. Rec: 15 Nov 1748.

P. 495   Mortgage.   Elias Diotrick of the Forks of Delaware, mason, to secure a debt of £200, to Mary Grafton of Philadelphia, widow, a messuage and 379 acres of land in the Forks of Delaware bounded by the lands of William Allen and Thomas Craig. To be repaid 11 Nov 1749. Made 11 Nov 1748. Wit: Robert Levers, Arthur Forster. Ackn: 11 Nov 1748. JP: Abraham Chapman. Rec: 6 Dec 1748.

P. 496   Mortgage. John Plumley of Northampton and his wife Alice, to secure a debt of £100, to Mary Plumstead of Philadelphia, widow, 221¾ acres of land in Northampton bounded by the lands of Robert Heaton, Robert Hockdale and James Logan. To be repaid in one year. Made 6 Jun 1747. Wit: Arthur Forster, Paul Isaac Voto. Ackn: 6 Jun 1747. JP: John Kinsey. Rec: 6 Dec 1748.

P. 498   Mortgage. Samuel Faires of Warwick, clothier, to secure a debt of £50, to Mary Plumstead of Philadelphia, widow, a fulling mill and press and 30 acres and 10 perches of land in Warwick by Neshaminy Creek and by Claypoole's land, by Thomas Dungan's land, and by land belonging to Hugh Hughston. To be repaid in one year. Made 12 Dec 1745. Wit: Arthur Forster, Paul Isaac Voto. Ackn: 13 Dec 1745. JP: John Kinsey. Rec: 6 Dec 1748.

P. 499   Mortgage. James Stewart of Hilltown, yeoman, to secure a debt of £200, to James Logan of Stenton, Philadelphia Co., gent., 200 acres of land in Hilltown bounded by the lands of Jeremiah Langhorne, John Williams and Thomas Jones. Said land part of 329 acres which Thomas Marple and Susannah his wife by indenture of release dated 25 Dec 1741 and recorded in Book B, Vol 3, pg 132 conveyed to Bernard Young and his wife Susannah, who conveyed 200 acres of the land to James Stewart by deed dated 16 Jul 1748. To be repaid in one year. Made 18 Jul 1748. Wit: John Hewston, Ruth Steer, Christian Lehman. Ackn: 15 Sep 1748. JP: John Kinsey. Rec: 22 Dec 1748. Memo: On the 1st of 9 in 1757, John Smith, executor for James Logan, received from Thomas Jones £150. On 18 Oct 1757 Hugh Roberts showed a receipt to Lawrence Growdon, Recorder of Deeds.

P. 501   Deed. Charles Plumly of Middletown, yeoman (the eldest brother and heir of William Plumly, late of the same place, yeoman, deceased) and his wife Ann, for £535, to Garret Vansandt of Middletown, yeoman, 214 acres and 17 perches of land by Neshaminy Creek, bounded by the lands of James Paxon, Joseph Richardson, Thomas Walmsley and _____ Goodwin. Said land is part of a tract of 500 acres, which by indentures of lease and release dated 27 and 28 Nov 1681 William Penn granted to Henry Paxon. James Claypool and Robert Turner, William Penn's Commissioners, by patent dated 17th da 3rd mo 1686 confirmed the 500 acres laid out in Bucks Co. to Henry Paxon, said documents are recorded in Bucks Co. Book B, Vol 1, pg 196.

By deed dated 10th da 10th mo 1698, Henry Paxon and Margery his wife and Elizabeth Burgess, Henry's daughter, conveyed to James Plumly and John Plumly, Henry's sons-in-law, the 500 acres of land (recorded in Book B, Vol 1, pg 196.) Henry and Margery Paxon died, and the said James Plumly also died. Although the land rightfully belonged to John Plumly by right of survivorship, the said James Plumly, in his Last Will and Testament dated 16 Oct 1702, made his wife Mary his sole executrix and his brother Charles and Uncle William Budd overseers. On the advice of Charles Plumly and William Budd, the widow Mary Plumly granted the moiety of the land by deed dated 10 Mar 1702 to John Plumly (recorded in Book C, Vol 1, pg 147.) John Plumly made his Last Will and Testament dated 24 Mar 1731 and bequeathed the half of the tract of land on which he was then living (the half adjacent to Neshaminy Creek) to his son Charles Plumly and to his son William he bequeathed the other half of the land. John Plumly the father died shortly after making his will and his son William also died soon after, under age and without issue, and the 500 acres of land descended fully to Charles Plumly. Made 10 Jan 1748. Wit: Lewis Rue, Jo'n. Vanhorn. Ackn: 12 Jan 1748. JP: Mathew Rue. Rec: 20 Jan 1748.

P. 504 Deed. Nathaniel Bye of Buckingham, yeoman, and Martha his wife, for £100, to his son Thomas Bye, a plantation and 172 acres and 129 perches of land in Buckingham bounded by the lands of Enoch Pearson, Thomas and Samuel Kinsey and by Nathaniel Bye's other land; also by land surveyed to Edward West. Said land part of a tract of land which Thomas Bye, grandfather of said Thomas Bye, by deed dated 9 Sep 1706, granted to Nathaniel Bye, recorded in Book D, Vol 1, pg 193 [a note on the side of the page says Book 4, pg 141.] Made 20 Oct 1746. Wit: John A. Queen, John Watson, Jr. Ackn: 6 May 1747. JP: John Wells. Rec: 27 Jan 1748/9.

P. 505 Lease. Enoch Pearson of Buckingham, yeoman, and Margaret his wife, for 5 shillings, to Thomas Bye of Solebury, yeoman, 50 acres of land bounded by the lands of Samuel Kinsey, Nathaniel Bye and Enoch Pearson's other land. Made 15th da 1st mo 1744. Wit: John Hurst, Jonathan Ingham, Jno. Watson, Jr.

P. 506 Release. Enoch Pearson of Buckingham, yeoman, and Margaret his wife, for £80, to Thomas Bye of Solebury, yeoman, 50 acres of land in Buckingham [see previous entry.] Said land is part of a greater tract of land granted to Nathaniel Bye from his father Thomas Bye by deed dated 9 Sep 1706 and was granted to Thomas Bye by patent dated 12 Jan 1702. Made 16th da 1st mo 1744. Wit: John Hurst, Jonathan Ingham, John Watson, Jr. Ackn: 25 Jun 1744. JP: John Wells. Rec: 27 Jan 1748/9.

P. 507 Mortgage. Jonkin Philips of Rockhill, yeoman, to secure a debt of £120, to William Coleman and James Pemberton of Philadelphia, merchants and executors of the Last Will and Testament of Samuel Powell, Jr., late of Philadelphia, merchant, deceased, a plantation and 150 acres of land in

Rockhill bounded by the lands of Philip Henry, James Roboson and Cornelius Bryant. Said land that which Thomas Freame of Philadelphia and Margaret his wife by deed dated 2 Aug 1735 conveyed to Abraham James and wife who by deed of 24 Nov 1741 conveyed it to Jonkin Philips. To be repaid in one year. Said money loaned is properly the money and estate of the children of Samuel Powell, Jr. which was ordered to be put out for interest by the Orphans Court of Philadelphia dated 18 Nov last. Made 19 Nov 1748. Wit: Paul Isaac Voto, Arthur Forster. Ackn: 19 Nov 1748. JP: William Till. Rec: 20 Jan 1748/9. Memo: By power of attorney from William Coleman recorded in Book 6, Vol 3, pg 299, Richard Gibbs acknowleded satisfaction of the mortgage on 19 Sep 1761 before Lawrence Growdon, Recorder.

P. 508   Mortgage. Thomas Philips of Hilltown, yeoman, to secure a debt of £200 due on 29 Nov 1749, to William Coleman and James Pemberton of Philadelphia, merchants and executors of the estate of Samuel Powell, Jr., late of Philadelphia, merchant, deceased, a plantation and 275 acres of land in Hilltown bounded by the lands of John Lewis, Lawrence Growdon and _____ Hamilton. Said money loaned is properly the money and estate of the children of Samuel Powell, Jr. which was ordered to be put out for interest by the Orphans Court of Philadelphia dated 18 Nov last. Made 29 Nov 1748. Wit: Robert Levers, Arthur Forster. Ackn: 29 Nov 1748. JP: John Kinsey. Rec: 28 Jan 1748. Memo: On 10 Jul 1755, William Coleman acknowleded to have received from Thomas Philips full satisfaction of the mortgage before Lawrence Growdon, Recorder.

P. 510   Mortgage. John Shaw of Tohickon, yeoman, to secure a debt of £100, to William Coleman and James Pemberton, both of Philadelphia, merchants and executors of the estate of Samuel Powell, Jr., deceased, a plantation and 200 acres of land in Tohickon bounded by the lands of _____ Streiper and Mathew Hughs. To be repaid on or by 21 Dec next. Made 21 Dec 1748. Wit: Jos. Galloway, Jonah Frances, Jr. Ackn: 21 Dec 1748. JP: Thomas Grame. Rec: 28 Jan 1748. Memo: William Coleman acknowledged to have received from John Shaw £104 before Lawrence Growdon on 3 Jun 175[?]

P. 511   Release. Thomas Howell of Warwick, yeoman, and Catharine his wife, for £4, to James Craven of Warminster, John Gray of Warrington, Alexander Jemyson of Warwick, Robert Walker, John McCollough, George Hiear, Henry Jemyson, Jr., all yeomen and of the same place, and John Scott of the same place, weaver, 2 acres and 2 perches of land in Warwick bounded by the lands of William Miller, Jr., William Miller, Sr. and by Thomas Howell's land, part of 325½ acres.

James Boyden of Philadelphia, merchant, John Boyden of the same place, taylor, and Jacob Shute of said city, cooker, and his wife Mary (the said James Boyden, John Boyden and Mary Shute are the children of James Boyden, late of said city, merchant, deceased, who was the only son and heir of James Boyden of Buckingham in Bucks Co., also deceased) by indentures of lease and release conveyed to Thomas Howell 325½ acres of land, part of 484 acres which by warrant dated 25th da 5th mo 1684 was laid out to James Boyden the grandfather on the 25th da 9th mo 1684 as part of his original purchase of 1,000 acres. Made 2 Jul 1743. Wit: Robert Jemison, William Leech. Ackn: 25 Apr 1745. JP: Matt Hughes. Rec: 2 Feb 1748.

P. 513   Declaration of Trust. James Craven of Warminster, John Gray of Warrington, Alexander Jemyson of Warwick, Robert Walker, John McCollough, George Heiar, Henry Jemyson, Jr., all yeomen of the same place, and John Scott of the same place, weaver, to Richard Walker, Daniel Craige, William Craigton and Thomas Craige, all yeomen of Warrington, Robert Jemyson, Samuel Faries and James Peak, all yeomen of Warwick, Archibald Kelsey of New Britain and James Carrell of Northampton, yeomen, all members of the Protestant Congregation at Warwick and adjacent townships of Presbyterians of the Church of Scotland usually assembling for worship at their meeting house in Warwick under the care of the Reverend W. Charles Peaky, land in Warwick on which to build a meeting house and a burying ground [see previous entry for history of this land.] Made Feb 1744/5. Wit: Moses Crawford, Archibald Crawford. Ackn: 12 Jun 1745. JP: Simon Butler. Rec: 3 Feb 1748.

P. 515   Mortgage. John Town of Bristol, yeoman, to secure a debt of £100 due 23 Dec 1754, to John Abraham Denormandie of Bristol and John Snowdon of Philadelphia, surviving executors of the Last Will and Testament of David Murray, deceased, a plantation with 118 acres of land in Bristol by Neshaminy Creek by land formerly John Clawson's and by _____ Spencer's land. Made 23 Dec 1748. Wit: John Denormandie, John Frohock. Ackn: 24 Dec 1748. JP: William Buckley. Rec: 14 Feb 1748/9.

P. 516   Deed. Lawrence Growdon of Trevose in Bensalem, gent., and his wife Sarah and Langhorne Biles of Falls Township, gent., for £197.18s.6p, to John Lewis of Hilltown, yeoman, 188½ acres of land in Hilltown bounded by the lands of Colonel Mildway and Thomas Morris which is part of a 200 acre tract formerly belonging to Jeremiah Langhorne.

     William Penn's Commissioners, by warrant dated 8 Mar 1706 caused to be surveyed and laid out to John Rowland in right of an original purchase of 4,250 acres made by John Rowland, his wife Priscilla (formerly

Priscilla Shepherd) and Thomas Rowland, his brother (both Priscilla and Thomas by the time of the survey were deceased) 500 acres of land in Hilltown. By deed dated 16 Jun 1711, John Rowland conveyed to Charles Brockden, then of Bensalem, the 500 acres. Charles Brockden conveyed by deed dated 13 Nov 1711, 200 acres of the land to William Hingston. By patent dated 9 Apr 1712, the Proprietary Commissioners confirmed the 500 acres to Charles Brockden. William Hingston died intestate shortly after and Josiah Hingston, his younger brother, granted the 200 acres to Thomas Sober of Philadelphia, merchant, by deed dated 31 May 1728. Thomas Sober then conveyed the 200 acres to Jeremiah Langhorne by deed dated 25 Sep 1730. Josiah Hingston and James Hingston, the eldest brother of the said deceased William Hingston, by deed made 25 Sep 1730 by their attorney Peter Evans granted the said 200 acres to Jeremiah Langhorne.

Shortly before he died, Jeremiah Langhorne made his Last Will and Testament dated 16 May 1742 and empowered his executors to dispose of the land and the residue of his estate was to go to his nephews the said Lawrence Growdon and Langhorne Biles. He appointed as his executors Lawrence Growdon, Langhorne Biles and Joseph Turner. Made 11 Dec 1746. Wit: Thomas Morris, Mary Harris. Ackn: 11 Dec 1748. JP: Mark Watson. Rec: 28 Feb 1748.

P. 518   Mortgage. Christian Moyer of Shippack in Philadelphia County, yeoman, to secure a debt of £60 to be repaid in one year, to William Coleman and James Pemberton of Philadelphia, merchants and executors of the Last Will and Testament of Samuel Powell, Jr., late of Philadelphia, merchant, deceased, 215 acres of land in the Manor of Perhesie bounded by the lands of Henry Seibel, Jeremiah Langhorn, Bartholomew Young and Thomas Philips. Said money loaned is properly the money and estate of the children of Samuel Powell, Jr. which was ordered to be put out for interest by the Orphans Court at Philadelphia dated 18 Nov 1747. Made 8 Mar 1748/9. Wit: C. Brockden, Paul Isaac Voto. Ackn: same day. JP: Thomas Greene. Rec: 28 Mar 1749. Memo: By power of attorney recorded in Book C, Vol 1, pg 102, full satisfaction of the mortgage was received by Richard Gibbs on 15 May 1760 before Lawrence Growdon, Recorder.

P. 519   Mortgage. Henry Seibel of Franconia, Philadelphia Co., yeoman, to secure a debt of £120 to be repaid in one year, to William Coleman and James Pemberton of Philadelphia, merchants and executors of the Last Will and Testament of Samuel Powell, Jr., late of Philadelphia, merchant, deceased, 160 acres of land in the Manor of Perhesie in Bucks Co. bounded by the land of Jeremiah Langhorne, Christian Moyer and Bartholomew Young. Said land that which Walter McCoole of Bucks Co., yeoman, and his wife

Mary sold to Henry Seibel by deed dated 15 Dec 1747. Said money loaned is properly the money and estate of the children of Samuel Powell, Jr. which was ordered to be put out for interest by the Orphans Court at Philadelphia on 18 Nov 1747. Made 8 Mar 1748/9. Wit: C. Brockden, Paul Isaac Voto. Ackn: same day. JP: Thomas Greene. Rec: 8 Apr 1749.

P. 520   Mortgage. William Newman of Lower Milford, yeoman, and his wife Margaret, to secure a debt of £800, to Morris Morris, Jr. of Philadelphia, merchant, a messuage and 500 acres of land in Lower Milford in the Great Swamp bounded by Joseph Growdon's land. To be repaid in one year. Made 25 Oct 1748. Wit: Hananiah Pugh, David Morris. Ackn: 28 Nov 1748. JP: John Jemison. Rec: 15 Apr 1749. Memo: On 15 Jul 1752 before Lawrence Growdon, Morris Morris, Jr. acknowledged full satisfaction of the mortgage.

P. 521   Deed. John Sample of Badminster, weaver, and Elizabeth his wife, for £81, to Richard Peters of Philadelphia, a plantation and 175 and 1/3 acres of land on the Delaware River and Tohickon Creek and bounded by the land of William Gooden. Said land was patented to John Sample 12 Mar 1738 and recorded at Philadelphia in Patent Book A, Vol 1, pg 239. Made 12 Jun 1746. Wit: James Devies, William Adams, Joseph McFarland, Matt Hughes. Ackn: 6 Dec 1746. JP: Robert Ellis. Rec: 15 Apr 1749.

P. 522   Deed. Thomas Bishop Vickries of Chew Magna, Somerset Co., Great Britain and his attorney Richard Hockley of Philadelphia, merchant, for £175, to Peter Lerew of Makefield, yeoman, 216 acres and 152 perches of land, part of a tract of 483 acres, bounded by the lands of James Tunniclif, _____ Baker, Abel Jenny, _____ Yardley and by Peter Lerew's other land.
     In April 1683, by the late William Penn's order, 483 acres of land in Bucks Co. on the Delaware River above the falls was surveyed for Richard Vickries, then of Bristol in Great Britain, since deceased, and was later confirmed to him by warrant dated 16 Aug 1700 and returned to the Governor's Secretary's Office on 3 Sep 1700 and recorded in that office. This land was part of 2,000 acres purchased by Richard Vickries.
     Thomas Bishop Vickries, who is the only surviving son of Richard Vickries, inherited his father's land and by letter of attorney dated 24 Apr 1740 and recorded at Philadelphia in Book G, Vol 1, pg 186 made Thomas Penn his attorney to sell his lands. Thomas Penn by letter of substitution dated 8 Dec 1740 appointed Richard Hockley to act as Vickries attorney. Made 13 Jun 1743. Wit: William Peters, Richard Peters. Ackn: 17 Sep 1743 before Justice of the Peace Richard Hough by William Peters' oath that the witnesses signatures were his and his brother Richard Peters. Rec: 15 Dec 1749.

P. 524   Deed. Nicholas Weiser of Smithfield, yeoman, and Elizabeth his wife, for £58, to Richard Peters of Philadelphia, gent., a plantation and 244 acres of land in Smithfield. Said land is that which by patent dated 28 Mar last intended to be recorded at Philadelphia was granted to Nicholas Weiser. Made 2 Apr 1744. Wit: George Boone, Edward Scull. Ackn: 1 Feb 1748 by Edward Scull of Philadelphia, surveyor, before John Kinsey, JP. Rec: 15 Apr 1749.

P. 526   Mortgage. Ralph Dracord of Northampton, yeoman, and Susanah his wife, to secure a debt of £60, to Anthony Morris of Philadelphia, brewer, a plantation and 28 acres and 25 perches of land in Northampton by the road leading to Philadelphia and bounded by Benjamin Scott's land. To be repaid on 26 Nov 1750. Made 26 Nov 1748. Wit: George Randall, Abrah. Chapman. Ackn: 9 Dec 1748. JP: Abraham Chapman. Rec: 26 Apr 1749. Memo: On 10 Nov 1752 Anthony Morris acknowledged having received full satisfaction of the mortgage from Ralph Dracord. Lawrence Growdon, Recorder.

P. 527   Mortgage. James Morgan of Derby, Chester Co., miller, to secure a debt of £150 to be repaid in one year, to Jacob Duche of Philadelphia, gent., a plantation and 200 acres of land in Richland, Bucks Co., bounded by the lands of Abraham Griffith and George Phillips. Made: 1 Mar 1748. Wit: Robert Levers, Arthur Forster. Ackn: 20 Mar 1748. JP: John Kinsey. Rec: 26 Apr 1749. Memo: On 21 Mar 1754 Jacob Duche acknowledged receiving full satisfaction of the mortgage from James Morgan. Lawrence Growdon, Recorder.

P. 528   Deed. John Mitchell of Middletown, carpenter, Thomas Janney of Newtown, mason, and Martha his wife, Joseph Clarke of Bristol, taylor, and Sarah his wife, for 5 shillings and because they are moving, quit claim to Henry Mitchell of Durham, blacksmith, 2 tracts of land in Bristol, the first near Neshaminy Creek and by land late of John Town's containing 125 acres. The other tract, also by Neshaminy Creek, is 106¼ acres of land and is bounded by land late of Robert Hall and by Bristol Road.

Henry Mitchell, late of Bristol, carpenter, who died intestate, (father of the said John Mitchell, Martha Janney, Sarah Clarke and Henry Mitchell) owned 2 tracts of land in Bristol in his lifetime. The first tract of 125 acres is that which Joseph Growdon of Trevose sold to him by indenture of release dated 25 Dec 1714. The second tract of 106¼ acres is that which Hannah Carpenter of Philadelphia, widow and sole executrix of the Last Will and Testament of Samuel Carpenter, late of Philadelphia, merchant, deceased, sold to him by indenture of release dated 13 Oct 1716. Made 6 Nov 1742.

Wit: John Lloyd, John Duncan. Ackn: 18 Mar 1748 by John Duncan before John Abraham Denormandie, JP. Rec: 1 May 1749.

P. 530   Mortgage. Isaac Shans of New York City, merchant, to secure a debt of £700 due 4 Apr 1750, to Alexander Brown Huston of Philadelphia, merchant, a plantation and 173 acres of land in Falls Township by the Delaware River, by Joshua Boare's land and by land formerly belonging to Richard Ridgeway. Also another plantation and 120 acres of land in Falls by the Delaware and bounded by the lands of William Biles and John Achesman. Made 4 Apr 1749. Wit: Chas. Brockdon, Paul Isaac Voto. Ackn: same day. JP: William Till. Rec: 1 May 1749. Memo: On 25 Jul 1750 Alexander Brown Huston released the mortgage. Recorded by Lawrence Growdon.

P. 532   Release. John Burden of Bristol, carpenter, for 5 shillings and because he is moving, quit claims to Henry Mitchell of the same place, blacksmith, 2 tracts of land in Bristol. The first near Neshaminy Creek is bounded by land formerly belonging to John Town and contains 125 acres. The second parcel of 106¼ acres of land is bounded by land formerly Robert Hall's and is near Neshaminy Creek.

Henry Mitchell of Bristol, carpenter, who died intestate, was the grandfather of the said John Burden, and owned 2 tracts of land in Bristol at the time of his death. The first of 125 acres was land which Joseph Growdon of Trevose sold to him by indenture of release dated 25 Dec 1714. The other tract of 106¼ acres of land is that which Hannah Carpenter of Philadelphia, widow and executrix of the Last Will and Testament of Samuel Carpenter, late of said city, deceased, sold to him by indenture of release dated 13 Oct 1716. Made 14 Jun 1746. Wit: Philip White, Geo. Mitchell, Wm. Atkinson. Ackn: 18 Mar 1748/9 before JP William Buckley by oath of William Atkinson of Bristol. Rec: 2 May 1749.

P. 534   Mortgage. James Baldwin of Bensalem, joyner, to secure a debt of £160 due 11 Mar 1749/50, to William Coleman and James Pemberton, merchants of Philadelphia and executors of the Last Will and Testament of Samuel Powel, Jr., late of said city, merchant, deceased, a plantation and 120 acres of land in Bensalem on the Delaware River by lands formerly belonging to Dunk Williams and John Abraham Denormandie. Said land that which John Abraham Denormandie and his wife sold to James Baldwin by indenture dated 4 Apr 1746. Money loaned is properly the estate of the children of Samuel Powel, Jr., which, by order of the Orphans Court held at Philadelphia 17 Nov 1747, is to be put out for interest Made 11 Mar 1748/9. Wit: Ch. Brockden, Paul Isaac Voto. Ackn: 11 Mar 1748/9. JP: John Kinsey. Rec: 5

May 1749. Memo: Full satisfaction of mortgage acknowledged by Court Decree and recorded 22 May 1873 by Recorder of Deeds J. Watson Case.

P. 535　　Mortgage. Henry Hartsell of Hilltown, yeoman, to secure a debt of £500 due 25 Mar 1750, to Isaac Norris of Fair Hill in the northern liberties of Philadelphia, merchant, 530 acres of land in Hilltown by land late of Thomas Freame, deceased, and by James Logan's land. This land is that which Isaac Norris sold to Henry Hartsell. Made 25 Mar 1749. Wit: Eliz. Norris, Mary Lloyd, Charles Vinager. Ackn: 3 May 1749. Lawrence Growdon, JP. Memo: 2 Oct 1754 Isaac Norris acknowledged having received full satisfaction of the mortgage from Henry Hartsell.

P. 537　　Deed. John Rich of Plumstead, yeoman, and his wife Sarah, for £450, to Patrick Poe of the same place, taylor, 200 acres of land in Plumstead bounded by the lands of Alexander Brown, Thomas Brown, Ephraim Fenton and Francis Hough. Said land part of 1,250 acres which William Penn granted to William Kent by indenture of release dated 18 Oct 1681. By indenture of release dated 11 Sep 1685, William Kent sold the land to Walter Hill who sold it to Thomas Milner by indenture of release dated 29 Sep 1685. Thomas Milner then sold it to John Davis by indenture of release dated 8 Apr 1721.

　　　　John Davis wrote his Last Will and Testament dated 7 Dec 1720. He bequeathed to his daughters £500 each and to his wife Mary the residue during her widowhood, but if she marry then she should have only £100 and the rest to be divided equally between his daughters. One of his daughters, Mary Davis, by indenture of release dated 13 Sep 1726, granted her equal and one-third share of the said 1,250 acres to her mother Mary Davis. Mary Davis the mother, with Elizabeth Davis and Ann Davis (the other daughters) sold the whole 1,250 acres of land to Ebenezer Large by indenture of release dated 17 Sep 1726. Elizabeth Davis released her share to Ebenezer Large by indenture of release dated 26 May 1733. Ann Davis married Awberry Bevan and by indenture dated 20 Nov 1733 released to Ebenezer Large her rights to the land.

　　　　By deeds of lease and release dated 1 and 2 Nov 1734, Ebenezer Large of Burlington, NJ, currier, and Dorothy his wife, sold to Richard Lundy of Plumstead, yeoman, 200 acres of land in Plumstead, which was part of the said 1,250 acres. Richard Lundy and Elizabeth his wife, by indentures of lease and release dated 26 and 27 May 1735, sold the 200 acres to Francis Borden, who by his deed dated 12 Mar 1741, granted the same to John Rich. Made 22 Feb 1748. Wit: Will. Hamilton, Will. Tea. Ackn: 25 Apr 1748/9. JP: Matthew Hughes. Rec: 11 May 1749.

P. 539   Deed. Ebenezer Large of Plumstead, yeoman, and his wife Ann, for £40, to John Russell of the same place, cordwainer, 40 acres of land in Plumstead bounded by the lands of Evan Jones, Nathan Preston and William Ewings, part of a tract of 100 acres. Joseph Large, late of Buckingham, deceased, died owning a plantation consisting of 2 adjoining tracts of land in Plumstead totaling 200 acres. In his Last Will and Testament dated 21st da 10th mo 1745 and recorded in Book B, folio 68, he devised the land to his son Ebenezer Large. 100 acres of this land was granted by patent dated 17 Nov 1736 and recorded at Philadelphia in Patent Book A, Vol 8, pg 102, to Joseph Large by the proprietors of the province. Made 15 May 1748. Wit: William Hough, Paul Kester. Ackn: 4 Jun 1748. JP: Matthew Hughs. Rec: 12 May 1749.

P. 541   Mortgage. Richard Hough of Makefield, yeoman, to secure a debt of £137, to John Shallcross of Oxford, Philadelphia Co., yeoman, a plantation and 115½ acres of land in Makefield by the Delaware River and bounded by the lands of Abel Janney, Thomas Janney, Joshua Heap, Thomas Kirl, Peter Worrell and Andrew Elliet. The part of the said land which Richard Hough recently sold to Jonathan Palmer and Daniel Palmer is excepted. To be repaid on or before 28 Apr 1751. Made 28 Apr 1749. Wit: Chas. Brockden, Paul Isaac Voto. Ackn: 11 May 1749. JP: Lawrence Growdon. Rec: 13 May 1749.

P. 543   Mortgage. Patrick Poe of Plumstead, taylor, and his wife Abigail, to secure a debt of £150, to Patrick Baird of Philadelphia, gent., a plantation and 200 acres of land in Plumstead and bounded by the lands of Alexander Brown, Thomas Brown, Ephraim Fenton and Francis Hughes. Said land part of 1,250 acres which William Penn granted to William Kent by indenture of release dated 18 Oct 1681. William Kent sold it to Walter Hill by indenture of release dated 11 Sep 1685 who by indenture of release dated 29 Sep 1685 granted it to Thomas Millner who sold it to John Davis by indenture of release dated 8 Apr 1721.

John Davis then died, having written a Last Will and Testament dated 7 Dec 1720, bequeathing to his daughters £500 each and the residue to his wife Mary (but if she should remarry, she should have £100 and the remainder divided equally among the daughters.) Mary Davis, one of John Davis' daughters, by indenture of release dated 13 Sep 1726, granted one equal one-third part of the 1,250 acres to her mother Mary Davis who along with the other two daughters, Elizabeth Davis and Ann Davis, by indenture of release dated 17 Sep 1726, granted the whole 1,250 acres to Ebenezer Large. Elizabeth Davis and Ann Davis (who married Awbery Bevan) both released their share of the land to Ebenezer Large by indentures of release dated 26 May 1733 and 20 Nov 1733 respectively.

Ebenezer Large and his wife Dorothy conveyed 200 acres of the 1,250 acre tract to Richard Lundy, Jr. and his wife Elizabeth by indentures of lease and release dated 1 and 2 Nov 1734. By indentures of lease and release dated 26 and 27 May 1735 the Lundy's sold the 200 acres to Francis Borden who then sold it to John Rich by deed dated 12 Mar 1741. John Rich and his wife Sarah, by deed dated 22 Feb this instant conveyed the 200 acres to Patrick Poe. To be repaid on or by 24 Feb 1749/50. Made 24 Feb 1748/9. Wit: Gariod Cunningham, John Rich. Ackn: 13 May 1749. JP: Lawrence Growdon. Rec: 18 May 1749.

P. 546   Deed of Trust. Anthony Burton of Bristol, gent., because he is moving and for love and affection for God Almighty, gives to the Rev. Mr. Robert Weyman, the present minister of the Church of St. James in Bristol, and to his successors, a lot in Bristol on which the Church has been built bounded by Cedar and Wood Streets (except to reserve for Anthony Burton a burying place and a pew for him and his family.) Made 7 Mar 1733. Wit: Matthew Rue, Thomas Worrell. Ackn: 18 May 1749 by Matthew Rue before JP Lawrence Growdon.

547   Release. James Journey of Middletown, yeoman, for £400, to Benjamin Abbit of Makefield, yeoman, 358 acres of land in 2 tracts in Makefield. The first tract contains 240 acres and is bounded by the lands of John Whitacre and Samuel Baker. The second tract adjoins the first, contains 118 acres of land and is bounded by the lands of Benjamin Taylor, John Milner, Samuel Baker, John Bauldwin and Samuel Runtin.

The first tract of land was granted to James Journey by John Addis by indentures of lease and release dated 30 and 31 May 1738. John Addis acquired the land from John Baldwin, Jr. by indentures of lease and release dated 11 and 12 Nov 1737. It was granted to John Baldwin, Jr. by John Baldwin, Sr. by deed dated 16 Dec 1736. This tract of land was 2 tracts of which 100 acres of it John Baldwin, Sr. purchased from Samuel Baker by deed dated 8th da 10th mo 1708 and recorded in Book D, Vol 1, pg 54 and was granted to Samuel Baker by proprietary patent dated 10th da 9th mo 1702. The other part of the tract was conveyed to John Baldwin, Sr. by proprietary patent dated 28 Oct 1701.

The second tract of land was conveyed to James Journey by John Baldwin, Sr. by indentures of lease and release dated 15 and 16 Dec 1736. It was granted to John Baldwin, Sr. by Thomas Maybury by indentures of lease and release dated 5 and 6 Sep 1729. Thomas Maybury acquired the land from John Milnor by indentures of lease and release dated 1 and 2 Mar 1722/3.

William Penn, by indentures of lease and release dated 15 and 16 Mar 1681, granted 250 acres of land to Joseph Milnor and Daniel Milnor, and 245 acres of the 250 acres of land was surveyed by warrant dated 9th da 8th mo 1682 and laid out to Joseph and Daniel Milnor in Makefield. Daniel Milnor died without issue soon after and the land descended to Joseph Milnor as joint tenant. Joseph Milnor died and the land descended to John Milnor, his only son, who conveyed part of the 245 acres of land to Thomas Maybury. Made 28 Sep 1739. Wit: John Burroughs, Jr., Chas. Bryan. Ackn: 29 May 1740. JP: Abraham Chapman. Rec: 24 May 1749.

P. 550   Release. John Wally of Newtown, yeoman, and his wife Elizabeth, for £403, to Benjamin Taylor of Bucks Co., blacksmith, 403 acres of land in Newtown bounded by the lands of James Gould, Thomas Stradlin, Charles Read, Francis Hague and by the road leading from Newtown to the Falls meeting house. Said land part of a tract of 1,500 acres.
    Edward Shippen, Griffith Owen and James Logan, Commissioners for William Penn, granted to Shadrick Wally, late of said County, yeoman, and father of said John Wally, 1,500 acres of land in Bucks Co., by patent dated 17 Oct 1705. Shadrick Wally died intestate and the land descended to his only son and heir John Wally. Made 11 Apr 1730. Wit: James Arbuckle, Thomas Buckman, Chas. Bryan. Ackn: 13 Mar 1734/5 by Charles Bryan before JP Abraham Chapman. Rec: 23 May 1749.

P. 552   Mortgage. Oliver Hart of Warminster, carpenter, and his wife Sarah, for £100, to Joseph Hart of the same place, yeoman, a messuage and 50 acres of land in Warminster bounded by the lands of Joseph Delworth, Able Noble, Job Noble and by Jacob Cadwallader's land. Said land the same which Jacob Cadwallader of Warminster and Magdalen his wife conveyed to Oliver Hart by deed dated 13 Jul 1748 and recorded in Book B, Vol 3, pg 470. To be repaid in 5 semi-annual payments; final payment due 16 May 1751. Made 31 Dec 1748. Wit: William Gilbert, Miles Hart, Edith Hough. Ackn: 18 Mar 1748/9. JP: Simon Butler. Rec: 5 Jun 1749. Memo: On the 18th of Mar 1752 Joseph Hart acknowledged full satisfaction of the mortgage from Oliver Hart before Lawrence Growdon, Recorder of Deeds.

P. 555   Release. Alice Nelson, widow of Henry Nelson, deceased, late of Middletown, yeoman, and Thomas Nelson, son of said Henry Nelson, and Euclidus Longshore of Middletown, cordwainer, for £115, to William Bidgood of Bristol, yeoman, 89 acres and 53 perches of land in Bristol by the land that Thomas Dowdney recently purchased from Anthony Willson and his wife Ann and bounded by the lands of Thomas Marriot, Richard Bidgood and Thomas Sisom. This land is part of 250 acres which formerly belonged to

Rebeccah Hague and was taken to satisfy a lawsuit of William Trent. It was sold by Sheriff John Hall to Joseph Bond by deed dated 11 Jun 1719. Joseph Bond sold it to Henry Nelson by deeds of lease and release dated 12 and 13 May 1721. Henry Nelson made his Last Will and Testament recorded in Book B, Vol 2 and dated 11 Apr 1744 wherein he named his wife Alice, Thomas Nelson and Euclidus Longshore his executors. Made 2 Jul 1748. Wit: John Kirl [also spelled Keirll,] Henry Tomlinson, William Atkinson. Ackn: 1 Aug 1748. JP: John Abraham Denormandie. Rec: 5 Jun 1749.

notes

Abbit, Benjamin, 193
Abbot, Jonathan, 125
Achesman, John, 190
Ackerman, John, 104
Acreman, Hannah, 70, 72
Adams, James, 44, 148
  William, 188
Adamson, Anthony, 172
Addington, John, 10
Addis, John, 164, 193, 33
Agilly, John, 152
Aishelle, James, 148
Aiskell, James, 177, 178
Aiskill, James, 137
Alberson, Abraham, 15, 29
  Mary, 15
  Rebecca, 15, 29
  William, 15, 29
Alborsbrult, Duck, 5
Alfreth, John, 102
Algan, John, 161
  Martha, 161
  Martha (Dyer), 161
Allen, Elenor, 66
  Elizabeth, 44
  Ephraim, 44
  James, 13, 98, 117
  Jedediah, 44, 117
  Margaret, 76, 101, 107, 121, 126, 166, 173, 177
  Nathaniel, 66, 107, 163
  Nehemiah, 13, 57, 66
  Reuben, 153
  Samuel, 4, 14, 17, 25, 30, 32, 38, 39, 42, 45, 65, 99, 120, 133, 169, 176, 16, 33
  Samuel, 1
  Will, 62
  William, 55, 58, 61-63, 76, 77, 91, 92, 101, 103, 107, 108, 110, 116, 118, 120, 121, 123, 125, 126, 128, 129, 131, 133, 150, 151, 156, 163, 166, 167, 171-173, 176, 177, 182

Alley, Abraham, 97
Alling, Samuel, 49
Allman, Benjamin, 159
Ambler, Joseph, 49
Ames, Ann, 136
Amos, Ann, 116, 136
  Richard, 111
  William, 111
Anderson, Archibald, 99, 133
  Lawrence, 147
  Mary, 99, 133
Andrews, Martha, 137
  Mary, 103
Annis, Thomas, 30, 99
Antes, Henry, 166, 167
Anthony, Stephen, 140
Antis, Henry, 173
Appleton, Josiah, 104
Arbuckle, James, 76, 87, 88, 194
Archbald, Elizabeth, 94
Armitage, Benjamin, 55, 82, 83
  Jane, 82
Armstrong, Richard, 73
Arnett, James, 113
Ashbourn, William, 49, 106
Ashburn, Wm., 170
Ashburne, William, 68
Ashburnet, William, 59
Ashburnett, William, 109
Ashcraft, Daniel, 55, 63
Ashfield, Richard, 107
Ashmead, John, 136
Ashton, Rob, 50
  Robert, 50, 79
  Thomas, 78, 113
Aspden, Mathias, 68
Aspdin, Mathias, 70
Aspen, Mathias, 68
Atkinson, Christopher, 60
  Hannah, 171
  Isaac, 41
  Joseph, 108, 110, 142, 168, 174, 175
  Margaret, 25, 83, 91, 108, 126, 142, 168, 169
  Mary, 6, 117
  Ruth (Stacey), 118

Atkinson *cont'd*
  Thomas, 2
  William, 2, 4, 6, 7, 67, 69, 91, 98, 101, 102, 108, 111, 122, 126, 132, 142, 168, 171, 190, 195
  William, Jr., 133
  Wm., 25, 26, 47, 66, 78, 81, 84, 86, 91, 96, 98, 100, 107, 110, 113, 115, 130, 132, 142, 148, 171, 178, 190
Attwood, William, 142, 160, 181
Atwood, William, 103
Avalon, Nicholas, 162
Axford, John, 104

Bagley, William, 142
Bailey, Edward, 89
Baily, Hannah, 117
  Henry, 107
  William, 117
Bainbridge, Elizabeth, 113
  John, 112, 113
  Sarah, 112, 113
  Sarah (Clowes), 113
Baines, Hannah, 90
  James, 90
  Joseph, 90
Baird, Patrick, 192
Baker, Henry, 18, 22
  John, 13, 25, 57, 66, 67
  Mary, 23
  Mary (Radclift), 35
  Rachel, 133
  Samuel, 15, 22, 52, 76, 83, 98, 193
  Widow, 73
  William, 25, 57
  William W., 13
  _____, 118, 140, 188
Bakin, Simon, 115
Baldwin, Ann, 51, 171
  James, 154, 175, 190
  John, 1, 2, 15, 20, 51, 52, 59, 67, 82, 109, 112, 171

Baldwin *cont'd*
  John, Jr., 193
  John, Sr., 193
  Joseph, 171
  Sarah, 171
  William, 13, 69, 105, 106, 109
Ballard, William, 73
Banes, Joseph, 160
  Thomas, 102
Banges, Benjamin, 165
  John, 165
Bangs, Benjamin, 165
  Elizabeth, 165
  John, 165
  Joshua, 165
  Mary, 165
Banks, Thomas, 114
Banksen, Daniel, 66, 67
Bansted, Caleb, 101
Barber, Elizabeth, 123
Barclay, John, 101
Barcroft, Ambrose, 117, 118
  Elizabeth, 117
  Hannah, 117
  John, 117
  William, 117
Bard, Mary, 172
  Peter, 172
Barker, Samuel, 64
  Thomas, 145
Barkes, Benjamin, 5
Barnard, Robert, 148
Barnes, Thomas, Jr., 115
Barnett, Elizabeth (Burrowes), 105
  Robert, 105
Barnetvanhood, Christian, 24
Barnetvanhorn, Christian, 24, 25
Barnson,
  Barnard, 2
  Christian, 2, 24, 25, 80, 81, 86, 96, 123, 174
  Nicholas, 122
  Rebeckah, 122
  Williamkee, 80
  WilliamKee, 81
  Williamkee, 123, 174

Barnsonvanhorne,
  Christian, 24
Bartholomew, Ellen, 84
  Ellen (Cutler), 84
  Ellin, 87
  Jeremiah, 39, 84-87, 99, 119, 161
  John, 179
  Mary, 179
  Rachel, 179
Bartolet, Philip, 177
Barton, Thomas, 158
Bass, Jeremiah, 16
Bates, Humphrey, 74, 75
  John, Jr., 182
Bathurst, Frances, 175
  Mary (Colby), 175
Bauldwin, John, 193
Bavington, Jonathan, 125, 146
Baxter, John, 99
  Samuel, 82
Bayard, Samuel, 31, 45, 52
Bayley, Henry, 27, 34
  Thomas, 75
Baynes, Joseph, 89
  Thomas, 80, 174
  Timothy, 134
Beak, Samuel, 70
Beake, Samuel, 44, 72
  ____, 4
Beakes, John, 41
  Samuel, 8, 26, 29, 104
  Stephen, 26
  William, 138
  Wm., 38
Beaks, John, 161
  Samuel, 134
  Stephen, 8
  William, 139
Beal, George, 131, 159
  William, 79
  Wm., 35
Beale, Alexander, 55
  George, 38, 39, 93
  John, 55
  William, 9, 39
Bealurs, William, 3
Bealy, Charles, 155
Beams, Jacob, 153
Bearley, John, 140

Beaumont, John, 105, 150
Belms, Edward, 136
Benbow, George, 129
Benezet, J. Stephen, 101
  John Stephen, 101, 173
Bennet, Abraham, 125, 181
  Abram, 181
  Ader John, 86
  Adrian, 86
  Annace, 125
  Jacob, 125, 148
  William, 141
Bennett, Edmond, 42
  Edmund, 4
  Elizabeth, 4, 42
  William, 7
Berkerk, Barnard, 90
Besonet, John, 59, 102
Best, Jeremiah, 107
Betredge, William, 17
  Wm., 18
Bettris, Edward, 138
Bevan, Ann (Davis), 191, 192
  Awberry, 191
  Awbery, 192
Biddle, Thomas, 1, 7, 31, 98
  William, 64
  Wm., 71
Bidgood, Richard, 194
  William, 194
Biles, Anne, 18
  Charles, 100, 152, 167, 169
  George, 70, 72, 73
  John, 18
  Langhorne, 118, 136, 138, 152, 158, 159, 162, 164, 169, 186, 187
  Martha, 70
  Sarah, 110, 158
  Sarah (Langhorne), 158
  Tho., 41, 50
  Thomas, 31, 34, 37, 41, 45, 52, 53, 57, 69, 115
  William, 4, 10, 14, 18, 20, 26, 30, 31, 38, 41, 43, 53, 54, 57, 60, 67-69, 79,

Biles, William *cont'd*
    104, 106, 118,
    125, 132, 154,
    158, 190
  William, Jr., 7, 18, 29, 66
  William, Sr., 29
  Wm., 26, 58, 68, 82
Bill, Thomas, 98
Bills, Thomas, 7, 21, 98
Bingham, James, 107, 108,
    116, 121-123,
    126, 131, 156,
    166, 173
  James, Jr., 77
  William, 173
Bissonet, John, 52
Bitts, Thomas, 117
Black, Randal, 117
Blackden, Barbara, 60
  Mary, 60
  Widow, 69
Blacker, Johanne, 2
  Johannes, 42
Blackshaw, Nehemiah, 70-
    72, 83, 84, 107
Blacot, Peter, 149
Bladgen, Widow, 14
Blagden, Widow, 57, 64
Blagdon, Widow, 39, 47,
    119
Blair, Thomas, 151
Blake, Paul, 141
Blaker, Johannes, 110, 148
  John, 148
  Peter, 148
  Samuel, 125
Blakey, William, 135
  William, Jr., 134
Bland, N., 97
Blangdon, Barbara, 4
Bleker, Peter, 97
Blongdon, Barbara, 42
Bloodgood, William, 53
Boare, Joshua, 104, 190
Bockhill, Jos., 78
Bogert, Geysbert, 156
Bollen, James, 64
Bolton, Isaac, 152
Bond, Ann, 81, 114, 130,
    170
  John, 92, 93

Bond *cont'd*
  Jos., 98
  Joseph, 4, 13, 15, 16, 20,
    22, 36, 69, 81, 82,
    98, 113, 114, 119,
    130, 170, 176, 195
  Sarah, 92
  Thomas, 26
Bonde, Thomas, 131
Bonds, Joseph, 117
Bood, John, 144
Boogaert, Geysbert, 156
Boone, George, 189
Borden, Benjamin, 19, 29,
    40
  Francis, 71, 191, 193
  John, 19, 29, 40
  Samuel, 144
  William, 19, 29, 40
  _____, 145
Boron, Samuel, 2
Bossenett, John, 119
Boude, Thomas, 144
Bouger, William, 44
Bougher, William, 43
Boulding, William, 144
  _____, 145
Bound, John, 41
  Samuel, 23, 41
Bowen, John, 16, 25, 38, 39
  Richard R., 3
Bowman, Jeremiah, 120
  Thomas, 100, 155
Bown, Abraham, 166
  Samuel, 23, 24, 125
Bowne, John, 13, 23
  Samuel, 23
Boyden, James, 14, 42, 186
  John, 186
  Margaret, 14
  Mary, 186
  Miriam, 17, 16
Boyles, James, 111
Bradford, Andrew, 61
  Thomas, 66
Brays, John, 101
Breas, Hannah, 81
Brees, Hannah, 151, 156,
    157
  Henderick, 81
  Henry, 90, 150, 151, 156,

Brees, Henry *cont'd*
    157
  John, 150, 151, 156, 157
  Margaret, 156, 157
  Nealeha, 150, 151
  Nealiha, 157
  Sarah, 151, 157
Breese, Henderick, 81
Breezely, John, 140
Breinlnall, Joseph, 71
Breintall, Joseph, 36
Breintnal, Joseph, 120
Breintnall, Joseph, 61, 118,
    120
  Owen Joseph, 103
Brelsford, Samuel, 69, 102,
    119, 159
  William, 35
Brice, Henry, 61
Bridgeman, William, 27
  _____, 1
Bridgman, Walker, 122
Brierly, John, 38
Briggs, William, 39, 103,
    105, 108
Brilsford, William, 47
Bringhurst, George, 58
  John, 164
  Mary, 164
Brinson, Daniel, 70, 72
Brise, Henry, 61
Britain, John, 144
  Nathaniel, 149
  William, 105, 176
Brittain, Nathaniel, 149
Brittin, William, 131
Britton, William, 132
Brock, Elizabeth, 3
  John, 3, 57
  Oddy, 16
  Ralph, 3, 43, 57, 58, 91
  Robert, 91
  Samuel, 63
  Thomas, 24, 37, 98
Brockden, C., 48, 50, 51, 61,
    75, 76, 83, 97,
    100, 101, 104,
    107, 156, 163,
    169, 173, 187, 188
  Ch., 190
  Cha., 28, 31, 36, 40, 73,

Brockden, Cha. cont'd
  82, 91, 141, 142
  Charles, 16, 21, 23, 31,
    35, 61, 73, 83, 92,
    125, 142, 144,
    146, 148, 166,
    167, 173, 187
  Chas., 24, 39, 190, 192
  Susannah, 21
Brockdon, Charles, 20
Brodnax, Catherine, 181
  Christian, 181
  Robert, 180, 181
Bromley, Elizabeth, 55
  Hannah, 55
  Katherine, 55
  Nathaniel, 55
Brooks, Charles, 148
  James, 95
  John, 74
  Thomas, 117
Broomly, Nathaniel, 9
Brown, Alexander, 28, 71,
    127, 191, 192
  Elecksander, 127
  George, 26, 86, 127
  Isaac, 92
  John, 26, 28
  Samuel, 133, 143
  Sarah, 127
  Thomas, 19, 28, 29, 71,
    191, 192
Browne, Isa, 22
Brownell, George, 39
Bryan, Charles, 194
  Chas., 106, 194
Bryant, Cornelius, 185
Buckles, Robert, 60
Buckley, William, 175, 186,
    190
  Wm., 178
Buckman, Thomas, 194
  William, 9, 110
Budd, Jno., 55
  William, 184
Buley, Ann, 155
  John, 155
Bulkley, Samuel, 17, 46, 67
Bur___, John, 159
Burchan, Henry, 8
Burden, John, 164, 190

Burge, Henry, 8
  Mary (Sanford), 8
Burges, Daniel, 2, 13, 18,
    167, 168
  Daniel, Jr., 167, 168
  Dorothy, 167, 168
  John, 2, 4, 9, 13, 18, 167,
    168
  Joseph, 43, 167, 168
  Richard, 14
  Samuel, 2, 3, 7, 13, 18,
    167
Burgess, Ann, 139, 176
  Daniel, 107
  Dorothy, 107
  Elizabeth, 79
  Elizabeth (Paxon), 183
  Hannah, 138
  John, 107, 138, 139
  Joseph, 107, 138, 139
  Richard, 79
  Samuel, 107, 139
  ___, 117
Burgis, John, 67, 69-73
Burk, John, 101, 102, 119,
    140
Burke, Edward, 104
  John, 123, 147, 174
Burkerdike, Gael, 52
Burling, John, 158
Burroughs, John, Jr., 194
Burrowes, Elizabeth, 105
  Francis, 105
  John, 105
  Roger, 105
Burton, Anthony, 2, 13, 24,
    29, 36, 37, 67, 69,
    107, 108, 114,
    130, 163, 164,
    172, 193
  Elizabeth, 67
  Elizabeth (Gibbs), 67
  Sarah, 130
Busby, John, 77
  Mary (Taylor), 77
Bush, Joseph, 136
Bushill, Samuel, 112
  Unity, 112
Buskirk, Andreas, 106
  Andrew, 91
  Peter, 86, 87

Buskirk cont'd
  ___, 92
Butler, S., 154
  Simon, 51, 92, 154, 159,
    176, 179, 186, 194
  Thos., 170
Buttons, Jacob, 116
Bye, John, 10, 24
  Martha, 184
  Nathaniel, 184
  Thomas, 24, 83, 184
Byes, John, 156

Cadwaladar, Jno., 154
Cadwalader, Jno., 74, 92
  John, 134, 135
  Tho., 92
Cadwallader, Jacob, 180,
    194
  John, 48, 59
  Magdalen, 194
  Timothy, 129
Cadwallador, Jacob, 180
  John, 180
  Magdalen, 180
  Margaret, 180
Caille, Robert, 116, 137, 138
Cain, Thomas, 21, 90
Caldwell, James, 144
Call, Caleb, 18
Callahan, John, 94, 95, 114,
    116, 124, 127-
    129, 133, 137,
    148, 155, 177, 178
Callowhill, Thomas, 34, 153
Campion, George, 144, 145
Camron, David, 129
Canby, Thomas, Jr., 156
Canby, Benjamin, 101, 102,
    115, 122, 142, 156
  Jane, 156
  John, 161
  Sarah, 115, 142, 156
  Thomas, 156
  Thomas, Sr., 156
Candonet, Francis, 25
  Mary, 25
Carliell, Abraham, 12
Carlile, Jonah, 127
  Jonathan, 30
Carmick, Peter, 97

Carmick cont'd
Sarah, 97
Carn, Thomas, 44
Carpenter, Hannah, 4, 15, 20, 21, 69, 82, 97, 114, 119, 189, 190
John, 9, 20, 21, 82, 97
Samuel, 2, 4, 8, 9, 15, 20, 21, 28, 30-32, 42, 45, 52, 69, 73, 86, 87, 97, 98, 111, 114, 117, 119, 133, 171, 189, 190
Samuel, Jr., 82
Samuel, Sr., 20, 21, 69, 82
Carr, Hannah, 41
Hannah (Willets), 23
Job, 23, 41
Carrell, Barnard, 181
Dinah, 181
Elizabeth, 181
James, 181, 186
Lydia, 181
Sarah, 181
Carruthers, James, 143
Carry, Samuel, 106
Carson, John, 44
Cart, John, 115
Samuel, 164
Sarah, 164
Cartar, John, 48
Sarah, 87
Wm., 87
Carter, Edward, 5, 46, 50
James, 1, 4, 26, 36, 43, 120, 133, 169
John, 7, 25, 26, 87
Mary, 175
Robert, 7, 15, 25, 26
Sarah, 87
Susanna, 36
William, 16, 36, 39, 51, 56, 74, 85, 87, 111, 112, 121, 154, 161
Wm., 161
_____, 68
Carts, John, 148
Samuel, 91
Carver, James, 17

Carts cont'd
John, 55
William, 55, 56
Cary, Abigail, 109
Jane, 109
Joseph, 109
Mary, 100, 117, 155
Saml., 137, 138
Sampson, 100, 109, 116, 117
Samson, 57, 100, 109, 117, 155, 171, 172
Samson, Jr., 100, 171
Samuel, 100, 107-109, 116, 117, 130, 147, 148, 156, 163, 164, 171, 172
Sarah (Stackhouse), 163
Thomas, 116, 117
William, 117
Case, J. Watson, 191
Cassly, John, 27
Catchill, Thomas, 9
Catlen, Isabel, 152
Cawley, Anne, 97
John, 18, 120, 135
Chalkley, Thomas, 135
Chamberlain, Peter, 9
Chamberlin, Jacob, 71
Peter, 5
Chambers, Williams, 165
Chapman, Abr., 35
Abra, 55, 77, 78, 88, 106
Abra., Jr., 88, 125
Abrah., 189
Abraham, 22, 35, 49, 59, 63, 68, 74, 78, 79, 82, 83, 88, 93, 101, 106, 109, 113, 125, 146, 147, 150, 169, 182, 189, 194
Abrm., 22
John, 49, 83, 109, 113, 131, 132
John, Jr., 109, 150
Joseph, 35, 44, 49, 113, 150
Chatham, Joseph, 100
Childs, John, 97
Christian, Barnard, 2, 24,

Christian, Barnard cont'd
49, 86
Bernard, 25, 42, 78, 86
Christy, Thomas, 176
Church, Joseph, 175
Richard, 170
Sarah, 170
Clare, William, 68
Clark, Benjamin, 49
John, 8, 13, 18, 24, 50
Thomas, 14, 16, 17, 119
William, 1
Clarke, John, 132, 154
Joseph, 189
Martha (White), 132
Rachel, 132
Sarah (Mitchell), 189
Thomas, 104, 119, 121, 159
Clarridge, Elizabeth (Bangs), 165
Clauson, John, 14, 16, 17, 23, 30, 47, 57, 99, 133
Clawson, Gustavas, 67
John, 5, 111, 186
Clay, John, 27, 142
Claypool, James, 7, 91, 146, 183
Rebecca, 146
Claypoole, Abraham, 153, 172
George, 34
Helena, 125
James, 6, 25, 33, 67, 103, 107, 125, 155, 157, 164
Joseph, 34, 125
William, 170
_____, 183
Clement, James, 53
Clews, Joseph, 3
William, 145
Clifford, Tho., 86
Thomas, 133
Clifton, John, 175
Climer, Margaret, 169
Cloak, Peter, 48
Closson, John, 14
Clough, George, 4, 14, 15, 69, 98, 101, 102,

Clough, George *cont'd*
   115, 122, 134
Clowes, John, 57, 113
   Margary, 113
   Rebecca, 113
   Rebeckah, 113
   Sarah, 113
Clows, Joseph, 58
Clymer, William, 120, 132, 133, 169
Coat, John, 49
   Samuel, 49
Coates, Roger, 72
Coats, Elizabeth, 1
   Enoch, 146
   John, 72, 144
   Thomas, 1
Cobbert, Robert, 12
Cock, Timothy, 48
Cockshaw, Jona., 154
Colbert, Robert, 12
Colby, Mary, 175
   Theodore, 175
Coleman, William, 182, 184, 185, 187, 190
   Wm., 63, 77
Coles, Samuel, 64
Colhoun, Andrew, 85
Collet, Tobias, 50, 137
Collett, Tobias, 50
Collins, Benjamin, 137
   Elizabeth, 98
Collison, Robert, 136, 174
Colonelly, William, 142
Colter, William, 95
Combe, Ann, 143
   Benjamin, 143
Combs, Joseph, 95
Comly, Henry, 1, 147
   Henry, Jr., 147
Conel, Adrian, 141
Conley, John, 114
Connoly, Cain, 27
   Deborah, 131
   William, 27
Conolly, Deborah, 131
Conoly, Deborah, 130
Constable, Thomas, 1, 27, 122
Conway, Philip, 154
   Phillip, 73

Cook, Arthur, 6, 17, 18, 40, 33, 73, 154
   Francis, 125
   John, 17, 22, 33, 40
   Margaret, 22, 33, 40
   Patrick, 68
Cooke, Francis, 15
   John, 79
   Margaret, 79
Coombe, Benjamin, 51
   Hannah, 51
   Samuel, 51
Cooper, James, 39
   John W., 87, 88, 160
   Jonathan, 23, 35, 63
   Mary, 160
   Samuel, 146
   Sarah, 23
   William, 33, 39, 80, 160, 170, 174
Cope, George, 95
Corfons, Cornelus, 148
Corker, Samuel, 144
Corn, Edward, 10
Cornish, Andrew, 92
Corns, Edward, 134
Corrie, James, 60
Corson, Benjamin, 33
   Cor., 49
Corsons, Cornelus, 148
Cotton, Benjamin, 164
Cotty, Abel, 144
Coupland, Caleb, 104
Course, James, 114
Cowgill, Edmund, 79
   John, 122
   Rachel, 122
Cowpland, Sarah, 33
Cox, Tho., 90
Coxe, Tho., 59, 60, 89
Coyle, _____, 145
Craig, Thomas, 133, 150, 182
Craige, Daniel, 186
   Thomas, 186
Craigton, William, 186
Crap, Mary, 34
Craske, Sell, 89, 90
Craven, James, 71, 140, 185, 186
Cravens, James, 125

Crawford, Archibald, 186
   Moses, 181, 186
Crellins, Joseph, 133
Cremere, George, 171
Crewson, Elizabeth, 124
   Francis, 124
Cridland, John, 68
Crispen, Silas, 119
Croasdale, Ezra, 3, 77, 86, 106, 109, 120
   Jeremiah, 55, 96
   John, 5, 122, 146, 161
   Thomas, 48, 122, 161
   William, 2, 4, 14, 47, 48, 69, 106, 109, 111, 122
Croasdele, Ezra, 43
Croasdell, Ezra, 135
   Jeremiah, 135
   John, 122
   William, 24
Crosdal, William, 57
Cross, John, 115
Crowley, James, 26
Cruickshanks, George, 120, 121
Crusen, Derick, 47
   Derrick, 90
   Henry, 90
   John, 90
Cruson, Derick, 29, 40
   Derrick, 9
   Nicholas, 181
Culler, John, 67
Cuming, Robert, 88
Cumings, Robert, 160
Cumming, Robert, 88
Cunningham, Gariod, 193
Curly, Thomas, 29
Currie, James, 60
Curry, Thomas, 29
Cuthbert, William, 64
Cutler, Benjamin, 80, 135
   Edmund, 10, 162
   Ellen, 84
   Isabel, 100, 162, 167
   John, 2, 10, 16, 28, 79, 83, 86, 87, 126, 127, 135
   Thomas, 9, 10
   William, 84

Cutter, John, 1, 2, 4, 5, 67, 68
   William, 24

D'Avenant, Frances (Bathurst), 175
   Henry, 175
Dagge, Hen., 56
Danby, John, 100, 167
   Sarah, 100, 167
Dark, John, 14, 169
   Samuel, 13, 18
Darke, Martha, 104, 143
   Samuel, 29, 41, 73, 104, 143
   William, 80
   ____, 80
David, Ben, 146
   Thomas, 59
Davids, Thomas, 6, 54, 58
Davies, Robert, 38
   William, 158
Davis, Ann, 191, 192
   Ben, 147
   Dinah, 145
   Elizabeth, 191, 192
   Elizabeth (Huddleston), 135
   Elizabeth (Hudleston), 130
   George, 176, 177
   John, 51, 71, 191, 192
   Mary, 71, 191, 192
   Mirick, 42
   Thomas, 130, 135
Dawson, Daniel, 144
   John, 19, 170
   Katharine, 19
Day, John, 145
   Mathew, 165
De Berholt, Catherine, 133
   Johanne Philip, 133
DeBertholt, Johannes Philip, 150
DeCew, Is., 71
   Isaac, 71
Decow, Isaac, 9, 28, 136, 138
   Susannah, 136
Deiver, John, 93, 94
Delworth, Joseph, 194

Demeyer, H., 46
Dempsy, Joseph, 176
Denmark, Christopher, 77
Denning, Chris, 40
Denormandie, Abram, 118
   Andrew, 137
   Elizabeth, 67
   Henrietta (Gandovett), 97
   Henryeta (Gandovet), 66
   Jn. Ab., 99
   Jn. Abrah., 143
   John, 134, 186
   John Abra., 67
   John Abraham, 66, 97, 98, 100-102, 111, 116, 119, 121-123, 130-132, 134, 137, 147, 154, 159, 168, 170, 171, 174, 175, 186, 190, 195
   John Anthony, 116, 137
   John, Jr., 134, 146
DeNormandie, Jno. Anthony, 36, 37
DeNormandy, John Abraham, 36, 37
Desting, Constance, 47
Devies, James, 155, 188
Dicken, James, 129
   ____, 127
Dickens, James, 127
Dickinson, John, 69
Dikes, Thomas, 36
Dillon, Nicholas, 124
Dilwin, William, 11, 12
Dilworth, James, 68, 104, 130, 135
Dimsdall, Sarah, 50
Diotrick, Elias, 182
Dixon, Joan, 145
Doan, Daniel, 3, 102
Doane, Daniel, Jr., 68
Dole, Joseph, 15, 29
Dolworth, Joseph, 180
Dongan, William, 143
Donham, Nathaniel, 48
Doraugh, James, 178
Dougall, John, 164
Dougan, James C.H., 90

Doughty, Francis, Jr., 79
   Will., 53
   Wm., 53
Dove, Frances, 158
Dowd, Michael, 110, 123
Dowdney, Thomas, 113, 142, 194
Downey, James, 78, 140, 170
Doyl, Edward, 27
Doyle, Clement, 139
   Edward, 139, 181, 182
   William, 182
Dracor, Philip, 96
Dracord, Ralph, 189
   Susanah, 189
Dracot, Philip, 68
Dracott, Philip, 43, 162
   Ralph, 36, 43
Draker, Ralph, 120
Draycot, Ralph, 1, 133, 169
Draycott, Ralph, 4
Drinker, Joseph, 47, 56, 57
   Mary, 47, 57
Drummond, Evan, 101
Duche, Jacob, 189
Duer, John, 101, 108
   Joseph, 101, 108
Dufay, Jane, 137
   Marie, 137
Duffield, Benjamin, 22, 33, 36
   Thomas, 160
Dun, George, 162
   Ralph, 163
Duncan, Jno., 81, 84, 85, 88-91, 93, 96, 97, 102, 122-124, 130, 161
   John, 102, 110, 116, 119, 190
   William, 57, 61
Dungan, Clement, 33
   George, 88, 160
   Jacob, 115
   Jeremiah, 33, 55, 159, 160
   John, 115
   Jonathan, 115
   Joseph, 125
   Mary, 33

Dungan cont'd
Samuel, 115
Thomas, 33, 115, 125, 140, 159, 160, 181, 183
William, 27
____, 29, 40, 47
Dunging, David, 148
Jeremiah, 148
Dunkan, David, 156
Edmund, 8, 55, 56, 114, 156
George, 7, 8
Jno., 87
John, 55, 56
Margaret, 55, 56
William, 7, 55, 56, 114
Dunker, Rebeckah, 96
Dunn, George, 163
Torrence, 181
Dupree, Nicholas, 163
Dupue, Nicholas, 61-63
Dupui, Nicholas, 62
DuPui, Nicholas, 77
Durborow, Jn., 57
Durborrow, John, 145
Dure, Thomas, 26
Durham, Edmund, 156
Mathew, 131
Dussay, Jane, 137
Marie, 137
Dusting, Constance, 57
Dyer, Benjamin, 161
Charles, 161
Comfort, 161
Deborah, 161
Elizabeth, 161
Freelove, 161
Hannah, 161
James, 39, 161
John, 144
Joseph, 99, 161
Martha, 161
Samuel, 95, 161
____, 127
Dymock, Sarah, 19
Tobias, 19, 57, 141, 142
Dymocke, Tobias, 83
Dyre, James, 49, 64
Joseph, 64

Eaglesfield, Barnard, 50
Earle, John, 144
Oliver, 40
East, Benjamin, 164
Eastbourn, Benjamin, 30
Eastburn, Benjamin, 166
John, 100, 167, 169
Thomas, 100
Eastburne, Elizabeth, 151, 152
John, 151, 152
Margaret, 151, 152
Mary, 151, 152
Sarah, 151
Thomas, 151, 152
Eaton, Edward, 176
Wm., 132
Eayre, Elizabeth (Brock), 3
Richard, 3
Edgell, Simon, 144
____, 145
Edmonds, Deborah, 26
Rodger, 26
Edmunds, Deborah, 25
Roger, 25
Edward, Thomas, 54
Edwards, Da., 99
Robert, 43, 77, 109, 110, 153
Thomas, 118
Eglin, Richard, 90
Ehrenhart, Jacob, 166, 167
Elfreet, John, 47
Elfreth, Elizabeth, 116
Elis, Robert, 188
Ellet, Andrew, 40
Ellets, Andrew, 65
Elliet, Andrew, 192
Elliott, Andrew, 104
William, 104
Ellis, Katherine, 60
Robert, 60, 61, 151, 155
Rowland, 92
Rowland, Jr., 92
Thomas, 111
Ellwood, Mary, 64
Thomas, 64
Emblen, George, 71
Emerson, ____, 172
Emlen, George, 126, 133, 169

Emlen cont'd
George, 71
Emlon, Samuel, Jr., 182
Emmot, George, 32
Mary, 33
Emott, George, 65
Mary (Tatham), 65
English, Joseph, 24, 37
Enoch, Britta, 5
Henry, 31, 45, 89
John, 5
Esnaugh, Eliza, 50
Estaugh, Eliza, 50
Jno., 50
John, 50
Evan, Alice, 124
Evan B., 109
Lewis, 124, 159
Thomas, 124, 179
Evans, David, 42
Edward, 6
Elizabeth (Musgrove), 22, 27
Evan, 22, 27, 33, 45
James, 127
John, 66, 67, 109
Lewis, 179
Lewis, Jr., 179
Madlen, 179
Magdalen H., 179
Mathew, 35
Pet, 29, 35, 59
Peter, 35, 187
Thomas, 99, 151, 179, 180
Ewings, William, 192
Eyre, Rebekah, 129

Faires, Samuel, 153, 172, 183
Fairies, Samuel, 115
Fairman, Robert, 16
Tho., Jr., 41
Thomas, 11, 16
Falesner, Daniel, 148
Faries, Samuel, 186
Farr, Thomas, 97
Faulkener, Edward, 117
Faulkner, Edward, 117
Fearon, Peter, 7
Fell, John, 182

Fell *cont'd*
  Jonathan, 181
  Joseph, 94
  Leonard, 59, 60
Fenton, Ephraim, 28, 71,
    191, 192
Ferguson, Hugh, 144
  Samuel, 144
Field, Ambrose, 136
  Benj'a., 87
  Benj., 122
  Benjamin, 20, 30, 53-55,
    64, 65, 79, 104
  Susannah (Decow), 136
Fields, Benjamin, 80, 146
Finley, James, 85
  Zachias, 85
Finney, William, 177
Fishborn, Hannah
    (Carpenter), 20
  William, 20
Fishbourn, Hannah, 97,
    114, 115, 130
  Hannah (Carpenter), 82
  Jane, 114, 115
  William, 30, 34, 36, 69,
    73, 81, 82, 97,
    114, 115, 130
  Wm., 34, 119
  _____, 117
Fishbourne, Jane, 102
  William, 86, 87, 102, 104
Fishburn, Hannah
    (Carpenter), 21
  William, 21, 164
Fisher, Tabitha, 47, 57
  William, 47, 56, 57
Fishwater, George, 139
Fithian, Joseph, 146
  Josiah, 147
Fitzwater, George, 14, 42,
    44, 51, 61, 146,
    158
Fletcher, Elizabeth, 119
  Robert, 70, 71, 119
  Widow, 160
Floyd, David, 42
Ford, Philip, 38, 39
  Thomas, 79
Forest, Daniel, 175
Forrest, Ann, 15, 29

Forrest *cont'd*
  Walker, 67
  Walter, 15, 29
Forst, Hendrick, 134
  Henry, 134
Forster, Arthur, 140, 144,
    146, 150, 153,
    156, 160, 163,
    169, 175, 176,
    182, 183, 185, 189
Foster, Bassillian, 27
  Josiah, 46
Fowler, Jeremiah, 30
  William, 30
Fox, Jos., 20, 21, 23, 24, 28,
    82
  Justinian, 1
  Susannah, 31
Frances, Jonah, Jr., 185
Francis, Elizabeth, 150
  Elizabeth (Frost), 18, 76,
    149, 150
  John, 76, 149, 150
  Tench, 123
Frazor, William, 38
Freame, Margaret, 185
  Thomas, 185, 191
Freams, William, 137
Frederickson, Michael, 45
Fredrickson, Michael, 35
Frelick, Michael, 128
Frelly, Jacob, 128
French, Nath'l., 82
  Nathaniel, 20, 21
Frogley, Henry, 144, 145
Frohock, Elizabeth, 178
  Jn., 116
  Jno., 77, 105-107, 109,
    110, 156, 158,
    162, 166
  John, 106, 112, 117, 120,
    121, 130, 134,
    146, 154, 159,
    168, 170, 173,
    174, 176, 178, 186
  John, Jr., 173
  Jon., 140, 147
Frost, Edmond, 149
  Edmund, 18, 76
  Elizabeth, 18, 76, 149
  Hannah, 18, 76, 147

Frost *cont'd*
  John, 18, 22, 76, 149
  Joseph, 18, 76, 147, 149
Fry, William, 81, 93, 116,
    119
  Wm., 58, 60, 61, 75-77,
    80, 85-88, 94, 95,
    130, 141
Fryday, Samuel, 31
Frylick, Michael, 127
Fullerton, John, 177, 178
Furley, Benjamin, 17
Furniss, Joseph, 69
Futham, John, 134

Galloway, Jos., 185
  Joseph, 153, 182
Gambley, Jacob, 133
Gandovet, Alexander, 66
  Francis, 25, 66
  Francis, Jr., 67
  Francis, Sr., 67
  Henrieta, 66
  Jeremiah, 66
  Lewis, 66
Gandovett, Alexander, 97
  Francis, 97
  Henrietta, 97
  Jeremiah, 97
  Mary, 97
  Solomon, 97
Gardinell, F., 34
Gardiner, Thomas, 64
Garland, Hum., 93, 94
  Humphrey, 73, 93, 94
Gatohels, Andrew, 128
George, David, 131
Ghiselin, Cesar, 66
Gibbs, Elizabeth, 67
  Richard, 94, 128, 185,
    187
  Samuel, 58
Gibson, Lanslot, 44
  William, 104
Gifford, Sam'l., 83
  Saml., 100, 131
Gilbert, Elizabeth (Carrell),
    181
  Esther, 155
  H., 155
  John, 15, 29, 70, 116

Gilbert *cont'd*
   Joseph, 78, 92
   Mary, 169
   Nicholas, 48, 59, 155
   Samuel, 155, 181
   Thomas, 27, 169
   William, 155, 194
Gill, Thomas, 55
Gilleylan, John, 167
Gilleylen, John, 169
Ginn, Ann, 99
   William, 99
Ginne, Ann, 60
   William, 60
Glover, Edward, 84, 87, 99, 122
   Rachel (Clarke), 132
   Richard, 25, 130, 132
Godeffroy, Cesar, 36, 66
Godfrey, Cesar, 97
Gold, James, 76
Goldney, Henry, 50, 137
Gonne, Henry, 35
Gooden, William, 188
Goodgeen, Rebecca (Johnson), 176
   Robert, 176
Goodin, William, 95
Goodson, Job, 42, 44, 51, 139, 158, 164
   John, 1, 8, 111
Goodwin, _____, 183
Gookin, Charles, 16
Goold, James, 18, 56, 146, 147
Goslin, John, 132
Gould, James, 34, 57, 194
   John, 144
Gouldney, Henry, 36
Grafton, Mary, 182
Graham, William, 129
Grahame, Wm., 67
Grame, Thomas, 185
Gramey, Thomas, 173
Grant, Elizabeth, 112
   Elizabeth (Lambert), 113
   Neal, 101, 108
   Neel, 112, 113
   Niell, 26
Gray, John, 31, 32, 45, 185, 186

Graydon, Alexander, 102, 147, 173-175
   Rachel, 174
   _____, 172
Grayson, Alexander, 122
Green, Samuel, 154
   Sarah, 154
Greene, Thomas, 54, 103, 165, 171, 187, 188
Greenway, Rob, 132
   Rob., 120, 167, 172
   Robt., 133
Gregg, James, 120
Gregory, John, 59
   William, 12
Grey, Elizabeth, 46
   John, 46, 65
Grier, John, 179
   Mathew, 144
Griffith, Abel, 179
   Abraham, 118, 189
   Ben, 59
   Benj., 160
   Benjamin, 33, 179
   Bn., 60
   Evan, 91, 162
   John, 1, 4, 123
   Katherine, 2
   Samuel, 1, 36
   Timothy, 102
Griffiths, David, 129
   Evan, 92
Griffits, Thomas, 91
Griffitts, Thomas, 107
Grifith, Abel, 179
   Benjamin, 179
Grigg, James, 171
Griscom, Tobias, 15, 29
Groom, Peter, 38, 41, 167
   Thomas, 2, 42
Groome, Peter, 152
Groosbeck, Jacob, 41
Grosebick, Jacob, 90
Groves, Joseph, 175
Growden, Joseph, 124
   Lawrance, 89
Growdon, Ann, 17, 81, 93
   J., 83
   Jos., 84
   Joseph, 3, 6-10, 15-17, 21, 29, 31, 32, 33,

Growdon, Joseph *cont'd*
   35, 37-39, 45, 46, 52, 57, 61, 67, 81, 83, 90, 93, 110, 111, 114, 116, 118, 135, 156, 157, 180, 181, 188-190
   Law., 22, 48, 94
   Lawr., 66
   Lawrance, 80, 81, 85, 89, 93-96, 99, 100, 104-108, 110, 114, 118, 158
   Lawrance, Jr., 81
   Lawrence, 16, 38, 56, 80, 111, 114, 116, 119-121, 123-126, 128, 130, 132-138, 140, 141, 144, 146-149, 151-153, 156-159, 161, 163, 164, 167, 169-173, 176-178, 180-183, 185-194
   Mary, 56
   Sara, 10
   Sarah, 108, 114, 136-138, 172, 186
Gruber, Peter, 127
Guineys, Elizabeth, 142
   George, 142
Gulick, Gertrude H., 155
Guy, Edward, 41
   John, 41

Hack, Roland, 94
Haddock, Isaac, 105
Haddon, Edward, 75
Hage, William, 100, 155
   Wm., 100
Hague, Francis, 59, 68, 109, 194
   Jane, 68
   Jeane, 59
   Rebeccah, 195
Haig, Peter, 137
Hair, Nathaniel, 57
Haire, Richard, 125
Hale, Lemuel, 155

Halfpenny, James, 176
Hall, Agnes, 75
  Hannah, 117
  Jno., 52, 81
  John, 2, 4, 7, 12-14, 19, 24, 29, 31, 32, 36, 52, 59, 64, 69, 91, 98, 100-102, 117, 122, 140, 154, 166, 171, 172, 182, 195
  Jon., 29, 66
  Jos., 40, 47
  Joseph, 43
  Rebecca, 2, 7
  Robert, 31, 32, 45, 50, 52, 119, 189, 190
  Sarah, 98, 171
  Sarah (Baldwin), 171
  William, 43
Hambleton, James, 27
Hambly, Joshua, 149
Hamilton, A., 100
  An., Jr., 62
  And., Jr., 62
  Andrew, 15, 45, 60, 86, 103-105, 108
  Ann, 45
  James, 60, 91, 134, 161
  James Andrew, 138
  John, 65, 101
  John, Col., 48
  Will., 191
  _____, 185
Hampton, Joseph, 44
Hamson, Margaret, 111
Hant, Joseph, 140
Harcomb, John, 172
Hardin, Francis, 19
  Nathaniel, 16
Harding, John Thomas, 169
  Nathaniel, 25, 38, 39
  Thomas, 4, 94, 100, 120, 133, 152, 169
Hardman, _____, 14
Harker, Adam, 68, 80, 82, 124, 146, 174, 178
  Grace, 178
  James, 150
  Sam'l., 69

Harker *cont'd*
  Samuel, 82
Harman, George, 145
Harody, Robert, 18
Harriott, Samuel, 145
Harris, Benj'a., 90, 91
  Benj., 132
  Benjamin, 6, 91, 130
  George, 48, 59, 70
  Mary, 172, 182, 187
  Walter, 116
Harrison, Benjamin, 45
  Daniel, 144, 145
  Elizabeth, 70, 72
  James, 16, 25, 35, 38, 39, 75
  John, 45, 70, 72
  Phebe, 35, 75
  Rachel, 45
Harrys, Sarah, 92
  Thomas, 92
Hart, John, 33, 70, 73, 109, 115, 144, 155, 159, 160, 180, 182
  Joseph, 180, 194
  Miles, 194
  Oliver, 180, 194
  Sarah, 194
Hartsell, Henry, 191
Hartshorne, R., 104
Harvelans, Jeffry, 72
Harvey, Benjamin, 171
  John, 78, 153
  Robert, 13, 132, 178
  Thomas, 170
Harwood, William, 145
Hasell, Samuel, 109
Hastings, Peter, 82
Hatfield, George, 145
Haughhead, Hannah, 124
  Jacob, 124
Hawkins, Geoffrey, 70
  _____, 73
Haydon, Andrew, 40
Haye, William, 155
Hayes, Henry, 85
  John, 137
  Richard, 104, 129
Hayhurst, Cuthbert, 10, 80, 85, 99, 130, 135
  John, 2, 39, 64, 119

Hayhurst *cont'd*
  Rachel, 23
  Rachel (Radclift), 35
  William, 23, 35, 80, 104, 130, 135
Hays, Richard, 86
Head, John, 170
  Jonathan, 64
  Thomas, 170
Headerickson, Michael, 32
Headley, Hannah, 182
  John, 182
  Joseph, 112, 182
  _____, 119
Headly, Daniel, 171
  John, 10
  _____, 159
Healey, Joseph, 102
Heap, John, 145
  Joshua, 192
Heart, Widow, 57
Heastand, Abraham, 126
Heath, Andrew, 7, 9
  Ann, 141, 142
  Elizabeth, 142
  Hannah, 142
  Mary, 142
  Richard, 66, 141, 142
  Susana, 141
  Susanna, 142
Heathcote, George, 117
Heaton, Alice, 10, 147
  Ann, 169
  Grace, 10, 119
  Jacob, 34, 129
  James, 24, 33, 73
  Robert, 39, 43, 55, 60, 64, 68, 77, 80, 81, 85, 90, 104, 119, 120, 132, 133, 135, 147, 148, 168, 169, 183
  Robert, Jr., 4, 10, 55, 80, 85, 86
  Robert, Sr., 10
Heed, Thomas, 19
Heiar, George, 186
Helby, Joseph, 64
Hellings, Elizabeth, 115
  Nicholas, 115
Helstyn, Jacob, 3

Hembury, Elinor, 51
   Joseph, 51
Henderson, Andrew, 85
   Cha., 74
Hendrick, James, 93
Henry, Philip, 185
Herding, Thomas, 152
Herman, Jacob, 127, 128
Heston, Jacob, 33, 129
Hewarth, Isabel, 43
Hewlet, John, 40
Hewston, John, 183
Hibbs, William, 77, 78, 168
Hicks, Isaac, 23
   J., 140
   _____, 128
Hiear, George, 185
Hiet, John, 78
Hiett, John, 13
Higginbotham, Joseph, 51
Hilborn, Samuel, 3
Hilbourn, Thomas, 77, 106, 135
Hilburne, Thomas, 146
Hiley, Peter, 47
Hill, Agnes, 13, 18
   Elizabeth, 166
   Hannah, 145, 146
   James, 13, 18
   John, 126, 169
   Joseph, 60
   Nicholas, 151
   Richard, 2, 12, 13, 18, 20, 23, 24, 28, 34, 62, 77, 143-146, 159
   Richard, Dr., 143, 146
   Sarah, 126, 169
   Thomas, 56
   Walter, 71, 191, 192
   William, 101, 102, 122, 166
Hillborn, Elizabeth, 79
   Margaret, 79
   Robert, 22
   Samuel, 79
   Thomas, 22, 79
Hillbourn, Robert, 88
   Thomas, 87, 88, 109, 135
Hillbourne, Thomas, 43
Hillburn, Thomas, 76
Hilliard, Mary, 12

Hilliard *cont'd*
   Mary (Steel), 175
   Richard, 12
Hinekson, Abel, 32
Hingston, Abel, 31
   Abell, 10
   James, 35, 187
   Josiah, 35, 187
   William, 35, 187
Hingstone, William, 21
Hinkson, Abel, 45
Hinkston, Abel, 57, 79
Hinsy, John, 180
Hinton, Gabriel, 33
   Joseph, 141
   Mary, 141
   William, 129
Hixon, William, 38
Hixson, William, 38
Hoare, Richard, 166
Hobson, William, 43
Hockdale, Robert, 183
Hockley, Ann, 103
   Richard, 103, 118, 139, 140, 188
Hodge, Henry, 57
Hodgly, Henry, 50
Hodgson, Daniel, 25, 38, 39
   Sarah, 38
Hodson, Thomas, 26
Hoffman, Geo., 167
Holcomb, Ja., 51
   Jacob, 142
Holcombe, Ja., 23, 51
   Jacob, 10, 141
Holgates, Robert, 122
Hollis, John, 165, 166
Holloway, Tobias, 15, 29
Holme, Elizabeth, 60
Holmes, James, 44
   Samuel, 19
Home, Thomas, 149
Homer, Elizabeth, 8, 21
   Tho., 157
   Thos., 150, 151
   William, 8, 21
Hoope, Joshua, 40
Hooper, Sarah, 142
   Sarah (Jones), 142
   William, 142
Hoopes, Daniel, 47, 48, 180

Hoopes *cont'd*
   Jane, 47, 180
   John, 180
   Joshua, 180
Hoops, Joshua, 65
Hooton, Elizabeth (Stanley), 11
   Thomas, 11
Hope, Rebecca, 115
   William, 102, 115
Hopkins, John, 61, 172
Horne, Edward, 70
Horneybroock, Samuel, 19
Hornibroock, Samuel, 18
Horohock, Jno., 77
Horsefield, Timothy, 166, 167
Hoster, Benjamin, 136
Hough, Deborah, 65
   Edith, 194
   Francis, 71, 191
   John, 18, 19, 22, 24, 27, 50, 59, 61, 68, 84, 109, 113, 120, 154, 171
   Joseph, 42, 44, 147
   Margary (Clowes), 113
   Margery, 112, 113
   Mary (Bangs), 165
   Richard, 29, 40, 50, 52, 60, 65, 66, 74, 75, 89, 104, 118, 140, 188, 192
   Samuel, 7, 9
   Thomas, 165
   William, 192
Howard, Thomas, 161
Howel, John, 180, 181
Howell, Catharine, 185
   Jane, 58
   Jane (Luffe), 12
   Job, 73
   Joseph, 58
   Philip, 12
   Thomas, 185, 186
Howgland, Derrick, 90
Huddleston, Dorothy, 135
   Elizabeth, 135
   Henry, 135
   William, 102, 135
   Wm., 104

Huddlestone, William, 80
Hudleston, Dorothy, 104, 129, 130
    Elizabeth, 130
    Henry, 55, 118, 130, 174
    William, 80, 104, 129, 130
Hudlestone, Henry, 80
____, 86, 87
Hudson, Thomas, 20, 30, 53, 54, 79
Huff, Jennet, 98
    Michael, 98
Hughes, Francis, 192
    George, 124
    James, 144
    Mathew, 64, 100, 118, 138, 142, 170
    Mathew, Jr., 69
    Matt, 8, 47, 124, 127, 186, 188
    Matthew, 35, 43, 169, 191
    Samuel, 74, 75
    Uriah, 94
Hughs, Elias, 118
    Mathew, 185
    Matthew, 192
Hughston, Hugh, 183
Huings, John, 115
Hulme, George, Jr., 8
Hulms, George, 146
Humphrey, John, 92
Hunloke, Tho., 78
Hunt, Job, 154
Hunter, James, 60, 65, 105
Hurst, John, 184
Huston, Alexander Brown, 190
    James, 177
Hutchinson, George, 64
    John, 2, 7, 54, 55, 128, 137, 167, 175
    Michael, 94
    Randal, 182
    Randle, 143
    Sarah, 107
    Tho., 111
    Thomas, 134
    Thos., 140
Hyatt, John, 34

Iliff, Richard, 106
Ingals, John, 136
    Rebecca, 136
Ingels, John, 91
Ingham, Jonathan, 184
Ingram, John, 144
Ingrams, John, 145
Inslee, Sarah, 164
Inyard, Charles, 70, 155
Irish, Nat, 122
    Nathaniel, 120, 121, 125, 131, 156, 166, 173
Iselstein, Isaac, 173
Isillteas, Elias, 46
Islestein, Isaac, 120
Islestone, Jacob, 12
Ivory, Theophilus, 149
Izelstein, Jacob, 11

Jackman, George, 9
____, 59
Jackson, Daniel, 3, 7, 10, 15, 25, 26, 90, 117, 127
    Hannah, 25
    Hannah (Baines), 90
    Jo., 99, 147
    John, 41, 90
    Joseph, 90, 110, 111, 115, 119, 121-123, 174, 176
    Ralph, 19
    Sarah, 19
    Sarah (Dymock), 19
Jacob, Bartholomew, 32, 64
    James, 9, 12
Jacobs, Bartholomew, 2, 14, 31, 37, 45, 50-53, 63, 132
James, Aaron, 159
    Abigail, 109
    Abigail (Cary), 109
    Abraham, 185
    George, 177
    James, 105
    John, 19, 20, 42, 44, 54
    Richard, 109
    Thomas, 19, 20, 51, 159
    William, 154
Jamison, Henry, 153
Janney, Abel, 40, 60, 65, 75,

Janney, Abel *cont'd*
    89, 118, 192
    Abel, Jr., 89
    Amos, 60, 75, 76, 118
    Elizabeth (Stacey), 118
    Hannah, 136-138
    Jacob, 67
    Jos., 67
    Joseph, 60
    Martha (Mitchell), 189
    Mary, 75, 76
    Rachel, 78
    Rachel (Pownall), 78
    Thomas, 40, 57, 65, 78, 118, 136, 138, 189, 192
Jarvis, John, 76
Jefferson, Edward, 165
    Robert, 165
    Winifred, 165
Jemison, Henry, 172
    John, 174, 188
    Robert, 186
Jemyson, Alexander, 185, 186
    Henry, Jr., 185, 186
    Robert, 186
Jenkins, Abigail, 74
    Abigail (Pemberton), 74, 75
    Mary, 132
    Stephen, 74, 75
Jenks, Harman, 129
    Thomas, 100
Jenney, Jacob, 108
    Thomas, 108, 159, 167
Jennings, Abraham, 86
    Benjamin, 85, 86
    John, 11, 12
    Margery, 9
    Samuel, 64
Jenny, Abel, 188
Jervis, John, 76
Joan, Forrest, 170
Joans, Benjamin, 148
Johnson, Abraham, 63
    Benjamin, 176
    Catherine, 63
    Claus, 16, 25, 31, 32, 38, 39, 45, 57, 176
    Clause, 10, 23, 33, 35, 69

Johnson *cont'd*
  Deborah, 176
  Gotha, 176
  Grace, 63
  Hendricky, 63
  Henricky, 63
  Henry, 119
  Jacob, 49, 63, 176
  James, 40
  John, 5, 22, 23, 31-33,
    45, 52, 63, 64,
    120, 172, 176
  Lawrence, 63, 176
  Margaret, 22, 29, 64
  Peter, 5, 49, 137, 176
  Rebecca, 176
  Richard, 134, 176
  Samuel, 170
  Sarah, 49
  Willmuth, 176
  Wilmeth, 172
  Yanica, 63
Johnston, John, 91
Jolliffe, Mary, 99
  Mary (Sheppard), 99
  William, 99
Jolly, Lewis, 26
Jones, Benj., 25, 93, 141,
    168
  Benjamin, 33, 48, 70, 73,
    93, 102, 104, 110,
    114-116, 132,
    140, 141, 148,
    149, 152, 155,
    157, 160, 168,
    175, 180, 181
  Catharine, 93
  Daniel, 142, 155
  Edward, 179
  Elizabeth, 142
  Evan, 51, 192
  George, 68, 82, 83, 100,
    117, 147
  Grace, 142
  Griffith, 6, 42, 145, 149
  Henry, 42
  Jno., 125
  John, 9, 11, 12, 34, 60,
    118, 152
  Joseph, 16, 79, 16
  Josh, 168

Jones *cont'd*
  Mary, 142
  Richard, 97
  Samuel, 27
  Sarah, 142
  Thomas, 30, 42, 43, 77,
    138, 159, 170,
    179, 183
Journey, James, 193

Kaighin, Ann, 15, 29
  Ann (Forrest), 15, 29
  John, 15, 29
Kearney, Joanna, 104
Kearny, Edmund, 57
Kearsley, Anna, 137
  John, 137
Keen, Frances, 180
  James, 89
  Jonas, 177, 180, 181
  Mathias, 108, 121, 130,
    163, 164, 172
  Susannah, 130
Keene, Mathias, 134
Keerny, Edmund, 140
Keirll, John, 195
Kekewich, Peter, 56
Kelley, James, 95
Kelly, Pat, 154
Kelsey, Archibald, 186
Kemp, Edward, 2, 7, 15,
    136, 138
Kempe, Edward, 2, 3, 24, 26
Kennard, John, 124
Kensey, Edmund, 83
  John, 101
Kent, William, 71, 191, 192
Kester, Paul, 192
Key, John, 145
Keyser, Dirck, 173
Kid, Thomas, 176
Kilbran, Richard, 43
Kilpatrick, James, 127, 128
Kinderdine, Joseph, 111
King, Christian, 124
  Cornelius, Jr., 124
  Francis, 124
  Katherine, 124
  Leo. Vandegrift, 124
King Charles II, 89
King Edward I, 90

Kingey, John, 57
Kingsley, John, 182
Kinsey, John, 104, 133, 137,
    140, 153, 156,
    160, 163, 172,
    183, 185, 189, 190
  John, Jr., 153
  Samuel, 184
  Thomas, 184
Kinsy, John, Jr., 47
Kirk, Godfrey, 35
  Godfrie, 55
  Isaac, 151
  Joseph, 33
  Thomas, 160
Kirkbride, Jane, 3, 139
  Jean, 139
  John, 51, 83, 154
  Jos., 94
  Jos., Jr., 36, 37, 54, 55, 58
  Joseph, 2, 3, 5, 6, 13, 18-
    20, 29, 30, 38, 40,
    44, 51, 53, 54, 60,
    64, 65, 70-72, 77,
    79, 81, 93, 94, 97,
    99-101, 104, 107-
    109, 118, 122,
    127, 131, 133,
    136, 138, 139,
    143, 150, 154,
    164, 181
  Joseph, Jr., 19, 42, 43, 58,
    68, 72, 78, 81, 83,
    98, 106
  Joseph, Sr., 72, 73
  Mahlon, 43, 105, 118,
    138, 139
  Mary, 44, 51, 181
  Mathew, 60, 65, 139
  Matthew, 3
  Robert, 65
  Sarah, 138, 139
  Sarah (Stacey), 118
  Thomas, 3, 43, 72, 73,
    105, 139
Kirkbride, Joseph, 42
Kirl, John, 108, 195
  Joseph, 67
  Thomas, 50, 65, 192
  ____, 59
Kirle, Joseph, 12, 13

Kirle cont'd
  Thomas, 40, 104
Kirll, Brett, 27
  Joseph, 66
Kirton, John, 95
Kitchen, Gotha (Johnson), 176
  Joseph, 176
  William, 142
Kitchin, Ann (Wheeler), 153
  Henry, 153
Knaufs, Henry Sebastian, 167
  Sebastian Henry, 166
Knight, Daniel, 170
  John, 164
  Lydia, 164
  Sarah, 164
  Sarah (Cart), 164
  Thomas, 9, 13, 25, 57, 58
  Thomas, Jr., 13
  _____, 61
Knowles, Francis, 47, 56, 57
  John, 83
  Mary, 83
Kolluck, Jacob, 17, 21
  Mary, 21
Kroensen, Garret, 141
Kroesen, Derrick, 90
  Derricke, 90
Kroewsen, Henry, 90
Krosen, Francis, 33
Kuster, Reiner, 182

Lacey, Thomas, 88
Laehary, Loyd, 48
Lamb, Daniel, 79
  Hugh, 78, 79
  Joseph, 79
Lambert, Achfah, 58
  Elizabeth, 113
  Hannah, 112, 113
  John, 3, 26, 43, 44, 58, 112, 113
  Rebecca (Clowes), 113
  Rebeckah (Clowes), 113
  Sarah, 112, 113
  Thomas, 23, 58
Lamways, Edward, 158
Lancaster, Thomas, 128,

Lancaster, Thomas cont'd 150
Landis, John, 173
Landus, John, 126
Langdale, John, 68
  Josiah, 36, 82, 178
  Margaret, 36
Langhorn, Jer., 169
  Jeremiah, 1, 8, 9, 13, 14, 16
Langhorne, Grace, 3, 31
  Jer., 23, 24, 29, 31, 33, 35, 36, 40, 46, 47, 52, 53, 58, 60-63, 70-72, 75, 76, 82-84, 89-91, 96, 102, 118, 119
  Jere., 62
  Jeremiah, 1-7, 9-12, 14, 16, 17, 19, 20, 22-25, 30, 31, 33-35, 37, 38, 40, 42, 44, 49, 51, 52, 55, 56, 58, 60-64, 66, 67, 73-81, 83-97, 99, 101-108, 110, 119, 120, 123-125, 131, 132, 136-139, 148, 157-159, 161, 173, 174, 181, 183, 186, 187
  Sarah, 158
  Thomas, 106, 158
Lanings, John, 84
Lanins, John, 126
Lantry, David, 115
Lardner, Lynford, 103, 128, 129, 137, 155, 176-178
Lardnor, Lynford, 116, 127
Larew, Isaac, 156
Large, Ann, 192
  Dorothy, 191, 193
  Ebeneser, 143
  Ebenezer, 71, 84, 101, 102, 122, 165, 191-193
  Elizabeth, 143
  John, 69, 101, 102, 122, 126, 134, 148,

Large, John cont'd 169, 171
  Joseph, 5, 143, 192
  Samuel, 15
  Widow, 69
  William, 9
LaRow, Peter, 89
Lasey, Thomas, 71
Laster, Adam, 175
Latham, Richard, 59
Laurence, Peter, 78
Lawrance, Johannes, 113
  Thomas, 107
  William, 53, 55
Lawrence, Giles, 132, 172
  Jas., 52
  Joa., 21
  Jos., 22, 125
  Josa., 56, 68
  Joshua, 6
  Peter, 49
  Thomas, 120, 140
  William, 20, 30, 53, 54, 79
  Wilmeth, 172
  Wilmeth (Johnson), 172
Lawton, Adam, 46
  Thomas, 46
Lay, Thomas, 160
Laycock, John, 44
Lea, Hannah, 124
  John, 124
Leadame, Richard, 94, 95
Leardner, Lynford, 127
Leatherman, Theobald, 123
Lee, Ralph, 109
Leech, Ephraim, 178
  Thomas, 134, 135
  Toby, 19
  William, 177, 178, 186
Lehman, Christian, 137, 174, 183
Leibkap, Solomon, 128
Lerew, Peter, 118, 188
Lerner, Peter, 140
Lester, John, 92, 151
  Peter, 151
Letham, Richard, 160
Levalley, Charles, 9, 31
Levally, Charles, 52, 64, 98
Levering, Jacob, 21

Levers, Robert, 182, 185, 189
Leverton, Thomas, 56
Levesley, Elizabeth (Heath), 142
Thomas, 142
Lewis, Francis, 128
John, 138, 159, 185, 186
Mary, 105
Richard, 45
Lightcap, Solomon, 129
Lightwood, Edw., 55
Lindley, Thomas, 61
Lindrey, Guy, 165
Linter, John, 48, 54, 58, 59, 70
Linton, Joseph, 84, 87, 94, 161
Lirkfold, William, 39
Livezey, Jonathan, 111
Lloyd, Da'd., 66
David, 6, 7, 11, 28, 34, 107
John, 190
Mary, 191
Mordecai, 11
Morr., 92
Patience, 11
Thomas, 11, 42, 107
Lock, John, 153
Locke, Jo'n., 97
Lodge, Henry, 47
Loftus, Jane, 164
Ralph, 164
Logan, George, 93, 94
James, 10, 12, 13, 18, 20, 21, 24, 34, 46, 49, 50, 61, 62, 77-79, 81, 91-94, 99, 103, 122, 126, 131, 136, 137, 159, 160, 183, 191, 194
Jane, 94
Sarah, 91, 92
William, 94
Londeau, Daniel B., 97
Longshore, E., 100
Eucledus, 121
Euclidus, 194, 195
Euclydes, 22

Longshore *cont'd*
Euclydus, 135, 147, 161
Longstreet, Bartholomew, 181
Longstreth, Bartholomew, 71, 140, 147
Longstrett, Bartholomew, 115
Longworth, Roger, 23
Lovett, Edmond, 10, 13
Edmond, Jr., 13
Lowther, Ann Sharlot, 173
John, 173
Lucas, Edward, 14, 80
Giles, 80, 169
John, 67
Luck, Thomas, 134, 135
Luff, Mitchell, 9
Luffe, Jane, 11, 12
John, 11, 12
Lufs, John, 8
Lukin, Robert, 165
Lunday, Richard, 83
Lundy, Elizabeth, 191, 193
Richard, 10, 191
Richard, Jr., 193
Lupton, Jos., 48, 49, 87
Joseph, 48, 55
Lynde, Joseph, 150
Lynn, Joseph, 96

McCarty, Sarah (Carrell), 181
MacCollester, James, 33
Mackay, John, 85
MacKelon, Margaret, 55, 56
Macorume, Samuel, 41
Maddox, Ann, 27
Madox, Joshua, 135
Maleigh, Thomas, 94
Maley, ____, 83
Malone, Patrick, 181
Mann, John, 18
Margarum, Henry, 43
Margerinus, Henry, 140
Margerum, Henry, 3, 143
Mariots, Thomas, 163
Marjorum, Henry, 104, 138, 139
Mark, Jacob, 105

Mark *cont'd*
John, 139
Marke, Thomas, 36
Marker, Adam, 116
Markham, Joanna, 175
William, 1, 8, 111, 175
Marple, David, 71, 131, 132
Jane, 131, 132
Susannah, 131, 183
Thomas, 131, 132, 183
Marriot, Thomas, 114, 115, 194
Marriott, Thomas, 2, 101, 102, 122
Thos., 69, 139
Marsh, Thos., 163
Marshall, Moses, 95
William, 140
Martin, Dan, 58
John, 67
Lancelot, 142
Mary, 142, 143, 148
Mary, Jr., 166
Thomas, 145
Martindale, John, 5
Mary, 5
Martyn, Samuel, 117
Mather, Elizabeth, 74, 75
Mathews, Simon, 51
Mathias, Evan, 176
Maugridge, William, 144, 145
Maurer, Jacob, 177
Mawd, Tho., 67
May, Daniel, 83
Maybury, Tho., 22
Thomas, 19, 22, 48, 56, 76, 88, 106, 109, 146, 147, 193, 194
Mayos, Ann, 163
Edward, 163
McCarty, Silas, 144, 181
McCollough, John, 185, 186
McComb, James, 43
John, 16
McCool, Walter, 118
McCoole, Mary, 188
Walter, 187
McFarland, Joseph, 188
McGlauglin, John, 95
Mead, William, 140

Meed, Ellen, 143
   Ellen (Worrall), 143
   William, 143
Mein, Hugh, 172
Meredith, Thomas, 24, 42, 44
Mern, Hugh, 153
Merrell, Amos, 149
Merriot, Anna, 33
Metchener, William, 144
Michener, Burroughs, 49, 110
Mickle, Samuel, 114
Mildmay, Coll., 136, 138
Mildway, Colonel, 186
Mildways, Colonel, 35
Miller, David, 166, 167
   Ralph, 52
   William, 155
   William, Jr., 185
   William, Sr., 185
Millner, Thomas, 192
Milner, John, 193
   Thomas, 191
Milnor, Daniel, 194
   John, 48, 59, 193, 194
   Joseph, 194
   Martha, 59
   Thomas, 71
Mitchel, Henry, 118, 119
   John, 130
   Richard, 63
   William, 170
Mitchell, Elizabeth, 155
   Geo., 190
   George, 44
   Hen., 40
   Henry, 5, 9, 32, 33, 40, 45, 47, 63, 69, 102, 189, 190
   John, 76, 99, 102, 189
   Martha, 189
   Richard, 37, 93, 121, 129, 146, 150, 153, 155
   Sarah, 189
   _____, 119
Mogridge, Thomas, 14, 17, 16
Moland, John, 127-129, 132, 137, 156
Molloy, Harry J., 100

Monington, Wm., 75
Monnington, John, 153
Montgomery, John, 36
Mood, Alexander, 7, 8
   Joseph, 42
Moode, Andrew, 182
Moon, Agnes, 170
   James, 4, 26, 97, 170
   Jonas, 106
   Roger, 13, 18
Moone, Roger, 13
Moor, _____, 18
Moore, Alexr., 102
   Hannah, 143, 144
   Hannah (Hill), 146
   Nicholas, 12
   Samuel Preston, 143, 144, 146
   William, 16
   _____, 17
More, Anah, 90
   Nicholas, 11
Morgan, David, 51, 158
   James, 189
Morice, Moses, 105
Morrey, Humphrey, 55
   Richard, 55
Morris, Anthony, 60, 61, 142, 189
   Anthony, Jr., 145
   David, 188
   Evan, 34
   Isaac, 34
   Israel, 79, 106, 109
   John, 12, 33, 34, 63, 92, 159, 160
   Maurice, 141
   Morris, 92, 93, 126, 141, 142
   Morris, Jr., 188
   Robert Hunter, 107
   Susanna, 141
   Susanna (Heath), 141, 142
   Thomas, 186, 187
   Thomas, 21
   William, 115
   _____, 181
Morry, Humphrey, 83
Mountain, Joseph, 143
   Richard, 15, 20, 171

Mountaine, John, 148
   Richard, 82
Mountjoy, William, 92
Moyer, Christian, 187
Murphy, Anthony, 154
   Arthur, 154, 164
Murray, David, 100, 130, 173, 186
   Rebecca (Richardson), 44
   Thomas, 44
   William, 166, 173
Murrey, Richard, 155
Murry, Humphrey, 144
   Richard, 144
Murton, Brita, 5
   Matts, 5
Musgrave, Thomas, 5
Musgrove, Abraham, 28
   Elizabeth, 22, 27, 28
   Gaynor, 28
   Hannah, 27, 28
   Thomas, 1, 22, 27, 28
   Widow, 28, 29
   William, 22, 27, 28
   _____, 18
Mussleman, Jacob, 126
Mutell, Charles, 97

Naylor, John, 4, 10, 85, 100, 120, 133, 152, 162, 167, 169
Neefies, Cornelius, 148
   George, 148
   John, 148
Neild, John, 180
Neilson, Henry, 102
   James, 57
Nelson, Alice, 113, 194, 195
   Henry, 1, 3, 22, 27, 35, 36, 49, 100, 113, 163, 164, 194, 195
   Henry, 5
   Thomas, 194, 195
Nephew, Cornelius, 148
   George, 148
   John, 148
Newburne, George, 129
Newlin, Nathaniel, 30, 73, 87, 104
Newman, Margaret, 188

Newman cont'd
William, 188
Nicholas, John, 38
Nicholls, John, 25
Joshua, 16
Nichols, Joshua, 39
Nickle, Samuel, 114
Noble, Abel, 125, 140, 180
Able, 194
Isaac, 166, 167
James, 166, 167
Job, 180, 194
John, 30
Mary, 166, 167
Thomas, 166, 167
William, 71, 125
Noot, Nicholas, 113
Norcross, John, 28, 137
William, 59, 137
Normandie, ____, 102
Normandy, ____, 122
Norris, Eliz., 191
Isaac, 11, 12, 20, 62, 77, 103, 107, 122, 126, 159, 191
Thomas, 164
Nut, Nicholas, 104

Offley, Caleb, 98
Elizabeth, 98
Ogden, David, Jr., 77, 78
Jos., 77, 78
Josiah, 78
Ogdon, Josiah, 49
Ogilby, John, 86, 87
Okely, J., 129, 166, 167
John, 173
Okill, George, 167
Oland, Edward, 2
Oldale, Ann, 100
Samuel, 100
Oldmant, Joseph, 47
Oliphant, Ann, 153
David, 153
Ord, J., 107
Jno., 99, 108
John, 83
Orlton, Elizabeth, 151
Hugh, 151
Orphan, King, 61
Orr, Elizabeth, 85

Orr cont'd
Humphrey, 85
John, 85
Osborn, Charles, 21
Osborne, Cha., 66, 91, 92, 141, 142
Charles, 92
Chas., 23, 39, 16
Osburne, Charles, 21, 24
Otter, John, 1, 8, 14, 16, 17, 22, 30, 47, 57, 99
Otterson, Otter, 14
Overholts, Martin, 46
Overton, Constantine, 43, 58
Hannah, 43, 58
Joseph, 43, 58
Samuel, 3, 43, 44, 58, 60
Sarah, 43, 44
Owen, David, 182
E., 160
Evan, 42, 44, 51, 139, 145, 158
Griffith, 10, 21, 24, 50, 51, 61, 81, 141, 194
Mary, 145
Thomas, 173

Packcom, Joseph, 64
Pages, Sol, 97
Pain, James, 13
Palmer, Amos, 180
Daniel, 47, 48, 113, 180, 192
John, 180
John, Jr., 180
John, Sr., 180
Jonathan, 48, 180, 192
Palsyunk, Margaret, 178
Samuel Helton, 178
Parker, Nicholas, 94
Parr, Samuel, 140
Parrock, James, 69, 146
Parrott, John, 73
Parry, David, 149
James, 74
Parsons, John, 49, 73, 138, 139, 154, 169
Robert, 159, 160
Thomas, 83

Parsons cont'd
William, 48, 50, 51, 61, 125
Wm., 61, 75, 76, 126, 166
Parsyunck, Margaret (Langdale), 36
Samuel Preston, 36
Pascall, Thomas, 66
Paschall, Benj., 23
Pastonus, Henry, 58
Patridge, Peter, 127
Patterson, Andrew, 148
Margaret, 155
Paul, Joseph, 28, 154
Paulin, Henry, 26, 91, 157
Paull, Joseph, 28
Pawlin, Henry, 79
Pawlins, Henry, 15
Paxon, Elizabeth, 183
Henry, 183
James, 183
Margery, 183
Mary, 184
William, 135
____, 135
Paxson, Abigail, 78
Abigail (Pownall), 78
Deborah, 158
Henry, 4, 5, 10, 14, 15, 19, 26, 93, 157, 158, 169, 170
Henry, Jr., 4, 14, 169
James, 14, 157, 158, 169
John, 158
Martha, 170
Mary, 158
Reuben, 26, 27
Thomas, 157, 158
William, 7, 13, 15, 26, 37, 44, 52, 68, 69, 78, 80, 83, 91, 157, 158, 169, 170
William, Sr., 162
Paxton, Alexander, 11
Elizabeth (Stanley) (Hooton), 11
William, 80
Wm., 39
Peace, Joseph, 36, 41, 42, 69, 100, 114, 115,

Peace, Joseph *cont'd*
    119, 123, 131,
        134
    Mary, 114, 115
    Widow, 47
Peak, James, 186
Peaky, Charles W., Rev., 186
Pearce, Benjamin, 34
    Edward, 34
    Joseph, 37, 161
    Mary, 34
Pearson, Aaron, 120
    Enoch, 184
    John, 120
    Lawrance, 94
    Margaret, 184
Peart, Mary (Hilliard), 12
    Thomas, 12
Peck, William, 148
Peckcom, John, 39
    Joseph, 39
Peckel, Baltes, 94
Peckom, John, 39, 119
    Joseph, 39
Pedcock, John, 132
Peekover, Edmund, 165, 166
Pegg, Daniel, 20
Peggs, Daniel, 82
Pegy, Elizabeth, 1
Peirce, Edward, 34
Pellison, Jacob, 2, 12
Pemberton, Abigail, 74, 75
    Israel, 9, 34, 35, 49, 67,
        69, 75, 84, 88, 91,
        122, 123, 126,
        130, 142, 182
    James, 182, 184, 185, 187, 190
    Phebe, 35
    Phebe (Harrison), 35, 75
    Phineas, 2, 13, 23, 35, 74, 75
    Priscilla, 75
    Rachel, 74, 75
Pemborne, Christian, 49
Penington, Edward, 110, 168
    Is., 58, 74, 84, 86, 89, 99, 100

Penington *cont'd*
    Isaac, 161, 168, 177
    Paul, 146
Penn, Hannah, 103
    John, 46, 91, 95, 99, 103,
        105, 106, 114,
        116, 127-129,
        136-138, 150,
        151, 153, 155,
        173, 179
    Letitia, 145
    Margaret, 103
    Richard, 46, 95, 99, 103,
        106, 114, 116,
        127-129, 137,
        150, 151, 155,
        173, 176-179
    Springet, 126
    Thomas, 46, 94, 95, 99,
        103, 106, 114,
        116, 127-129,
        137, 140, 150,
        151, 153, 155,
        173, 177-179, 188
    William, 6-8, 10-15, 20,
        21, 24, 25, 27, 28,
        30-35, 38, 39, 41,
        44-46, 50, 54, 55,
        58-60, 62, 63, 65,
        67, 68, 71, 75, 77-
        79, 81, 83, 89-93,
        95, 97, 101, 103,
        106, 107, 111-
        113, 116, 122,
        125, 126, 131,
        136, 138, 140,
        141, 147, 149,
        155, 156, 158,
        159, 165, 166,
        168, 174, 183,
        186, 188, 191,
        192, 194
Pennington, Edward, 2, 42, 44, 49
    Is., 77
    Isaac, 40, 47, 73, 78, 120
Pennock, William, 49
Penquite, John, 49, 103
    Nicholas, 103, 118
Perce, Benjamin, 34
    Mary, 34

Perks, Edmd., 54
Perry, Samuel, 97
    Thomas, 114
Perttinse, George, 48
Peters, John, 133
    Reese, Jr., 165
Rice, 131
Richard, 94, 95, 114, 116,
    124, 127-129,
    133, 137, 140,
    148, 155, 156,
    167, 177, 178,
    188, 189
William, 56, 114, 116,
    124, 127-129,
    151, 188
Wm., 108, 114, 116, 118,
    121-123, 140,
    176, 177
Petty, John, 162, 163
Philips, Benjamin, 92
    Jonkin, 184, 185
    Mary, 165
    Sage, 92
    Thomas, 185, 187
Phillips, Benjamin, 92
    George, 32, 33, 45, 189
    Henry, 150
    Jenkin, 156
    John, 34
    Nancy, 104
    Thomas, 142
Phipps, Samuel, 150
Pickering, Samuel, 10
    William, 103
Pidgeon,
    Ann, 72
    Joseph, 42, 44, 51, 72, 158
    _____, 145
Pidgion, Joseph, 139
Pike, Jos., 19
    Joseph, 84
Pilling, Thomas, 26
Pilston, Thomas, 18
Pleadwell, Edwd., 152
Plumbley, John, 37
Plumbly, John, 37, 52, 61, 63
    William, 157
Plumer, Richard, 153

Plumley, Alice, 183
 Ann, 74
 Ann (Stackhouse), 163
 Charles, 74, 163
 James, 67
 John, 5, 46, 74, 110, 111, 183
 Margery, 67
 Mary, 5
Plumly, Ann, 183
 Charles, 91, 182-184
 James, 183, 184
 John, 14, 47, 63, 133, 160, 183, 184
 Mary (Paxon), 184
 William, 183, 184
Plumstead, Clement, 57, 61, 92, 117
 Francis, 28
 Mary, 176, 183
Plumsted, Clem, 105
Poe, Abigail, 192
 Patrick, 191-193
Pollard, Jeffrey, 17, 20, 57
 Jeffry, 14, 30, 47, 82, 117
 Jefry, 16
 Rebecca, 14, 17, 30, 47, 16
Pool, Joseph, 48, 80
Poole, Joseph, 80, 96, 116
Porue, E., 33
Potter, Thomas, 6
Powel, Samuel, 182
 Samuel, Jr., 185, 190
Powell, Samuel, 61
 Samuel, Jr., 60, 61, 184, 187, 188
Pownal, George, 134
 Mary (Stacey), 118
 Reuben, 93
 Ruben, 101
Pownall, Abigail, 78
 George, 26, 27, 78
 Rachel, 78
 Reuben, 27, 108
 Ruben, 78
Poynter, Henry, 114
 Mary, 114
Praul, Harris, 52
 Johanes, 61, 63
 Johannes, 37, 52, 63, 64,

Praul, Johannes *cont'd*
 74, 96
 John, 110, 111, 132, 182
Praules, Peter, 162
Preestly, John, 43
Presmall, Robert, 59, 67
Preston, Amos, 8
 Esther (Sanford), 8
 Nathan, 192
 Samuel, 15, 21, 26, 32, 62, 77, 126, 145
Price, David, 27, 28
 Hannah (Musgrove), 27, 28
 Jonathan, 172, 173
 Sarah, 164
Prichard, Joseph, 163
Prickett, Ann (Turner), 104
Prior, Silas, 150
Pritchard, Daniel, 73
 Joseph, Jr., 173
Pritcherd, Jo., Jr., 120
Prompoor, Andres, 105
Pryor, Norton, 38
 Thomas, 38, 133
Puckle, Anne, 15
 Deborah, 15
 Nathaniel, 15
Pugh, Hananiah, 188
 Hugh, 74, 75
Pursel, Denis, 55
 Peter, 55
Pursill, Thomas, 35
Pyke, Joseph, 79

Quare, Daniel, 50, 137
Queen, John A., 184
Quimby, Isaiah, 115
Quinby, Rachel, 142

Radcliff, John, 155
Radcliffe, Edward, 23
 Rebecca, 23
 Richard, 23
Radclift, Edward, 35
 James, 35
 Mary, 35
 Rachel, 35
 Rebecca, 35
 Richard, 35
Radley, John, 41

Ramsey, William, 107
Randal, Fredrick W., 161
Randall, Frederick W., 87, 88
 George, 189
 Nicholas, 8, 9, 12, 43, 67
Ratcliff, Edward, 27
Rawle, Frances, 145
Rawlings, Thomas, 118
Raymon, Mary (Steel), 175
 Presly, 175
Read, Alice, 93
 Cha., 64
 Charles, 23, 42, 44, 51, 68, 78, 86, 93, 94, 101, 104, 108, 139, 158, 194
 Chas., 52
 James, 93, 108
 John, 145
 Sarah, 101, 108
Redman, Ric., 47
 ———, 145
Reed, Charles, 61
 James, 101
Reeder, Charles, 172
Reese, Evan, 54
 Ulrich, 175
Reilles, Charles, 150
Reily, Edwd., 128, 129
 G., 108
 J., 107, 164, 173
 Jno., 165
 John, 125, 126
Renshaw, Ann (Steel), 175
 Richard, 175
 Thomas, 175
Revel, Thomas, 46
Revell, Thomas, 7
Rew, James, 46
 Mathew, 52
Reynolds, John, 9
Rich, John, 191, 193
 Sarah, 191, 193
Richard, David, 47
 John, 145
Richards, James, 154
Richardson, Francis, 36, 44
 John, 44
 Joseph, 52, 81, 87, 96, 104, 105, 107,

Richardson, Joseph *cont'd*
    122, 123, 129, 141,
    146, 157, 174, 183
  Mary (Paxson), 158
  Rebecca, 44
  Tho., 40
  Thomas, 19, 46, 109
Richmond, Silvester, 64
Ridge, Daniel, 144
  William, 85, 105
Ridgeway, Richard, 104, 190
Ripert, Peter, 137
Ritcher, Sarah, 115
Roberts, Deliverance, 74
  Edmund, 74
  Edward, 40, 115
  Edwd., 164, 163
  Hugh, 183
  Jane (Howell), 58
  John, 48, 57, 58, 74
  Jonathan, 74
  Owen, 134, 135
  Susanna, 74
  Thomas, 74
  Timothy, 109, 111, 180, 181
Robertson, Andrew, 155
Robeson, Jonathan, 104
Robins, Roger, 56
Robinson, Andrew, 47, 57
  Jno., 93, 94
  John, 93, 94
  Sep., 71
  Sept., 120
  William, 34
Roboson, James, 185
Rochford, Denis, 54
Rockford, Dennis, 144, 145
Rockhill, Jos., 74, 139
Rodeman, Elenor, 151
  Eleoner, 150
  John, 151
  John, Jr., 150
  Nealeha, 151
  Nealeha (Brees), 151
Rodgers, William, 114
Rodman, John, 46, 65, 150, 151, 157
  John, Jr., 45, 46, 52, 151, 157

Rodman *cont'd*
  Jos., 33
  Joseph, 89
  Nealeha (Brees), 150
  Nealiha (Brees), 157
  Wm., 153
  & Co., 83
  ———, 134
Roe, Uriah, 64
Rogers, Alex'r., 85
  Alexander, 85
  Thomas, 85
  Thomas, Jr., 88
Rogson, John, 9
Rootledge, John, 119
Ross, George, Jr., 169
  Jno., 59
  John, 119, 153, 169
Rowland, Elizabeth (White), 112
  John, 1-4, 21, 88, 107, 112, 130, 132, 136, 138, 167, 170, 186, 187
  Owon, 179
  Priscilla (Shepherd), 186, 187
  Thomas, 107, 132, 167, 179, 187
Rowledge, John, 119
  Margaret, 119
Royton, John, 2
Ruck, Thos., 48
Rue, James, 46, 65, 89, 180, 181
  Lewis, 132, 184
  Mathew, 50, 74, 76, 88, 106, 109, 110, 112, 114, 116, 119, 124, 132, 134, 141, 152, 159, 180, 181, 184
  Matthew, 162, 193
Rumford, John, 18
  Mary, 18
Runtin, Samuel, 193
Rush, Thomas, 140
Russ, James, 180
Russell, John, 192
  Michael, 50
Rutledge, John, 39, 79

Rutledge *cont'd*
  Margaret, 39
Rutlidge, Margaret, 149
Rye, John, 83

Sacket, Simon, 130
Salter, Anna, 11
Salthouse, Elijah, 60
Sample, Elizabeth, 188
  John, 95, 188
Samuel, Isaac, 173
  Joseph, 182
  Sarah, 182
Samuels, Joseph, 166, 173
Sandeford, Ralph, 68
Sanders, Stephen, 175
Sandilands, Robert, 101
  Robert, Rev., 48
Sands, John, 43, 67, 68
  Richard, 85
  Stephen, 67, 85
Sanford, Esther, 8
  Mary, 8
  William, 8
Sansom, Samuel, 164
Satcher, Robert, 83
Saterthwait, Wm., 88, 89
Saterthwaite, Eliza, 41
  Wm., 41
Saterthwate, Elizabeth, 57
  Wm., 57
Satterwait, Joseph, 29
  Rebecca (Alberson), 29
Satterwaite, Joseph, 15
  Rebecca (Alberson), 15
Say, William, 83
Scaif, Jane, 28
  Jeremiah, 28
Scaife, Jonathan, 27
Scarborough, John, 10, 83, 102, 174
  Mary, 10
Scarbrough, John, 24, 156
Scarfe, Jonathan, 18, 22
Scattergood, Tho's., 71
  Tho., 71
Schoonhoven, Nicholas, 58
Schout, Avie, 71
Schutt, G., 106
Scot, ———, 61
Scott, Abraham, 170

Scott *cont'd*
  Benjamin, 67, 96, 108,
    141, 161, 189
  Henry, 139
  John, 106, 109, 185, 186
  Richard, 118, 177
  Samuel, 7, 57, 108, 156,
    16
  Thomas, 50, 57, 120,
    137, 171
  _____, 30
Scriepers, John, 50
Scull, Edward, 189
Seams, Henry, 134
Searl, Arthur, 157
  Francis, 29, 157
Searle, Arthur, 7, 61
  Francis, 7-10, 29, 31, 32,
    45, 57, 61, 81, 93
  _____, 61
Sebering, Jai., 58
Seely, Jonas, 156
Sefferts, Saffert, 141
Seibel, Henry, 187, 188
Sell, Henry, 165
  Winifred (Jefferson), 165
Serbor, Rudolph, 129
Seull, Nicholas, 134, 135
Severens, Joseph, 89
Severns, John, 41
  Joseph, 46
Seward, Benjamin, 101
  William, 101
Shaffer, Adam, 127, 128
Shalcross, John, 59
Shallcross, John, 30, 40, 65,
    66, 68, 109, 192
  Leonard, 109
Shans, Isaac, 190
Shattick, James, 1, 5
Shaw, Amos, 85
  George, 73
  James, 28, 73, 74, 154
  John, 6, 73, 74, 111, 154,
    168, 185
  Joseph, 69, 73, 115, 160,
    174
  Mary, 73, 115
  Robert, 8
  Susanah, 73
Shawcross, John, 170

Shawcross *cont'd*
  Leonard, 180
Sheals, William, 140
Sheels, William, 140
Sheiffer, Adam, 127
Shellton, John, 44
Shepherd, Priscilla, 187
Sheppard, Mary, 60, 99
  Mary , 60
Sherrard, Fra., 45
Shewell, Robert, 158
  Walter, 158
Shiart, Alex., 171
Shier, George, 20
Shiers, Geo., 82
  George, 21
Shillingford, James, 136
Shippen, Edward, 10, 21,
    24, 42, 43, 50, 81,
    122, 124, 141,
    160, 164, 194
  Joseph, 164
  William, 146
  _____, 160
Shoards, Samuel, 41
  Sarah, 41
Shoemaker, Benjamin, 125
  George, 116
  Jacob, 125
  Jacob, Jr., 133
Shook, Christian, 123
Showel, Robert, 140
Shreve, Freelove, 161
  Freelove (Dyer), 161
  William, 161
Shrieve, William, 84, 87
Shute, Allwood, 160
  Elizabeth (Steel), 175
  Jacob, 186
  Mary (Boyden), 186
  William, 175
Sidon, Joseph, 119
Simans, William, 39
Simcock, Joseph, 113
Simples, John, 137
Simrell, Elizabeth, 85
Sisom, Jno., 17, 18, 98
  John, 98, 101, 102, 122
  Thomas, 194
Sison, Jno., 97
  Thomas, 69

Siver, Samuel, 72
Skelton, Thomas, 54
  Thos., 54
Slater, George, 3, 139
  Sarah, 3
Sloams, James, 129
Smart, Lydia (Allen), 66
Smith, Daniel, 134, 155
  Isaac, 31
  James, 35
  Jane, 139
  John, 7, 26, 27, 62, 84,
    126, 130, 134,
    142, 143, 157,
    163, 183
  John, Jr., 126
  Jonas N., 70
  Joseph, 106, 148, 156
  Mary, 115
  Richard, 84
  Richard, Jr., 84
  Robert, 84, 102, 114,
    115, 126, 127,
    129, 143
  Rowland, 148
  Samuel, 100, 139, 155
  Sarah, 143
  Thomas, 145
  Timothy, 30, 43, 48, 72,
    77, 82, 84, 85
  William, 6, 11, 24, 49,
    83, 150
  William S., 6
  _____, 7
Smout, Edward, 10
Smyth, James, 3, 5, 6
Snowden, John, 143
Snowdon, John, 43, 104,
    134, 186
  William, 43
  Wm., 109
Sober, Thomas, 35, 187
Solcher, Robert, 78
Sotcher, John, 11, 42, 54,
    154, 163, 164
South, William, 148
Spakeman, Randall, 27, 134
Spanagenberg, Joseph, 167
Spangenberg, Joseph, 166
Spencer, _____, 186
Spiller, Henry, 56

Springett, Harb't., 89, 90
Sprogell, Lodowick
    Christian, 38
Stacey, Mahlon, 75, 76, 89,
    118
  Rebeckah, 118
Stackhous, John, 79
Stackhouse, Ann, 163
  Ann (Mayos), 163
  Isaac, 147
  Jacob, 163, 164
  John, 7, 79, 80, 84, 116,
    126
  John, Jr., 116
  Joseph, 135, 147, 174
  Samuel, 30, 36, 44, 146
  Sarah, 163
  Thomas, 5, 10, 22, 36,
    43, 44, 68, 69, 77,
    80, 84, 85, 101,
    102, 108, 116,
    122, 130, 135,
    147, 163, 173
  _____, 159
Stacy, Mahlon, 60, 118
Stanbury, Nathan, 17, 18
Stanley, Elizabeth, 11
  William, 11
Statts, Peter, 156
Steel, Ann, 175
  Elizabeth, 175
  James, 42, 45, 70, 79, 99,
    155, 175
  Martha, 70
  Mary, 175
  Rebecca, 175
  Ruth, 175
Steer, Ruth, 183
Stell, Peter, 47
Stephens, Abraham, 131
Stephenson, Thomas, 46
  William, 46
Stevens, Abraham, 132
  David, 51
  Mary, 51
Stevenson, Ann, 65
  Ann (Jennings), 64
  Edward, 65
  Elizabeth, 65
  Henry, 177
  Jno., 53

Stevenson *cont'd*
  John, 64, 65
  Mary, 181
  Mercy (Jennings), 64
  Olive, 65
  Samuel, 65
  Sarah, 3, 9, 19, 20, 31,
    32, 40, 45, 54, 55,
    65
  Sarah (Jennings), 64
  Tho., 43, 70, 71, 79
  Thomas, 1-3, 5-7, 9, 10,
    15, 19, 20, 28, 31-
    33, 35, 40, 45-47,
    52-55, 64, 65, 79,
    177, 181, 33
  William, 64, 65
Stevese, Abraham, 87
Steward, Thomas, 179
Stewart, James, 145, 183
  Rachel (Witchall), 145
Stillman, Augustine, 140
Stockdale, Dorothy, 5
  William, 5
Stockdell, William, 4, 70
Story, Thomas, 10, 21, 50,
    123, 141, 160
Stradlin, Thomas, 56, 76,
    88, 146, 194
Stradling, Thomas, 43, 77
Streater, James, 169
Streator, James, 83
Streeter, James, 126
Streiper, _____, 185
Streiter, Johann Philip, 108
  Juliana, 108
  Rev. John Philip, 105,
    108
Stretch, Joseph, 164
  Lydia (Knight), 164
Strettell, Robert, 129, 172
Strettle, Amos, 64
Strickland, Amos, 146, 147
Stringer, Comfort (Dyer),
    161
  Humphrey, 161
Strutt, William, 11
  Wm., 91, 169
Stuart, Alex., 176, 177
Studam, Mary, 152
  Mary (Eastburne), 152

Studam *cont'd*
  Richard, 152
Studdam, Mary
    (Eastburne), 151
  Richard, 151
Stutchbury, Robert, 49
Suite, Thomas, 20
Sutton, James, 10
  Mary, 56
Swarthoot, Barnardus, 76,
    77
Swarthout, Bernardus, 58
Swift, Elizabeth, 136
  Frances, 11, 12
  John, 1, 4, 8, 9, 11, 12,
    25, 36, 38, 43, 59,
    67, 136, 152, 162
  John, Jr., 4
  Peter, 100
  Sam'll., 68
  Samuel, 59, 136
Swinton, Is., 59, 60
  Js., 59, 60
Symons, Tho., 56
  Thomas, 56
Sysom, Thomas, 145
  _____, 159

Tallman, John, 30, 79
Talman, John, 20, 53-55
Tatham, Elizabeth, 46, 65
  George, 9
  John, 6, 17, 31, 32, 45,
    46, 65
  Mary, 65
Taylor, Benj'a., 109
  Benjamin, 76, 88, 193,
    194
  Christopher, 1, 4, 7, 77,
    123, 168
  Elizabeth, 12
  Henry, 114
  Israel, 1, 3, 4, 7, 48, 77,
    162
  Jacob, 20, 62, 77, 126
  John, 157
  Jonathan, 38, 41
  Joseph, 7, 77
  Mary, 77
  Peter, 83, 111
  Philip, 86

Taylor *cont'd*
  Rebecca, 111
  Thomas, 121
Tea, Will., 191
Teague, Elizabeth, 47, 56, 57
  Pentecost, 14, 17, 30, 47, 57, 99, 16
  _____, 133
Tecck, Wm., 109
Tennant, Charles, 177, 178
Tennyclift, Thomas, 43
Terry, Jasper, 13
  Susanna, 13
  Thomas, 10, 13, 78
Thackrey, James, 135
Thatcher, Bartholomew, 84
  Jos., 83
  Joseph, 5, 84
  Richard, 42, 104, 130, 135
  _____, 80, 104
Thatchers, _____, 174
Thomas, Evan, 105, 176
  John, 92
  Joseph, 176
  Thomas, 92
  William, 91, 92, 124, 179
Thompkins, Anthony, 49
Thompson, James, 175
  Nich., 143
  Nick, 107
  Ruth (Steel), 175
  William, 153
Thorn, Samuel, 45, 53
  William, 30
Thorne, Joseph, 20, 30, 53-55, 79
  Samuel, 20, 30, 53-55, 79
  Samuel, Jr., 53
  Thomas, 32, 53, 79
Thornton, Joseph, 63, 105-107
  Margaret, 105, 107
Thwailrs, Thomas, 147
Thwaits, Thomas, 10, 67
Tidmarsh, William, 146
  Wm., 92
Till, William, 172, 176, 177, 185, 190
Tilley, Peter, 57

Tilleyer, Phillip, 157
Tillico, Jacobus Clough, 98
Tillyer, Philip, 151
Tinings, John A., 3
Tippenderver, Alexander, 116
Tod, Joseph, 60
Todd, Thomas, 12
Tomkin, Anthony, 110
Tomkins, Anthony, 42, 149
  Hannah, 149
  Joshua, 149
  Lydia (Carrell), 181
  Robert, 181
Tomlinson, Benjamin, 96, 130, 141, 152, 161, 162
  Elizabeth, 96, 161
  Harry, 117
  Henry, 13, 20, 36, 69, 82, 98, 101, 102, 112, 122, 171, 195
  Joseph, 10, 30, 43, 67, 68, 96, 141, 152, 162
  Mary, 30, 112
  Sarah, 171
  Thomas, 96, 97, 108, 114, 130, 152, 161, 162, 164
  Thos., 141
Tompkins, Anthony, 148
Tompson, Nich, 105
Tool, John, 173, 174
Topham, Christopher, 35
Topsham, Christopher, 23
Town, Benjamin, 69
  John, 5, 186, 189, 190
Towns, John, 118
Townsend, George, 23, 41
  Jacob, 41
  James, 23
  John, 108
  Joseph, 124
  Nathaniel, 41
  Stephen, 85, 86
  Thomas, 108
Treame, Margaret (Penn), 103
  Thomas, 103
Treat, Richard, 149
Tredwen, John, 56

Treeck, William, 109
Trent, William, 32, 195
Tresck, William, 109
Trotter, Joseph, 164
  William, 49
Tucker, Richard, 104
Tuckett, Edw., 74
Tuckney, Henry, 87, 88
Tunclife, James, 58
Tunicklief, Thomas, 75
Tunly, Richard, 49
Tunniclif, James, 188
Turner, Ann, 104
  Joseph, 61, 95, 119, 159, 172, 187
  Peter, 125
  Robert, 7, 23, 25, 33, 41, 67, 91, 103, 111, 148, 149, 155, 157, 183
Turniclift, James, 139
Turniclofts, James, 118
Twining, John, 48
  Nathaniel, 48
  Stephen, 48, 120
Underwood, John, 101, 102, 122
  _____, 117
Ustine, Abraham, 176

Van Ahen, Henry, 176
Van Dam, Rip, Jr., 46
VanBaskirk, Jan, 33
Vanbreskirk, Hans, 24, 25
Vanbuskek, John, 92
  Mary, 92
VanBuskirk, Andreas, 12, 92
Vanbuskirk, Andreas, 105
  Antie, 105
VanBuskirk, John, 106
  Lawrence, 42
Vanbuskirk, Yoost, 105
Vandegrift, Abraham, 124
  Frederick, 41
  Jacob, 124
  Leonard, 41, 124
  Mary, 124
  Nicholas, 41
  Sarah, 124
Vanderbelt, Ram, 148

Vandergrift, Abraham, 73, 152
  Barentye, 21
  Foulkert, 21
  Frederick, 21
  Jacob, 73, 124, 176
  Johanes, 152
  Johannes, 25, 90
  Nicholas, 21, 116
  Tolehart, 152
  Willmuth (Johnson), 176
Vandicke, Henry Johnson, 10
Vandike, Hendrick Johnson, 67, 68
  Henry Johnson, 80, 81, 174
  Lambert, 59
  Yanica, 80, 81, 174
Vandine, Abraham, 63
  Garrat, 52, 53, 93
  Garret, 37
  Jarret, 37
Vandlecy, Susan, 80
  Susanna, 80, 81
Vanhooten, Christian, 120
Vanhorn, Abraham, 24, 25, 42, 163
  Barnard, 42
  Barnet, 155
  Bernard, 110
  Christian, 77, 78, 80, 96, 102, 135, 161, 168
  Christian Barnson, 174
  Elisabeth, 152
  Elizabeth, 172
  Henry, 80, 122, 174
  Isaac, 42, 110, 149
  Jo'n., 184
  Johannes, 25
  John, 168
  Margaret, 172
  Nicholas, 147
  Peter, 74, 132, 152, 153, 172, 182
  Peter Barnson, 86
  Susanna, 80, 174
  Susanna (Vanvlieg), 174
  Williamkee, 80, 174
Vanhorne, Barnard, 124, 141

Vanhorne *cont'd*
  Bernard, 87
  Christian, 96, 123, 130, 163
  Christian Barnson, 80, 81, 96, 123, 174
  Henry, 80, 81, 96, 102, 104, 116
  Isaac, 105
  Peter Barnson, 86, 87
  Pieter Barson, 86
  Susanna, 80
  Susanna (Vandlecy), 81
  Susannah, 102
  WilliamKee, 96
  Williamkee, 123, 174
  Williamkee Barnson, 80
  WilliamKee Barnson, 81
Vankerck, Bernard, 90
Vansand, Albert, 5
  Cor., 6
  Cornelius, 5, 6, 177
  Derica, 6, 177
  Elizabeth, 6
  Garret, 5
  George, 5, 6, 177
  Harman, 3, 5, 6
  Jacobus, 5
  Johannes, 3, 5, 6
  John, 6
  Lea, 3
  Leah, 6
  Leah O., 6
  Micah, 5
  Stoffel, 63, 64
  Stopfell, 6
  Stophel, 24, 63
  Stophell, 5, 63
  Stophfell, 5, 6
Vansandt, Derica A., 6
  Garret, 183
  George, 52, 61
  Hannah, 89
  Horman, 152
VanSandt, Jacobus, 90
Vansandt, James, 129, 150, 151
  John, 91
  Stoffel, 61
  Stophel, 52, 61, 91
Vansant, Albert, 124

Vansant *cont'd*
  Cornelius, 35, 180
  Dorica, 180
  Garrat, 152
  Garret, 49, 157
  Garret, Jr., 157
  George, 37, 46, 111
  Harman, 31, 45
  Jacob, 157
  James, 129
  John, 109, 110, 157
  Margaret (Brees), 157
  Stophel, 24, 37
Vanvlieg, Susanna, 174
Vanzant, Cobus, 16
  James, 129
Vaughan, John, 102
Verkerck, Bernard, 90, 91
  John, 90, 91
Vickeris, Thomas Bishop, 118
Vickries, Richard, 188
  Thomas Bishop, 188
Vickris, Richard, 140
  Thomas Bishop, 139
Vinager, Charles, 191
Vining, Benj., 26
Voto, Paul Isaac, 126, 129, 140, 144, 146, 150, 153, 163, 172, 175, 176, 181, 183, 185, 187, 188, 190, 192
  Sarah, 172
Votring, Elizabeth, 159

Wait, William, 94
Waite, Hannah, 70
  Joseph, 70-73
  Martha, 70-73
Waitrell, Thos., 98
Waley, John, 106
Walker, Francis, 46, 65
  Joseph, 55, 130, 135, 146
  Richard, 186
  Robert, 185, 186
  William, 177, 178
Walley, John, 24, 56, 59, 68
  Shadrach, 24
  Shadrack, 18, 149
Wallige, Samuel V., 31

Walln, Ann, 141
  Ann (Heath), 141, 142
  Richard, 141, 142
Wally, Elizabeth, 194
  John, 48, 49, 76, 109, 146, 194
  Shadrach, 49
  Shadrick, 194
Walmsley, Henry, 67, 96, 105
  Mary, 32, 45, 105, 33
  Thomas, 9, 10, 31-33, 45, 57, 153, 162, 172, 183
Walmsly, Henry, 108
  Mary, 108
Waln, John, 180
  Nicholas, 44, 116
Walton, Benjamin, 60
  Elizabeth, 152
  Elizabeth (Eastburne), 151, 152
  Isaac, 127
  Jacob, 127
  M., 103
  Malachi, 122, 140
  Mary, 103
  Nathaniel, 17
  Thomas, 151, 152
Walver, Nicholas, 175
Wanton, Edward, 27
Ward, Steph'n., 70
  Stephen, 70
Warder, Elisabeth, 143
  Elizabeth, 133, 143
  Elizabeth (Worrall), 143
  John, 164
  Joseph, 133, 143
  Mary, 83
  Solomon, 72
  Willoughby, 4, 21, 83, 133
Wares, William, 137
Warner, Isaac, 17
  Swan, 97
Warrell, Thomas, 104
Water, Nathan, 147
Waterman, Isaac, 74, 75
  Priscilla, 74
  Priscilla (Pemberton), 75
Wathel, Tho., 72

Wathel *cont'd*
  Thomas, 131
Watkins, Abraham, 91
  Abram, 144
Watson, Hannah, 170
  Jno., Jr., 184
  Jo., 36
  John, 94, 100, 161
  John, Jr., 170, 184
  Jos., 21, 23, 24, 30, 31, 73
  Joseph, 92
  Js., 92
  Mark, 78, 147, 158, 174, 178, 180, 187
  Nathan, 52, 68, 69, 81, 86, 97, 103, 112, 122, 123, 132, 158, 161, 178
  Rebecca, 78, 81
  Rebecca K., 78
  Rebeckaw, 68
  Tho., 43, 47, 54, 55, 67, 70, 71, 78, 93, 97
  Thomas, 1, 3, 7, 10, 15, 17, 20, 24, 30, 67, 68, 70, 71, 74, 75, 78, 81, 94, 106, 132, 161, 181, 182
  Will'm., 98
  William, 2, 5, 7, 170
  ———, 117
Watts, Stephen, 140, 160
Wealtherill, Christopher, 4
Weatherel, Christopher, 169
Weatheril, Christian, 133
Weaver, Thomas Jones, 179
Webb, John, 173
  Joseph, 31
  Richard, 97
Webbe, Jno., 71, 101, 102
  John, 102
Webster, John, 14
  Peter, 3, 4
Weiser, Elizabeth, 189
  Nicholas, 189
Welch, James, 102, 104, 172
  Joseph, 1
Welding, Ely, 55
Wells, John, 115, 121, 141, 142, 156, 169,

Wells, John *cont'd*
  170, 184
  Mary, 170
  Moses, 74
Welsh, George, 35
Welver, George, 116
West, Edward, 9, 129, 184
Westbrook, John, 38
Weston, Edward, 149
  Hannah, 149
  Hannah (Tomkins), 149
Wetherill, Christopher, 120
Weyman, Robert, Rev., 193
Wharley, Daniel, 92
Wheeler, Ann, 153
  Gilbert, 29, 50, 153, 154
  Robert, 83
Whitacre, John, 120, 193
  William, 147, 174
Whitacres, John, 171
Whitaker, John, 50
  William, 101, 102, 123
White, Benjamin, 112
  Elizabeth, 112
  Francis, 3, 5-7, 31, 32, 45, 50, 52, 64, 102, 119, 132, 153, 182
  Francis, Jr., 174, 175
  George, 10, 14, 15, 26, 28, 63, 111, 112
  Gilbert, 132
  Joan, 112
  John, 50, 63, 69, 101, 102, 111, 112, 117, 122
  Joseph, 4, 12, 13, 15, 69, 176
  Martha, 132
  Peter, 112, 121, 182
  Philip, 190
  Thomas, 143, 144
  Unity, 112
  William, 10, 169
Whitecar, John, 36
Whitefield, George, 101
Whitehead, George, 145
  Wm., 132
Whittemore, Joseph, 149
Whitton, Thomas, 22
  Thos., 111

Wigans, William, 158
Wilcox, Joseph, 1, 12, 16, 42
  Roger, 46
Wildey, Obediah, 46
Wildman, Deborah, 157
  Deborah (Paxson), 158
  Elisabeth, 146
  Jacob, 146
  John, 1, 22, 83, 146, 161
  Joseph, 5, 146, 161
  Mathew, 68
  William, 130, 157
Wilkins, Samuel, 131
  Sarah, 131
Wilkinson, John, 74, 75, 146
  John, Jr., 146, 153
  Josiah, 155
Willard, George, 6, 73, 74, 107, 154, 164, 181
  Mary, 181
Willets, Hannah, 23
  Jacob, 23
Williams, Christian, 124
  Dank, 154
  David, 42
  Duncan, 46
  Dunk, 175, 190
  Em, 71, 81
  Em., 100
  Emion, 142, 143, 148
  Emmon, 70, 100-103, 113
  Emon, 71, 74, 88, 108, 112, 133
  En, 182
  En., 156
  Enion, 116, 130, 138, 182
  Ennion, 114, 115, 122, 131, 134, 136, 174, 175, 177, 178
  Evan, 66
  Jane, 109
  Jane (Cary), 109
  Jenkins, 124
  John, 134, 144, 159, 179, 183
  Nicholas, 17, 49
  Peter, 134

Williams *cont'd*
  Richard, 109, 179
  Stephen, 182
  William, 25, 124, 179
Williamson, John, 66, 67, 73
  Sarah, 73
  William, 73
Williard, George, 73
Willing, Charles, 164
Willis, Jacob, 23
Wills, William, 23
Willson, Ann, 194
  Anthony, 194
  David, 135
  John, 69
Wilson, Ann, 100
  Anthony, 100, 147
  David, 46, 59, 85, 94, 95
  James, 105, 170
  John, 23, 114, 115, 130
  Mary, 170
  Mary, Jr., 170
  Saml., 44
  Samuel, 43
  Stephen, 30, 171
  William, 179
Wincope, Cornelius, 160
Winder, Thomas, 24, 57, 120
Winecope, Mr., 49
  Nicholas, 148, 149, 168
Winecup, Nicholas, 168
Winekoop, Garret, 149
  Nicholas, 149
Winner, John, 72
Wisel, Michael, 128
Wislar, Cosbar, 22
Wistair, Casper, 151
Wistar, Caspar, 121, 125
  Catherine, 125
  Katherine, 121
Witchall, Mary, 145
  Rachel, 145
  Thomas, 145
Wittanam, Jacob Carl, 105
Wolf, Paul, 44
Wood, James, 153
  Peter, 69
  Philip, 179
  Richard, 11, 12

Woodford, Joseph, 153
Woods, Abraham, 120
  Joseph, 70, 72
Woodward, Samuel, 71
Woolf, Thomas, 67
Woollston, John, 65
  Jonathan, 65, 85
Woolston, Jeremiah, 108
  John, 100
  Jonathan, 10, 55, 63, 72, 87, 96, 123
  Sarah, 55
Woolstone, Jonathan, 80, 146
Wootman, John, 128
Worms, Daniel, 177
Worrall, Elisabeth, 143
  Ellen, 143
  Martha, 143
  Peter, 40
  Tho., 59
  Thomas, 143
Worrel, Peter, 65
Worrell, Hannah (Heath), 142
  Peter, 192
  Richard, 142
  Thomas, 193
Worstall, Jno., 23
Worth, James, 88, 160
  Joseph, 30
Wright, Andrew, 100, 155
  Anthony, 41, 48, 112, 121, 153, 159, 172
  Barak, 174
  Benjamin, 13
  Charles, 121, 143, 159
  Daniel, 100, 143, 148, 155, 171, 178
  Jacob, 38
  John, 104
  Jonathan, 23
  Joshua, 102, 119, 122, 159
  Rebecca, 178
  Sarah, 21
  Thomas, 121, 159
Wynkoop, Nicholas, 163

Yardley, Ann, 109
  Samuel, 109

Yardley *cont'd*
   Tho., 39
   Thomas, 51, 58, 60, 65,
       68, 70, 78, 83, 89,
       101, 109, 118
   _____, 188
Yates, Agnes, 3
   Francis, 53
   James, 3, 48, 106
   Joseph, 100
Yeales, Agnes, 106
Yeardley, Tho's., 72, 73
   Thomas, 73, 85, 115, 170
   Thos., Jr., 133
   W., 138
   Wm., 133, 137, 138
   _____, 140
Yearley, Thos., 78
Yeats, Jos., 125
Yoder, Peter, 33
Yong, Barnard, 159
Young, Barnet, 138
   Bartholomew, 105, 176,
       187
   Bernard, 105, 131, 183
   John, 137
   Susannah, 183

Zane, Jonathan, 164
Zuber, Johannes, 81, 93

_____, Arthur, 133
   John, 165
   Nicholas, 141

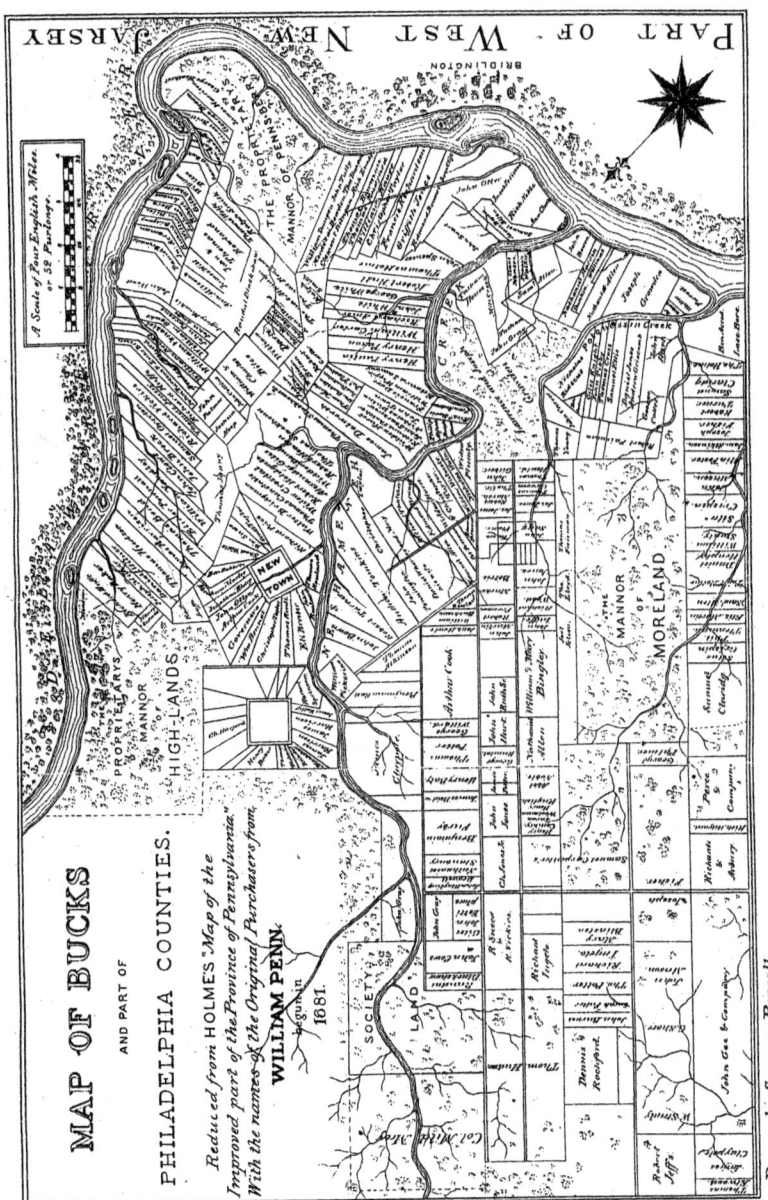

www.ingramcontent.com/pod-product-compliance
Lightning Source LLC
Chambersburg PA
CBHW050142170426
43197CB00011B/1932